MW01253048

Analyzing Affective Societies

In recent years, research in the social sciences and cultural studies has increasingly paid attention to the generative power of emotions and affects; that is, to the questions of how far they shape social and cultural processes while being simultaneously shaped by them. However, the literature on the methodological implications of researching affects and emotions remains rather limited.

As a collective outcome of the Collaborative Research Center (CRC) *Affective Societies* at Freie Universität Berlin, *Analyzing Affective Societies* introduces procedures and methodologies applied by researchers of the CRC for investigating societies as affective societies. Presenting scholarly research practices by means of concrete examples and case studies, the book does not contain any conclusive methodological advice, but rather engages in illustrative descriptions of the authors' research practices.

Analyzing Affective Societies unveils different research approaches, procedures and practices of a variety of disciplines from the humanities, arts and social sciences. It will appeal to students and researchers interested in fields such as Qualitative Research Methods, Emotions, Affect, Cultural Studies and Social Sciences.

Antje Kahl is a postdoctoral researcher in Sociology currently heading the method lab at the CRC *Affective Societies* at Freie Universität Berlin, Germany.

Routledge Studies in Affective Societies

Series Editors:
Birgitt Röttger-Rössler
Professor of Social and Cultural Anthropology at Freie Universität Berlin, Germany
Doris Kolesch
Professor of Theater and Performance Studies at Freie Universität Berlin, Germany

Routledge Studies in Affective Societies presents high-level academic work on the social dimensions of human affectivity. It aims to shape, consolidate and promote a new understanding of societies as Affective Societies, accounting for the fundamental importance of affect and emotion for human coexistence in the mobile and networked worlds of the 21st century. Contributions come from a wide range of academic fields, including anthropology; sociology; cultural, media and film studies; political science; performance studies; art history; philosophy; and social, developmental and cultural psychology. Contributing authors share the vision of a transdisciplinary understanding of the affective dynamics of human sociality. Thus, *Routledge Studies in Affective Societies* devotes considerable space to the development of methodology, research methods and techniques that are capable of uniting perspectives and practices from different fields.

Affect in Relation
Families, Places, Technologies
Edited by Birgitt Röttger-Rössler and Jan Slaby

Image Testimonies
Witnessing in Times of Social Media
Edited by Kerstin Schankweiler, Verena Straub and Tobias Wendl

Affective Societies
Key Concepts
Edited by Jan Slaby and Christian von Scheve

Analyzing Affective Societies
Methods and Methodologies
Edited by Antje Kahl

For more information about this series, please visit: www.routledge.com/Routledge-Studies-in-Affective-Societies/book-series/RSAS

Analyzing Affective Societies

Methods and Methodologies

Edited by Antje Kahl

Routledge
Taylor & Francis Group

LONDON AND NEW YORK

GUELPH HUMBER LIBRARY
205 Humber College Blvd
Toronto, ON   M9W 5L7

First published 2019
by Routledge
2 Park Square, Milton Park, Abingdon, Oxon OX14 4RN

and by Routledge
52 Vanderbilt Avenue, New York, NY 10017

Routledge is an imprint of the Taylor & Francis Group, an informa business

© 2019 selection and editorial matter, Antje Kahl; individual
chapters, the contributors

The right of Antje Kahl to be identified as the author of the
editorial material, and of the authors for their individual chapters,
has been asserted in accordance with sections 77 and 78 of the
Copyright, Designs and Patents Act 1988.

All rights reserved. No part of this book may be reprinted
or reproduced or utilised in any form or by any electronic,
mechanical, or other means, now known or hereafter invented,
including photocopying and recording, or in any information
storage or retrieval system, without permission in writing from
the publishers.

Trademark notice: Product or corporate names may be trademarks
or registered trademarks, and are used only for identification and
explanation without intent to infringe.

British Library Cataloguing-in-Publication Data
A catalogue record for this book is available from the British Library

Library of Congress Cataloging-in-Publication Data
A catalog record for this book has been requested

ISBN: 978-1-138-38879-6 (hbk)
ISBN: 978-0-429-42436-6 (ebk)

Typeset in Times New Roman
by Apex CoVantage, LLC

Contents

Contributors

Bilgin Ayata is Professor for Political Sociology at the University of Basel in Switzerland. Her research interests are the politics of emotions, migration, social movements, and memory with a regional focus on the Middle East and Europe. She is an associate member of the CRC *Affective Societies* where she co-directs with Cilja Harders the project "Political Participation, Emotion and Affect in the Context of Socio-Political Transformations".

Jonas Bens is trained both as a lawyer and an anthropologist. Currently he is a postdoctoral researcher working in the project "Sentiments of Justice and Transitional Justice" at the CRC *Affective Societies* at Freie Universität Berlin. His research interests include legal and political anthropology, international law and criminal justice, and theories of democracy.

Anna L. Berg is completing her PhD in Sociology at the University of Chicago. For her doctoral research, she looks at the role of emotions for political participation in Germany and France. Her main research interests are sociology of emotion, affect theory, sociology of secularism and religion, and political sociology.

Hansjörg Dilger is Professor of Social and Cultural Anthropology at Freie Universität Berlin. His research interests include the anthropology of religion, medical anthropology, transnationalism and migration, urban anthropology, and the anthropology of education and learning. He is co-editor of the forthcoming book *Affective Trajectories: Religion and Emotion in African Cityscapes* (with A. Bochow, M. Burchardt, and M. Wilhelm-Solomon, Duke University Press, 2019).

Samia Dinkelaker is Volkswagen Stiftung Research Fellow in the project "The Researchers' Affects" at the Institute of Social and Cultural Anthropology at Freie Universität Berlin. She is also a PhD candidate at the Institute for Migration Research and Intercultural Studies at Osnabrück University and studies the Indonesian labor migration program. Her research interests include global migration studies, feminist and postcolonial perspectives on subject formation, as well as political affects.

Anne Fleig is Professor of Modern German Literature at the Institute of German and Dutch Languages and Literatures at Freie Universität Berlin. Her research interests include affects, feelings, and belonging in literature, literature around 1800, modernist literature and contemporary literature, Gender Studies, female authorship, and drama and theatre.

Eric Hahn is a psychiatrist and cognitive behavioral psychotherapist at Charité Universitätsmedizin Berlin, CBF. He is head of a project within the CRC *Affective Societies*, and his research interests include cultural and anthropological psychiatry as well as migration and mental health.

Meike Haken is a doctoral researcher in Sociology at Technische Universität Berlin. She is currently working in the project "Audience emotions in sports and religion" at the CRC *Affective Societies*. Her research interests are the sociology of religion, knowledge, and culture, especially religious events and emotions, as well as celebrity studies.

Cilja Harders is Professor of Political Sciences and the director of the Centre for Middle Eastern and North African Politics at Freie Universität Berlin. Her research interests are in the field of transformations of statehood in Egypt and the Arab World. She worked on "politics from below", protest and affect, violence, and gender relations.

Edda Heyken is a social and cultural anthropologist and currently a doctoral researcher working in the project "Affective Efforts of Migration: South and North Vietnamese Lifeworlds in Separated and Reunified Berlin" at the CRC *Affective Societies* at Freie Universität Berlin.

Thomas John is an anthropologist and a doctoral researcher currently working in the project "The Affective Creation of 'Home': Patron Saint Fiesta Videos in the Transnational Context of Mexico/USA" at the CRC *Affective Societies* at Freie Universität Berlin. His research interests include visual and media anthropology as well as the indigenous media and art scene in southern Mexico.

Antje Kahl is a postdoctoral researcher in Sociology, currently heading the method lab at the CRC *Affective Societies* at Freie Universität Berlin. Her research interests include methods and methodologies, sociology of knowledge, science research, medical sociology, sociology of the body, and death and dying.

Hermann Kappelhoff has been a professor in the Department for Film Studies at the Freie Universität Berlin since 2003. He has published extensively on Weimar cinema, melodrama, cinematic realism, and the Hollywood war movie. His research interests lie in the nexus between the aesthetics and politics of the cinematic image.

Omar Kasmani is a postdoctoral researcher in Social and Cultural Anthropology at the CRC *Affective Societies* at Freie Universität Berlin. With a cross-cutting interest in affect and spatiality, his research is invested in ideas of public intimacy, queer futurities, and the politics of Sufi religious lifeworlds. He is co-editor of the volume *Muslim Matter* (with S. Maneval, Revolver Publishing, 2016).

Hubert Knoblauch is Professor for General Sociology and Theory of Modern Society at the Technical University of Berlin. His major areas of research are the sociology of knowledge, communication, and religion as well as qualitative methods.

Doris Kolesch is Professor of Theatre and Performance Studies at Freie Universität Berlin and co-director of the DFG-funded collaborative research center "Affective Societies. Dynamics of Social Coexistence in Mobile Worlds", where she heads a research project on "Reenacting Emotions. Strategies and Politics of Immersive Theater". Her research interests include theory and aesthetics of theatre, voice and acoustic culture, and affect and emotion theory.

Ingrid Kummels is Professor for Cultural and Social Anthropology at the Institute for Latin American Studies at Freie Universität Berlin. She is head of the project "The Affective Creation of 'Home': Patron Saint Fiesta Videos in the Transnational Context of Mexico/USA" at the CRC *Affective Societies*. Her major areas of research are migration, transnationalism and identity politics, anthropology of knowledge and media, and visual anthropology.

Anh Thu Anne Lam is a doctoral researcher in social and cultural anthropology, currently working in the project "The Formation of Feeling in Vietnamese Berlin" at the CRC *Affective Societies* at Freie Universität Berlin.

Jörg-Christian Lanca is an area specialist on Southeast Asia and currently a doctoral researcher working in the project "Affective Efforts of Migration: South and North Vietnamese Lifeworlds in Separated and Reunified Berlin" at Freie Universität Berlin.

Hauke Lehmann is a film scholar and postdoctoral researcher currently working in the project "Migrant Melodramas and Culture Clash Comedies" at the CRC *Affective Societies* at Freie Universität Berlin. He has published on the affectivity and temporality of cinematic images, especially with regard to New Hollywood and the relation between cinema and migration.

Margreth Lünenborg is Professor in Media and Communication Studies focusing especially on journalism studies at Freie Universität Berlin, where she also serves as the Director of the Margherita-von-Brentano-Center for Gender Studies. Her research focuses on hybrid forms of public communication, gender media studies, and media and migration.

Tanja Maier is a senior lecturer (Privatdocent) in media and a communication researcher and currently working as an associate member at the CRC *Affective Societies* at Freie Universität Berlin. Her research interests include visual communication and culture, cultural studies and digital media, affect studies and transcultural communication, and gender media studies.

Dominik Mattes is a postdoctoral researcher in Social and Cultural Anthropology at the CRC *Affective Societies* at Freie Universität Berlin. His research interests include medical anthropology, anthropology of religion, urban anthropology, sensory ethnography, and the study of affect and emotion. His most recent publication is "Spatialities of Belonging: Affective Place-Making Among Diasporic Neo-Pentecostal and Sufi Groups in Berlin's Cityscape" (with H. Dilger and O. Kasmani, in *Affect in relation: families, places, technologies*, ed. by B. Röttger-Rössler and J. Slaby, Routledge, 2018).

Rainer Mühlhoff is a postdoctoral researcher in philosophy, currently working in the project "Changing Repertoires of Emotion: A Theory of Affective Relationality and Transformativity" at the CRC *Affective Societies* at Freie Universität Berlin. His research focuses on the crossroads of theories of power, affect, and subjectivity. He has expertise in social philosophy, political philosophy of affect, and critical theory of the digital age.

Thi Main Huong Nguyen is a psychologist and currently a doctoral researcher working in the project "Affective Efforts of Migration: South and North Vietnamese Lifeworlds in Separated and Reunified Berlin" at Freie Universität Berlin.

Derya Özkaya is a doctoral researcher in Political Science, currently working in the project "Political Participation, Emotion and Affect in the Context of Socio-Political Transformations" at the CRC *Affective Societies* at Freie Universität Berlin. Her research interests include social movements, collective memory, commemorative practices, revolutionary movements in Turkey, collective emotions, and affect.

Birgitt Röttger-Rössler is Professor of Social and Cultural Anthropology at Freie Universität Berlin. Her research focuses on the study of emotions and affect, childhood, socialization and schooling, social inequality, and migration. Regionally, she is specialized on Southeast Asian societies. Since 2015, she is director of the CRC *Affective Societies: Dynamics of Social Coexistence in Mobile Worlds.*

Elgen Sauerborn is a doctoral researcher in sociology at the Freie Universität Berlin. Next to finishing her PhD research on affective work of women in leadership positions, she is currently working as a research assistant at the Europa-Universität Viadrina Frankfurt (Oder). Among her research interests are sociology of emotions and affects, sociology of organizations and elites, gender studies, qualitative research methods and methodologies, and computer-assisted analysis of qualitative data.

Kerstin Schankweiler is an art historian and currently postdoctoral researcher in the project "Affective Dynamics of Images in the Era of Social Media" at the CRC *Affective Societies* at Freie Universität Berlin. Her research areas include image practices in social media, contemporary art from Africa, and art history in a global context. She is the author of *Die Mobilisierung der Dinge* (transcript 2012) and co-edited *Images Testimonies: Witnessing in Times of Social Media* (Routledge, 2018). In 2017 she co-curated the exhibition *Affect Me. Social Media Images* in Art (KAI 10 Düsseldorf).

Gabriel Scheidecker is a postdoctoral researcher in social and cultural anthropology, currently working in the project "The Formation of Feeling in Vietnamese Berlin" at the CRC *Affective Societies* at Freie Universität Berlin. His research focuses on emotion, affect, and childhood in Madagascar and the Vietnamese community in Berlin.

Jan Slaby is Professor for Philosophy of Mind at the Institute of Philosophy at Freie Universität Berlin. His research interests are philosophy of emotion and affect, and he has expertise in phenomenology, critical theory, and social philosophy.

Thomas Stodulka is Junior Professor for Social and Cultural Anthropology at Freie Universität Berlin. He is the co-founder and convenor of the European Network for Psychological Anthropology (ENPA), and his research focuses on affect, culture, emotion, illness, stigma, childhood, youth, and relational methodologies.

Thi Minh Tam Ta is a psychiatrist and psychotherapist at Charité Universitäts-medizin Berlin, CBF. She is head of a large outpatient clinic for Vietnamese migrants in Germany and head of a project within the CRC *Affective Societies*. Her research interests include transcultural psychiatry and development of migration and culture-sensible psychotherapies, including MBCT.

Ferdiansyah Thajib is a PhD candidate at the Institute of Social and Cultural Anthropology at Freie Universität Berlin. He is also a DAAD scholarship recipient and an Associate Research Fellow of "The Researchers' Affects" project, funded by Volkswagen Stiftung. His work is situated in the intersections of theory and praxis, with specific research interests on queer modes of endurance and forms of affective entanglement in everyday life.

N. Yasemin Ural is a postdoctoral researcher in Sociology, currently working in the project "Feelings of Religious Belonging and the Rhetorics of Injury in Public and in Art" at the CRC *Affective Societies* at Freie Universität Berlin. Her main research interests are sociology of religion, Islam in Europe, secularism studies, and sociology of immigration.

Dina Wahba is a doctoral researcher in Political Science, currently working in the project "Political Participation, Emotion and Affect in the Context of Socio-Political Transformations" at the CRC *Affective Societies* at Freie Universität

Berlin. Among her research interests are social and revolutionary movements, women's rights activism, and gender studies.

Robert Walter-Jochum is a postdoctoral researcher in German Literature, currently working in the project "Feelings of Religious Belonging and the Rhetorics of Injury in Public and in Art" at the CRC *Affective Societies* at Freie Universität Berlin. Among his research interests are literature and affect, literature and religion, theory of autobiography, and narratology. He has mostly worked on contemporary and 18th-/19th-century literature from Germany and Austria.

Matthias Warstat is Professor of Theatre Studies at Freie Universität Berlin. Between 2008 and 2012, he was Chair of Theatre and Media Studies at Friedrich-Alexander-Universität Erlangen-Nuremberg. In 2012, he was awarded an ERC-Advanced Grant for the project "The Aesthetics of Applied Theatre". His main research areas are contemporary theatre and society, modern European theatre history (19th and 20th century), and theatricality of politics.

Michael Wetzels is a doctoral researcher in Sociology at Technische Universität Berlin. He is currently working in the project "Audience Emotions in Sports and Religion" at the CRC *Affective Societies*. His research interests are sociology of emotion, affect and sport, the study of masses, audiences, and collectivities, and he has expertise in social phenomenology, qualitative research, and social and communicative constructivism.

Philipp Wüschner is a postdoctoral researcher of philosophy at Freie Universität Berlin. His interests are aesthetics, philosophy of emotion and affect, and theories of habits, which he approaches from the point of view of French poststructuralism and German media philosophy.

Anita von Poser is a social and cultural anthropologist at Freie Universität Berlin and head of a project within the CRC *Affective Societies*. The core themes of her research engage psychological anthropology, the anthropology of aging and care, the anthropology of migration, as well as the anthropology of foodways.

Christian von Scheve is Professor of Sociology at the Institute of Sociology at Freie Universität Berlin. His main research interests are in the sociology of emotion, social stratification, social psychology, and economic sociology.

Acknowledgments

Affects, emotions and relational affective dynamics are key themes in ongoing social and political processes. To analyze those often very subtle dynamics represents not only an important task but also an ongoing methodological challenge, to which this volume is intended to contribute.

Although it is generally considered a matter of course that science is produced in a methodically specifiable fashion, it is actually not that simple to transparently present how this happens in practice in a way that is comprehensible for others. That is why I owe enormous gratitude to all the authors who rose to this challenge, making the publication of this book possible by doing so. I would like to thank the authors for the fundamental disposition to make their own work methodologies transparent, investing work and time to do so. In addition, I would like to express thanks for the sometimes challenging but always constructive and inspiring collaboration during the workshops and reviews which accompanied the compositions of this book and significantly contributed to its final version. I am certain that this exchange about different work processes and procedural methodologies represents an advantage of interdisciplinary cooperation, which in turn strengthens and deepens such collaboration. A look at our different methodological grasps of social phenomena helps to raise our understanding of such phenomena – regarding the variety of disciplinary perspectives as well as the reflection of one's own perspective.

To realize this volume, I relied upon the support of many people and institutions. I would particularly like to thank the editors of the Routledge book series *Studies in Affective Societies*, Birgitt Röttger-Rössler and Doris Kolesch, for their trust and support. I also owe enormous gratitude to Jan Slaby and Christian von Scheve for their excellent and inspiring support and encouragement. Besides my colleagues at the Collaborative Research Center *Affective Societies* at the Freie Universität Berlin, the German Research Council (DFG) was of uttermost importance for the successful completion of this book. Their financial support enables our research, the scientific exchange and publications in the first place. I am also very grateful to Routledge's Emily Briggs and Elena Chiu for their interest in this book project and their professional assistance during the publication process. I am enormously thankful to Tamar Blickstein for improving the English of many contributions and for giving hints towards improving the clarity and readability of the texts. Last but not least, many thanks to Linda Huke for her dedicated support in proofreading and formatting matters.

Berlin, June 2018
Antje Kahl

Chapter 1

Introduction
Analyzing affective societies

Antje Kahl

1. Researching the dynamic sociality of affect and emotion: a major challenge

Affect and emotion are fundamental to human sociality. This observation has increasingly been a focus of research in the social and behavioral sciences as well as in the humanities and cultural studies. These disciplines offer conceptual and empirical approaches to examining the role of affect and emotion in social life, ranging from general social and cultural theories of affect and emotion to applications of affect and emotion analyses in research about historically and culturally distinct societies.

Taking a broader view of the central developments in affect and emotion research over the preceding two or three decades reveals the emergence of a new general framework that foregrounds the sociality, relationality and situatedness of affect and emotion (Parkinson, Fisher, & Manstead, 2005; Greco & Stenner, 2008, Gregg & Seigworth, 2010; Burkitt, 2014; von Scheve & Salmela, 2014; von Scheve, 2017; Röttger-Rössler & Slaby, 2018). This new framework firmly reverses older approaches to affect and emotion, which were largely focused on human individuals and their psychological and biological properties (e.g., Izard, 1991; Lazarus, 1991; Panksepp, 1998). By contrast, at present, the sociality and dynamic relationality of affective and emotional phenomena is no longer a matter of much controversy in the social and human sciences.

However, it is one thing to proclaim a general theoretical and conceptual shift towards social-relational perspectives. It is quite another matter to equip this transformed conceptual terrain with feasible tools, methodological orientations and research methods. Whereas a growing field of research has begun to develop methodologies and techniques for investigating emotions in social and cultural contexts (e.g., Flam & Kleres, 2015 Holmes, 2014, 2015; Katz, 2004; Beatty, 2005; Kleres, 2011), scholarship on the methodological implications of researching affect, in particular, has remained rather limited (see Knudsen & Stage, 2015, for a promising start). This is certainly due to the practical challenges of researching relational and phenomenological issues more generally: how can we go about analyzing subtle affective and, to a lesser extent, emotional dynamics through social and cultural research that is empirical and that relies heavily on what can be observed, described or imagined? Affect is a particularly challenging category for this sort of research to address. Unlike emotions, affect is not restricted to specific observable forms of action, bodily behavior or even to discursive and language-based modes of articulation and enunciation. Instead, affect is often understood to elude and bypass these modes of accessibility (Blackman, 2012). A further methodological challenge lies in affect theory's grounding in process and relational ontology. Social research methods have not been developed for relational ontology in the way they have for more traditional ontologies, such as methodological individualism or holism. Finally, affect (and emotion) research is a transdisciplinary endeavor that encompasses a number of different methodological traditions and scientific paradigms. Hence, methods that would be considered adequate in one discipline might be less ideal in another field. However, this diversity is also a source of inspiration in that methods considered to be amongst the standard repertoire of a particular discipline might be adopted and lead to innovation in another discipline.

Given these challenges, how can affect – as a situated and relational dynamic – be meaningfully operationalized, observed and described in empirical research? Given their profound and constitutive entanglement with corporeality, discourse, media, materiality, space and technology, how can interpersonal affective dynamics be reconstructed and interpreted in ways that are meaningful beyond the individual researcher and across different cases? To put it more provocatively, how can we know that the phenomenon we conceptualize as affect exists in the first place? Is affect merely a tool for thought and analysis rather than a bodily force with causal repercussions? Which general methodological paradigms and approaches are viable for affective analysis, and how would we need to amend existing methods and techniques of data collection and analysis in order to successfully "capture" affect (and emotion) in their situational, material and discursive entanglements? Judging from this list of questions, it almost seems that the methodological challenges of researching the dynamic sociality of affect encapsulates many of the major challenges of cultural and social research at large. Obviously, then, the bar is set rather high for workable methodological approaches to advance affect and emotion research.

The aim of the present volume is to make focused advances in this novel terrain. The chapters bring together methodological inquiries, as well as specific methods and analytical techniques that are carried out in the Collaborative Research Center (CRC) *Affective Societies*, a research initiative based at Freie Universität Berlin that includes affect and emotion researchers from 11 disciplines across the social sciences, cultural and media studies, arts and humanities. Tightly interlocking different disciplinary orientations, the Center's researchers work collaboratively on grounded approaches capable of illuminating the affective dynamics of social coexistence within a range of salient domains of life in contemporary societies. This research initiative is the exemplary terrain on which the present volume draws for its contributions. This interdisciplinary context in itself provides a challenge as well as a source of potential innovation. One of the central assumptions of the CRC is that *Affective Societies* can only be understood in a comprehensive fashion when researchers simultaneously account for the social and cultural constitution of affect and emotion. This often requires finding a common ground from which exchange and mutual inspiration becomes possible, not only in terms of theories and concepts, but also regarding the fundamental methodological orientation of research. As a starting point, this common ground has been found in a methodological orientation that implies an inductive and interpretative-hermeneutic approach to empirical research – an approach that is well established in both the social sciences and cultural studies. Workable solutions to the challenges of researching affect and emotion can thus draw on the existing repertoires of methods in these different disciplines. Nevertheless, there is also a clear need to adapt and further develop these methods in new directions, so as to tackle the research questions through a shared transdisciplinary conceptual framework firmly anchored in social and cultural theory.[1]

More generally, it is vital that the development of methods proceeds in-step with the conceptual and theoretical elaboration of the phenomena under study. Concepts are the building blocks on which any empirical research, no matter what methodological orientation it subscribes to, rests. The present volume is therefore complemented by another book entitled *Affective Societies: Key Concepts* (Slaby & von Scheve, 2019), which appears in the same *Routledge Studies in Affective Societies* book series. In an expanded glossary and review article–style format, this other book presents 29 working concepts that comprise the theoretical and conceptual core of the *Affective Societies* initiative. The particular approach to concepts reflected in that volume is research-oriented, pragmatic and grounded in specific domains, instead of offering detached and abstract "theory" in the classical sense. The present volume, in turn, orients its methodological and methods-based elucidations closely to the conceptual perspective explicated in the *Key Concepts* book. Thus, these two works function as "sister volumes", offering complementary perspectives. While they can of course be used independently of each other, they may be read together for a fuller picture of the *Affective Societies* perspective and its methodological and conceptual advances as well as challenges.

In this introduction, I will undertake the following tasks: I will first provide an overview and commentary of *Affective Societies* as the designator of an inter- and trans-disciplinary research perspective (section 2). I will then introduce the specific methodological and methods-based approaches collected in this volume, with particular emphasis on the methodological challenge posed by "affective relationality" (section 3). Finally, I will present overviews of the four parts of the book, the 16 separate chapters and the rationale of arranging them in this particular manner (section 4).

2. Affective societies: theoretical outlook

Affective Societies is more than just the title and general theme of the Berlin-based interdisciplinary research initiative. It is also, and predominantly, a general designator of a theoretical and diagnostic approach to affect and emotion research. This approach centers on a social-relational and situated understanding of affect and emotion and their foundational – both constructive and disruptive – involvement in the social fabric of contemporary societies. The contributors to this volume and other researchers at the CRC use the title to focus on the affective dynamics that circulate within and underpin contemporary societies in both a theoretical and a diagnostic perspective. As a theoretical orientation, *Affective Societies* draws on a basic theory of sociality centered on embodied affective relations, affective situatedness, performativity and collective agency, and combines that theory of sociality with approaches that theorize societies along the lines of particular historical exemplars. These latter approaches analyze concrete societal formations under a specific "optic" focusing on a salient element or development that is characteristic of the formation in question (as, for example, "post-industrial society", "knowledge society", "risk society"). The two orientations – a *social theory* perspective and a more diagnostic and critical *theories of societies* perspective – are often undertaken as separate endeavors with only partial overlap. This is different in the case of *Affective Societies*. Here, sociality as such and the broader outlook on society at large are theorized in terms of affectivity. Accordingly, the social theory perspective on relational affect is tightly interwoven with the broader diagnostic angle on contemporary societies – that is, societies characterized by an intensification and acceleration of affective modes of address and relatedness. This adds complexity to the overall picture but makes for a richer and more timely outlook on affect and emotion compared to theories that focus on affect and emotion in isolation from their embeddedness within extant social, cultural and political life. I will now briefly consider both dimensions of the approach separately, beginning with the understanding of relational affectivity as a central category of social theory.

Relational affect in social theory

The first thing to note about contemporary theories of affect and emotion is that the long-standing assumption of a sharp opposition between affectivity and rationality is now decidedly outdated. The dichotomy between emotion and reason has given way to views that emphasize their entanglement and co-dependence. Even fields that have little in common and are rarely in agreement, such as social philosophy, cognitive psychology and the affective neurosciences, share the same basic assumption that affectivity is an indispensable dimension of human world-relatedness. Affective and emotional processes are vital for assessments of relevance, for the formation of value and valuation, and for keeping social practices focused on what is ultimately at stake in them. Without affectivity, evaluation and decision-making would not be possible – whether at the individual or the collective level. This is not merely an add-on view that loosely joins separable affective and rational "components", but an integrated perspective that posits the inextricable entanglement of affective, cognitive and volitional elements. Based on this new consensus across fields, a number of key points have been empha-sized and theoretically elaborated. These include the social situatedness of affect and emotion, the dynamic relationality of affective processes, their embodied and intercorporeal character, and in particular, their efficaciousness as drivers of social relations and collective action in various local and trans-local contexts. With these characteristics, relational affect is a central force of social connectedness, ranging from face-to-face encounters to various interactive dynamics between individuals and collectives as well as inter- and intra-group relations. All these points give shape to the foundational involvement of affect and emotion among the processes that enable, create, sustain – but also threaten or disrupt – human social and soci-etal life.

Developed in this way, the relational understanding of affect rivals other prominent concepts in social theory that provide a focused outlook on central dimensions of sociality, such as agency, reciprocity, interaction, communication or intention in earlier approaches. It is a central theoretical aim of the *Affective Societies* initiative to develop and solidify this perspective and demonstrate its value in various areas of research.

Relational affect as a diagnostic notion

In addition to its role as a conceptual anchor for social theory, relational affect – along with related relational approaches to emotion[2] – have diagnostic purchase with regard to contemporary societies. Here, the *Affective Societies* perspective resembles diagnostic "theories of societies" that are prominent in the German tra-dition of sociology and social analysis (i.e., *Gesellschaftstheorie*). Such theories circumscribe specific and historically situated societal formations, often drawing on modern Western nation-states as prime examples. Drawing on assumptions and concepts from general social theory, these theories often combine a range of concepts and approaches to phenomena that scholars deem important for a spe-cific local or historical societal formation, such as the risk society (Beck, 1992) or the information and network society (e.g., Castells, 2010). Loosely in line with these earlier approaches, but with a significantly different organizing idea, the *Affective Societies* initiative considers affect and emotion to be a signature fea-ture of contemporary social and societal life. In particular, the assumption is that recent developments signal a tipping point when it comes to manifestations of affect in public discourse, in mediatized social interactions, and in broader efforts at managing, controlling and governing affect and emotion.

To note just one significant dimension of this trend, consider how recent politi-cal events and developments have managed to transform public communication and global politics in a matter of just a few years. Thanks to the new possibilities brought on by social media, political movements emerge and rally around salient issues with increased speed and a much broader reach than ever before. Relat-edly, spontaneous, highly sensuous modes of affective associations are high in demand, resulting in transient collectives or affective communities that can make their presence felt rapidly within a thoroughly reformatted public realm. At the same time, one cannot fail to notice the widespread emergence, public appeal and sustained success of right-wing populist parties across Europe and the world, and their reliance on – and, one must admit, increasing mastery of – affective modes of communication. All this has led to a substantially altered political climate, evidenced by the increasingly divisive nature of political debate and practices in the context of the so-called European "refugee crisis" since 2015. This trend has many facets – one of them directly pertaining to the public production and dissemination of knowledge. In times where it seems that what "feels true" wins the day over knowledge claims grounded in evidence, including those brought forth by acknowledged experts, acclaimed scientists or members of the intellectual establishment, the whole epistemic fabric of society seems to be at risk. Given these developments, it is urgent to find ways to diagnose with precision what is going on, and to come up with conceptual and methodological tools that are effective in highlighting what is new amidst a complex confluence of factors that make up the present conjuncture.

"Affective societies" in this respect functions as a sensitizing concept that helps to direct attention to the increasing *intensification* and *reflexivity* of affective modes of interaction and communication within the fragmented domain of contemporary public spheres. Affective modes of address have risen to unprecedented prominence, often to the detriment of other forms and styles of interaction. But which precise forms of sociality and modes of political participation will consolidate in this reformatted and contested public landscape remains an open question and a pressing issue for current research.

Beyond the relevance of affect and emotion for general social theory, *Affective Societies* also designates a historical formation of a specific and unprecedented kind: societies whose modes of operation and means of integration increasingly involve efforts and new techniques to mobilize and strategically deploy affect and emotion in a highly intensified and often one-sided manner. These novel and much intensified modes of affective communication and affective relatedness require powerful new research tools, concepts and methods. These new research tools must be designed to capture the energies and impulses of contemporary affect within highly complex and rapidly changing mediatized publics, or within institutions and organizations that have come under pressure recently (such as, for example, mainstream journalism, establishment politics, certain religious congregations or parts of the educational sector). It is the aim of the present volume to supply such tools.

However, the diagnostic perspective outlined here can only succeed if it is grounded in historical and theoretical knowledge of the structure, development and modes of operation of contemporary societies, as well as on sophisticated scholarship on affect and emotion. Such a perspective must be able to draw on an understanding of the manner and extent to which affective processes have always been a central element in the functioning of societies or social formations at various scales of development, to distinguish what is truly new from a background of the familiar. Above all, this perspective requires methods and methodologies capable of elucidating the intricacies of affective dynamics that operate at various levels of contemporary social life. Ideally, these methods and methodologies will combine different disciplinary practices and traditions, while also arising from research engagements with concrete sites and settings in which currently salient developments take place.

The *Affective Societies* center has sought to address this methodological need through theoretically informed empirical research. This body of research is organized into 16 subprojects, each of which addresses a specific field or domain in which affect and emotion have become salient features of social life, for instance, in transnational communities, politics and the arts. Within these domains, the projects investigate and sometimes compare concrete empirical cases of, for instance, specific religious communities, theatre performances or works of art. First and foremost, this kind of research provides an understanding of the questions, issues and challenges that relate to these cases or their role in contemporary dynamics of social coexistence. In addition, these modes of research allow for the development of empirically grounded theoretical concepts on the one hand (see Slaby & von Scheve, 2019) and for more "middle-range" theories of the fields and domains in question on the other hand. These middle-range theories, in turn, are an essential ingredient in any attempt at developing viable diagnoses of present-day societies (cf. Lindemann, 2009). The methods discussed in this volume are an essential part of the engine driving this kind of conceptual and diagnostic research.

3. Affective societies: researching affect and emotion as a methodological challenge

In recent years, research in the social sciences and cultural studies has increasingly paid attention to the generative power of emotions and affects to shape – and be shaped by – social and cultural processes. While affect and emotion research in social psychology and other behavioral and natural sciences has paid substantial attention to the development of research methods in this regard (e.g., Quigley, Lindquist, & Barrett, 2013; Coan & Allen, 2007; Heise, 2006), this is less the case for approaches to emotion in the social sciences, let alone for scholarship on affect in cultural studies. Notable exceptions to this tendency in the social sciences are the volume *Methods of Exploring Emotions* (Flam & Kleres, 2015) and the special section *Methodological Innovations in the Sociology of Emotions Part Two – Methods* in the journal *Emotion Review* (Olson, Godbold, & Patulny, 2015). In the field of cultural studies, the volume *Affective Methodologies: Developing Cultural Research Strategies for the Study of Affect* (Knudsen & Stage, 2015) has paved the way for this kind of inquiry. Evidently, as these works show, it is anything but trivial to empirically observe emotions and affective dynamics. Even though affects and emotions are ubiquitous in human social life, it is a major challenge to observe, describe and understand them in rich and yet precise and reliable ways. This holds irrespective of the specific methods and techniques used, whether in interviews with or observations of actors and informants, in literary texts or in an artistic performance, in recordings of audiences or in discourses.

The theoretical understanding of how affectivity and emotions are to be understood strongly influences the possibilities of methodological access to corresponding social phenomena and processes. For example, if we were to understand affect as Brian Massumi (1995, 2002) does, namely as non-symbolized, pre-conscious and pre-discursive *intensity*, this would make empirical research on affective phenomena almost impossible. Affect understood as the "invisible glue that holds the world together" (Massumi, 2002, 217) would basically exclude scientific observability. After all, where and how should researchers look to collect their data if the phenomenon under study is by definition invisible? If affect were strictly opposed to and ontologically distinct from culturally classified and regulated emotion, and if it were thus seen as existing independently of meaning-making and eluding conceptualization and reflection, social scientists would indeed have a hard time conducting empirical research about it.

Much research in the social sciences, humanities and cultural studies has focused on the situated and historically contingent processes of meaning-making among human agents. It is of course important to note the ontological specificity of affectivity in assessing its fundamental role in the constitution of sociality, as Massumi and others point out (e.g. Clough, 2009). However, doing so does not resolve the challenges related to empirical research on affective phenomena. Accordingly, scholars have criticized definitions of affect as a non-phenomenal background of sociality or as an indeterminate potential, as too empirically inaccessible and vague (e.g. Hemmings, 2005; Leys, 2011; Wetherell, 2012). These critics argue against strict dichotomies of affect and language as well as of body and cognition. From this perspective, it is precisely because affect, body, cognition and language are indissociable that affects are traceable in the effects they have on social and cultural phenomena.

However, even with the following understanding of affect, provided by Blackman (2012), matters remain complicated: "[A]ffect refers to those registers of experience which cannot be easily seen and which might variously be described as non-cognitive, trans-subjective, non-conscious, non-representational, incorporeal and immaterial" (p. 4). Developing an empirical research design that would be capable of analytically examining such registers of experience would be a major challenge. Blackman (2012) is herself aware of this challenge: "[A]ffect is not a thing but rather refers to processes of life and vitality which circulate and pass between bodies and which are difficult to capture or study in any conventional methodological sense" (p. 4). In her contribution to the volume *Affective Methodologies* (Knudsen & Stage, 2015), Blackman identifies the development of methodological strategies "that are sensitive to human and nonhuman agencies, entanglements, and thresholds" (Blackman, 2015, 26) as one of the major challenges in empirical affect studies. To this end, she presents an experimental-performative strategy that she describes as an "embodied hauntology", which works "with the traces, fragments, fleeting moments, gaps, absences, submerged narratives, and displaced actors and agencies that register affectively" (ibid.). Her focus on the spectral, on tiny traces and elusive fragments, sits uneasily with established disciplinary methods and methodologies, but is all the more innovative for it. In their introduction, Knudsen and Stage (2015) emphasize the importance of inventing experimental, performative and action-oriented research approaches by collecting and producing embodied data as well as affective textualities.

Though the authors in this volume are largely sympathetic to Knudsen and Stage's (2015) plea for more creative and innovative methodological approaches to affect, they also pay close heed to the creative potential of applying already established methods and methodologies to the study of affect. Before calling for the invention of entirely new methods, one is well advised, in my view, to think imaginatively about the further development, refinement and combination of existing and well-established and thus "battle-proven" methods and methodologies from the social sciences, the humanities and the more empirically oriented cultural disciplines. Methods such as discourse analysis (Chapter 3), interview analysis (Chapters 4 and 5), image and film analysis (Chapters 6 and 7), videography (Chapters 8 and 9), participant observation (Chapters 10, 11, and 15), or performance analysis (Chapter 12) are adapted and calibrated to the relational, embodied and situated understanding of affect sketched in the first section of this introduction. These methods and methodologies are potentially powerful, yet largely unexplored tools for identifying, describing and understanding how affectivity unfolds in local arrangements of relational dynamics.

"Relational affect" is a broad concept, and this breadth offers several advantages – over and beyond its utility as both a theoretical and a diagnostic notion within social theory. For instance, it is applicable to very different methodological approaches in empirical research and is sufficiently broad to integrate heterogeneous research perspectives from the humanities, the social sciences and cultural studies, all of which investigate aspects of the affective and emotional foundations of contemporary societal coexistence. It allows for interdisciplinary integration, while also accommodating disciplinary differences. Given that most disciplinary approaches to affect theory emphasize the importance of *bodies*, it is methodologically important to ascertain which concrete "bodies" are examined in each particular discipline and research case. Emphasizing the situated relatedness and interactive dynamics of bodies – human as well as non-human, natural and cultural, simple and complex, salient or inconspicuous – allows for very different bodies to become the objects of investigation. As the chapters in this volume will illustrate, different disciplines tend to study different sorts of bodies: human bodies in social interaction, the imbrication of human bodies with other material bodies, including equipment, technologies and media, as well as image bodies, discourse bodies or other textual bodies. Only when we manage to address the differentiated multiplicity of concrete bodies with sufficient precision can we explore the ways different bodies make a difference for situated affective dynamics. The social-relational and situated understanding of affect and emotion thus crucially requires interdisciplinary cooperation to explore the manifold aspects and facets of contemporary affective phenomena.

The conceptual breadth of affect and emotion thus evidently comes with a host of challenges for empirical research. In light of this challenge, the theoretical and analytical work carried out in the CRC *Affective Societies* and elsewhere seeks to generate social-theoretical *working concepts* that can be useful to any kind of social research (e.g., affective relationality, affective arrangement, affective communities, affective practice; cf. Slaby, Mühlhoff, & Wüschner, this volume; Slaby & von Scheve, 2019). Working concepts essentially bridge theory and research in a twofold way that is well-known in social science methodology, in particular when it comes to the acquisition and analysis of empirical data. Concept formation can proceed predominantly in an inductive fashion, wherein concepts are developed from examples and observations of empirical reality. Of course, this does not happen in research practices that are devoid of any conceptual assumptions, as some methodologies would like us to have it. In the social sciences, there is an abundant literature on the various techniques of this kind of data-driven concept formation (e.g., Corbin & Strauss, 2008). However, concepts are also widely used in more deductive ways, where some description of a concept that is already known is then used to make sense of empirical observations. In the case of the latter, many works have discussed the criteria that useful concepts should fulfill, such as resonance, consistency, or fecundity, to name but a few (e.g., Gerring, 2012).

Concepts can thus be put to "work" in social and cultural research in myriad ways and with an endless spectrum of concrete research methods. Different methods put different burdens on the concepts and operationalizations they require. For example, large-scale survey research that aims at making valid claims about the features and characteristics of a population, for instance, regarding voting intentions or social mobility, is well advised to have clear-cut concepts and reliable measures of *voting intentions* and *social mobility*. If, however, one is interested, for example, in the intricacies of social interactions and how they unfold in a specific social and material setting (say, in a protest gathering) or in the meanings of cultural artifacts or performances (say, in a theatre audience) and has only a vague and initial idea of what might be relevant in these situations, more open-ended concepts and methods, such as interviews and ethnographies, might be the more promising approaches. This is certainly the case when one is interested in understanding how affectivity unfolds in local arrangements of relational dynamics. Concepts then always inform the theoretical sensibilities of researchers and their uses of specific methods. They help shape viewpoints and angles on complex subject matters and research domains (*sensitizing concepts*, Blumer, 1954), and they can specifically "sharpen the senses", in particular when a new conceptual articulation breaks with established habits of sorting and judging matters, offering novel modes of access to reality accompanied by newly configured capacities for recognition and judgment on the part of researchers (cf. Slaby & von Scheve,

2019). More often than not, the overall research process advocated in this volume therefore proceeds in a circular fashion in that concepts that have been derived from examples and observations of empirical reality are used as sensitizing concepts in a different context.

Aside from these considerations, and given the strong interdisciplinary scope of research on affect and emotion in the humanities, cultural studies and the social sciences, there is no unified set of methods or analytical techniques that would do justice to the broad variety of research questions that are pertinent in the different disciplines. However, given the broader stance of the questions and the conceptual background outlined earlier, the approaches assembled in this volume are characterized by a *common methodological orientation* that implies an inductive and interpretative-hermeneutic approach to research, which is well established in both the social sciences and cultural studies. Based on this common understanding, the methods discussed in this volume are geared towards generating theoretically informed and empirically grounded insights into specific cases and domains.

The contributions to this volume are also aware of what others have called the "double social life of methods" (Law, Ruppert, & Savage, 2011), or the notion that research methods are not only constituted by the social world of which they are inevitably a part but are also implicated in the social world – they are "performative of the social" (ibid., 8, emphasis omitted). Moreover, this volume's contributions recognize that working with the social-relational and situated concept of affect often means involving the person and perspective of the researcher in an explicit and ideally reflexive way. When researching the affective dimensions of social coexistence, researchers cannot easily be separated from the research they conduct. Inevitably, they are part of the unfolding of the affective dynamics and relationality they investigate – often actively as a participant (see Prosser, 2015). Affect can be located neither in the subject nor in the object of the investigation, but is instead produced jointly. Thus, researchers of affect must account for the ways they are affected by their own object of research. Needless to say, these influences must be critically reflected and accounted for. For instance, researchers can do so by reflexively linking their own ways of being affected to specific identifiable affecting elements of the empirical configuration under investigation (cf. Mattes, Kasmani and Dilger in this volume). In so doing, researchers should not consider their own affects as purely subjective impressions, let alone as disturbances or irritants within the research process. On the contrary, their affects can be turned into epistemological resources for producing knowledge and insights (cf. Stodulka, Dinkelaker, & Thajib, in this volume; see also Loughran & Mannay, 2018). For this to happen successfully, however, researchers benefit from following a certain protocol for enabling a systematic "emotional reflexivity in research" that specifically includes the vital reflexivity with regard to the researchers' own affects and emotions. This is a central aspect of the broader methodological perspective that emerges in the pages that follow.

4. Aim of this volume

In light of this information, the purpose of the volume is twofold: First, separately and together, the chapters aspire to gain insight into different subject areas that are relevant for understanding affective societies. Second, the volume presents – by means of concrete examples and case studies – possible methodological procedures for investigating these subject areas and hence for analyzing affective societies. Methodologically, the volume's explorative orientation implies a strongly inductive and interpretative-hermeneutic approach to empirical research. Its broad range of methods and approaches for the study of affects and emotions includes discourse analysis, the analysis of qualitative interviews, the photovoice technique, the analysis of images and audiovisual movement-images such as films and videos, theatre studies' performance analysis as well as ethnographic and literature studies' approaches. Because the methodology is directed more toward an empirically based generation of concepts and hypotheses, it differs substantially from deductive and hypothesis-testing approaches that dominate research on affect and emotion in the natural and behavioral sciences. The volume's novelty lies not only in the methodological approaches it describes but, above all, in the practical application of these approaches to research on affects and emotions in the humanities, cultural studies and the social sciences. In laying out the different ways affects and emotions can be studied as central elements of social processes, this volume aims to contribute new research models for empirically examining affect within those processes.

Accordingly, the book presents concrete scholarly research practices as works-in-progress. It does not contain any conclusive "this is how it is done" advice, but rather engages in illustrative descriptions of how the authors go about their research. The chapters contain descriptions and critical reflections about different research approaches, procedures and practices from a variety of disciplines, such as sociology, social and cultural anthropology, literature, media, theatre and communication studies, art history, political science and philosophy. In so doing, the volume aims to bridge the gap between the study of affect in a cultural studies tradition and the study of emotion in a social science tradition. It does so, on the one hand, by opening up the social science tradition of the study of emotions to more recent approaches from the field of affect studies. On the other hand, it seeks to ground the exploratory and methodologically disjointed elements of affect studies with examples of more concrete approaches to the empirical investigation of affect-relevant phenomena. Thus, rather than imposing methodological strictures on this heterogeneous field, this volume seeks – through example – to further maximize the field's potential for generating novel, innovative and fruitful research perspectives on the complex realities of affect and emotion within social and cultural life.

In order to achieve this goal, the volume presents insights drawn from the concrete investigative work of research on affects and emotions. Thereby, it demonstrates the radical exercise in creativity, imagination and experimentation required to conceive of affect in a methodologically and empirically rigorous manner, and it does so across a wide array of distinct disciplinary traditions that, to date, have rarely been combined in a constructive fashion. The volume thus makes an innovative methodological contribution – not only by adding a decidedly methodological perspective to affect studies, but also by enhancing the qualitative methods for research in this domain. In showcasing how reflexive affect and emotion research is conducted, the book seeks to make such research comprehensible – and, perhaps, inspirational – for other researchers in the field.

5. Structure of the volume and outline of chapters

The first chapter of the book sets the stage for most of the following chapters. In their contribution "Concepts as Methodology – A Plea for Arrangement Thinking in the Study of Affect", the philosophers Jan Slaby, Rainer Mühlhoff and Philipp Wüschner lend insight into the development and refinement of concepts as a philosophical method that can serve as a cross-disciplinary methodology in the study of affect and emotion. Concepts – understood by the authors as working concepts – are not pre-given entities, but are dynamic and operative templates for scientific articulation and understanding, constantly made and modified during the research process. Concepts thus inform and inspire empirical research while also being informed by this research. Once they gain a certain salience, concepts are able to connect different fields and perspectives and to bridge theory with empirical data. The authors illustrate their considerations with the exemplary case of the concept of an affective arrangement – one of the central concepts of the entire CRC that will be referred to in a number of other chapters in this volume. Affective arrangements are dynamic formations comprising heterogeneous elements such as persons, artifacts, discourse, behaviors and expressions, all coalescing in a particular spatial setting. In such local formations, relational affect unfolds in a characteristic mode of composition, which can be empirically investigated by systematically analyzing how the human and non-human, material and immaterial elements relate to each other in the case at hand, and how they jointly produce distinct interactional dynamics. By presenting three examples for affective arrangements (contemporary white-collar work environments, street protests during the revolutionary uprisings in Egypt in 2011, and ceremonies of worship at saints' shrines in Sehwan, Pakistan) the authors illustrate how the arrangement perspective can be applied as a methodological orientation in the study of affect. In this way, they refine and deepen the relational, situated and transindividual understanding of affect common to all contributions of this volume.

Part I – Textualities

Following this initial chapter, Part I of this volume focuses on text- and narration-based methodological approaches for the study of affects and emotions. Exploring the entanglement of language, emotion and affect is a difficult task, as research in the social and behavioral sciences, linguistics and literary studies has shown. If it were true that affect precedes any form of language and is located beyond the reach of linguistic "capture", as some proponents of affect theory propose (most notably, Massumi, 1995, 2002), this would render most conventional social science methods incapable of providing access to affective phenomena. In light of these challenges, and building on a relational understanding of affect, the chapters in this part explore the potential for discourse analysis, qualitative interviews and photovoice techniques to further empirical analyses of emotional and affective dynamics. In so doing, they seek to overcome the conceptual divide between affect and language. Instead, they propose that language itself is imbued with affect and is thus a key conduit of relational affect in its own right. The textual materials analyzed in Part I include documents that can be found by researchers, in the sense that they already exist in the world before the researcher becomes active, as is the case in discourse analysis (Chapter 3). Yet Part I also considers textual material produced by the researchers themselves for analytical purposes during the research process, as is the case for interview transcripts or fieldnotes (Chapters 4 and 5).

The first contribution in Part I, "Reading for Affect – A Methodological Proposal for Analyzing Affective Dynamics in Discourse", was written by an interdisciplinary team of sociologists and literary scholars. Based on a review of works on the relationship between language, discourse, affect and emotion in social sciences and cultural studies, Anna L. Berg, Christian von Scheve, Yasemin Ural and Robert Walter-Jochum developed a methodological approach for analyzing affective dynamics in discourse. Bringing together affect theory and methods of discourse analysis, they argue that focusing on different "bodily" aspects of language, and on the relations between discursively produced bodies, provides insights into the affective potential of language. To this aim, the authors introduce the term "discourse bodies", which refers to entities in discourse that are produced and defined by their relation to one another. Discourse bodies are entities that are portrayed and characterized in texts *as if* they had qualities of sensitive (human or animal) bodies, a linguistic technique the authors dub "bodification". The chapter is grounded in the work of a research project investigating the role of affect and emotion in public debates on feelings of religious belonging, moral injury and hate speech. Here, the authors are specifically interested in the bodification of social collectives and the political implications of this linguistic strategy. Reporting on a case study centering on German news coverage after the *Charlie Hebdo* Attack in Paris, the proposed approach *Reading for Affect* is illustrated in three dimensions: (1) *the discursive ascription of emotions to bodies*: Here the authors suggest that discursive bodies come into existence by ascribing feelings, emotions or affective capacities to abstract and non-material entities; (2) *the relations between discourse bodies*: In a second step, the chapter analyzes how these bodies become linguistically related to each other, as these relations constitute the affective dynamics between bodies; and (3) *the bodily material characteristics of discourse itself*: Here the materiality of language itself is considered, as well as discourse products beyond the textual sphere, for example, T-shirts or posters. By providing an exemplary analysis that includes all three dimensions, the authors show how an analytical perspective informed by affect theory can be applied effectively to the study of the discursive formation of antagonistic social collectives.

By exploring the potential of qualitative interviews for empirical research on affect in political science, Chapter 4 deals with a second central method of data collection in the social sciences. In their contribution, "Interviews as Situated Affective Encounters – A Relational and Processual Approach for Empirical Research on Affect, Emotion and Politics", the political scientists Bilgin Ayata, Cilja Harders, Derya Özkaya and Dina Wahba note that empirical research on affect is very limited in the discipline of political science, and argue that the discipline's positivist understanding of interviews is too narrow to accommodate empirical studies of affect. Thus, as an alternative, the authors advance a relational and processual understanding of interviews informed by methodological approaches in neighboring fields such as anthropology and feminist studies. Moreover, they conceptualize qualitative interviews as situated affective encounters in their own right. Such encounters, they argue, cannot be reduced to the interview situation itself, but must be seen in a broader temporal context, in which the relation between interviewer and interlocutor must be considered with regard to its affective and emotional dimensions and to changing intensities or dissonances. To illustrate such an understanding of qualitative interviews, the authors draw from their research on the affective dynamics of political participation during the occupations of Tahrir Square in Cairo in 2011 and of Gezi Park in Istanbul in 2013, which included more than 90 semi-structured qualitative interviews with activists and participants in the occupations in addition to ethnographic participant observation. Their empirical examples show how the experiences of their interlocutors are narrated and how they reverberate the affective intensities of the past moment. Moreover, through their case study, they demonstrate the importance of translating the immediacy of affect into descriptions by documenting bodily expressions, silences, cracks and non-verbal interactions during the interview, in addition to documenting the researchers' own affects and emotions during the research process.

Chapter 5, written by the social anthropologists Birgitt Röttger-Rössler, Gabriel Scheidecker and Anh Thu Anne Lam, presents another facet of qualitative interviews that incorporates photography as a method for gaining access to the emotional worlds of young people. Their chapter, entitled "Narrating Visualized Feelings – Photovoice as a Tool for Researching Affects and Emotions among School Students", describes an approach to investigating the formation of feelings among school children. Ninety students were asked to take pictures of situations, objects, places or persons that evoke feelings in them. Afterwards, they were interviewed about these pictures. Through this intersection of visualization and narration, the researchers obtained rich material and profound insights into the students' emotional experiences and affective relations. Some of their findings are illustrated in three examples of salient themes: pets, objects and relaxation. The authors highlight the third topic, relaxation, as especially relevant for an affect-theoretical perspective. In discussing the methodological implications of their approach, the authors emphasize its collaborative nature and argue that the photovoice method is much better suited to grasp the meanings that children and adolescence ascribe to their lifeworlds than the conventional interview, which depends on an adult-privileged code of words. The authors also stress the narrative-generating potential of the photos and their capability to embody and anchor the student's particular ways of seeing, feeling, resonating and verbalizing. They also note that, from an affect-theoretical perspective, it is methodologically important that this procedure begins with images instead of words, because in this way, it is precisely the materiality of the emotional lifeworlds of the interlocutors and the various affective relations therein that come into view and becomes empirically traceable.

Part II – Audiovisualities

Given the increasingly central role of visuality in contemporary societies, it is vital to understand the relationship between images and affectivity, and to explore empirical methods for doing so. Part II thus turns decisively to the important role of images in the analysis of affective societies. It concentrates on methodological approaches to analyzing both visual and audiovisual materials. The contributions in this part span the perspectives of art history, film and media studies, and sociology. They deal with (audio-)visual materials which are either produced by persons other than the researchers (Chapters 6 and 7) or by the researchers themselves during the research process for documentary or analytical purposes (Chapters 8 and 9).

In Chapter 6, "Images that Move – Analyzing Affect with Aby Warburg", art historian Kerstin Schankweiler and philosopher Philipp Wüschner address the theoretical and methodological foundations of image analysis. Starting with Erwin Panofsky's difference between iconography and iconology, the authors emphasize the relevance of precise image descriptions and well-grounded interpretation for aesthetics and art history. They illustrate how the practice of these basic techniques leads to a deeply embodied expertise of the researcher, which can be described as a constantly refined capacity to be affected by one's research objects. Though image analysis accordingly relies on the researcher's perception, observation and reflection, it is objectifiable when the researcher accounts for her own process of being affected by relating it back to visible formal elements of the image. Based on examples from their own research, the authors illustrate how affective qualities such as movements or intensities can be identified and described, and how affect accordingly materializes in images. In order to analyze images as "storage" of affect in terms of materialization and formalization, the authors refer to Aby Warburg's concept of the "pathos formula" (Warburg, 1905). Clarifying this notion, the authors show that the formulaic depiction of expressive gestures of heightened affective intensity is central. By analyzing exemplary images, the authors illustrate how pathos formulas capture moments of affective intensity (for example, movement), formalize them and thus enable their circulation. In this respect the authors emphasize the renewed relevance of Warburg's concept for analyses of recent social media phenomena, in which the circulation of images, and thus also of affects, is of utmost importance.

While Chapter 6 addresses single images with a focus on pathos formulas, Chapter 7 is devoted to the analysis of audiovisual movement-images, in which pathos scenes are central. In their contribution, "The Temporal Composition of Affects in Audiovisual Media", film scholars Hermann Kappelhoff and Hauke Lehmann develop the term "audiovisual dramaturgy of affect" to analyze the compositional structures of audiovisual movement-images with regard to strategies, means and patterns of affectively engaging spectators. Based on the theoretical background of the film analytic concept of expressive movement, they explain the complex relationship between aesthetic techniques and the poetics of affect established and canonized through these techniques and the affective involvement of the spectator, which is activated and shaped by these techniques. Audiovisual rhythm is central to cinematic expressive movement. Such rhythm includes all aspects of cinematic staging, such as light, color, music, space or montage, and unfolds temporally with ever-changing intensities. In order to analyze this audiovisual dramaturgy, the authors developed the method eMAEX (electronically based media analysis of expressive-movement-images). They illustrate this method through the exemplary analysis of the war film genre. To do so, they subdivide the material into scenic units as the basis for the subsequent identification of pathos scenes, which are characterized by distinguishable realms of affect. These realms are activated by the expressive movement, which can also be divided into different units within a single pathos scene. By analyzing the audiovisual composition of each scene, as well as the temporal arrangement of the scenes, the authors are able to reconstruct the dramaturgy of affect. In their conclusion, the authors discuss the possibilities and challenges of adapting their method to different subjects of study.

The relationship between moving images and spectators is also the focus of Chapter 8, "Analyzing Affective Media Practices by the Use of Video Analysis". Here, in contrast to the previous chapter, media and communications scholars Margreth Lünenborg and Tanja Maier apply an affect-theoretical perspective to empirical audience research. They combine textual television analysis for investigating TV shows (*Germany's Next Topmodel*) and digital video analysis for studying media audiences while watching these shows. With this combination of approaches, they explore the affective dynamics that occur between what is happening on the television screen and what goes on in front of that screen. They describe their approach to affective media practices with regard to the collection and analysis of their video material. Informed by the mapping approach of Clarke's (2005) situational analysis, they develop a relational method of video analysis that enables them to identify those elements of the reception situation that are relevant for tracing affective dynamics. To do this, the authors devise situational maps based on the coding of their empirical material. They illustrate their approach through the example of the material "sharing the excitement" – which led them to develop one of their central concepts – and show how this affective media practice is meaningfully enacted on the TV screen as well as in front of it. Furthermore, they note that viewers are not only involved corporeally but also cognitively – for instance, by commenting, evaluating or judging what they see on the screen. In the last part of their contribution, Lünenborg and Maier address the impacts of affects by discussing the connection of affective media practices to the production of belonging and affective orientations.

The next Chapter (9) deals with the analysis of video material from a sociological perspective. The contribution "Videography of Emotions and Affectivity in Social Situations", by sociologists Hubert Knoblauch, Michael Wetzels and Meike Haken, exemplifies a productive method of analyzing emotions and affectivity through the use of videography – a technique that combines video analysis with ethnography. Following an overview of the development and key features of videography, the authors outline the connections among audiovisual studies, emotion and affectivity. They consider emotions as relational communicative actions, since emotions are communicated by the body in certain gestures or postures that can be observed and understood by others. This, in turn, is the precondition for a social scientific exploration of emotions through video analysis. The authors then turn to their central example of jubilation at a football match. Since their empirical research is based on a project about audience emotions in sports and religion, the authors use the example of jubilation in the sports arena to demonstrate the relationality of emotion. After reviewing their process of video data selection, coding and transcription, the authors take a closer look at the multimodal bodily gestalt of jubilation. The authors show that different degrees of audience involvement can be observed through an analysis of the different ways actors perform jubilation at the match. Furthermore, their sequential analysis shows how a specific affective dynamic unfolds temporally. By considering the institutional context of the football game in comparison to religious contexts, it becomes clear that this affective dynamic is strongly related to the contingency and agonality of the game.

In sum, the contributions to part II on audiovisualities of affective relations provide a diverse range of methods that use the modalities of image and sound to focus on local and media-specific formations of affect and emotion. In this way, the chapters collectively enhance the scope and sophistication of methodologically sound research into recurring formats, modalities and expressive patterns of affect.

Part III – Performativities

Part III addresses performativity as a cornerstone of empirical affect research. Performativity is central to an affect-theoretical perspective for at least two reasons. First, unlike internal, individual states, affects become apparent in relational situations and through actions. Performativity is thus central to the way affective relationality unfolds temporally in specific local configurations or dynamic sequences. Second, this unfolding of affective relationality often takes place in public performance arenas in which politically contested issues of social coexistence are both acted out and debated. Accordingly, Part III includes four chapters focusing on performativity in social situations, theatre performances, texts, and talk, and drawing on approaches from anthropology, theatre and performance studies, and literary studies. These chapters show how affective and emotional dynamics can be analyzed in performative settings, such as media practices in transnational contexts, discourse production events, multilingual literary texts or the theatre.

In Chapter 10, cultural anthropologists Ingrid Kummels and Thomas John propose "Investigating Affective Media Practices in a Transnational Setting". They do so from a media anthropology perspective by exploring the transnational relations between the inhabitants of a Zapotec village called Yalálag in Mexico and their relatives living in the United States. The authors analyze the affective dimensions of mediatized social relations and argue that these affects are central to processes of transnational community building. In particular, they highlight the value of applying a multi-layered methodology when studying affective media practices as an object of research. Their empirical example of a fiesta in Yalálag deals with a female dance group from Los Angeles, which became the first group of women to perform a Zapotec ritual dance previously reserved for men in the community of origin. The first methodological layer consisted of participant observation and informal conversations centering on the affective media practices of this group's dance performance, its remediation through video and social media, and the larger affectively laden debates which these media events triggered. Several further methodological layers were then applied to the initial empirical data gathered, including videos of actors, such as those produced by Zapotec professional videographers, as well as the researchers' own videos. Finally, formal interviews were conducted in Yalálag and Los Angeles, during which the interviewees explained their Facebook pages and proposed their exegesis. By basing the final analysis on all four methodological layers, the authors show that this approach is able to discern step-by-step how particular actors residing either in Yalálag or Los Angeles "do affects"; that is, how they resignify emotions and transculturalize emotion repertoires when remediating Zapotec dances and culture via video and social media.

In his contribution, "The Ethnography of Affect in Discourse Practice – Performing Sentiment in the Time Machine", legal anthropologist Jonas Bens offers an example of how to ethnographically investigate discourse practices as socially embedded affective dynamics. In order to do so, the author introduces the term "discourse practice event", which he understands "as a specific place in the world and a specific moment in time in which people communicate in order to be heard by a public". Building on this notion, Bens reconstructs how linguistic performances co-constitute discourse practice events as affective arrangements. His empirical case study draws on his research about the International Criminal Court's outreach activities in Uganda in the context of the trial against Dominic Ongwen, the former leader of the rebel force Lord's Resistance Army in Northern Uganda. Through detailed description and analysis of a selected outreach scene,

Bens gives profound insight into the relational affective dynamics at work among the co-present bodies of speakers and listeners as well as among the material setting, the atmosphere, and audiences not physically present, such as the ICC itself or the international community. Finally, the author argues that in order to understand exactly what is happening in this scene, it is necessary to include broader structural forces and long-term processes in the ethnography of discourse practice. Arguing through his case study that sentiments are re-enactments of the past and pre-enactments of the future, the author shows that sentiments are invoked, enacted and transformed in discourse practice events.

Chapter 12 tackles one of the most central settings of performativity in social life: the theatre. In their contribution, "Affective Dynamics in the Theatre: Towards a Relational and Poly-Perspectival Performance Analysis", Doris Kolesch and Matthias Warstat interrogate the potential of Theatre Studies' performance analysis for research on affect. Since performance analysis is the most important method in Theatre and Performance Studies today, the authors begin by presenting its central characteristics and reviewing its complex genealogy. In turning to the role of emotions and affectivity in performance analysis, the authors introduce the memory protocol. Memory protocols enable researchers to link their own affects to specific scenic constellations on the stage. As such, they are an important tool with which researchers can account for their own ways of being affected by particularly intense and memorable experiences during a performance, enabling a retrospective analysis of the relational dynamics on the stage as well as between stage and spectator. Based on two case studies from the contexts of postmigrant and immersive theatre, Kolesch and Warstat illustrate their methodological perspective in practice and discuss the challenges of a performance analysis that draws on affect theory, especially with regard to novel theatre forms. By drawing on exemplary theatre cases such as these, the authors are able to demonstrate how affectivity can be analyzed as a performative process involving relations among materials, actors, objects, voices, languages and spatial dispositions. In so doing, they are able to propose a new way of analyzing performances from a stance they describe as multi- or poly-perspectivism: a stance that takes the polyphonic and relational structure of affective experiences fully into account.

Part III's final chapter addresses the performativity of literary texts through Anne Fleig's contribution, "Shared and Divided Feelings in Translingual Texts of Emine Sevgi Özdamar – Performativity and Affective Relationality of Language, Writing and Belonging". Fleig, a literary scholar, investigates the affective dimensions *of* as well as *in* contemporary literature. Fleig's approach stresses that affect is not only a result of writing but is also an integral part of the writing process itself, so that the performativity of language is one of its key dimensions. Starting with the relationship of language and textuality, Fleig emphasizes the bodily dimension of language with reference to Bakhtin's (1984 [1929]) concepts of heteroglossia and of dialogism. Her analysis is empirically grounded in her study of the translingual texts of Emine Sevgi Özdamar, a multilingual German author of Turkish ancestry. Fleig shows that Özdamar's transligual writing reflects on the act of literary writing, as well as on the processes of acquiring a new language and of moving in and between languages – all of which gesture poignantly to the question of belonging. Fleig argues that this moving between languages is an affective encounter between bodies and words, and that the texts themselves perform the difference between speaking and writing in the artistic representation of those processes. Her empirical case of a translingual author offers a useful template for further literary investigations of performativity and affective relationality more broadly.

Part IV – Reflexivities

The fourth part of this volume focuses on reflexivity as a condition for methodological development in research on affect. The contributions in this part address such topics as the role of researchers' own affects and emotions during research, the need for novel tools to enable researchers to fruitfully make use of their own emotions as an epistemic resource, and the value of multi-perspectivity as a methodological approach in interdisciplinary research teams. In addition, this section also comprises a chapter on the investigation of emotions by using computer-assisted qualitative data analysis software.

The first contribution in this part, "Researching Affects in the Clinic and Beyond – Multi-perspectivity, Ethnography, and Mental Health-Care Intervention", comes from a team of authors with distinct disciplinary backgrounds. Here, two psychiatrists (Eric Hahn and Thi Minh Tam Ta), one psychologist (Thi Main Huong Nguyen) and three anthropologists (Edda Heyken, Anita von Poser and Jörg-Christian Lanca) draw on their experiences as an interdisciplinary research team to develop a methodological approach that is multi-perspectival. In particular, they draw on their experience developing an innovative affect- and emotion-focused group therapy for first- and second-generation Vietnamese migrants and Germans of Vietnamese descent in Berlin, in the context of their research project "Affective Efforts of Migration: South and North Vietnamese Lifeworlds in Separated and Reunified Berlin". To achieve the goal of establishing a cultural and context-sensitive form of therapy with a person-centered approach, the anthropologists in the team accompanied the patients outside the clinic across their various social, spatial and structural environments. The authors describe how their different spatial, methodological and disciplinary perspectives enabled them to collectively develop a deeper understanding of the affective complexities of their patients' lives. However, they also discuss potential risks that may arise from the systematic application of multi-perspectivity in this constellation. In addressing this concern, they build on their practical experience as a multi-perspectival team to isolate replicable factors that strengthened their study and that can serve future research projects of this kind. Notably, they observe how a clearly defined distribution of roles and tasks as well as intra- and interdisciplinary team "intervisions" were central for being able to learn from each other.

In Chapter 15, " 'All Eyes Closed' – Dis/Sensing in Comparative Fieldwork on Affective-Religious Experiences", social anthropologists Dominik Mattes, Omar

Kasmani and Hansjörg Dilger highlight the importance of using the researcher's own bodily perceptions and ways of sensing the field as a crucial component of ethnographic research. Their chapter draws on their ongoing comparative research project in Berlin, which explores how affective experiences and practices are shaped and embodied in a neo-Pentecostal church attended largely by West African migrants, and in a predominantly Turkish-speaking Sufi prayer circle. This experience confronts the authors with important limitations of the main methods of ethnographic fieldwork. They note that standard ethnographic procedures – such as listening to interlocutors and observing in the field – usually fall short when it comes to understanding and representing the affective atmosphere of religious gatherings. In two case studies, they discuss their decision to pay closer attention to their own senses and to close their eyes as part of the believers' practices. These unconventional decisions enabled them to open and enrich their understanding of what it is like to be affected in such a space and of the affective power of these gatherings' atmospheres. In doing so, they gained access to sensations of intensity, intimacy, bonding, belonging and immediacy, as well as moments of struggle and resistance, awkwardness and discomfort. In their conclusion, the authors stress that while their focus on their own bodily involvement enhanced their access to affective dynamics, this method should be used as a meaningful addition to the existing methodological repertoire of ethnographic fieldwork, rather than a wholesale replacement of it. Overall, their chapter suggests that a reflexive inclusion of the researchers' own sensing and dis-sensing, of her own manner of being affected, broadens an access to potential elements that can become relevant for the empirical analysis of affective dimensions of social phenomena in many domains.

This reflexive perspective on the researchers' own bodily perceptions is complemented and substantively enriched in Chapter 16. The social anthropologists Thomas Stodulka and Ferdiansyah Thajib and the political scientist Samia Dinkelaker provide an encompassing and field-proven toolbox for an affectively aware methodology of ethnographic research. At the beginning of their chapter "Fieldwork, Ethnography, and the Empirical Affect Montage", the authors highlight fieldwork as relational processes of encountering the so-called "other" and discuss the methodological dilemma of ethnographers' immersion and detachment during participant observation. They argue that ethnographers' affects and emotions, their affective positionalities and practices have thus far been inadequately discussed as a systematic methodological heuristic with significant epistemological potential. To counter this lack of attention, Stodulka, Dinkelaker and Thajib have designed templates for semi-structured emotion diaries to encourage and support fieldworkers' systematic reflection and documentation of their own affective experiences and to train their emotional literacy. These emotion diaries facilitate an interpretation of ethnographic observations that is sensitized to their multifarious affective dimensions. By describing their own experiences of using these diaries for their research, the authors highlight a number of ways these devices act as a complement to more established techniques of ethnographic data construction. They stress emotion diaries' psychological, strategic, epistemic and representational dimensions, and introduce the concepts of *field emotions* and *epistemic emotions* as core analytical concepts for relating to and analyzing the phenomena studied. Based on their experience, they propose an ethnographic writing technique of "empirical affect montage" to juxtapose researchers' affects and emotions with the behavior and talk of those they study.

The final contribution by sociologist Elgen Sauerborn proposes using computer-assisted qualitative data analysis software to investigate emotions. Sauerborn notes that this methodological approach goes against the grain of commonplace assumptions about data analysis software in emotion research. Qualitative research in the sociology of emotions often draws on constructivist or phenomenological approaches. Considering emotions as social constructions comes along with methodological paradigms that seek to reconstruct and understand social dimensions of emotions such as meaning, interpretations and knowledge as well as norms, values or discourses. This, however, is generally considered incongruous with computer-assisted qualitative data analysis software (CAQDAS) since the use of software is mostly associated with positivist approaches and quantifying techniques of data analysis. Sauerborn advocates for the methodological value of using CAQDAS in constructivist emotion research. To do so, she discusses three ways in which software can facilitate and broaden the investigation of emotions in qualitative data. Firstly, she demonstrates CAQDAS features that are useful for inductive analyses. For example, she shows how codes, memos, linkages and comments can help identify pivotal data segments for in-depth analysis. These tools also simplify the use of a variety of different data sources that are crucial for certain kinds of emotion research. Secondly, by drawing on an understanding of qualitative analysis as a set of material practices, she demonstrates how researchers modify their own data with their interpretations. Since CAQDAS provides a visualization of the researcher's interpretations, it can be used as an instrument for materializing the social dimensions of emotions. Thirdly, she examines the importance of including the researcher and her own emotions in the analysis process. In particular, she focuses on the significance of the researcher's own emotional biography as well as the role of her feelings towards the data. In so doing, Sauerborn suggests that CAQDAS can improve the reflexivity of subjective emotional narratives, while also enabling researchers to visualize feelings they have towards certain data segments. These methodological improvements can significantly facilitate the researchers' understanding of the patterns that underlie emotions.

6. Outlook

In light of the broad spectrum of methodologies and methods assembled in the 16 chapters of this volume, it becomes clear that affective phenomena can be investigated in countless domains of social and cultural life: in the discursive formations of public debate and artistic articulation, as part of the actions and strategies in politics and social movements, in the quotidian worlds of children and adolescents, in concrete social situations, in constellations of performances and spectators, in visual worlds, in the negotiations of legal issues or in contemporary literature. All of these fields provide researchers with rich data of various sorts, data that require working concepts, methodological perspectives and analytical tools and methods for researchers to make sense of them.

The chapters in this volume clearly show that affectivity as both a fundamental and formative process of sociality is by no means beyond empirical research. Contrary to existing misconceptions, the analysis of affective phenomena is not limited to the observation and description of material bodies alone, thereby side-stepping their potential to verbalization and articulation. Affectivity as a socially relevant process is also evident in the various ways through which material bodies become related to one another: spatially, visually and linguistically. Moreover, researchers as well as their "objects" of research, such as interlocutors, collabora-tors or artifacts, can very well develop a descriptive and analytical repertoire for affective dynamics to which actors are exposed and which they co-constitute at the same time.

Obviously, affectivity poses a number of challenges for empirical research. The contributions to this book show that these challenges are by no means insurmount-able. On the contrary: they can be made productive for thinking about methodo-logical innovation and the cross-fertilization of different disciplinary fields and methodologies. The chapters and their broad range of methodological proposals from different disciplinary backgrounds show that affective phenomena can be made "visible" and accessible in many different and promising ways. It is my hope that our attempt to adapt and refine existing methods and methodologies and to describe and reflect concrete scholarly research practices will substantially advance empirical research on affect and emotion in different fields.

Notes

1 There are, of course, other methodological perspectives and methods that might prove valuable for researching affect, such as social network analysis, but these approaches would be more adequate for research interests and questions that are currently not at the heart of the *Affective Societies* center.
2 For example, Burkitt (2014) and Parkinson, Fisher, and Manstead (2005).

References

Bakhtin, M 1984, *Problems of Dostoevsky's Poetics*, ed. and transl. C Emerson, University of Minnesota Press, Minneapolis.
Beatty, A 2005, 'Emotions in the field: What are we talking about?' *Journal of the Royal Anthropological Institute*, vol. 11, no. 1, pp. 17–37.
Beck, U 1992, *Risk Society: Towards a New Modernity*, Sage Publications, London.
Blackman, L 2012, *Immaterial Bodies: Affect, Embodiment, Mediation*, Sage Publications, London.
Blackman, L 2015, 'Researching affect and embodied hauntologies: Exploring an ana-lytics of experimentation', in BT Knudsen & C Stage (eds.), *Affective Methodologies:*

Developing Cultural Research Strategies for the Study of Affect, pp. 25–44, Palgrave Macmillan, Basingstoke.

Blumer, H 1954, 'What is wrong with social theory?' *American Sociological Review*, vol. 19, no. 1, pp. 3–10.

Burkitt, I 2014, *Emotions and Social Relations*, Sage Publications, London.

Castells, M 2010, *The Rise of the Network Society, the Information Age: Economy, Society and Culture*, vol. I., 2nd edn., Wiley-Blackwell, Cambridge.

Clarke, AE 2005, *Situational Analysis: Grounded Theory After the Postmodern Turn*, Sage Publications, Thousand Oaks.

Clough, PT 2009, 'The new empiricism: Affect and sociological method', *European Journal of Social Theory*, vol. 12, no. 1, pp. 43–61.

Coan, JA & Allen, JJB (eds.), 2007, *Handbook of Emotion Elicitation and Assessment*, Oxford University Press, New York.

Corbin, JM & Strauss, AL 2008, *Basics of Qualitative Research: Techniques and Procedures for Developing Grounded Theory*, Sage Publications, London.

Flam, H & Kleres, J (eds.), 2015, *Methods of Exploring Emotions*, Routledge, London.

Gerring, J 2012, *Social Science Methodology: A Unified Framework*, Cambridge University Press, Cambridge.

Greco, M & Stenner, P (eds.), 2008, *Emotions: A Social Science Reader*, Routledge, London.

Gregg, M & Seigworth, GJ (eds.), 2010, *The Affect Theory Reader*, Duke University Press, Durham.

Heise, DR 2006, *Expressive Order: Confirming Sentiments in Social Actions*, Springer VS, Wiesbaden.

Hemmings, C 2005, 'Invoking affect: Cultural theory and the ontological turn', *Cultural Studies*, vol. 19, no. 5, pp. 548–567.

Holmes, M 2014, *Distance Relationships: Intimacy and Emotions Amongst Academics and Their Partners in Dual-Locations*, Palgrave Macmillan, Basingstoke.

Holmes, M 2015, 'Researching emotional reflexivity', *Emotion Review*, vol. 7, no. 1, pp. 61–66.

Izard, CE 1991, *The Psychology of Emotions*, Plenum, New York.

Katz, J 2004, 'Everyday lives and extraordinary research methods', *Social Science Information*, vol. 43, no. 4, pp. 609–619.

Kleres, J 2011, 'Emotions and narrative analysis: A methodological approach', *Journal for the Theory of Social Behaviour*, vol. 41, no. 2, pp. 182–202.

Knudsen, BT & Stage, C (eds.), 2015, *Affective Methodologies: Developing Cultural Research Strategies for the Study of Affect*, Palgrave Macmillan, Basingstoke.

Law, J, Ruppert, E & Savage, M 2011, *The Double Social Life of Methods*. CRESC Working Paper Series, Working Paper No. 95. Available from: www.open.ac.uk/research projects/iccm/files/iccm/Law%20Savage%20Ruppert.pdf.

Lazarus, RS 1991, *Emotion and Adaptation*, Oxford University Press, New York.

Leys, R 2011, 'The turn to affect: A critique', *Critical Inquiry*, vol. 37, pp. 434–472.

Lindemann, G 2009, *Das Soziale von seinen Grenzen her denken*, Velbrück, Weilerswist.

Loughran, T & Mannay, D (eds.), 2018, *Emotion and the Researcher: Sites, Subjectivities, and Relationships*, Emerald, Bingley.

Massumi, B 1995, 'The autonomy of affect', *Cultural Critique*, vol. 31, pp. 83–110.

Massumi, B 2002, *Parables for the Virtual: Movement, Affect, Sensation*, Duke University Press, Durham.

Olson, R, Godbold, N & Patulny, R 2015, 'Introduction: Methodological innovations in the sociology of emotions part two – methods', *Emotion Review*, vol. 7, no. 2, pp. 143–144.

Panksepp, J 1998, *Affective Neuroscience: The Foundations of Human and Animal Emotions*, Oxford University Press, New York.

Parkinson, B, Fisher, A & Manstead, ASR 2005, *Emotion in Social Relations: Cultural, Group, and Interpersonal Processes*, Psychology Press, New York.

Prosser, B 2015, 'Knowledge of the heart: Ethical implications of sociological research with emotion', *Emotion Review*, vol. 7, no. 2, pp. 175–180.

Quigley, KS, Lindquist, KA & Barrett, LF 2013, 'Inducing and measuring emotion: Tips, tricks, and secrets', in HT Reis & CM Judd (eds.), *Handbook of Research Methods in Social and Personality Psychology*, pp. 220–250, Cambridge University Press, New York.

Röttger-Rössler, B & Slaby, J (eds.), 2018, *Affect in Relation – Families, Places, Technologies*, Routledge, London.

Slaby, J & von Scheve, C (eds.), 2019, *Affective Societies – Key Concepts*, Routledge, London.

von Scheve, C 2017, 'A social relational account of affect', *European Journal of Social Theory*, vol. 21, no. 1, pp. 39–59.

von Scheve, C & Salmela, M (eds.), 2014, *Collective Emotions*, Oxford University Press, New York.

Warburg, A 1905, 'Dürer und die heidnische Antike', in A Warburg (ed.), 1998, *Die Erneuerung der heidnischen Antike. Kulturwissenschaftliche Beiträge zur Geschichte der europäischen Renaissance*, G Bing (ed.), 1932, reprint 1998, H Bredekamp & M Diers (eds.), pp. 443–448, Akademie Verlag, Berlin.

Wetherell, M 2012, *Affect and Emotion: A New Social Science Understanding*, Sage Publications, London.

Chapter 2

Concepts as methodology

A plea for arrangement thinking in the study of affect

Jan Slaby, Rainer Mühlhoff and Philipp Wüschner

Introduction

'Work on the concept' is a key component in all scholarly and scientific work, regardless of whether it takes place in the humanities or in the sciences, in cultural studies, ethnology, sociology or the arts. By 'work on the concept' we mean the creation, development and continuous refinement of contentful yet concise concepts that are capable of opening up focused perspectives on selected segments of reality. Concepts enable and advance understanding by aiding a robust yet open-textured grasp of how phenomena hang together systematically. We understand concepts in a pragmatist key as *action schemata* that function as dynamic templates for thinking and understanding, informing observation, trained judgment, experimental and technical practices of all kinds and persuasions. What we will work toward here is a more reflective and self-conscious understanding of how well-made *working concepts* inform and actively drive ongoing research – and intellectual activity more broadly – across a significant spectrum of approaches dealing with affect and emotion.

Researchers and scholars across the sciences and the humanities share a widespread sense for the importance of concepts. But several misconceptions about concepts hamper a clear understanding. Sometimes, concepts get conflated with terminology. This raises what we call the 'myth of definition': the assumption that substantive concepts have a simple and stable definition that might be stated in a few sentences and will then settle most controversial issues surrounding a given concept. A nuisance that accompanies the myth of definition is that concepts for which such a concise definition cannot be easily provided might be disqualified from learned discourse. Concomitant to the first myth is a second myth, to which contemporary philosophers are particularly prone to succumb: the 'myth of precision'. Here, the idea is that concepts must be capable of a precise and unambiguous elucidation that legislates most or all instances of their application in terms of adequacy. Even where issues of vagueness have been accommodated, the logic behind this second myth is that concepts can be detached from their situations of application, as if there was a neutral vantage point from which one could specify concept and object independently from one another and compare them in an aspect-by-aspect manner. This is a remnant of Cartesian-style representation-alism. As we will illustrate in the present chapter, a different framing for issues involving precision and ambiguities is required, in order to distinguish reasonable requests for clarity from excessive acts of policing conceptual practice.

A third myth is the conflation of concepts with words of natural language (the 'myth of concepts as words'). The assumption is that what a concept amounts to is the meaning of a word of common use, where everyday linguistic practice is the decisive authority for specifying a concept's content. While it is true that ordinary language is a central resource, playing field and consolidating factor for conceptual understanding, it is not true that it holds in store self-standing and nor-matively binding elucidations of all possible concepts. Nor can the development or clarification of concepts be decisively arbitrated with recourse to established linguistic usage. Everyday linguistic practice works as a sustaining backdrop, a formative milieu that in part enables, informs and aids, but does not determine conceptual practice, let alone exhaustively.

All three myths underestimate the extent to which those concepts that are con-tentful enough to be of more than auxiliary use in the sciences and in academic scholarship are a matter of creative invention and deliberate crafting, both in response to an object domain and grounded in the practical and theoretical situ-ation of the researchers or scholars working with them. As the history of science and historical scholarship in general amply illustrate, de facto intellectual practice speaks massively in favor of this latter perspective. Concepts prove changeable, are subject to much inventive development, often in surprising, unanticipated ways, and undergo a lot in the way of historical change and semantic drift, not in irregular ways but by answering to significant new developments in their domains of application. Moreover, concepts are tied up in complex ways with the articula-tive and judgmental capacities of concept users, and thus with these individuals' particular learning histories and skillsets. Concepts are in this regard a matter of "Urteilskraft" ('powers of judgment'), and this gives them an irreducibly qualita-tive and even personal note.[1]

In this chapter, we do not want to dwell at length on these general issues. We do not aspire to provide a theory of concepts, or engage with the many differ-ent approaches to the nature of concepts in philosophy. Favoring a pragmatist approach in a broadly Aristotelian lineage, we understand concepts as dynamic tools for thinking, as intellectual *action schemata*.[2] In line with this, we adhere to the methodological maxim of *practical elucidation* of an exemplary instance – case-based understanding instead of generalization.[3] Thus, we single out an exam-ple of what we deem a productive working concept in interdisciplinary affect research and develop it in detail. This serves a double purpose. For one, we illus-trate in a concrete case much of what we mean by the phrase 'concepts as meth-odology'. Furthermore, we contribute directly to an understanding of relational affect, which has the advantage of closing the gap between reflection on method-ology and content-based inquiry within affect studies. Our choice of example is the concept of an *affective arrangement* – a working concept that we have adapted for our purposes from a precursor notion in continental philosophy, the concept of *agencement* in the work of Deleuze and Guattari (1987). With this concept, we aim to elucidate those complex socio-material settings in which a heightened affective intensity and affective relationality among actors, material conditions and equipmental set-up ensues. The concept thus counters the assumption that affect is always and necessarily a matter of what individuals feel or experience. We are convinced that 'affective arrangement' can become the linchpin of a productive perspective on affect across a number of fields and disciplines (Slaby, Mühlhoff, & Wüschner, 2017).

There is another advantage that this choice of example provides. Concepts themselves can be understood as *agencements*, and thus as arrangements not entirely unlike, in general structure, what we mean when we speak of *affective arrangements*: concatenations of heterogeneous components – usually other concepts – unified by a dynamic mode of composition into a characteristic formation. Accordingly, we assume that the same principles that govern the concept of an affective arrangement also apply to issues pertaining to concepts in general. *Arrangement thinking* – a style of thought we introduce later in this chapter – not only works in affect and emotion research, but also provides an angle for understanding working concepts and their methodological employment. Ideally, then, what we provide in the following is a dual elucidation: of concepts as a methodological device in qualitative affect research on the one hand, and of relational affect and affective arrangements on the other hand.

Working concepts

In philosophy, contrasting approaches to concepts are a central fault line between analytic and continental philosophy. Pragmatism comes closest to a common ground between these traditions, and we indeed adhere to a non-orthodox pragmatist outlook on concepts. On this view, concepts are not pre-given entities (as Platonists or intuitionists would have it), but dynamic constructs that need to be made and re-made by concept users in response to the practical purposes of a given situation of inquiry. Concepts are not detached representations of reality, but action schemata operative in normatively accountable relations to the world – regardless of whether these relations are predominantly cognitive, practical, rhetorical, aesthetic or otherwise. One might gloss this point by saying that, strictly speaking, *there are no concepts* (in the sense of discrete *entities*), but just *conceptual capacities* on the part of intellectually competent agents (see Rouse, 2015 for a related point). Yet, at the same time, such capacities are beholden to historical legacies of use practices and established articulations (codified, for example, in handbooks, compendia or theoretical manifestos). Important precursors in this pragmatist, enactivist, operationalist and dynamic-historical legacy of understanding concepts are Aristotle (both in his notion of 'practical wisdom' or *phronesis* and in his own 'philosophical lexicon', i.e. book Delta of his *Metaphysics*), Kant with his *Critique of Judgment* (especially his idea of reflective – as opposed to determinative – judgments), Nietzsche – with his knack for conceptual invention and creativity and also his thorough genealogical critique of established ideas – and also the later Wittgenstein, with his insistence on rules as not existing outside communal practices of rule-following.[4] In the more narrowly continental strands of the philosophical tradition, an influential articulation of an understanding of concepts – echoing several impulses from the authors and traditions just mentioned – is Deleuze and Guattari's *What Is Philosophy?* (1994, esp. ch. 1). These authors likewise develop a dynamic, enactive and constructivist approach to concepts, but they emphasize the aspect of a concise dynamic formation of elements – stressing the self-standing character of concepts as 'intensive' ideational complexes that are rooted in both a historical trajectory of conceptual development and the concrete articulative capacities and postural orientation of philosophers or theorists (see Schmidgen, 2015).

Before we dip into our case-based exposition, a few remarks on what we mean specifically by the expression *working concept* are in order. In line with the theoretical lineage just sketched, we understand concepts as dynamic templates for articulation – formations of significant elements that can be put to use in intellectual practice, for instance, as schemata for constellating and framing reality in specific ways. For a simple example to start with, one might compare a well-crafted concept to a fire escape plan: it does not purport to give a precise representation of the surroundings (like a map would), but provides a coherent instruction on *how to act* when it matters (and – contrary to the fire escape plan – also specifies *when* it matters). A fire escape plan does not only *show* escape routes but highlights them, renders them salient. It does not represent the world, but articulates – dynamically *prescribes* – a possible event (i.e., an act of escape). As such dynamic templates, concepts actually *do the primal work* within qualitative inquiry. Much like artistic concepts – for example, different shots in cinema (close-ups, long shots, jump-cuts etc.) – they are not only ways to look at things, but also ways to *make things seen*. Concepts enable and facilitate this making-present by way of *intensifying* elements and characteristics of a given domain, just like a camera shot intensifies aspects of what is visible so as to contribute to the constitution of a filmic scene as a coherent arrangement of moving images.[5]

In an effort to stress the (re-)arranging and creative power that concepts unfold within an open discourse, one could also compare their ways of working to a successful or 'viral' *hashtag* in social media. A hashtag not only binds together discursive elements (texts, tweets, comments) and non-discursive elements (affects, experience, desires) but also makes complex phenomena, for instance, social justice issues, addressable in a concise way. Thereby, it might fill a critical gap in a society's hermeneutical repertoire (see Fricker, 2007, ch. 7). On the flipside, just like hashtags, concepts are never safe from misappropriation, bifurcation or bold bias. In relation to the theme of affect, the example of the hashtag also indicates that concepts are not only the lens *through* which an affective scene can be made specifically visible and debatable. At the same time, concepts *themselves* may become the target or carrier of affects as they may catch attention, circulate virally and become detached from their original field of inquiry, potentially inspiring further articulations in other fields. Yet, this comes with the inherent danger of superficiality in that a viral, trending, possibly politicized concept is sometimes perceived as a silver bullet or turns into a universal plane for projection, putatively resolving a long-standing issue but without actually expanding on it. The hashtag example highlights the ambivalence or oscillation of focal concepts between their concise, gripping, reality-illuminating efficacy (in the best case) and their potential to turn into a mere catchphrase, a piece of jargon, an empty abstraction mindlessly reproduced without contact to the original insights that had inspired the creation of the concept (in the worst case).

With the adjective 'working', we therefore not only aim to indicate the provisional character of the concepts in question, i.e., that they might be coarse-grained and open-textured initially, expected to be refined during the course of inquiry. We also assume that concepts themselves do work. They create realities and affects, the circulate and travel to the degree that they can become independent of the original scholarly scope of their invention – for better, when they aspire insightful articulations elsewhere, or for worse, when they degenerate into jargon. This is also why working concepts have to be understood as operating on a plane that is a level up from specific domains of inquiry. Working concepts are generic templates for articulation and understanding – framing devices that are adaptable to a range of different domains and subject matters and capable of different kinds of uptake and case-based specification. They delineate and render salient strategies for framing and embellishing reality while excluding other possible strategies for doing so. We call them *operative templates for articulation*, where 'articulation' refers to a range of different activities of sense-making, spanning forms of verbal description, ways of meaningfully dealing with artifacts, modes of artistic practice and various expressive and aesthetic activities of other kinds (see Rouse, 2015).

Yet, on a pragmatist and enactivist perspective, working concepts cannot be completely generic and formal, on pain of losing any specific content. As we will show later, a contentful concept has both a particular history and is embedded within a specific context, it is rooted in a domain. A concept's genealogy inspires present articulations and provides resources for further work with, and 'on', the concept. In all instances there is an intricate balance between a concept's rootedness in its formative historical trajectory and its openness and versatility with regard to novel elaborations and adaptations. Viewed as such partially domain- and theory-independent devices, working concepts are indeed prone to *travel* through different object domains and fields of inquiry – at times through quite diverse landscapes, which won't leave the concept itself unchanged. Thus, concepts in intellectual practice are what Mieke Bal calls *traveling concepts* – a notion she puts forth as a methodological orientation for the humanities and cultural studies: "They travel – between disciplines, between individual scholars, between historical periods, and between geographically dispersed academic communities. Between disciplines, their meaning, reach, and operational value differ" (Bal, 2002, 24).

In keeping with this orientation, our exemplary elucidation of the concept of an affective arrangement will do both: chart a historical trajectory as well as zoom into different areas of elaboration. We will draw on precursor concepts and hint at neighboring concepts, but we will also craft the concept itself into a specific and – in its present guise – unprecedented concise formation of significance. Inextricable from the characterization of the concept itself comes the illustration of a particular perspective, style of thought or 'optic' that we will call *arrangement thinking*. This is a characteristic of at least those working concepts that reach a certain focality. Concepts that have enough substance and specificity to be suited as anchors of an effective epistemic formation provide those who work with the concept with a characteristic perspective and intellectual posture in approaching and working with their respective subject matter. Such a posture combines a trained theoretical receptivity with a set of practical skills for crafting and framing one's materials, down to the minutiae of technical operations within the process of inquiry.

Conceptual practice across wide swathes of academic and scientific fields already heeds the points and principles we discuss in this chapter. Yet, this is often not acknowledged and not reflected upon, and also not respected enough as a self-standing intellectual practice with its own merits and pitfalls – as something in need of cultivation and, at times, protection, for instance, against ill-advised attempts to establish quantification-based methods in all corners of the academy. What we provide here is meant to be an exemplary account rendering explicit some of what is implicit in day-to-day conceptual practice across a variety of fields of inquiry into affect and emotion. We do this in the hope that working concepts, despite their tentativeness and incompleteness, may become veritable ingredients in the toolbox of interdisciplinary qualitative inquiry and important signposts at the intersection of empirical and theoretical work on relational affect.[6]

Affective arrangement: basic characterization

The concept we chose to be our exemplary case is that of an *affective arrangement*. This is a working concept whose operative purpose is to help provide as much concreteness as possible to the understanding of affect as relational, situated and "transindividual", in critical distinction to individualistic and mentalistic perspectives (see Slaby, Mühlhoff, & Wüschner, 2017). The concept of an affective arrangement bridges instantaneously elements from a relational theory of affect with a number of local domains of inquiry, as it brings the specific concatenations of elements and materials into focus as part of which relational affect unfolds locally. In each case, relational affect transpires as part of local arrays of elements that operate as dynamic formations, comprising, for instance, persons, things, artifacts, spaces, discourse, behaviors and expressions in a characteristic 'intensive' mode of composition. The concept of an affective arrangement not only *refers* to heterogeneous ensembles of materials but also makes them conceivable as such dynamic ensembles in the first place.

Affective arrangements often bring multiple human actors into a coordinated conjunction, so that these actors' mutual affecting and being affected is the central dimension of the arrangement. The concept does neither pertain merely to socio-material settings nor to affective relations in isolation – but rather to *both* in their mutually formative combination. The concept – and the concomitant 'arrangement thinking' as the characteristic skillset, style of thought and optic this concept engenders – can help researchers come to terms with ongoing affective relationality in socio-material domains, in particular where actors with different positions, histories, roles, dispositions or habits engage and interact. Examples – randomly amassed – are corporate offices high on teamwork and affective labor, public events of sports or entertainment, street protests, religious or ceremonious rituals, many social gatherings of other kinds and also the interactive spaces of contemporary networked media. The concept can facilitate micro-analyses of such settings as it furthers both a perspective on the entities that coalesce locally to engender relational affect and also the overall affective tonality or affective atmosphere that prevails in these locales.[7]

As stated earlier, a substantive working concept is not merely a novel designator for creating new domains of examples for a pre-existing theory. Rather, it must be able to arrange theoretical elements and examples in a characteristic manner. A concept in this robust sense also inevitably suggests a critical de-emphasizing of alternative conceptual options. In the case at hand, this might be a sidelining of notions such as emotional contagion, collective emotions or affective atmospheres (these might still be invoked but only as auxiliary elements of affective arrangements). Accordingly, a given concept's history or 'travelogue' is of particular importance – both constructively and critically. In the case at hand, the concept of affective arrangements is inspired by Deleuze and Guattari's influential notion of *agencement* (Deleuze & Guattari, 1983, 1986, 1987; see also Buchanan, 2015; Nail, 2017). Another related precursor concept is Foucault's 'dispositif' (Foucault, 1980), which stresses materiality, historicity and visibility in the unfolding of power relations but does not place particular emphasis on affect. Deleuze and Guattari's "agencement" refers to local concatenations of diverse materials that actively run through a characteristic routine. Thus, their concept combines an understanding of affect with a notion of distributed *agency* in the sense of a performative sequence jointly enacted by a heterogeneous bundle of contributing elements. In line with this, we understand affective arrangements as comprising agency – both human and non-human – in inextricable entanglement with relations of affecting and being affected among their elements.

In order to function as a working concept for the study of affect, and especially as a notion capable of rendering salient the specificity of *affective relations*, it is important to construe the concept of an affective arrangement in a sufficiently open-textured manner. Historical precursor concepts, parallel notions and systematic approaches – also those by Deleuze and Guattari themselves – should best be viewed as inspirations and orientations, short of providing theoretical strictures or mandating particular articulations. A key aspect of the concept is the idea that an affective arrangement is a *fragmentary, open-textured* formation – a tangle of pieces, where the pieces keep their distinctness and autonomy no matter how densely they are enmeshed. Still, the concept only finds application when there is a characteristic 'intensive' mode of relatedness that holds the elements together, a *specific* mode of affecting and being affected. In such a dynamic interplay, the elements sustain a local sphere of affective intensity and thereby both initiate and give shape to characteristic affective relations and agentive routines. In view of this dynamic openness and heterogeneity, formations analyzed as affective arrangements often cannot be sharply demarcated from their surroundings. Yet, there will likely be a sensible difference between inside and an outside, marked by thresholds of intensity. Moreover, affective arrangements are understood as *performatively open-ended*, i.e., as capable of expanding into their surroundings by incorporating new elements.

Examples and focal dimensions

In line with the practical and local orientation of arrangement thinking, we will now present three brief examples from recent work on affect in which the conceptual perspective of the affective arrangement has found application. The cases are such that a particular domain of study has inspired further articulations and conceptual development at the ground level of research. Each will emphasize a particular dimension of affective arrangements, but it is not assumed that all these dimensions must appear together in a single case.

An intuitive example are contemporary work environments such as open-floor corporate offices with their dense communication and interaction routines among co-workers in a spatial set-up, wired up by networked media and interactive work-flow technologies (see Slaby, Mühlhoff, & Wüschner, 2017). Crucial in modern office workplaces where *affective labor* is paramount is both the momentary creation of a specific working atmosphere – an affective style of moment-to-moment interaction and engagement among the co-workers – and the longer-term habituation and cultivation of affective dispositions (Mühlhoff, 2019) and agentive routines (think of a veteran employee going at it in routine absorption contrasted with a novice staggering around the office insecurely). The affective arrangement is a dynamic formation that modulates individual dispositions and harnesses energies and potentialities, often to the benefit of the overall set-up of the company or institution. There is an element of self-organization as local interaction patterns and intra-active routines emerge in part spontaneously, but also a dimension of deliberate design that draws its techniques from long legacies of group dynamics research, organizational psychology, ergonomics or human factors research (among much else). Conceptual elaboration in these settings might suggest further notions capable of characterizing the dense mutual modulation of affectivity, behavior and habit in close-knit workplace interaction, for instance, concepts such as *affective resonance, affective disposition, immersive power* or *mind invasion* (see Mühlhoff & Schütz, 2017; Mühlhoff & Slaby, 2018; Slaby, 2016).

Significant political events and movements might be approached fruitfully through the lens of the affective arrangement. Recent qualitative work on the street protests during the revolutionary uprisings in Egypt in 2011 make use of the concept to bring the particular affective atmosphere, texture and temporality – and their various enabling conditions – of the movement into focus. The protests at issue are those on the Tahrir Square in downtown Cairo on the 18 days of the square's occupation in early 2011 (see Ayata & Harders, 2018). In interviews, activists speak of a palpable intensity and energy unfolding during the protests, and many of the participants describe their time on the square during those days as transformative, life-changing experiences. Approaching the dynamics on the square as a complex of interlocking affective arrangements provides a fruitful angle on the heterogeneity of contributing factors (material, bodily, architectural, practical, discursive, medial, imaginary etc.), on the uniqueness of certain transformative moments, but also on the tensions and differences among the participants or participant factions. Arrangement thinking lets researchers look at the Tahrir Square as a material-discursive site imbued with the sedimented traces of previous struggles, movements, epochs and balances of power that weigh into the particular affective texture of the 2011 uprisings. As a conceptual guide for qualitative research, the optic of arrangement thinking is capable of combining – not merging – individual experiential perspectives, gleaned from narrative interviews with activists, with fine-grained descriptions of the affective dynamics on the square. A socio-political *event* on the world-historical scale is thereby dissected into a confluence of enabling factors without imposing a reductive explanation. It is noteworthy that the political event itself can become the focus of arrangement thinking, as epitomized in the concept of "Midan moment", coined by Ayata and Harders to bring to attention the unique temporality of the exceptional situation of protest, including its manifest transformative force, as experienced by those actively involved at the scene (see Ayata & Harders, 2018).

The ethnographic study of rituals is another domain where the affective arrangement has provided useful conceptual guidance. Consider recent work on religious ceremonies at saints' shrines in Sehwan, Pakistan by the anthropologist Omar Kasmani. An arrangement optic is here brought to bear on the multi-layered temporality of practices of devotion at holy sites, with emphasis on the complex soundscapes, on the "sonic *mise-en-scène* of affect" (Kasmani, 2017). By foregrounding the local arrangement of sound, the thick sensuality and complex historicity of the audible comes into view as a powerful conveyor of affect. Practices of worship are seen as multiply layered soundscapes in which a panoply of tendencies, temporal dimensions, participant orientations, tensions and contestations coalesce at a historically charged site into a unique sonic formation:

> [T]he ordinary tinkering of tea-sellers, the guttural roar of motor-cycle rickshaws, the five calls to prayer, the daily bustle of surrounding markets as well as the occasional fights, brawls and conflicts on site are as much part of an emergent yet already drifting sonic-scene as are dissonances triggered by ritual performances themselves.
>
> (ibid.)

What we call arrangement thinking here entails a sensibility for the time- and site-specific complexities and ambivalences that inhere practices of worship at contested public sites. This prevents a mono-thematic approach that would fore-ground a focus on transcendence and view participants mainly in their role as dev-otees with few other stakes in their practice. Countering such readings, Kasmani emphasizes the political dimension audible at Pakistani shrines, pointing out other vital concerns besides religious ones, and discerning stirrings of a particular his-torical agency on part of those engaged in the rituals: "in publicly sounding alle-giance to Shia figures, events and temporalities, pilgrims long for other histories, they insist on other futures. They voice a historical-emotional consciousness that critiques, interrupts, and refuses a for-granted continuity of the present" (ibid.).

Arrangement thinking: key dimensions

As apparent in these examples, with the concept of affective arrangement comes a particular thought style and a practical as well as theoretical orientation – *arrangement thinking* – that lets theorists and researchers approach affective rela-tions in a specific manner, emphasizing certain aspects and connections while de-emphasizing others. In this section, we outline the focal elements of this orientation.

The first and most general assumption is that affect does not happen in a void: Relations of affecting and being affected are always situated; they unfold as part of local formations of elements, involving actors, materials and environmental conditions, sensory modalities, habits and patterns of practice – and much else – whose characteristics and potentials variously enter into, shape and channel the affective relations in question. The point of arrangement thinking is to bring the contributing elements and dimensions into focus in their specificity and with regard to their particular mode of composition: a particular degree and texture of organization or disorganization. This enables an understanding of a potentially wide-ranging and diverse multiplicity of elements in terms of how they coalesce locally into a concise, recognizable, potentially unique formation of affective relationality.

There is much leeway as to the forms affective arrangements may take, with regard to the elements that might figure in them and as to the types of related-ness holding them together. However, some recurrent features have proven use-ful for elucidating concrete cases. Among these are the aspect of *heterogeneous composition* (i.e., a non-unifying adherence of self-standing elements), the idea of a *polycentric tangle of relations* that nevertheless gives an impression of a *characteristic mode of relatedness*, the idea of *shifting thresholds of intensity* that provisionally demarcate the arrangement from its surroundings, and also the sense of an often (but not always) *pleasurable absorption, captivation or immersion* that an affective arrangement affords to individuals that are about to get involved with it. More globally, affective arrangements can be thought of as a combina-tion of two contrasting registers. They combine a dimension of materiality with a dimension of expression. These dimensions are tied together but operate independently (Deleuze & Guattari, 1987). When it comes to an arrangement's intrinsic dynamics, two counteracting tendencies can be observed. The first is a tendency towards the consolidation – even, at times, ossification – of the arrangement into a stable pattern. The second tendency runs counter to the first towards transformation or even dissolution. So there is both, relatively stable arrangements and relatively more fleeting ones, and the same agglomeration of elements might pass through successive phases of stability and destabilization. As such temporary consolidated meshworks of materials and expressions, affective arrangements may be approached as repositories and conservation devices, which points to their complex and multi-scale *historicity*. This importantly includes a sense for marginal strands of history: hidden traces and latent dimensions that could easily escape the purview of other analytical perspectives.

So over and above a general orientation toward the *situatedness* of affect (see Griffiths & Scarantino, 2009; Slaby, 2016), arrangement thinking lets researchers reckon with local concatenations, apparatuses and relational configurations, and in particular with surprising combinations of elements in one's attempts to situate a given instance of affect within an "intensive milieu" of formative relations, both synchronically and diachronically (see Angerer, 2017). Arrangement thinking might be considered a form of materialism, but it is a *vital* materialism that foregrounds the dynamics, liveliness and performativity of matter (Barad, 2007; Bennett, 2010). On this perspective, the individual subject will likewise be approached as an affective arrangement of sorts: as a shape-shifting, ecologically embedded, multiply temporal complex of elements only provisionally united by socially crafted modes of reflexivity.

Work with the concept: a methodological proposal

Taken in its full complexity, 'affective arrangement' is a philosophical concept that aims at bringing out the unique constellation of a particular affect-intensive site of social life. It drives toward disclosing the operative essentials of a social domain in terms of local machinations of relational affect, giving shape to a potentially idiosyncratic, highly specific affective formation inherent in a particular place or social site at a certain time. The methodology associated with this employment of the concept is accordingly qualitative, explicative and (in part) constructivist, as a given object domain will be described from a unique and potentially even personal angle, developed and crafted with the help of various aesthetic and stylistic means, as deemed appropriate for the case at hand. It will be hard – or even impossible – to separate this sort of work with the concept from an educated perspective and capacity for judgment on the part of the scholars working with it, a perspective derived from a unique learning history and experiential trajectory. More is required, it turns out, than the global orientation of arrangement thinking, which is an outlook comprising relatively clear-cut principles, as outlined previously. What is required, over and above this general orientation, is a specific 'take' or imprint on the part of the scholar or researcher – the adoption of a particular stance or posture over and above the mere application of a concept. Thereby, a scholar's – or a scholarly collective's – trained powers of judgment will not only be applied to some object or other, but also have to effectively coalesce with whatever object or domain is currently studied, forming an affective arrangement of its own kind between concept users and domain of inquiry (this points to a substantive notion of an 'intellectual posture'). A central role inevitably also accrues to an involved, highly immersive style of approaching and then writing about a subject matter. Hence what we propose especially with respect to the work in *affect studies* is a qualitative, involved and personal perspective that still proceeds *conceptually*, that is, by way of crafting, proposing and critically discussing explicative concepts in close engagement with the material and in alignment with fellow scholars and researchers.

At the same time, much in the foregoing has pointed also to other aspects of empirical research methodologies. For instance, social scientists, ethnographers, or researchers of media who approach a social domain might take up 'affective arrangement' as an explorative schema that guides their charting of the material layout and functional design of social spaces, domains or media platforms, focusing on those elements and their structured interplay that are presumably instrumental to the reliable production and/or continued circulation of affect. Here, what we call 'arrangement thinking' finds a readily workable application. The concept of affective arrangement functions as a generative template for hypotheses, research questions or initial domain descriptions. For example, the anthropological study of communal practice or interaction rituals might map out elements of the material propping and staging instrumental to the unfolding of affect during the practice's performances – up to the drawing of empirically grounded 'heat maps' and interaction diagrams in intricate and fine-grained ways. In studies of the nexus of affect and media, the arrangement optic inspires a focus on the milieus and apparatuses of contemporary media and on the immersive, usually transmediated environments and practical contexts of broadcast media and networked applications. In the sociology of organizations, the design of offices and workplaces might be approached with a refined sense for those factors and local set-ups which likely play a role in realizing the predominant forms of affective interactions or affective atmospheres in these settings. Work on individual experience by means of qualitative interviews can likewise make use of the concept, as interviewees might be asked about salient elements of spatial settings and local arrangements and about these items' presumed roles in generating moods or atmospheres.

These empirically oriented endeavors won't have to assume the full qualitative notion of an affective arrangement, but might highlight selected dimensions or focus on different elements of an arrangement sequentially during the research process. Accordingly, reckoning with an affective arrangement within affect and emotion research can take the form of an orientating blueprint that is sketchy and selective initially, with details being filled in as new data emerges. The research process takes the form of moving back and forth between arrangement sketches and their correction and elaboration in the light of new material.[8]

Conclusion

In closing, we want to address a tension that might have surfaced in our chapter. As we have argued, a robust element of skill, judgment and taste is required for competent conceptual practice. This seems to point to a certain individualism, even exceptionalism, with regard to the figure of the skilled scholar and her or his unique creative capacities. Yet, at the same time, we want to claim emphatically that concepts exist only as *collectively* shared, as that which successfully *travels* between domains and research contexts and thus as something essentially social. Is there a way to reconcile these requirements?

As versatile yet open-textured templates for object-oriented articulation, concepts cannot be understood independently of the conceptual capacities and powers of judgment on the part of scholars or researchers that develop, employ, refine and elaborate them – capacities that are not only a product of each individual's personal history of affective involvement in the world, but also stemming from particular histories of learning, of being embedded within traditions of scholarship and thought collectives. Accordingly, thought styles, intellectual tastes, tacit knowledge and powers of judgment ("Urteilskraft") are indispensable for devising an understanding of concepts as methodology. Yet, even as 'grounded' in practical capacities this way, concepts are not the property of individual scholars, nor do they 'exist' – if they exist at all – in the intellectual practice or orientation of a single individual. A concept derives its reality not from the status, authority or unique skillset of the person inventing or articulating it, but from the dynamic of being received by others, by its power of explication in the eyes – and the practices – of others, of those responding to and continuing an initial creative impulse of concept construction. Concepts are *real* in virtue of the *work they can do* on situated individuals and their practical orientations. The more 'dynamic stability' a concept gains in such spread-out webs of intellectual practice, the more it becomes a significant factor in its own right. Thus, one might say that a concept only exists in the plurality of its articulations, in a loose yet specific enough nexus of interrelated practices of explication, elaboration, reception, uptake, transformation, contestation and critique.

In light of this fact, it is a key criterion for whether a concept has indeed emerged and gained traction that it is employed and taken up by various scholars or researchers. Conceptual practice is inevitably social, since concepts are articulative templates *collaboratively* employed within an interrelated context of intellectual practice. This does not mean that different scholars need to share a homogeneous outlook and agree on all details of a concept's components, its structure and dynamics. What it does entail is a receptivity to the conceptual explications of others and to the style and outlook that a conceptual articulation brings with it, even where it cannot be rendered explicit in a widely agreed-upon way ('arrangement thinking' is a case in point). There is no neutral vantage point from which conceptual articulations can be decisively arbitrated, yet there are rich intellectual practices of collaboration, discussion, critique, centered on joined endeavors of explication and conceptual development. It is thus vital – and, indeed, part of conceptual practice itself – to build, cultivate, inform and advance what Ludwik Fleck called a "thought collective" (Fleck, 1979).

This is one respect in which our proposal implies, besides providing a methodological reflection, also a strategic plea with respect to the societal and economic framing of academia. It is a plea for preserving an intellectual culture of scholarly independence and creative diversity amidst growing trends pushing for quantification, objective assessment, digitalization and the dismantling of interpretive inquiry in favor of big-data-driven methodologies. While a discourse of methodology has often served the purpose of policing scholarship – to the point of rooting out individual specificity as deviant and troublesome – in our case it aims at restoring a culture of intellectual accountability among a global, inclusive community of scholars and researchers.

Acknowledgments

Our joint work on this paper was part of the activities of subproject B05 (*Changing Repertoires of Emotion*) of the CRC *Affective Societies*. We thank Philipp Haueis, Antje Kahl, Omar Kasmani, Henrike Kohpeiß, Dominik Mattes, Thomas Stodulka and Ferdiansyah Thajib for valuable reviews and insightful comments to an earlier version of the chapter.

Notes

1 This paragraph condenses insights from several decades of work in science and technology studies (STS), notably from the anthropological study of scientific research and from perspectives in the so-called "history and philosophy of science", drawing on Ludwik Fleck, Thomas Kuhn, Bruno Latour, Hans-Jörg Rheinberger and others. Our central philosophical source is philosopher of science Joseph Rouse, whose work might be read as an expansive running commentary on the philosophical significance of STS, history of science, ethnographic lab studies and related areas and is characterized by an original approach to concepts and conceptual articulation as a normatively accountable material-discursive practice. See Rouse (2002, 2015).

2 It is almost shocking how little the issues we address are covered in standard texts in mainstream debates of analytic philosophy. The entry 'concepts' in the *Stanford Encyclopedia of Philosophy* (Margolis & Laurence, 2014) is, for instance, totally silent on work by, to our estimate, heavyweight players in the debate on concepts such as Joseph Rouse and Mark Wilson (see especially Wilson, 2006 for a highly innovative study on the dynamics of conceptual behavior in the sciences).

3 With this orientation, our approach resembles Gary Gutting's (2009) case studies focusing on what he calls philosophical "pictures". While Gutting does not pay much attention to concepts, his understanding of "pictures" resembles closely our notion of concepts as anchoring an optic or thought style, exemplified for present purposes by what we call

"arrangement thinking". Echoes to Wittgenstein's (critical) employment of the notion of a 'picture' are evident, yet we focus here on the generative potential of such pictures.

4 Foucault and some of his methodological followers in philosophy, such as Ian Hacking, might also be mentioned here as further stages in this ongoing lineage (see Hacking, 2002).

5 Here our approach overlaps with the perspective on moving images and image analysis by Schankweiler and Wüschner in the present volume.

6 These considerations make our approach relatable to work in social and cultural anthropology; and much of our inspiration comes from interaction with anthropologists within the *Affective Societies* initiative. It would be worth exploring the many resonances with the contribution by Stodulka, Dinkelaker and Thajib to this volume, as they sketch a proposal for bottom-up conceptual development in contexts where established categories for emotions and affect are unavailable. See also Stodulka (2017).

7 Several authors in the field of affect studies have suggested comparable concepts, likewise drawing on Deleuze and Foucault; see, for instance, Anderson (2014), who speaks of affective apparatuses, and Seyfert (2012), who has coined the term "affektif". Bennett (2010) and Grossberg (1992) also hint at notions resembling our proposal.

8 With this, our approach has obvious affinities with the 'grounded theory' methodology in sociology and with the role assigned therein to 'sensitizing concepts' (see, e.g., Bowen, 2006).

References

Anderson, B 2014, *Encountering Affect: Capacities, Apparatuses, Conditions*, Ashgate, Farnham.

Angerer, ML 2017, *Ecology of Affect*, Meson Press, Lüneburg.

Ayata, B & Harders, C 2018, ' "Midan Moments" – conceptualizing space, affect and political participation on occupied squares', in B Röttger-Rössler & J Slaby (eds.), *Affect in Relation – Families, Places, Technologies: Essays on Affectivity and Subject Formation in the 21st Century*, pp. 115–133, Routledge, New York.

Bal, M 2002, *Traveling Concepts in the Humanities: A Rough Guide*, University of Toronto Press, Toronto.

Barad, K 2007, *Meeting the Universe Halfway: Quantum Physics and the Entanglement of Matter and Meaning*, Duke University Press, Durham.

Bennett, J 2010, *Vibrant Matter: A Political Ecology of Things*, Duke University Press, Durham.

Bowen, GA 2006, 'Grounded theory and sensitizing concepts', *International Journal of Qualitative Methods*, vol. 5, no. 3, pp. 12–23.

Buchanan, I 2015, 'Assemblage theory and its discontents', *Deleuze Studies*, vol. 9, no. 3, pp. 382–392.

Deleuze, G & Guattari F 1983, *Anti-Oedipus: Capitalism and Schizophrenia*, University of Minnesota Press, Minneapolis.

Deleuze, G & Guattari, F 1986, *Kafka: Towards a Minor Literature*, University of Minnesota Press, Minneapolis.

Deleuze, G & Guattari, F 1987, *A Thousand Plateaus*, University of Minnesota Press, Minneapolis.

Deleuze, G & Guattari, F 1994, *What Is Philosophy?* Columbia University Press, New York.

Fleck, L 1979, *Genesis and Development of a Scientific Fact*, University of Chicago Press, Chicago.

Foucault, M 1980, 'The confession of the flesh' in C Gordon (ed.), *Power/Knowledge. Selected Interviews and Other Writings 1972–1977*, pp. 194–228, Pantheon Books, New York.

Fricker, M 2007, *Epistemic Injustice: Power and the Ethics of Knowing*, Oxford University Press, Oxford.

Griffiths, PE & Scarantino, A 2009, 'Emotions in the wild' in P Robbins and M Aydede (eds.), *The Cambridge Handbook of Situated Cognition*, pp. 437–453, Cambridge University Press, Cambridge.

Grossberg, L 1992, *We Gotta Get Out of This Place: Popular Conservatism and Postmodern Culture*, Routledge, New York.

Gutting, G 2009, *What Philosophers Know: Case Studies in Recent Analytic Philosophy*, Cambridge University Press, New York.

Hacking, I 2002, *Historical Ontology*, Harvard University Press, Cambridge, MA.

Kasmani, O 2017, 'Audible spectres: The sticky Shia sonics of Sehwan', *History of Emotions – Insights into Research*, October 2017. DOI:10.14280/08241.54 [22 July 2018].

Margolis, E & Laurence, S 2014, 'Concepts' in EN Zalta (ed.), *The Stanford Encyclopedia of Philosophy*, Spring 2014 Edition. Available from: https://plato.stanford.edu/archives/spr2014/entries/concepts/ [22 July 2018].

Mühlhoff, R 2019, 'Affective disposition' in J Slaby and C von Scheve (eds.), *Affective Societies: Key Concepts*, Routledge, New York.

Mühlhoff, R & Schütz, T 2017, *Verunsichern, Vereinnahmen, Verschmelzen. Eine affekttheoretische Perspektive auf Immersion*. Working Paper SFB 1171 Affective Societies 05/17. Available from: http://edocs.fu-berlin.de/docs/receive/FUDOCS_series_000000000562 [22 July 2018].

Mühlhoff, R & Slaby, J 2018, 'Immersion at work: Affect and power in post-Fordist work cultures', in B Röttger-Rössler & J Slaby (eds.), *Affect in Relation – Families, Places, Technologies: Essays on Affectivity and Subject Formation in the 21st Century*, pp. 155–174, Routledge, New York.

Nail, T 2017, 'What is an assemblage?' *SubStance*, vol. 46, no. 1, pp. 21–37.

Rouse, J 2002, *How Scientific Practices Matter: Reclaiming Philosophical Naturalism*, University of Chicago Press, Chicago.

Rouse, J 2015, *Articulating the World: Conceptual Understanding and the Scientific Image*, University of Chicago Press, Chicago.

Schankweiler, K & Wüschner, P (this volume). 'Images that move: Analyzing affect with Aby Warburg'.

Schmidgen, H 2015, 'Cerebral drawings between art and science: On Gilles Deleuze's philosophy of concepts', *Theory, Culture and Society*, vol. 32, no. 7–8, pp. 123–149.

Seyfert, R 2012, 'Beyond personal feelings and collective emotions: Toward a theory of social affect', *Theory, Culture and Society*, vol. 29, no. 6, pp. 27–46.

Slaby, J 2016, 'Mind invasion: Situated affectivity and the corporate life hack', *Frontiers in Psychology*, vol. 7, no. 266. DOI:10.3389/fpsyg.2016.00266 [22 July 2018].

Slaby, J, Mühlhoff, R & Wüschner, P 2017, 'Affective arrangements', *Emotion Review*. DOI:10.1177/1754073917722214 [22 July 2018].

Stodulka, T 2017, 'Storms of slander – relational dimensions of envy in Java, Indonesia', in R Smith, M Duffy & U Merlone (eds.), *Envy at Work and in Organizations*, pp. 297–320, Oxford University Press, Oxford.

Stodulka, T, Dinkelaker, S & Thajib, F (this volume), 'Empirical affect montage'.

Wilson, M 2006, *Wandering Significance: An Essay in Conceptual Behavior*, Clarendon Press, Oxford.

Part I

Textualities

Chapter 3

Reading for affect

A methodological proposal for
analyzing affective dynamics
in discourse

*Anna L. Berg, Christian von Scheve,
N. Yasemin Ural and Robert Walter-Jochum*

Introduction

How are literary texts, media reports, or political commentaries involved in constituting social reality? How are they implicated in the drawing of boundaries, in the construction of communal bonds, or in the formation of antagonistic social collectives? And what is the role of affect and emotion – vis-à-vis calm deliberation and rational thought – in these processes? Understanding the intertwining of language, emotion, and affect is a notoriously difficult task, as decades of research in the social and behavioral sciences, linguistics, and literary studies have shown.[1] Ever since Aristotle's *Rhetoric*, scholars have been intrigued by the question of the emotional properties and consequences of not only spoken but also written language. This prolonged interest in how language and emotion go together is probably fueled by the conviction that the two are somewhat strange bedfellows, given that the former is thought of as a system of formal syntactic rules coordinating the use of symbols, whereas the latter is supposed to be an unpredictable idiosyncratic and somatic mode of engaging with the world.

Today, many endeavors in the humanities and the social sciences to understand how language and emotion are intertwined rely on theories and methodologies of discourse. Although some strands of discourse analysis have for a long time paid close attention to the importance of emotion, particularly those in the tradition of linguistic ethnography and conversation analysis, others have only partially accounted for this dimension, especially works taking a Foucauldian stance towards discourse. This latter tradition has rather eschewed emotions and affect, presumably because both are often conceived of as 'individual' or 'subjective' phenomena that are hard to reconcile with an understanding of discourse as a system of utterances that follows certain historically grounded rules of the (re)production of knowledge (Foucault, 2002 [1969]).

In this chapter, we suggest that the concept of *affect* is a promising candidate to reconcile this tension between 'the discursive' and 'the bodily subjective'. We do not propose a conceptual loophole for the fundamental body/discourse problem (Butler, 1989) nor develop concrete methods for analyzing the potential linkage between the discursive and the realm of bodily experience. Rather, we suggest a theoretical and methodological turn that moves away from the idea that – for the time being – we can come to terms with the actual 'effects' of discourse on how subjects 'actually' feel. Instead of relying on feelings and emotions in the traditional phenomenological understanding of these terms (i.e., feelings as conscious phenomenal experiences of human individuals), the concept of *affect*, as developed in cultural studies, may offer a valuable theoretical and methodological perspective for a novel take on the intertwinement of emotion, language, and discourse. In particular, the understanding of *bodies* implied in the concept of affect promises to overcome some of the dividing lines in research on emotions and discourse.

In what follows, we first provide a very brief review of different strands of research on the links between discourse and emotion, including a review of how different affect theories have conceptualized the potential intertwining of affect and language. In a second step, we will elaborate on our methodological propositions that involve the notions of 'discourse bodies' and 'reading for affect' as an analytical perspective for the close reading and interpretation of text. In a third part, we will illustrate this approach using concrete examples from our own research on the role of affect and emotion in debates over feelings of religious belonging, moral injury, and hate speech.

I. Emotions and discourse

Approaches to emotion and discourse in the social sciences can be roughly categorized along two lines. First, linguistic and ethnographic approaches, often in a pragmatist tradition, conceive of discourse predominantly as an interaction order that emerges in social situations and interactions, focusing on the 'talk' rather than the 'text' part of discourse (Angermüller, 2001). Here, the focus often is on the different ways in which emotions are expressed, communicated, and become manifest in social interactions through various modalities, for instance, speech, gestures, or body postures, and thus serve as an infrastructure of discourse and meaning-making (Potter, 2012; Ruusuvuori, 2012). Other approaches in this tradition are more specifically concerned with how people talk *about* emotions and what this talk reveals about emotions and their place in discourse and society. These views consider emotions to be a semantic domain and argue that language always classifies and categorizes emotional experience such that the emotion words used to signify and analyze emotional experience are always bound to culture, either in a representationist (Wierzbicka, 1999) or ontological (Bamberg, 1997) sense (see Besnier, 1990 for an overview).

Second, and contrary to these perspectives that understand discourse mainly as "language in use", emotions frequently have been part of discourse analyses in a post-structural, Foucauldian tradition. These approaches conceive of discourse as a system of utterances that produces knowledge and meaning and thus tend to focus more on encompassing political ideologies, historically circumscribed ways of constituting knowledge, and the social practices, subjectivities, and power relations that this entails. Research in Critical Discourse Analysis (CDA), which is rooted in linguistics and inspired by Althusser's theory of ideology, Bakhtin's genre theory, and critical theory of the Frankfurt School (Titscher et al., 2000, 144) has looked at how emotions are connected to social problems, ideologies, and power relations and how they become part of the "linguistic character of social and cultural processes and structures" (ibid., 146; see also Altheide, 2002; Furedi, 1997; Koschut et al., 2017). Matouschek and Wodak (1995), for instance, have shown how the public discourse on refugees and immigration in Austria in the 1990s creates 'we-groups' and operates on the attribution or rejection of guilt. These latter approaches assume that 'emotional' or 'emotionalizing' discourse is essential for subjectivation and the ways in which social reality and subject positions are constructed. Along similar lines, William Reddy has suggested the concept of 'emotives' as specific forms of speech acts that do not simply have emotions as referents but are performatives that 'do things to the world': "Emotives are themselves instruments for directly changing, building, hiding, intensifying emotions" (Reddy, 2001, 105).

This second line of inquiry, in particular, faces the (almost classical) challenge of conceptually bridging the realm of language and text on the one hand, and subjective emotional experience involving human bodies on the other hand. For example, what consequences does the use of an 'emotionalizing' language or the articulation of certain emotion words actually have for the subjective feelings and emotional experience of an audience? Although assumptions concerning these 'extra-discursive' effects – which are in-line with Foucault's idea of the material dimension of discourse – can be frequently found in the literature on discourse and emotion, the social processes involved in this translation usually remain opaque, and it is as yet unclear how they can be conceptualized, let alone investigated empirically (see Butler, 1989; Wrana & Langer, 2007 for discussions).

The affective turn

Crossing the fuzzy borders from the social sciences to the humanities brings to attention a cluster of alternative approaches to discourse and emotion that is much less interested in feelings and subjective emotional experience, but rather understands affects and emotions as deeply imbricating the public sphere. Lauren Berlant (1997, 2011), Ann Cvetkovitch (2003, 2012), and Eve K. Sedgwick (2003), for example, have investigated emotions as a mode of heteronormative power, showing how emotionality has been attributed to specific subject positions rather than others. This line of thought aims at developing a critique of the affectivity and emotionality of the public sphere, exposing the ways in which emotions contribute to creating hierarchical relationalities, but also valuing them as being conducive to emancipation and social change (Bargetz, 2015).

These endeavors are firmly anchored in the field of the "affect studies" as an outcome of what many call the "affective turn" in the humanities and in cultural studies (Clough & Halley, 2007). Some of the first works in this field originated as a response to the theoretical fatigue engendered by poststructuralist thinking and its strong emphasis on discourse in processes of subjectivation (Blackman et al., 2008). To counter this bias in attempts to bridge the divide between discourse and text, scholars have increasingly taken an interest in more body-centered, sometimes even psychological and physiological, frameworks of analysis. Most prominently, Sedgwick and Frank (1995) incorporated the concept of affect – as developed by psychologist Silvan Tomkins – into cultural studies to reinvigorate the relevance of the body and biology against an overemphasis on language. The concept of affect was (re)discovered from the natural and psychological sciences as a means to emphasize the bodily components of becoming – designed to describe how "the impulses, sensations, expectations, daydreams, encounters and habits of relating" felt, in a state of "potentiality and resonance that comes before representation" (Stewart, 2007, 2).

Aiming at a strict break with discourse, some approaches in affect theory locate affect strictly outside the realm of language. Affect (in singular) – distinct from the concepts of feelings and emotions which are conceived of as cultural expressions/manifestations and follow a certain 'social script' – is taken to describe dimensions of the body that cannot be apprehended by language. By the most fervent proponents of this strand of theorizing (e.g. in the works of Brian Massumi), affect is discussed as a phenomenon which is not linked to thought let alone language or discourse. For Massumi, affect is a pre-discursive and even pre-cognitive realm of pure intensity, of relating objects to one another without resorting to discourse or any other means of signification (Massumi, 1995, 2002). In reinterpreting Baruch de Spinoza's understanding of affect as depicted by Deleuze (1990 [1968]) and combining it with findings of modern neuroscience, Massumi makes it the cornerstone of an ontological theory of affect, thereby marking the starting point for a school of affect theorists who are interested in relationships between human and non-human agents beyond a liberal theory of subjectivity (Schaefer, 2015, 19).

Attempts at locating affect solely in the realm of intensity have, however, been thoroughly criticized for their vagueness and untenability (Hemmings, 2005; Leys, 2011). Moreover, critics have expounded on the idea of a temporal split between affect and discourse, where affect is in some sense supposed to precede language (Wetherell, 2012, 2013). To overcome these conceptual and methodological impasses, others have suggested to look at affect and discourse as tightly interwoven entities. In the introduction to her collection of essays *Senses of the Subject*, Judith Butler (2015) claims that affect is not to be conceived of in opposition to discourse, but as an important condition for a discursive subject to come into existence. Thus, there is no discourse without the basis of affectivity as "I am already affected before I can say 'I' and . . . I have to be affected to say 'I' at all" (Butler, 2015, 2). Butler also sees the methodological problem of the hierarchical temporal order pointed out by Wetherell (2013) and others: "if I say that I am already affected before I can say 'I', I am speaking much later than the process I seek to describe" (Butler, 2015, 2). In other words, it seems impossible to address affect at the origin of discourse in a direct way as it always takes place in a realm of non-discursivity, which remains inaccessible to discursive means. Butler stresses, however, that "remaining silent on such matters" given this problem is not the only option available. Importantly, she proposes to shift attention to the processual nature of affectivity that never ceases throughout a subject's lifetime as "the bodily dimension of signification does not fall away as talking begins" (ibid., 15), since indeed "affect and cognition are never fully separable – if for no other reason than that thought is itself a body, embodied" (Gregg & Seigworth, 2009, 2). Considering affect within discourse, according to Butler, we should "accept this belatedness and proceed in a narrative fashion that marks the paradoxical condition of trying to relate something about my formation that is prior to my own narrative capacity" (Butler, 2015, 2). Affect might therefore be accessible through a textual dynamic referring to bodily aspects of language and discourse.

Importantly, affect in these works is notably different from the concept of emotion as it is used in most theories in the social and behavioral sciences. One important aspect of this distinction is the different ontological status of affect and emotion that most scholars in affect studies assume. While emotions are often conceived of as – on the one hand – belonging to the realm of a person's subjective phenomenal experience and – on the other hand – as concepts which have acquired a rather fixed and culturally determined meaning, affect relies on a relational ontology following a Spinozian logic of appearing in between bodies and neither belonging to one certain body nor being reducible to a fixed set of attributes. Affect, in this sense, is a dynamic encounter between entities, which only appear as bodies through this encounter (Slaby, 2016, 2017; von Scheve, 2018).

How can this understanding of affect satisfy an interest in the links between emotion and discourse? How can it inform – beyond the realm of signification and representation – the analysis of literary texts, media reports, or political commentaries in their involvement in the constitution of social reality? And how can affect contribute to comprehending the drawing of boundaries, the construction of communal bonds, or the formation of antagonistic social groups through language and discourse? We suggest that two facets of affect are particularly conducive to addressing these questions: its *relational* and *bodily* dynamics. In a Foucauldian perspective, discourse itself is a system of relations between linguistic utterances, and these utterances in themselves are not void of materiality as they have a bodily dimension. Analytically capitalizing on affective dynamics in the realm of discourse thus means to concentrate on the relational couplings between bodies of various sorts (see section "Discourse bodies and reading for affect") which are constituted through and within discourse. While discourse itself does make use of the conceptual vocabulary of discrete emotions (e.g., anger, fear, shame, happiness) and the ascription of feelings to individuals or social groups, the lens of affect enables us to focus on the relational dynamics and bodily aspects related to these discursive phenomena – without the need to make vague and empirically hard-to-establish assumptions regarding the consequences of these ascriptions for individuals' subjective experiences.

2. Discourse bodies and reading for affect

The interrelatedness of affect and discourse, as elaborated by Butler and others, becomes evident in a fundamental concept of affect studies, namely their concept of the body. Drawing on Donna Haraway and echoing ideas of the New Materialism in sociology and other disciplines (Latour, 2005), Lisa Blackman (2012) argues that the body can no longer be understood to be of flesh and blood and that it is no longer the sole natural material carrier of social processes. Rather, the concept of body within affect studies is extended to "species bodies, psychic bodies, machinic bodies, vitalist bodies, and other-worldly bodies. Bodies do not have clear boundaries anymore, what defines bodies is their capacity to affect and be affected" (Blackman, 2012, X). For the methodological approach we seek to develop here, we suggest using such a concept of the body that does not distinguish between registers of biology, physiology, and discursive representations, but rather reflects a 'flat' ontology (Latour, 2005). We thus use the term 'discourse bodies' to refer to the various transpersonal entities within discourse that are defined by their relations to other entities, either material or representational/ideational. As we will elaborate in the following section, discourse bodies surface in language, for example, through processes of bodification, i.e. when objects or ideas are ascribed qualities of (human) bodies, such as the capacity for feeling and emotion (as in a 'feeling nation'). They also emerge through linguistic collectivization, i.e. when social collectives (as, for instance, the German term 'Körperschaft' indicates) are portrayed in their agentic and bodily qualities. They are also evident in the relationality of all the utterances that form the system of knowledge production we call discourse. And they are apparent in the materiality of discourse itself, in the ink of printed letters, the paper and the signposts, or the glare of a tablet's screen.

To identify these bodily relationalities in text, we suggest an approach we call *Reading for Affect*, a term that has, with partly different scopes, also been used by Christoffer Kolvraa (2015) and by Encarnación Gutiérrez Rodríguez (2007). In defining the elements of *Reading for Affect*, we take inspiration from Sara Ahmed, who presents a fruitful way for analyzing the emergence of relational bodies in discourse. With this, her approach shows a firm tendency towards affect studies, although in her earlier works, she uses the terms 'affects' and 'emotions' interchangeably. Talking about 'emotions', Ahmed does not center on the experiential and subjective realm of feeling, but instead capitalizes on affective dynamics for which emotion words and the (discursive) ascription of feelings play a vital role. Our understanding of Ahmed's methodological conjecture is that she focuses, analytically, on the use of an emotion-bound vocabulary in order to map the relational affective dynamics in which bodies are enmeshed.

Ahmed claims that emotions "work to align some subjects with some others and against other others" and shows how these alignments, circulating "between bodies and signs", "create the very effect of the surfaces or boundaries of bodies and worlds" (Ahmed, 2004a, 117). In her elaborations on right-wing and conservative rhetoric – e.g. of the Aryan Nation (Ahmed, 2004a), British nationalist parties (Ahmed, 2004b), or British Prime Minister David Cameron (Ahmed, 2014) – she shows in which ways the use of emotion words plays a crucial role in constructing and portraying subjects and groups and in aligning them with or against each other, for instance, based on a continuum of love and hate or an economy of fear. Essential to her analysis of right-wing politics is the intentional object of ascribed emotions that comes into play in a specific rhetoric: by showing its affection for a *nation*, Ahmed shows, nationalist speech aims at producing "affect aliens", namely, subjects not belonging to the specific community as they are said to lack the feelings that constitute it (Ahmed, 2014, 13). Ahmed's reading of (nationalist) political speeches and propaganda thus centers on one crucial dimension of affect in discourse: its potential to align subjects and to provide a framework of alignment that is not so much grounded in conceptual and propositional knowledge, but rather in the registers of affecting and being affected. What seems particularly valuable for the question tackled here is Ahmed's insistence on the relevance of affect for the formation of the very "skin" of subjects and her underlining the importance of tracing the implications of the uses of emotion words for issues of power (e.g. in terms of nationalism or racism). In this sense, and regarding the relationality of affect, Ahmed specifically points out the group dynamics that are presumably put into action through affective speech. Her understanding of these kinds of alignments thus resonates well with our notion of discourse bodies, although we would even more strongly account for the material side of discourse itself, as we will show in the following.

Within the field of affect studies, the idea of pursuing a certain *Reading* of text has been suggested by Sedgwick (2003). She argues that poststructuralist approaches to discourse have too much focused on subjectivation as subjugation. Instead, she proposes a different approach – a different reading – determined less by scholars' preexisting hypotheses, concerns, and critical stances (which she dubs "paranoid"), but instead a reading that aims at the reconstruction of a sustainable life, opening space for the unexpected and agency (which she dubs "reparative"; see Love, 2010 for a summary and discussion). Needless to say, this demand for openness and impartiality in encountering text reflects decades of work on qualitative research methods in the social sciences, including the analysis of discourse (see e.g. Diaz-Bone et al., 2007; Keller, 2005). *Reading for Affect* embraces the idea of taking a specific, if well-informed perspective on text, one that foregrounds affective phenomena as a hermeneutic lens, capitalizing on affect and emotion as sensitizing concepts in the interpretation of discourse.

3. Discursive bodies in media coverage of the *Charlie Hebdo* attacks

Reading for Affect traces emotion words and their genealogies, metaphors, and analogies involving bodies or a bodily becoming, vocabulary indicating subjective feelings and experiences, and the materiality of discourse itself to lay open how the affective relations between different bodies are established through language. This part is devoted to illustrating different dimensions on which the methodological approach of *Reading for Affect* can be translated into a heuristic for the analysis of textual discourse. We capitalize on three such dimensions: (a) the attribution of emotion words to specific actors, material, or ideational entities; (b) linguistic collectivization, i.e. social collectives being portrayed in their agentic and bodily qualities; and (c) the materiality of discourse itself. For illustrative purposes, we will use the public debates that ensued after the terrorist attack on the satirical newspaper *Charlie Hebdo* in January 2015, in which 10 members of the newspaper's editorial team and two police officers were killed. The examples cited here are taken from an ongoing research project, focusing on public discourse in Germany in particular.[2]

Ascribing emotions

In line with Ahmed's approach, one dimension of analysis is concerned with identifying to whom feeling and emotions are ascribed in discourse and how bodies come into existence through these ascriptions. The underlying assumption is that portraying a group, an individual, an idea, or an object in the registers of affect contributes to its bodily creation and perception. Abstract social entities, such as social categories, communities, groups, or nation-states, which are ascribed feelings or affective capacities are, in a sense, discursively constructed bodies.

This ascription is often made to mark a contrast with Western tradition, being skeptical about affectivity and emotions within a post-Enlightenment discourse (Hirschkind, 2011). On the other hand, if there is a social entity *feeling* the same way, this is framed as a connection much deeper than any attachment based on rational *thought*. Depending on whose feelings are at stake in a certain situation, ascribing emotions can thus have different effects ranging from the construction of a deeply felt solidarity up to the ultimate exclusion of certain entities on the grounds of their feelings (which are deemed inappropriate). The ascription of feelings and emotions to groups, collectives, or simply to arbitrary social categories thus entails the affect-based relational construction of what we call *discourse bodies*.

In this vein, the emergence of a collective *WE* within the discursive (and performative) reactions to the attack on *Charlie Hebdo* becomes visible: "We were all targeted by this attack" (Nelles, *Spiegel Online*, 7 January 2015), "We mourn" (Gürgen & Schulz, *taz*, 14 January 2015), "We have to defend ourselves" (Heinen, *Frankfurter Allgemeine Zeitung*, 9 January 2015). This collective body arising within the reactions after the attack becomes manifest predominantly through its ascribed emotional state. Shocked by the blatant offense of its public norms, mourning the victims, and at the same time raging against such provocative violation of its foundational values – democracy and freedom. The collective *WE* hence emerges through these ascriptions of bodily characteristics, for instance, semantics of vulnerability and injury. An article in the *Süddeutsche Zeitung* describes the "nation" as "heart-wounded" (Kock, 8 January 2015) and the *Neue Zürcher Zeitung* "us" as "hit at the heart" (Haltern, 9 January 2015). These visceral registers constitute the discourse body of the *WE*.

But not only the *WE* is ascribed feelings and emotions in these debates, but also 'Muslims' as a social category are 'emotionalized' in specific ways. In discussions around the legitimacy of the Mohamed cartoons – a question directly tied to *Charlie Hebdo*, as the magazine reprinted the infamous cartoons first published in the Danish *Jyllands Posten* in 2006 – Muslims are portrayed as light-tempered, easily provoked, angry, and aggressive. In this vein, articles report on the massive violent reactions of "Muslims" "in Afghanistan, Iraq, Iran, Gaza and Yemen" ("Tausende protestieren gegen 'Charlie Hebdo' und Frankreich", *Zeit*, 18 January 2015), following the first publication of *Charlie Hebdo* after the attack, which had a caricature of the prophet as its front cover (e.g. Prantl, *Süddeutsche Zeitung*, 19 January 2015). Frequently, articles also refer to the figure of "the fanatics" in order to convey the unpredictable aggressiveness of Muslims (e.g. Kuzmany, *Spiegel*, 8 January 2015; Salloum, *Spiegel*, 8 January 2015; Kister, *Süddeutsche Zeitung*, 9 January 2015). Images and metaphors, such as "the fanatics", have repeatedly been used to create affectively charged bodies seemingly alien to Western cultural norms and affect-regimes.

Relating discourse bodies

Emotions that are ascribed to collectivities like the *WE* or 'the Muslims' enact certain attractions and repulsions between bodies – they can be conceived of as the source of an affective dynamic. These affective constellations offer positions or affective subjectivities bodies become attached to by 'feeling the emotions' and hence by entering a certain subject-object-arrangement. Discourse thus provides affective subject positions that can be embodied by subjects.

One of the dominant affective relations through which the *WE* becomes visible is the frequent articulation of fear in public discourse. One dominant concern is that people could refrain from exercising their right to freedom of speech, scared by the drastic consequences their speech might engender. "Many people are scared to express their opinion or to criticize religion after this attack", the weekly *Der Spiegel* cites a French journalist (Salloum, 8 January 2015). Although we can only speculate that the protester is referring to Islam in particular and potential reprisals to blasphemy, other articles more clearly relate fear to a violent interpretation of Islam, invading the 'European body' from the outside. Other articles warn of a danger from 'within'. The *Süddeutsche Zeitung* cites security experts who contend that the real danger for Europe is the potential radicalization of European Muslim youth (Leyendecker, 8 January 2015). In the days following the attack, and in particular in connection to the so-called '*marches republicaines*' – huge mobilizations and protests in various European cities in solidarity with the victims – headlines commented that Europeans had proven their fearlessness. "Europe is united in solidarity – we don't have fear", reads the *Frankfurter*

Allgemeine Zeitung's coverage of the marches (Kohler, 8 January 2015). "Calmly, but strongly, in many countries of the world people have affirmed the right of journalists and cartoonists to express their opinion – without having to fear the consequences. . . . The terrorists' intention to spread fear has failed" (Ulrich, *Süddeutsche Zeitung*, 10/11 January 2015). Furthermore, fear after the attack is problematized as potentially exploitable by politicians who aim to justify excessive restrictions on individual freedom in the fight against terrorism (Kurz, *Frankfurter Allgemeine Zeitung*, 12 January 2015).

Engaging emotionally in this collective of fear ensures becoming part of the *WE*. The affective subjectivity reflected by this overwhelming *WE* of solidarity is one that is affectively determined by fearing the change of 'our' Western societies through the brutal acts of terrorism committed by others – the non-*WE*, namely, Islamist terrorists. Capitalizing on the emotion of fear within the discourse surrounding the attacks promotes an affectively charged construction of a subject position that gives way to identification on an affective basis and, with this, arranges a process of discursive inclusion and exclusion.

A second emotional relation that defines the *WE* is that of love: for freedom, liberal values, and freedom of speech. This becomes most evident in pleas for defense of and solidarity for such values, as in the following excerpt:

> The cruel assassinations in Paris were a well-targeted attack on the satirical magazine *Charlie Hebdo* and its journalists. At the same time, it was an attack on the Western world, on the foundations and values of an open society. . . . Let's defend ourselves, let's continue to insist on a plurality of opinions and the freedom to express them.
>
> (Heinen, *Frankfurter Allgemeine Zeitung*, 9 January 2015)

Through love, freedom of speech becomes an object of alignment and attachment. The positive and negative identification – with what is loved and feared – promotes the emergence of a collective *WE* that only comes into being and persists as affected by the continuous singular modalities of love and fear, yet it can never be fully taken – or inhabited – by the sum of singular human bodies.

Since freedom of speech figures as a "shared object of love" (Ahmed, 2004b, 135), as Sara Ahmed terms it, figuring in a process of collective alignment, Muslims can become part of the *WE* when they demonstrate their love for freedom of speech. If Muslims want to be integrated into the *WE*, if they do not want to be *feared* but *loved* by the *WE*, they have to affectively confirm their respect for freedom of speech and actively turn against those who "hate" freedom, thus joining the ranks of a collective "united against the fanatics" (Kister, *Süddeutsche Zeitung*, 9 January 2015). Emphasizing not so much the bodily but rather the cultural components of this affection, this can be interpreted as the demand for adopting a Western "emotion repertoire" (von Poser, Ta, & Hahn, 2018) and to subject the self under a specific "emotion regime" (Reddy, 2001). Ahmed discusses the relationality regarding the case of "multicultural love" (see Ahmed,

2004b, 122, 2014, 23). In multicultural settings, Ahmed argues, love allows for an affective dynamic that works through alignment and exclusion simultaneously. The love for those who follow the ideal in a way requires the exclusion of those who have not achieved it. In this vein, many Muslim organizations underline their attachment to values like freedom of speech and reach out to the "silent majority" to declare their fidelity to such values (e.g. J.A., *Frankfurter Allgemeine Zeitung*, 24 January 2015; Babayigit, *Süddeutsche Zeitung*, 15 January 2015). To belong to the *WE* emerging after 7 January 2015, one has to be emotionally committed to freedom of speech, and thus embody the affective subject positions offered by hegemonic discourse.

Bodies inside and outside texts

A third dimension of affectivity which can be analyzed regarding discourse is bound to the materiality of discourse itself – its language and rhetoric and the materiality it finds in forms transcending the merely textual sphere and becoming part of translinguistic phenomena within the social.

One can conceive of the materiality of the slogan "*Je suis Charlie*" as part of the body of the *WE*, for instance, on T-shirts, posters, slogans on buildings, as transmitted through social media profiles or as a full-page insert to Germany's bestselling newspaper *Bild* etc. The sentence "*Je suis Charlie*" gains much of its power through being disseminated via a huge variety of channels and media, thus becoming part of the everyday and transforming the social sphere. In its omnipresence, "*Je suis Charlie*" connects a multitude of different objects – bodies in Blackman's sense – and thus is transformed into a powerful measure to create an overarching affective arrangement (Slaby, Mühlhoff, & Wüschner, 2017), binding other bodies and transforming affective relations within society. "*Je suis Charlie*" thus is no longer only a (discursive) slogan, but through its widespread use through different modalities gains a materiality without which, we argue, its overwhelming effects could not be the same. This diverse materiality opens up opportunities to affect individuals and groups on different levels and through different channels. This phenomenon of the bodily in/through discourse leads us to label arrangements like these as 'discourse bodies', highlighting their discursive origins as well as their bodily material components.

In a less extensive sense – directed at the analysis of specific fragments of a discourse – talking of the 'discourse body' may mean to address the aspect of discourse's materiality more strictly, i.e. relating to the concrete language material used in a certain discourse. With Petra Gehring (2007), we can here speak of the "bodily power of language", a power she underlines stating that language cannot be seen as the other of the body, but that language itself is a bodily phenomenon (see Gehring, 2007, 213). While Gehring concentrates on acts of "*deadly* rage", i.e. the most massive linguistic attack possible, we argue that the bodily materiality she phenomenologically analyzes in these cases can also be found in less strong utterances (in a less powerful way). Even in cases in which it is not a "weapon", language itself still is a "physical thing", as "on the paths of language, bodies collide physically" (Gehring, 2007, 219, 221, our translation). Gehring, following up on Merleau-Ponty (1964), points to the necessity of including the bodily, material side of language into considerations on discourse, a point in which we follow her and which can be addressed through considering discourse a body in its own right. While Gehring continues her argument in a phenomenological realm considering scenes of individuals confronting each other verbally (and bodily) in speech acts, she also hints to the necessity of analyzing (not necessarily spoken) discourse in the same vein. Our concept of 'discourse bodies' concentrates on the materiality of language here, considering the ways the linguistic material is formed and distributed within discourse. This makes aspects of metaphor, rhetoric, onomatopoeia, and choice of vocabulary the realm in which this part of *Reading for Affect* proceeds.

In the debate analyzed here, an opinion piece published by the well-known German women's rights activist Alice Schwarzer in the *Frankfurter Allgemeine Zeitung* (25 January 2015) is particularly informative. Especially her use of metaphor is striking in this regard. Her subject is the problem of drawing a "demarcation line between Islam and Islamism", which German chancellor Angela Merkel is cited in seeing at the point "where religion is used to legitimate violence". Schwarzer writes: "Violence is only the tip of the iceberg of politicized Islam, i.e. Islamism. . . . Inciting hate towards others is the seed of violence. This seed shoots, the Kalashnikov in hand" (Schwarzer, 2015). In combining the naturalistic metaphor of the shooting seed with the picture of the iceberg of Islamism hiding below sea level, Schwarzer's text incites feelings of fear without naming this emotion. In the following, she criticizes Islamism for "dehumanizing the other" and thus forming the base for hate – while dehumanizing Muslim subjects herself by using the metaphors depicted. A central thread of her text is to posit a continuum between liberal Muslims and Jihadists, which becomes clear in the metaphors used – while on an argumentative level, she underscores the importance of differentiating between Islam and Islamism. Contrary to her argument, she then ends with the demand to end every form of "misleading tolerance" and stop being too considerate with religious minorities – a conclusion clearly at odds with her argument, but in line with the assumption of a continuity between Islam and Islamism suggested by the metaphors employed. The language material used in this case delivers its own story – a way to convey a message separate from the line of thought given in the argumentative parts of her text.

While metaphor is arguably one of the more covert forms in which affectivity becomes tangible in discourse, forms of hyperbole and linguistic excess are more clearly visible. Most explicitly, tabloid papers use these affectively charged techniques, as can be seen in the German *Bild*, which underlined the totality of its solidarity with the "*Je suis Charlie*" movement by dedicating the entire last page of its paper to the slogan, printed white on black, on 8 January 2015, and following up on this by putting online a picture of the paper's staff unanimously holding up this page in a depiction of the editorial office on the day's afternoon ('BILD zeigt Solidarität mit Pariser Terror-Opfern', *Bild*, 8 January 2015). Mass solidarity is thus depicted through a massive accumulation of the slogan within the paper. On the other hand, *Bild* uses shocking and hyperbolic headlines to strongly underline the threat Islamism poses to European societies, enhancing the messages given by the big size of the letters used for the paper's headlines. For example, *Bild* asks "Is there a whole terror network raging in Paris?" on January 9 ('Wütet in Paris ein ganzes Terrornetzwerk?', *Bild*, 9 January 2015b), after stating a day before that "This is war – real war" in quoting French newspaper *Le Figaro* (Hempel & Müller Thederan, *Bild*, 8 January 2015). And hyperbole is also used in depicting the movement of "*Je suis Charlie*", when *Bild* writes of "Limitless solidarity" ('Je suis Charlie – Grenzenlose Solidarität', *Bild*, 9 January 2015a) or delivers a count of "*Je suis Charlie*" trending on Twitter: "Five million times #JeSuisCharlie" ('Fünf Millionen Mal #JeSuisCharlie: Damit ist es eines der meistgenutzten Hashtags aller Zeiten!', *Bild*, 10 January 2015) – and also when it registers the economic value of "*Je suis Charlie*" as a brand, writing on "The million-Euro-business of 'Je suis Charlie'" ("Das Millionengeschäft mit 'Je suis Charlie': Ausgabe Nummer 1177 für knapp 100 000 Euro auf Ebay!", *Bild*, 14 January 2015). Here, textual measures of enhancing affectivity materially meet with the transtextual realm in which the phenomenon "*Je suis Charlie*" gains its power.

3. Conclusion

In this chapter, we have presented an interdisciplinary approach to analyzing the affective dynamics of discourse. Combining methodological approaches from the social sciences and the humanities, in particular literary studies, this approach seeks to overcome the conceptual divide present in many theories of affect between body and affect, on the one hand, language and discourse, on the other hand. We question those positions in the literature that prioritize material bodies over language and discourse – or vice versa – and instead argue to analyze the coincidence of bodies and language as shown in the affective arrangements in discourse and society. Many existing approaches to discourse analysis that focus on emotions, in particular those in a Foucauldian tradition, struggle with implicit assumptions on the links between discourse and the subjective emotional experience of an audience. Our methodological proposal of *Reading for Affect* seeks to transcend questions related to personal or collective feelings as qualities of the 'inner life' of human individuals.

Regarding the question of how media reports and political commentaries are involved in constituting social reality and how they are implicated in the drawing of boundaries and the formation of (antagonistic) social collectives, we suggest to look at the relational affective dynamics between discursive enunciations and the discourse bodies that emerge from the enunciations. Taking the vivid debates over freedom of speech and religious sensibilities after the *Charlie Hebdo* attacks as an example, the methodological approach of *Reading for Affect* allows to describe how these bodies are discursively constructed, which possibilities they offer an audience to align with distinct social collectives, and in which material ways they present themselves *as* bodies.

Reading for Affect proposes to coalesce affect theory and discourse analysis by opening up the latter to questions of affectivity, materiality, and the linguistic creation of social bodies. In this, it seems promising for other fields of research as well: considering, for example, that a Foucauldian (discourse analytical) theory of discipline or of governmentality also relates to bodies but is not sufficiently able to consider these aspects without integrating affective elements. Any analysis of power, we argue, should consider affects and emotions as well as the dynamics they create, which can be accomplished by incorporating bodily and affective characteristics of discourse into its analysis. Moreover, the proposed approach gives way to a perspective on affect studies that is able to come to terms with the textual embedding and relevance of affectivity beyond ideas of the impossibility to grasp affectivity at all. *Reading for Affect* proposes a methodology for working with affect in discourse, something many positions in the field, which postulate the entanglements between affect and discourse more abstractly, still lack or actively oppose.

Reading for Affect thus proposes to approach text through a specific lens or perspective that is informed by affect theories and to use their concepts as sensitizing concepts in the analysis and interpretation of language and discourse. Our proposal is not limited to specific techniques of analysis as they are used in the social sciences and humanities and can, in principle, be combined with established analytical procedures, such as close readings, dispositive analysis, or critical discourse analysis.

Notes

1 The work presented here stems from our interdisciplinary cooperation as scholars in sociology and German literary studies within our project "Feelings of Religious Belonging and Rhetorics of Injury in Public and in Art" at the Collaborative Research Center *Affective Societies* at Freie Universität Berlin, generously funded by the German Research Foundation (DFG).
2 Our analysis is based on a sample of approximately 70 newspaper articles published during the two weeks after the attack. For the purpose of our case study, it seemed adequate to concentrate on major print outlets of the German speaking market, namely, the daily newspapers *Süddeutsche Zeitung*, *Frankfurter Allgemeine Zeitung*, *Neue Zürcher Zeitung*, *Tageszeitung*, and *Tagesspiegel*, as well as the weeklies *Zeit* and *Spiegel*, as these media stand for a hegemonic thread of discourse which is also mirrored in other news coverage. As it is clear in this case that these parts of mass media do not represent the whole of the debate, in some parts of the case study we complement this data set through other materials for illustrative purposes. English translations from the German texts are our own.

References

Ahmed, S 2004a, 'Affective economies', *Social Text*, vol. 22, 79, no. 2, pp. 117–139.
Ahmed, S 2004b, *The Cultural Politics of Emotions*, Edinburgh University Press, Edinburgh.
Ahmed, S 2014, 'Not in the mood', *New Formations*, vol. 82, pp. 13–28.

Angermüller, J 2001, 'Diskursanalyse: Strömungen, Tendenzen, Perspektiven. Eine Einführung', in J Angermüller, K Bunzmann & M Nonhoff (eds.), *Diskursanalyse: Theorien, Methoden, Anwendungen*, pp. 7–22, Argument, Hamburg.

Altheide, D 2002, *Creating Fear: News and the Construction of Crisis*, De Gruyter Mouton, New York.

Babayigit, G 2015, 'Zwang zum Abstand: Muslime distanzieren sich vom Terror', *Süddeutsche Zeitung*, 15 January. Available from: www.sueddeutsche.de/politik/muslime-distanzieren-sich-zwang-zum-abstand-1.2304475 [18 June 2018].

Bamberg, M 1997, 'Emotion talk(s): The role of perspective in the construction of emotions', in S Niemeier & R Dirven (eds.), *The Language of Emotions: Conceptualization, Expression, and Theoretical Foundation*, pp. 209–225, John Benjamins, Amsterdam.

Bargetz, B 2015, 'The distribution of emotions: Affective politics of emancipation', *Hypatia*, vol. 30, no. 3, pp. 580–596.

Berlant, L 1997, *The Queen of America Goes to Washington City: Essays on Sex and Citizenship*, Duke University Press, Durham, London.

Berlant, L 2011, *Cruel Optimism*, Duke University Press, Durham, London.

Besnier, N 1990, 'Language and affect', *Annual Review of Anthropology*, vol. 19, pp. 419–451.

'BILD zeigt Solidarität mit Pariser Terror-Opfern' 2015, *Bild*, 8 January. Available from: www.bild.de/politik/inland/bild/zeigt-solidaritaet-mit-opfern-des-terroranschlags-von-paris-39252750.bild.html [18 June 2018].

Blackman, L 2012, *Immaterial Bodies: Affect, Embodiment, Mediation*, Sage Publications, London.

Blackman, L, Cromby, J, Hook, D, Papadopoulos, D & Walkerdine, V 2008, 'Creating subjectivities', *Subjectivity*, vol. 22, no. 1, pp. 1–27.

Butler, J 1989, 'Foucault and the paradox of bodily inscriptions', *The Journal of Philosophy*, vol. 86, no. 11, pp. 601–607.

Butler, J 2015, *Senses of the Subject*, Fordham University Press, New York.

Clough, PT & Halley, J 2007, *The Affective Turn: Theorizing the Social*, Duke University Press, Durham, London.

Cvetkovitch, A fehlt hier ein Leerzeichen? 2003, *An Archive of Feelings: Trauma, Sexuality, and Lesbian Public Cultures*, Duke University Press, Durham, London.

Cvetkovitch, A 2012, *Depression: A Public Feeling*, Duke University Press, Durham, London.

'Das Millionengeschäft mit "Je suis Charlie": Ausgabe Nummer 1177 für knapp 100 000 Euro auf Ebay!' 2015, *Bild*, 14 January. Available from: www.bild.de/geld/wirtschaft/charlie-hebdo/das-millionen-geschaeft-mit-charlie-hebdo-devotionalien-39322000.bild.html [18 June 2018].

Deleuze, G 1990 [1968], *Expressionism in Philosophy: Spinoza*, trans. M Joughin, Zone, New York.

Diaz-Bone, R, Bührmann, AD, Gutiérrez Rodríguez, E, Schneider, W, Kendall, G & Tirado, F 2007, 'The field of Foucaultian discourse analysis: Structures, developments and perspectives', *Forum: Qualitative Social Research*, vol. 8, no. 2. Available from: http://nbn-resolving.de/urn:nbn:de:0114-fqs0702305 [18 June 2018].

Foucault, M 2002 [1969], *The Archaeology of Knowledge*, trans. AM Sheridan Smith, Routledge, London, New York.

'Fünf Millionen Mal #JeSuisCharlie: Damit ist es eines der meistgenutzten Hashtags aller Zeiten!' 2015, *Bild*, 10 January. Available from: www.bild.de/news/ausland/

terroranschlag/je-suis-charlie-eines-der-meist-genutzten-hashtags-aller-zeiten-39280466.bild.html [18 June 2018].

Furedi, F 1997, *Culture of Fear: Risk-Taking and the Morality of Low Expectation*, Continuum, London.

Gehring, P 2007, 'Über die Körperkraft von Sprache', in SK Herrmann, S Krämer & H Kuch (eds.), *Verletzende Worte. Die Grammatik sprachlicher Missachtung*, pp. 211–228, Transcript Verlag, Bielefeld.

Gregg, M & Seigworth, GJ (eds.), 2009, *The Affect Theory Reader*, Duke University Press, Durham, London.

Gürgen, M & Schulz, B 2015, 'Berlin trauert mit', *taz*, 14 January. Available from: www.taz.de/!5248254/ [18 June 2018].

Gutiérrez Rodríguez, E 2007, 'Reading affect – on the heterotopian spaces of care and domestic work in private households', *Forum: Qualitative Social Research*, vol. 8, no. 2. Available from: http://nbn-resolving.de/urn:nbn:de:0114-fqs0702118 [18 June 2018].

Haltern, U 2015, 'Unbedingtheit der Satire', *Neue Zürcher Zeitung*, 9 January. Available from: www.nzz.ch/meinung/debatte/unbedingtheit-der-satire-1.18457390 [18 June 2018].

Heinen, H 2015, 'Wehren wir uns!' *Frankfurter Allgemeine Zeitung*, 9 January. Available from: www.faz.net/aktuell/politik/aufruf-der-zeitungsverleger-wehren-wir-uns-13361546.html [18 June 2018].

Hemmings, C 2005, 'Invoking affect: Cultural theory and the ontological turn', *Cultural Studies*, vol. 19, no. 5, pp. 548–567.

Hempel, D & Müller Thederan, D 2015, 'Das ist ein Krieg – ein richtiger Krieg', *Bild*, 8 January. Available from: www.bild.de/politik/ausland/terroranschlag/frankreich-unter-schock-das-ist-krieg-ein-richtiger-krieg-39252144.bild.html [18 June 2018].

Hirschkind, C 2011, 'Is there a secular body?' *Cultural Anthropology*, vol. 26, no. 4, pp. 633–647..

J. A. 2015, 'Es reicht! Muslime treten für Aufklärung ein', *Frankfurter Allgemeine Zeitung*, 24 January.

'Je suis Charlie – Grenzenlose Solidarität' 2015a, *Bild*, 9 January. Available from: www.bild.de/politik/ausland/politik-ausland/grosse-solidaritaet-mit-opfern-des-charlie-hebdo-39255052.bild.html [18 June 2018].

Keller, R 2005, *Wissenssoziologische Diskursanalye. Grundlegung eines Forschungsprogramms*, VS Verlag, Wiesbaden.

Kister, K 2015, 'Einig gegen die Fanatiker', *Süddeutsche Zeitung*, 9 January, p. 4. Available from: www.sueddeutsche.de/panorama/anschlag-auf-die-pressefreiheit-on-ne-passe-pas-sie-werden-nicht-durchkommen-1.2295114 [18 June 2018].

Kock, F 2015, 'Ins Herz der Nation getroffen', *Süddeutsche Zeitung*, 8 January. Available from: http://sueddeutsche.de/panorama/paris-nach-dem-anschlag-auf-charlie-hebdo-ins-herz-der-nation-getroffen-1.2295947 [18 June 2018].

Kohler, B 2015, 'Blut auf die Mühlen', *Frankfurter Allgemeine Zeitung*, 8 January. Available from: www.faz.net/aktuell/politik/kommentar-zum-anschlag-auf-satiremagazin-charlie-hebdo-13358326.html [18 June 2018].

Kolvraa, C 2015, 'Affect, provocation, and far right rhetoric', in B Timm-Knudsen & C Stage (eds.), *Affective Methodologies: Developing Cultural Research Strategies for the Study of Affect*, pp. 183–200, Palgrave Macmillan, Basingstoke.

Koschut, S, Hall, TH, Wolf, R, Solomon, T, Hutchison, E & Bleiker, R 2017, 'Discourse and emotions in international relations', *International Studies Review*, vol. 19, no. 3, pp. 481–508..

Kurz, C 2015, 'Seid wachsam in Zeiten der Terrorangst', *Frankfurter Allgemeine Zeitung*, 12 January. Available from: www.faz.net/aktuell/feuilleton/aus-dem-maschinenraum/folgen-des-terrors-mehr-zensur-und-ueberwachung-13364454.html [18 June 2018].

Kuzmany, S 2015, 'Wir sind alle Charlie', *Spiegel*, 8 January. Available from: www.spiegel.de/kultur/gesellschaft/anschlag-auf-charlie-hebdo-in-paris-kommentar-a-1011802.html [18 June 2018].

Latour, B 2005, *Reassembling the Social: An Introduction to Actor Network Theory*, Oxford University Press, Oxford.

Leyendecker, H 2015, 'Gefahr von innen', *Süddeutsche Zeitung*, 8 January. Available from: www.sueddeutsche.de/politik/anschlag-auf-satiremagazin-charlie-hebdo-gefahr-von-innen-1.2294201 [18 June 2018].

Leys, R 2011, 'The turn to affect: A critique', *Critical Inquiry*, vol. 37, pp. 434–472.

Love, H 2010, 'Truth and consequences: On paranoid and reparative reading', *Criticism*, vol. 52, no. 2, pp. 235–241.

Massumi, B 1995, 'The autonomy of affect', *Cultural Critique*, vol. 31, pp. 83–110.

Massumi, B 2002, *Parables for the Virtual: Movement, Affect, Sensation*, Duke University Press, Durham, London.

Matouschek, B & Wodak, R 1995, 'Diskurssoziolinguistik. Theorien, Methoden und Fallanalysen der diskurs-historischen Methode am Beispiel von Ausgrenzungsdiskursen', *Wiener Linguistische Gazette*, vol. 55, no. 6, pp. 34–71.

Merleau-Ponty, M 1964, *Le visible et l'invisible, suivi de notes de travail*, ed. C Lefort, Gallimard, Paris.

Nelles, R 2015, 'Anschlag auf uns alle', *Spiegel Online*, 7 January. Available from: www.spiegel.de/politik/ausland/charlie-hebdo-terror-in-paris-anschlag-auf-uns-alle-a-1011766.html [18 June 2018].

Potter, J 2012, 'Conversation analysis and emotion and cognition in interaction', in CA Chapell (ed.), *Encyclopaedia of Applied Linguistics*, Wiley-Blackwell, London. Available from: https://doi.org/10.1002/9781405198431.wbeal1316 [18 June 2018].

Prantl, H 2015, 'Aufforderung zum Faustrecht', *Süddeutsche Zeitung*, 19 January. Available from: www.sueddeutsche.de/politik/bestrafung-von-gotteslaesterung-aufforderung-zum-faustrecht-1.2309269 [18 June 2018].

Reddy, W 2001, *The Navigation of Feeling*, Cambridge University Press, Cambridge.

Ruusuvuori, J 2012, 'Emotion, affect and conversation', in J Sidnell & T Stivers (eds.), *The Handbook of Conversation Analysis*, pp. 330–349, Wiley-Blackwell, Malden, MA.

Salloum, R 2015, 'Frankreichs brüchige Einigkeit', *Spiegel*, 8 January. Available from: www.spiegel.de/politik/ausland/charlie-hebdo-frankreich-trauert-und-streitet-ueber-zukunft-a-1011917.html [18 June 2018].

Schaefer, D 2015, *Religious Affects: Animality, Evolution, and Power*, Duke University Press, Durham, London.

Schwarzer, A 2015, 'Hier irrt die Kanzlerin', *Frankfurter Allgemeine Zeitung*, 25 January. Available from: www.faz.net/aktuell/politik/inland/islamismus-debatte-hier-irrt-die-kanzlerin-13388949.html [18 June 2018].

Sedgwick, EK 2003, *Touching Feeling: Affect, Pedagogy, Performativity*, Duke University Press, Durham, London.

Sedgwick, EK & Frank, A (eds.), 1995, *Shame and Its Sisters: A Silvan Tomkins Reader*, Duke University Press, Durham, London.

Slaby, J 2016, *Relational Affect: SFB Affective Societies*. Working Paper, no. 2. Available from: www.sfb-affective-societies.de/publikationen/workingpaperseries/wps_2/index.html [18 June 2018].

Slaby, J 2017, 'More than a feeling: Affect as radical situatedness', *Midwest Studies in Philosophy*, vol. 41, no. 1, pp. 7–26.

Slaby, J, Mühlhoff, R & Wüschner, P 2017, 'Affective arrangements', *Emotion Review*, prepublished 20 October 2017. Available from: http://journals.sagepub.com/doi/abs/10.1177/1754073917722214 [18 June 2018].

Stewart, K 2007, *Ordinary Affects*, Duke University Press, Durham, London.

'Tausende protestieren gegen "Charlie Hebdo" und Frankreich' 2015, *Zeit*, 18 January. Available from: www.zeit.de/politik/ausland/2015-01/charlie-hebdo-karikaturen-protest-pakistan [18 June 2018].

Titscher, S, Meyer, M, Wodak, R & Vetter, E 2000, *Methods of Text and Discourse Analysis: In Search of Meaning*, Sage Publications, London.

Ulrich, S 2015, 'Freiheit', *Süddeutsche Zeitung*, 10, 11 January, p. 11.

von Poser, A, Ta, TMT & Hahn, E 2018 (in press), 'Emotion repertoires', in J Slaby & C von Scheve (eds.), *Affective Societies – Key Concepts*, pp. 241–251, Routledge, London, New York.

von Scheve, C 2018, 'A social relational account of affect', *European Journal of Social Theory*, vol. 21, no. 1, pp. 39–59..

Wetherell, M 2012, *Affect and Emotion: A New Social Science Understanding*, Sage Publications, London.

Wetherell, M 2013, 'Affect and discourse – What's the problem? From affect as excess to affective/discursive practice', *Subjectivity*, vol. 6, no. 4, pp. 349–368.

Wierzbicka, A 1999, *Emotions Across Languages and Cultures: Diversity and Universals*, Cambridge University Press, New York.

Wrana, D & Langer, A 2007, 'An den Rändern der Diskurse. Jenseits der Unterscheidung diskursiver und nicht-diskursiver Praktiken', *Forum: Qualitative Social Research*, vol. 8, no. 2. Available from: www.qualitative-research.net/index.php/fqs/article/view/253/557 [18 June 2018].

'Wütet in Paris ein ganzes Terrornetzwerk?' 2015b, *Bild*, 9 January. Available from: www.bild.de/politik/ausland/terroranschlag/terrornetzwerk-in-paris-taeter-kannten-sich-39265968.bild.html [18 June 2018].

Chapter 4

Interviews as situated affective encounters

A relational and processual approach for empirical research on affect, emotion and politics

Bilgin Ayata, Cilja Harders, Derya Özkaya and Dina Wahba

Introduction

Although the affective turn has given rise to more research on affect and emotions in the social sciences on the whole, there has been far less engagement with affect in the discipline of political science, and even less so in empirical approaches to the field. This reluctance may stem from the challenge that affect research poses for methodology: how can political scientists gather empirical knowledge about affect when the notion itself seems too elusive to be collected with the field's conventional research methods? Affect studies in the humanities regard the elusive character of affect as its productive potential, since this quality enables affect to overcome the dominance of language in textual analysis in cultural studies. For empirical research in political science, however, affect poses a big challenge. The strong positivist and behavioralist traditions in North American and European political science make it difficult to integrate affect studies into the disciplinary boundaries of the field. Compared to its neighboring fields, political science is much more conservative and less self-critical when it comes to methodological questions. Paradigmatic shifts in the humanities and social sciences, such as constructivism, poststructuralism, feminism and postcolonialism, were met with reluctance when they were first introduced into the discipline. Taking stock of these challenges, this chapter offers methodological propositions for doing empirical research on affects and politics. We focus on qualitative interviews, which are one of the central methods for collecting data in qualitative research in political science. Benefitting from the critical discussions and approaches in neighboring fields, we seek a synthesis and integration of existing methodological debates with the aim to amend and expand the methodological tools available in our own discipline for carrying out affect research.

In what follows, we critically discuss both the potentialities and the limitations of qualitative interviews for doing research on affect in political science. We highlight the very interview process itself, and explore what it entails for the methodological approach we propose. In political science research, interviews are commonly understood as straightforward conversations, in which rational actors engage in exchanging information, such as during expert interviews. Anything relating to atmosphere, emotions, or affects that occurs during the interview is neglected as a disturbance to the objectivity of data collection. Yet affect studies seek to destabilize this primacy of rationality, both in theory and in method. While this critique by affect studies pertains to all areas of social science research, it becomes particularly salient when researching the affective and emotional dimension of politics. How can we conceive interviews beyond this understanding of them as straightforward, rationalized conversations? To do so, we propose turning to feminist, anthropological, postcolonial and affect studies within the interpretative research paradigm. These fields offer a more complex understanding of interviews by considering power relations, as well as the emotional and relational dimensions of the interview process. Rather than neglecting, avoiding or "controlling" for moments of affective attunement as potentially disturbing factors (Gould, 2015), these contributions focus on the embodiments, intensities and dissonances of the interviewing process that relate both to the interviewer and interviewee. This means that feelings and emotions also have to be considered as part of the interview process. As Lee-Treweek notes, "ignoring or repressing feelings about research is more likely to produce distortion of data, rather than clarity" (Lee-Treweek & Linkogle, 2000, 128). Arguably, this is the case in all research designs that engage with meaning and meaning-making in the social world (Davis & Stodulka, 2019).

The perspectives developed here are based on our own research experience of studying the affective dynamics of political participation in Egypt and Turkey. More specifically, we are examining the affective dynamics, aftermaths and political transformations of the occupations of Tahrir Square in Cairo in 2011, and of Gezi Park in Istanbul in 2013. Both were highly affectively charged occupations of the public sphere, and both instigated a mass upheaval in their respective countries. As such they are critical examples for contemporary forms of protest that concentrate around the occupation of public squares. Our research project examined the affective dynamics in the squares during the occupation and explored whether and how these dynamics travel in time and space (Ayata & Harders, 2018, 2019). Empirically, we located the traveling of these moments in emerging new political practices at the local level in various neighborhoods in Turkey and Egypt (Harders & Wahba, 2017).[1] As part of this research, our team carried out ten months of ethnographic fieldwork in Egypt and Turkey and conducted more than 90 semi-structured qualitative interviews with activists and participants in the occupations. But we also employed a variety of experimental research methods such as memory walks and emotion cards[2] following the call for more innovative and creative methodological approaches in affect studies and in the sociology of emotions (Knudsen & Stage, 2015; Flam & Kleres, 2015; Flam, 2015). These methods supported and complemented our interviews which were our key method for data collection. When conducting the interviews, we approached interviews differently from more conventional practices in political science. For one, we approached qualitative interviews as *affective encounters* themselves, and more specifically as *situated affective encounters*. We begin first with the former and will introduce the latter in more detail further below. By affective encounters, we refer to the relationship between interviewer and interlocutor, which is dynamic and always shaped by different relational intensities. These affective intensities often already build up when the researcher is looking for access to her interlocutors. Sometimes they become clear only after the meeting is over. In addition, the temporal, spatial and emotional context of the encounters also influences the interview, which needs to be taken into account as systematically as possible. Thus, to approach interviews as affective encounters highlights the relationality among the settings, actors and contexts involved in the interview process, which is important for any interpretative research setting. In addition, and related to the previous point, we suggest approaching interviews as a *process* that encompasses the phases before and after the actual conversation. In conventional political science methods, only the conversation itself is understood as a dynamic site of action through the exchange between the interviewer and interlocutor, while everything else is regarded as a constant. We, on the other hand, highlight that the entire interview *process* is shaped by affective dynamics. Therefore, the thoughts, emotions, affects and interactions between the interviewer and the interview partner need to be documented. Likewise, the phases before, during and after the interview must be considered for a more comprehensive account for the dynamic and relational aspects of the interview process. Such an understanding and practice of interviewing collects more nuanced material since the notes, records and reflections regarding the affective dynamics of the interview process itself help to contextualize and analyze the interview beyond the mere textual analysis of the interview transcripts. This can create more space for self-reflection on the part of the researcher without turning data collection into an auto-ethnography. Moreover, such an approach invites and encourages researchers to be more attentive to non-lingual dimensions of the interview by cultivating an awareness of the affective intensities and embodiments during the interview process.

In what follows, we first engage with qualitative research methodologies and scholarship on interviews in political science and discuss their usefulness for doing research on affects and emotions. We then turn to methodological contributions by feminist, postcolonial, anthropological and affect studies scholars to present our own concept of the interview as a situated affective encounter. In a next step, we present examples from our fieldwork in order to illustrate how a relational and processual approach to interviewing can be put into practice. We conclude with an overall assessment of the potential of employing qualitative interviews based on our proposed amendments.

Qualitative interviews and affect research in political science

As we have indicated, political science has so far engaged much less with affect and emotions in empirical studies than neighboring disciplines have.[3] In terms of methodology, conventional approaches offer little entry points for researching affect due to the positivist and behavioralist traditions of empirical research in the discipline (King, Keohane, & Verba, 1994; for a critique, see e.g. Wedeen, 2007). A wide range of research methods is usually incorporated under the rubric of qualitative methods (Johnson, Reynolds, & Mycoff, 2016; Wood, 2007), but even among those studies that do employ qualitative methods, it has been argued that there is a tendency not to refer "to the traditions of meaning-focused or lived experience-focused research but to small-n studies applying large-n tools" (Yanow, 2009, 431). Rather than making wider use of the rich spectrum of interpretative approaches to social and political life, such an understanding of qualitative methods uses interviews intensively yet treats them with caution (Bruter & Lodge, 2013; Mosley, 2013). Concerns about objectivity and the validity of the data gathered through interviewing are some of the main issues (Brenner, Brown, & Canter, 1985) that limit the use of interviews in political sciences according to the positivist proponents of the discipline (Brady, Collier, & Box-Steffensmeier, 2011).

Lately, there has been an intensive conversation with anthropology in some parts of political sciences (Wedeen, 2010). This literature engages with interviews and focuses on the knowledge that is produced in the conversation, and addresses ethical issues that can arise at each stage of the research process. In most of these works, interviews are analyzed either as a "social event" (Seale, 1998; Rapley, 2004) or as a form of "conversation" with an emphasis on talking. While this is an important contribution, the data is here mainly retrieved from the words uttered during the conversation, which cannot account for the non-lingual dimensions of affect. To engage with the methodological challenges when researching affect with interviews, we find the work by Deborah Gould very helpful. In her seminal work on affect and social movements, Gould provides a case study of the ACT UP movement in the US (Gould, 2009). Here, Gould productively engages with affect studies, social movement studies and the sociology of emotions, offering important insights into how to do empirical research on affect. Based on her qualitative interviews with participants in the ACT UP movement who fought AIDS amidst public efforts to silence the issue, she develops a careful and attentive reading of texts, speech and bodily actions of the interviewed activists in a way that is sensitive to affect. This close reading enables her to get an understanding of the affective states in play in a given scene (ibid., 29). In addition to a close reading, Gould also stresses the importance of cultivating emotional self-knowledge as a researcher. Doing so "allows one to observe and read in a manner that can pick up the unspoken, the repressed, the less-than-fully conscious, the inarticulable" (ibid., 30). Such self-knowledge is critical for research on political phenomena involving intense collective and personal experiences that are difficult to talk about, such as violent uprisings, mass protests or resistance movements. Political disappointments, feelings of defeat, hope, loss and despair are hard to express in a straightforward manner during an interview. Yet this is precisely why such realms of silence and the unspoken are productive sites for exploration beyond textual analysis.

This understanding of the interview resonates well with certain debates in anthropology that conceptualize the "ethnographic interview" as more than just a conversation or an event (O'Reilly, 2005, 114). In this vein, Sarah Pink's *Doing Sensory Ethnography* (2009) describes interviews as "social, sensorial and emotive *encounters*" (p. 82). Pink thus proposes to treat interviews as "instances in which interviewer and interviewee together create a shared place" and as a "route to understanding other people's emplacement through collaborative and reflexive exploration" (ibid., 83). Building on the notion of the interview as an encounter, we follow the insights of anthropologists as well as feminist and postcolonial scholars who have stressed that such encounters can only be grasped contextually (Sherman-Heyl, 2001). Authors such as Abu-Lughod (1991), Clifford (1983), Haraway (1988), Harding (1986) and Smith (1999) have highlighted the contextual importance of positionality, power dynamics and hierarchies, the relevance of time and place, and the relationship between knowledge production and unequal power structures. In this sense, all interviews are situated, and the knowledge gathered through them is "situated knowledge," as Donna Haraway famously put it (1988). Haraway proposes using "the view from a body, always a complex, contradictory, structuring, and structured body" and contrasts this situated positionality with the seemingly neutral, godlike and scientific "view from above, from nowhere, from simplicity" (ibid., 589). Drawing on Haraway, we argue that the interview must be understood as an encounter that is itself situated. It unfolds in specific social, political, economic and cultural contexts, and is bound to time and space. Power relations based on gender, sexuality, class, race, religion and ethnicity profoundly shape interview dynamics. They influence data collection and field access, as well as data analysis. Yet we argue that interviews are not just situated encounters but rather situated *affective* encounters.

Interviews as situated affective encounters

Before elaborating on what we mean by interviews as situated affective encounters, we first need to briefly specify our understanding of affect and emotion in this chapter. Affects and emotions have been abundantly theorized and defined. Following contemporary affect studies, our use of the term "affect" refers to relational dynamics unfolding in interaction. As such, affect entails processes of "affecting and being affected" that not only ground and inform emotions, but also exceed discrete emotional states in moments of transgression and intensity (Massumi, 2002; Gould, 2009; Röttger-Rössler & Slaby, 2018). Thus, affect and emotion are closely intertwined and feed into each other; however, affect's characteristic elusiveness and fluidity poses challenges when doing empirically grounded research. In their volume *Affective Methodologies* (2015), Knudsen and Stage respond to this challenge by urging researchers to collect or produce "embodied data" (p. 3) when researching affect empirically. Researchers are encouraged to take an inventive approach to redefining established methods in their fields. Applying that intervention to the field of political science, we propose approaching interviews as situated affective encounters that enable researchers to collect such embodied data. This data can then be traced through careful observation, self-reflexivity and documentation in an interview.

But how does the process of affecting and being affected transpire in an interview, and how can we as researchers grasp sense, feel and collect embodied data? As a fundamentally relational impulse, affect constantly travels between or among people and artifacts and is registered in varying degrees of intensities, resonances or dissonances. As Teresa Brennan (2004) suggests, this traveling of intensities is a "flow" that can be traced in an interview. Affect moves through space or place and between people during encounters. The intensification of different feelings and emotions in such encounters bonds the researcher to the interlocutor. Kathleen Stewart described this connection as bodies "literally affecting one another and generating intensities: human bodies, discursive bodies, bodies of thought, bodies of water" (2007, 128). But, as Brennan rightly warns, it would be wrong to think that interlocutors are just receivers of feelings, affects and information. Rather, as Brennan holds, people should be perceived as interpreters. This is true for both researchers and their interlocutors, as we experienced consistently during our own field research. As researchers, we exchange multiple affects with our interlocutors, particularly in an interview setting or during longer periods of fieldwork. In turn, this exchange of affect generates further affective engagements with our research subjects and objects. This is a relational process in which both the researcher and the researched are open to affecting and to being affected. Sara Ahmed aptly describes the emotional and affective encounter that occurs in an interview, stating that, "through the work of listening to others, of hearing the force of their pain and the energy of their anger, of learning to be surprised by all that one feels oneself to be against; through all of this, a "we" is formed, an attachment is made" (2004, 188).

As affect travels, it creates attachments and accumulates value (Ahmed, 2003, 120). We thus argue that these shared affective states should also be recognized as relevant sources of knowledge during the interview process. It would be rather awkward to do research on affect and emotions with interviews by excluding the interviewers' affects from the research. This is not a call for turning every research into an auto-ethnography, but to understand what is entailed by regarding interviews as affectively situated encounters that inform the entire interview process.

Conducting interviews as a process

We further propose that an interview is not limited to the moment in which it actually occurs, but rather spans a constellation of different affective temporalities. Thus, we regard both the interview itself and its documentation as processual. A rigorous documentation of the interview must therefore attend to the informal conversations and various encounters that arise during the fieldwork.

This includes a wide variety of encounters that researchers in the field experience, such as attempts to set up interview meetings, the feelings of excitement, anxiety or frustration on the part of both researchers and interlocutors before, during and after the interview, and other expressed or embodied emotions arising during the interviews. It also includes the notes taken by the researcher as the interpretative part of an interview. All of these contexts are central components of the data and provide different layers of textualities for the data analysis. This is a productive and feasible way to generate qualitative material for systematic reflection about the affective entanglements at play in the entire interview process. It allows for an encompassing documentation of an interview's affective and emotional dynamics, thus creating empirical ground for its systematic inclusion and scrutiny of affect's role within the qualitative research dynamic. This processual understanding of interviews has several advantages. Firstly, it substantially broadens and deepens the material gathered through the interviews, and thus helps to reach data-saturation. Secondly, it allows researchers to operationalize interviews as situated affective encounters in the actual research practice. Thirdly, it offers a broadened understanding of qualitative, semi-structured interviews to those political scientists who wish to explore the dynamic relationship among emotion, affect and politics in any given subfield.

Such an understanding of qualitative interviews necessitates more than what can be captured in the acts of interviewing and documentation alone, as is the commonly accepted practice in political science. Thus, in addition to the conventional interview transcript, we suggest that political scientists employing interviews systematically generate field notes as well as field diaries. Corresponding to the phases before and after the interview respectively, field notes and field diaries are methods that have been long employed in anthropology. The purpose of the field diary is to document in detail how the interview encounter came about, and how the process evolved. Then, in the phase after the interview, the researcher actively reflects on the affective and emotional dynamics of the encounter in an effort to capture the subtle and often unspoken aspects of the interview, as well as the feelings that linger or arise afterwards. Considering these affective fields as empirical sources has the potential to make it easier to approach emotions and affect as analytical objects, opening a "useful avenue for seeking self-scrutiny and transparency of the context in which knowledge was produced" (Punch, 2012, 87). In contrast to field diaries, field notes are a more formal and less intimate way to document participant observation during meetings and informal conversations (Bøhling, 2015). As de Laine argues, researchers produce field notes to explain the social world (2000, 170). Hence, considering interviews as a process allows for using multiple text sources. These include the written reflections that the researcher collected through field diaries, field notes and participant observation notes before and after the interviews.

Interviews as situated affective encounters – examples from the field

But how might we implement an understanding of interviews as situated affective encounters within the interviewing process itself? In this section, we present examples from our own fieldwork to illustrate how we put these propositions into practice. These examples are drawn from our interviews in Turkey and Egypt, where we researched the affective dynamics of political participation and mass protest during and after the occupations of Tahrir Square in Egypt (2011) and of Gezi Park in Turkey (2013). We used ethnographic interviews to trace the feelings, memories and experiences of the political activists and protest participants interviewed by our research team. We explored the different kinds of affects and emotions that circulated among the protestors, how these shared intensities shaped political participation and the extent to which these intense experiences were reproduced through different practices at different times. According to Gabriel and Ulus (2015, 36), emotions can be observed in one of three ways: People might openly state how they feel, they might recount a story or anecdote intended to explain their feelings, or they might indicate feelings through their actions and bodily expressions. In a similar vein, Knudsen and Stage proposed attending to bodily expressions during the research process (2015, 5). Building on these suggestions, we approached the emotional and affective responses during the interview process as additional sources to analyze the emotional and affective dynamics of political participation and (im)mobilization. For instance, when we asked our interlocutors about their memories of the feelings they had felt during the protests events, we attended not only to their speech, but also to how they experienced the act of relating those memories at the time of our interview. Although interlocutors may narrate and interpret these memories differently over time, these altered narratives often reverberate the affective intensities of the past moment. An interview we conducted in Turkey will help illustrate the verbal and non-verbal interaction that often transpires between the interviewer and interlocutor. In this case, the interviewer is a member of our research team who by this time had already conducted several interviews and had actively sought to cultivate an emotional self-awareness when speaking with her interview partners. The interlocutor here is a 63-year-old retired, male teacher who was the leader of the teachers' union during the Gezi protests in Turkey and a prominent activist. Before the interview, both had met several times to arrange the interview and had developed a friendly and cordial rapport, facilitated by the age difference between the young researcher and the elderly, seasoned activists. The interview was conducted in the activist's own coffee shop, where most of the seasoned leftist political activists of the city meet. After some general questions regarding his memories of the Gezi protests, the interviewer slowly inquired into more personal memories that directly related to emotions and feelings. The interviewer's gradual approach to asking about his personal memories was informed by her awareness that speaking about emotions can evoke a range of unexpected reactions that can either disrupt or intensify the course of interview. Here is an excerpt, where the inquiry into past feelings evokes strong emotional reactions in the moment of narration:

D: How did you feel when you saw thousands of people on the streets?

A: It was the most beautiful feeling that I had until that time. I was very emotional then (*his eyes fill with tears, he is trying to hide them by reaching out to a glass in the table nearby, but there are other customers sitting there. He tries to hide his face from the interviewer by turning his upper body a bit away*).

[*Mutual silence of 0:43 minutes*]

D: (*with a quiet voice*) How did the masses start to walk through the AKP [*The Justice and Development Party*] building?

A: Who represents the political power in this city? (*raises his voice in an enraged way*) They!

The biggest target here was the AKP so we decided to go there. But no one expected that crowd. So what happened then? Somebody had to lead the crowd and people knew me because we were always in the streets and I had the megaphone. Thus, I made a call to the crowd to conduct a sit-in protest in front of the building. There was no empty space in the street. Maybe you saw that picture. [*Talks about a symbolic picture of the protests that shows tens of thousands of people in the streets and a group of police waiting in front of the party building.*]

D: Yes, yes, I know it. Almost all the protesters I know are proud of that scene. (*Mutual laughing*)

A: As if it was taken in a European country (*laughing*). I saw people who came with their babies. I looked at the people and then thought that hundreds of people would die if the police attack to the crowd. Why? Because the whole street was full of people and no one could move. I have the photo. Shall I show you? It is the most beautiful photo. (*He is laughing.*)

D: Okay! (*also laughing*)

[*A takes his mobile phone out of his pocket and shows the photo of the protest to the interviewer.*]

A: Look! (*Again, his eyes fill with tears and trying to hide them.*)

D: [*waiting for him to feel better*] Yes, I remember this photo well. Many people talked about that scene as a symbol of the protests.

(Interview excerpt with A., Eskisehir, 12 July 2017)

While transcribing the interview, the interviewer added some of the non-verbal parts of the sequence to the records based on interview notes she had taken during the interview. In the interview transcript, they are listed as brief pointers to convey the atmosphere and additional layers of communication that occurred at the non-verbal level between the interviewer and interview partner. They offer a glimpse of the affective attachments that develop in the course of the conversation between the two and illustrate the embodied and affective narration of the interlocutor. In her field diary, she noted more detailed reflections on that sequence in the aftermath of the interview:

> I was very perplexed how even the mere mentioning of "how did you feel" led so fast to an emotional response of his eyes filling with tears. He was in general a lively, emphatic and emotional person, but this was not even a question about a loss or painful moment, it was basically my first opening question and before raising even the others, he already had such a strong physical emotional response. The moment I asked about his feelings about four years ago, he was ready to cry, the emotion was right there. I am still surprised about this immediacy. Before that question, we had spoken about the increasing depression and hopelessness that is present among so many activists, how things have turned so bad and that no one dares to protest anymore. And then already at the first question on the Gezi protests, he got so moved. Did he cry because he was so happy back then? Or did he cry because everything is so politically desperate now, which my question about "the good times" may have him triggered to realize? I wanted to ask him this even at that moment, but I couldn't. For instance, I would have liked to ask "what do you mean this was the most beautiful feeling you had so far" or "how does this memory make you feel," but I got silent with him and wanted to respect his boundary. Now thinking back, I could have taken up the question again later, but at that moment, I just saw and felt that he wanted to hide his tears from me, and I didn't want to push this further. His emotional outburst made me also emotional, so I changed the question, to make him but also myself more comfortable. Once the atmosphere calmed down and the emotional release happened after he showed me the photo from his mobile phone, the conversation opened up and deepened. Ironically, it seems that he appreciated my respect towards his boundary and my affective affirmation of his photo, he felt somehow safer or more comfortable with me, because through the rest of the interview, it was him who kept talking about his feelings and emotions, without that I had to ask him explicitly about it anymore. He was so excited when talking about his memories, he was so vivid, intense and alive when talking about the days of the protest, I somehow got also excited with him, and remembered myself a couple of memories that I had totally forgotten from my own experiences when I had joined the protests myself back then.
>
> (Eskisehir, 12 July 2017)

These two excerpts illustrate how the collected data is enhanced when non-verbal and embodied material is documented and included in the analysis. When visiting the multiple textualities of field notes, interview transcripts and field diaries, the interview offers much richer insights to trace the affective dynamics of mass protests. Of particular significance, for instance, is the interlocutor's strong bodily and emotional reactions when narrating his memory of the protest he participated four years ago. These documented reactions transmit the intensity of the interlocutor's experience, and illuminate his mixed emotions of anger against the government, fear for the safety of his fellow co-protestors and excitement about his moments of leadership during a sit-in protest. Remembering a particular moment alongside its corresponding feelings is not always easy, and the emotions can change in different contexts. This becomes most vivid in the interlocutor's immediate urge to show a photo that captures the moment which had excited him the most. As if his own words would not suffice to express the feeling of the moment, he has the urge to complement them by showing the interviewer a picture saved on his mobile phone. This affectively charged moment, and the transmission of affect during the interview more broadly, open up other avenues for thinking about the emotional motivations of political activism and of the affective dynamics at a protest. The protests had high personal costs for him, as he lost his job due to his activism and was forced into retirement. By contrast, the interlocutor's vivid emotional response during the interview demonstrates the strongly felt affective resonances of the protests. This example shows how different types of intensities – the material environment of the interview, embodied manifestations of different emotions and the resonance between different components of the interview – provide rich sources of material for tracing the affective dynamics of political participation.

This example briefly illustrated how approaching interviews as situated affective encounters can generate a comprehensive body of material for tracing affects and emotions. In the following example, we highlight the importance of considering the affective encounters which unfold even before the actual interviews take place. Considering these contexts during the interview process itself can also help the interviewer to cultivate more emotional self-awareness as a researcher. Such an emotional self-awareness requires researchers to be sensitive to the constant re-negotiation of positionalities, and to how they impact our field access, the degree of intimacy we experience and the quality and relevance of our interaction. During the fieldwork of our research team in Turkey and Egypt, these issues arose before, during and after the interview. As we saw in the previous example, our interview contents related directly to emotions, feelings and personal memories of intense experiences during mass protests, and this content inevitably made the interview encounter itself an intimate and emotionally charged experience. Documenting and collecting field notes about these experiences create a productive space for self-reflection. This is illustrated in the following excerpt from the field diary of another member of our research team, in which she reflects on the difficulties of field access in Cairo. Such difficulties can occur in many research contexts. In her field diary, she reflects on the multi-layered class and gender hierarchies that she noted after several attempts to set up a semi-structured, open-ended interview with a young, Egyptian lower-class man, who is a political activist at one of our research sites. Arranging the interview required several preliminary meetings, during which they discussed some of the interview questions she was preparing.

Although he was interested in the interview and in the research, he repeatedly postponed the actual interview. In the following excerpt, the researcher reflects on the possible reasons for his reluctance to have a lengthy interview:

> I have been trying to have an actual, recorded interview with him for a few months now. I am not sure why he is reluctant. The security situation can surely scare anyone out of talking to a researcher; however, someone he knows very well introduced us. He was arrested before and spent two years in jail so he does not strike me as someone afraid to go back. We had a meeting for a brief, exploratory interview but he did not want me to record it. I was trying to write down everything he says. It was all very interesting for me even if not new. Yet, I had a feeling that he did not think what he said is worthy of being recorded. Several issues complicate the story further. I am perceived by the people in the informal area I am working in as a middle-class, unmarried woman. This can trigger all kinds of assumptions and layered gendered dynamics. I am an "outsider" to the area but I am still an Egyptian, so domestic gender norms still apply to me. Maybe for him, to meet with a young woman alone longer in a café feels a lot like a date. To explain to him what the interview was about, I needed to reach across Cairo's rigid class and gender boundaries to build a relationship that allows for a conversation about feelings.
>
> (Cairo, 26 September 2017)

The excerpt illustrates how setting up an interview over the course of several informal preliminary meetings already established a relationship that triggered affective resonance and dissonance. In her field diary, the researcher tries to make sense of the prospective interlocutor's reluctance to be interviewed by reflecting on the ways class and gender matter for emotions. She feels that her interlocutor depreciates his own experiences in front of her, maybe because of an emotional habitus towards the condescending ways middle- and upper-class Egyptians can treat marginalized urban young men. Reflecting on the dynamics of their efforts to meet, the researcher also wonders about possible gendered anxieties concerning the "appropriateness" of the situation. Asking for an interview about emotions and politics could sound quite intimate. Such feelings of intimacy may intersect with and at times clash with class, gender, racial or religious borders, thus influencing the interaction before and during the interview. The excerpt from the field diary shows how the researcher actively explores her own emotions (anxiety, frustration, patience, trying to be careful and respectful) in order to cultivate emotional self-knowledge as an interviewer. However, this might also be stifling if situations become too complex to navigate. In addition, the excerpt also speaks to the importance of class and gender for "feeling rules" (Hochschild, 1979) and for the "emotional habitus" (Gould, 2009) that inform the experiences of researchers and interlocutors. In this example, reflecting in writing about the difficulty of setting up an interview triggered important considerations and awareness about how the context of the Egyptian gender and class order may have affected the actual interview.

Conclusion

This chapter has explored the potentials of employing qualitative interviews as a method of empirical research on affect and emotions. It is important to highlight that we refer here to our discipline in political science, which has a rather straight-forward understanding of conducting interviews. Considering the difficulty of collecting empirical data in affect research, we propose to integrate interview methods from neighboring disciplines, and suggest approaching qualitative semi-structured interviews as *situated affective encounters*. This enables researchers to analyze affect and emotion in an empirically grounded way while adhering to the main tenets of the interpretative paradigm in social science research. Furthermore, rather than a circumscribed event, we conceptualize the interview as a process that spans the encounters while setting up interviews as well as the phases after the interviews are concluded and transcribed. On the ground, of course, fieldwork is much messier than it is on paper. Encounters, observations and self-reflections merge into an affectively charged assemblage of collected material. With our procedural understanding of the interview, we aim to expand the methodological practices in political science. We suggest that researchers of affect and emotion in political science can benefit from cultivating emotional self-knowledge and from documenting their own affects and emotions during the research process. We have stressed that the interview is a constellation of different affective temporalities. As such, the interview provides access to the more cognitive and emotional phrasings at play and to the unspoken intensities that unfold during the interview. Research-ers are urged to document the embodiments of such affective flows in their field diaries both before and after the interview. In so doing, they can translate the immediacy of affect into descriptions of bodily states. Keeping this record makes it possible to pay closer analytic attention to the silences and cracks or to the sud-den strange feelings that sometimes impose themselves in situ, and which often only become legible in hindsight when reading the interview transcript. It is of course important to emphasize that, by themselves, the empirical advantages of a heightened emotional self-awareness and self-documentation during the interview process will hardly satisfy the criteria of conventional positivists in political sci-ence. The limits of our concept are rather clear in this regard. Yet therein lies also its potential. By pushing the methodological boundaries of the discipline from within, our approach makes those disciplinary boundaries more permeable and thus more productively open, so to speak, to affecting and being affected.

Notes

1 In order to collect the data for an affective reading of the events and their aftermath, team members Dina Wahba and Derya Özkaya spent more than ten months in Egypt and Turkey respectively between 2016 and the end of 2017. Cilja Harders and Bilgin Ayata joined them for shorter field visits.
2 We also used more experimental methods such as "emotion cards" in a focus group, memory walks, "show-and-tell" situations including artifacts, pictures or videos, and mental mapping. But, for the purpose of this chapter, we want to focus on interviews as the main method of data collection.

3 In the subfields of political psychology, political theory and social movement studies, emotion and affect attracted some interest in the last 20 years. Still, these literatures are only of limited use for our purposes due to the individualist understanding of emotions in political psychology, which is different from the concept of emotions used here. Political theorists do not collect empirical data and movement studies, which mostly depend on interview data, do not engage in detailed methodological debates about the kind of data they gather.

References

Abu-Lughod, L 1991, 'Writing against culture', in R Fox (ed.), *Recapturing Anthropology: Working in the Present*, pp. 137–162, School of American Research Press, Santa Fe.

Ahmed, S 2003, 'Affective economies', *Social Text*, vol. 22, 79, no. 2, pp. 117–139.

Ahmed, S 2004, *The Cultural Politics of Emotion*, Edinburgh University Press, Edinburgh.

Ayata, B & Harders, C 2018, 'Midan moments: Conceptualizing space, affect and political participation on occupied squares', in B Röttger-Rössler & J Slaby (eds.), 2017, *Affect in Relation: Families, Places and Technologies*, Routledge, London, New York.

Ayata, B & Harders, C 2019, 'Midan moments' in J Slaby & C von Scheve (eds.), *Affective Societies: Key Concepts*, Routledge, New York.

Bøhling, F 2015, 'The field note assemblage: Researching the bodily-affective dimensions of drinking and dancing ethnographically' in B Knudsen & C Stage (eds.), *Affective Methodologies: Developing Cultural Research Strategies for the Study of Affect*, pp. 161–182, Palgrave Macmillan, London.

Brady, HE, Collier, D & Box-Steffensmeier, JM 2011, 'Overview of political methodology: Post-behavioral movements and trends', in RE Goodin (ed.), *The Oxford handbook of political sciences*, pp. 1005–1063, Oxford University Press, Oxford.

Brennan, T 2004, *The Transmission of Affect*, Cornell University Press, Ithaca.

Brenner, M, Brown, J & Canter, D (eds.), 1985, *The Research Interview: Uses and Approaches*, Academic Press, New York.

Bruter, M & Lodge, M (eds.), 2013, *Political Science Research Methods in Action*, Palgrave Macmillan, London.

Clifford, J 1983, 'On ethnographic authority', *Representations*, no. 2, pp. 118–146.

Davis, J & Stodulka, T 2019, 'Emotions in fieldwork' in P Atkinson, S Delamont, M Hardy & M Williams (eds.), *The SAGE Encyclopedia of Research Methods*, Sage Publications.

Flam, H 2015, 'Introduction: Methods of exploring emotions', in H Flam & J Kleres (eds.), *Methods of Exploring Emotions*, pp. 1–18, Routledge, New York.

Flam, H & Kleres, J (eds.), 2015, *Methods of Exploring Emotions*, Routledge, New York.

Gabriel, Y & Ulus, E 2015, ' "It's all in the plot": Narrative explorations of work-related emotions', in H Flam & J Kleres (eds.), *Methods of Exploring Emotions*, pp. 36–45, Routledge, New York.

Gould, D 2009, *Moving Politics: Emotion and ACT UP's Fight Against AIDS*, University of Chicago Press, Chicago.

Gould, D 2015, 'When your data make you cry', in H Flam & J Kleres (eds.), *Methods of Exploring Emotions*, pp. 163–171, Routledge, New York.

Haraway, D 1988, 'Situated knowledges: The science question in feminism and the privilege of partial perspective', *Feminist Studies*, vol. 14, no. 3, pp. 575–599.

Harders, C & Wahba, D 2017, 'New neighborhood power: Informal popular committees and changing local governance in Egypt', in T Cambanis & MW Hanna (eds.), *Arab*

Politics Beyond the Uprisings: Experiments in an Era of Resurgent Authoritarianism, pp. 400–419, The Century Foundation Press, New York. Available from: https://tcf.org/content/report/new-neighborhood-power/ [30 April 2018].

Harding, S 1986, *The Science Question in Feminism*, Open University Press, Milton Keynes.

Hochschild, AR 1979, 'Emotion work, feeling rules, and social structure', *The American Journal of Sociology*, vol. 85, no. 3, pp. 551–575.

Johnson, JB, Reynolds, HT & Mycoff, JD 2016, *Political Science Research Methods*, Sage Publications, Los Angeles.

King, G, Keohane, R & Verba, S 1994, *Designing Social Inquiry: Scientific Inference in Qualitative Research*, Princeton University Press, Princeton.

Knudsen, B & Stage, C (eds.), 2015, *Affective Methodologies: Developing Cultural Research Strategies for the Study of Affect*, Palgrave Macmillan, London.

de Laine, M 2000, *Fieldwork, Participation and Practice: Ethics and Dilemmas in Qualitative Research*, Sage Publications, London.

Lee-Treweek, G & Linkogle, S (eds.), 2000, *Danger in the Field: Risk and Ethics in Social Research*, Routledge, London.

Massumi, B 2002, *Parables for the Virtual: Movement, Affect, Sensation*, Duke University Press, Durham, New York.

Mosley, L 2013, *Interview Research in Political Science*, Cornell University Press, Ithaca.

O'Reilly, K 2005, *Ethnographic Methods*, Routledge, Abingdon.

Pink, S 2009, *Doing Sensory Ethnography*, Sage Publications, London.

Punch, S 2012, 'Hidden struggles of fieldwork: Exploring the role and use of field diaries', *Emotion, Space and Society*, no. 5, pp. 86–93.

Rapley, T 2004, 'Interviews', in C Seale, G Gobo, JF Gubrium & D Silverman (eds.), *Qualitative Research Practice*, pp. 16–34, Sage Publications, London.

Röttger-Rössler, B & Slaby, J (eds.), 2018, *Affect in Relation: Families, Places and Technologies*, Routledge, London, New York.

Seale, C 1998, 'Qualitative interviewing', in C Seale (ed.), *Researching Society and Culture*, Sage Publications, London.

Sherman-Heyl, B 2001, 'Ethnographic interviewing', in P Atkinson, A Coffey, S Delamont, J Lofland & L Lofland (eds.), *Handbook of Ethnography*, pp. 369–383, Sage Publications, London.

Smith, LT 1999, *Decolonizing Methodologies*, University of Otago Press, Duneden.

Stewart, K 2007, *Ordinary Affects*, Duke University Press, Durham.

Wedeen, L 2007, 'Scientific knowledge, liberalism, and empire: American political science in the modern Middle East', *Social Science Research Council*, 14–15 June. Available from: www.ssrc.org/publications/view/8A197ABF-ED60-DE11-BD80-001CC477EC70 [31 July 2018].

Wedeen, L 2010, 'Reflections on ethnographic work in political science', *The Annual Review of Political Science*, no. 13, pp. 255–272.

Wood, E 2007, 'Field methods' in C Boix & S Stokes (eds.), *The Oxford Handbook of Comparative Politics*, pp. 123–146, Oxford University Press, Oxford.

Yanow, D 2009, 'Interpretative ways of knowing in the study of politics', in S Pickel, G Pickel, HJ Lauth & D Jahn (eds.), *Methoden der vergleichenden Politik- und Sozialwissenschaft*, pp. 429–439, VS Verlag für Sozialwissenschaften, Wiesbaden.

Chapter 5

Narrating visualized feelings

Photovoice as a tool for researching affects and emotions among school students

Birgitt Röttger-Rössler, Gabriel Scheidecker and Anh Thu Anne Lam

Seeing comes before words. The child looks and recognizes before it can speak.

But there is also another sense in which seeing comes before words. It is seeing which establishes our place in the surrounding world; we explain that world with words, but words can never undo the fact, that we are surrounded by it. The relation between what we see and what we know is never settled.

(Berger, 1972, 7)

Introduction

Within the context of a school study designed to investigate the formation of feelings among school children with differing socio-cultural backgrounds, we provided 90 students of different age grades (10–18 years) with small digital cameras. With these cameras, we asked them to "picture their feelings" by taking photos that show or symbolize what triggers emotions in them. We gave them two weeks to perform this task in order to give them enough time to reflect on it. Afterwards, we asked the children and adolescents to select the 15 most important photos out of their sample, and we interviewed them about these pictures. The method turned out to be extremely efficient. In relation to the photos of situations, objects and persons, which are key to their daily experiences, the students produced dense narrations about their feelings. The school study was embedded in the work of a larger social-anthropological project addressing the formation of feeling ("Gefühlsbildung") in Vietnamese Berlin. This transnational field is composed of families with Vietnamese ancestry or identities and the wider socio-material context of Berlin. As part of the CRC *Affective Societies. Dynamics of Social Coexistence in Mobile Worlds*, the project investigates how second-generation Vietnamese immigrants contend with altering emotional models and corresponding modes of emotional education that confront them in diverse social spheres (family, peers, pre-schools, day-care centers, schools, clubs etc.). It analyzes the dissonances and frictions that this second generation experiences while navigating different social spaces and dealing with multiple incompatibilities of emotion repertoires and emotional interaction styles. And, in turn, it considers how these factors shape the formation of feeling in that younger generation. To conduct this study, we used a mixed-methods approach encompassing photovoice, biographical and focus group interviews, as well as systematic observation in different educational and childcare institutions.

A key methodological challenge consisted in accessing the emotions of children and adolescents within the scattered field of Vietnamese Berlin. Building such a rapport with children and youths is far less difficult in the context of long-term ethnographic fieldwork in small local communities, where one can easily observe their emotional expressions and interaction styles on a daily basis.[1] However, things are much more complicated in larger urban settings like Berlin. Furthermore, it is generally a difficult task to talk with children and adolescents about their experiences in formal interview settings. There are several reasons for this. Firstly, young children are still acquiring language skills, and even older ones are not as verbally mature as adults are. Thus, the classical interview situation gives a communicative advantage to the adult and accentuates adult authority, especially if the interviewer does not belong to the children's social world. Researchers working with children emphasize that a conventional interview with its dependence on the adult-privileged code of words is not suited to capturing the meanings children and teens ascribe to their lifeworlds (Clark, 1999, 40; Epstein et al., 2006, 2; Schratz, 1993). In order to avoid these pitfalls, we decided to conduct a photovoice study among school children; that is, to apply the auto-driven photo elicitation method as a first entry into the emotional worlds of young people.

The photovoice study was conducted in a "Gymnasium" (German academic high school) with which we were already collaborating.[2] It is located in the eastern part of Berlin, where many Vietnamese immigrants live, and thus has a high percentage of children whose parents immigrated from Vietnam. We discussed the project extensively with the school director, teachers and the school's social worker, who originates from Vietnam, and together we decided to address the whole student body instead of defining a particular sample beforehand. Our main arguments behind this decision were that it would be interesting to see which factors (age, gender, family background) corresponded with the students' choice to partake in the study, and that it would not be a good signal to exclude certain groups and age grades from participating. We hoped, of course, that the participation would mirror the proportions at the school, although the Vietnamese social worker presumed that few of the Vietnamese parents would approve of their children's participation in the project, unless it were mandatory or likely to foster school success. The school's social worker turned out to be right: With barely 10%, the participation of students with parents born in Vietnam was clearly underrepresented, as the overall proportion of students with this background at the school was roughly 15%. From this small number, we could not ground any valid analysis concerning the formation of feeling among the children of Vietnamese immigrants. However, the photovoice study produced deep insights into the emotional experiences and affective relations of children and teens at a German "Gymnasium". Most notably, it provided unforeseen and highly surprising results that challenge some basic affect-theoretical assumptions.

In this contribution, we shall (1) describe the photovoice technique and its methodological foundations in more detail; (2) outline how we conducted the photovoice study at the Berlin gymnasium; (3) represent some of the most striking results of our study; and (4) discuss the affect-theoretical implications of these results and reflect on the intersection of narration and visualization, which constitutes one of the biggest challenges in analyzing and interpreting the data of this study.

The use of photovoice in social anthropology, sociology, and research with children

Photovoice and photo elicitation studies include photographic images in the interview process in order to elicit information from research participants. The photos used can either originate from the researcher (photos taken during the research process or selected from various sources like photo archives, books, or newspapers) or stem from the research participants. In the latter case, the researcher asks the participants to either select some pictures from his or her private photo collections or to take their own photos about the particular research topic. In social anthropology and sociology, this kind of photo-based interview method is mostly referred to as *auto-driven photo-elicited interview* (Clark-Ibánez, 2004; Samuels, 2004), while in health and educational studies it is usually labeled *photovoice* (Wang & Burris, 1997; Wang & Redwood-Jones, 2001). We prefer the term photovoice because it implies that image and voice are inseparable in this method: The photos not only cause participants to speak but are speaking themselves in the sense that they add a visual dimension to the narration. They are a constitutive part of the meaning-making process that takes part in the interview. We will turn to this aspect later.

Using photo elicitation as a field method is not new. The method was first mentioned in 1957 by the visual anthropologist John Collier, who used photo elicitation to examine how rural Canadian families adapted to new forms of residence and work in urban factories. Collier and his team found it difficult to explore the subtle processes of psychological adaption to new environments in the form of conventional surveys and in-depth interviews, and therefore tried to invent a new interview technique using photos of the old and new residential areas of their informants. They found that this method triggered not only much more but also more precise and detailed information than word-only interviews. Collier related this to the "more subtle function of graphic imagery. This was its compelling effect on the informant, its ability to prod latent memory, to stimulate and release emotional statements about the informant's life" (Collier, 1957, 858).

The photo elicitation method was introduced by a founding figure of visual anthropology, who described it during the following decades in his introductory books to visual anthropology, which became reference works within the discipline (Collier, 1967; Collier & Collier, 1986; Collier, 1987). Nevertheless, the method never attracted many anthropologists, and very few anthropological studies today rely on photo elicitation.[3] In visual sociology, however, photo elicitation has played a greater role, especially in more recent developments.[4] Douglas Harper, one of the leading figures in this subdiscipline, describes photo elicitation as "a postmodern dialogue based on the authority of the subject rather than the researcher" (Harper, 2002, 15). This applies in particular to auto-driven photo elicitation studies. Interviews based on photographs taken by the participants themselves are more likely to mirror the participants' lifeworlds, and thus facilitate a bridging between the worlds of researcher and the researched (Samuels, 2004, 1530). The potential of the auto-driven photo elicitation method to "break the ethnographer's frames" (ibid., 1540) has also made this technique especially attractive to researchers in the domains of public health, education and social work, who find the method as a valuable means to assess participatory needs (e.g. Wang & Burris, 1997). In childhood studies, photovoice proves to be a highly effective tool for gaining access to the worlds and viewpoints of children (e.g. Clark, 1999; Lal, Jarus, & Suto, 2012; Wahle et al., 2017).

Methodological considerations

One of the biggest advantages of photovoice is its collaborative nature. During the interview session, researcher and researched usually sit side by side in order to look together at the photographs and thus *share* the same line of sight and focus of attention. This fact alone implies a collaborative aspect and decenters the authority of the adult researcher. Furthermore, if the photos originate from the participants, the authority during the discussion shifts primarily to them. The participants are the ones who made or selected the photographs, who know what the pictures represent and who understand why they are important. In other words, this method creates an affective arrangement that softens the social distance and unequal power relations that usually guide conventional interview sessions. This empowering character makes the photovoice method especially valuable in research with children and adolescents. We were surprised by how smoothly and effectively this method worked and by the richness and density of the material we gathered about the children's emotional experiences and affective relations.

A key issue of the method concerns the role of the photographs. Photos are not mere representations of social realities but are also generators of meaning. In social meaning-making processes like conversations or interviews, photos enfold their own agency. Abel and Deppner view photos as "hybride Wesen zwischen Bild und Gestalt, ausgestattet mit Akteursstatus und bildlicher Wirkmacht" ("hybrid beings in-between image and figure, provided with agency and illustrative power") (2012, 15). The agency of photographs is rooted in their polysemic quality: They store much more information than just the sight the photographer had in mind, and therefore continuously enable new (in)sights. In other words, photos always embody subjective ways of seeing, but as mechanical processes they also 'memorize' aspects that were not in the photographer's focus of attention. Thus, taking photos and looking at them constitute different acts of meaning-making that might become highly diverse. Even a person who took a photo with a particular intention, a particular scene in sight, may only a little bit later see this image in new light, discover 'new' elements in it, or be reminded of events behind the scene portrayed in the photo. For the purpose of our research, we were mainly interested in the potential of pictures to embody and reactivate the photographer's ways of seeing, resonating, and feeling.

In his reflections on the photovoice method, Samuels (2004, 1539) notes that the photographs his informants had taken functioned not only as an anchor for grounding their descriptions in their lifeworld and daily experiences, but also as a "catalyst for remembering". The capacity of photographs to trigger a multitude of memories is, according to neurobiological research, grounded in the particularities of human memory: Visual stimuli are processed and stored differently from verbal information. While words belong to declarative or *explicit memory*, visual and other sensory perceptions are processed through *implicit memory*; that is, in brain regions that are also considered relevant for processing emotions (Siegel, 2006, 23–26, see also Harper, 2002, 13). However, researchers experienced in working with photovoice state that photo-elicited interviews evoke more "affectively charged responses" (Samuels, 2004, 1529) or are "capable of reaching deeper centers of reaction, [and] triggering spontaneous revelations of a highly-charged emotional nature" (Collier, 1957, 858). Applying the photovoice technique thus affords an awareness of the complex relationship among words and images, memory, emotions and affects.

Because photovoice is able to ground the participants' descriptions in their daily lifeworlds and to access their more implicit memories and experiences, we viewed this method as suitable for studying the emotional and affective worlds of children and adolescents. While a conventional interview would rely primarily on verbal categories as starting points of narratives, we aimed at starting from the affectively charged lifeworlds the participants represented with their pictures. Rather than trying to directly observe them in their daily lives and interactions, and thus risking to impose our own (adult) presumptions of priorities and affective responses to them, we wanted to start with the children's own observations of and responses to their own lifeworlds. We thus prompted them to observe their daily lives and to reflect on whether it makes them feel positive or negative to picture these aspects and to explain the meaning of these photographs to us. It is noticeable that such a design has rarely been used in research on emotion and affect. Nevertheless, this design is built on a common practice to convey and share affecting experiences by showing and commenting on how one's photographs represent one's experiences, whether in the form of a photo album, an evening slide show, or by circulating pictures online.

The photovoice project 'FeelingPictures'

After we received the consent to conduct the photovoice project from the elected representatives of the teachers, students, and parents, we visited all 26 classes from grade 5 to 10 to introduce our project to the students.[5] We explained that we were interested in their feelings and would like them to think about what makes them feel, for example, happy, sad, angry, proud, scared, or cheerful, and to take a picture of it. We explained that anything could be pictured, whether people, objects, places, events, or symbols, as long as it evokes feelings, whatever they are. In our explanations, we avoided the terms emotion and affect, and instead used the German word "Gefühl" (feeling). This is, in part, because the word "Gefühl" is embedded in everyday language and is more comprehensible to children and teens, but also because it encompasses a strong bodily connotation and thus relates to phenomena which are perceived on a more implicit, sensual level rather than as a necessarily distinct and nameable emotion. The students were encouraged to pose questions, which allowed us to check if the task had been understood and to clarify it if necessary. In the end, we distributed small leaflets to the students, which contained the description of the task as well as the procedure, and a consent form, which had to be signed by the parents of children under the age of 14.

Having outlined the task, we proceeded as follows. The students who were willing and permitted to participate and who had returned the consent form were gathered in the school hall, where they each received a small digital camera. On this occasion, the task was explained again. The students got two weeks to take the pictures, so that they had enough time to reflect upon and photograph whatever evokes feelings in them. They were told that they could make as many photos as they wanted, but they should select the 15 most important photos of their sample and note on an extra protocol sheet why they had taken each of these 15 photos. When the cameras with the pictures were returned, we interviewed each participant individually.[6] After completing a short socio-demographic questionnaire, the interviewees were invited to comment on each of their pictures that were represented one after another on a computer screen. The initial narrative for each picture served as a starting point for further investigations concerning the photo subject as well as the feelings connected to it. A semi-structured interview guide ensured a similar procedure across interviewers and interviews, most of which took around half an hour. In the end, the participants received the pictures and the audio recording of the interview on a USB memory stick.

Two aspects of the preparatory process are particularly remarkable. First, while some of the teachers and parents questioned the task as such and doubted that it would be possible to take pictures of feelings, none of the students expressed a similar skepticism. The task to take *FeelingPictures* ("GefühlsBilder") seemed unproblematic for them, which might be due to the fact that taking and sharing photographic images via smartphones has become a common everyday practice for the younger generations, who are often portrayed as the *natives* of an increasingly *photographic society* (Abel & Deppner, 2012, 11). The second aspect relates directly to the phenomenon of "photographic networking" through the sharing of images in digital platforms like Instagram, WhatsApp, Facebook etc. We found that the students preferred to use our small digital cameras instead of their own, often highly potent, smartphones. They argued that using our cameras, which were marked with a small university sticker, would (1) hinder them from posting the images on different platforms; (2) stop them from using photos taken earlier and stored in their mobiles; and (3) remind them of the task through their pure physical presence. They clearly separated the photovoice task from their everyday photographic activities.

Exemplary findings

The photovoice material can be analyzed on multiple levels. Even the characteristics of the sample offer some interesting insights into feelings, emotions, and affects. Of the 163 students who registered, 90 went through all of the stages, from the distribution of cameras, to taking the pictures, to returning the camera, and finally conducting the interview. As participation was open to every one of the 1,171 students of the school, the registrations may shed some light on which social parameters make it likely to participate by reflecting and communicating one's feelings. Figure 5.1 breaks down the students' proportional participation according to their gender and grade in school, which was indicated on the questionnaire.

There is a clear peak of registrations for students from grade 6, who are around the age of 12 and 13 years. Almost half of the sixth graders registered for participation. These facts can be interpreted in light of impressions during the class

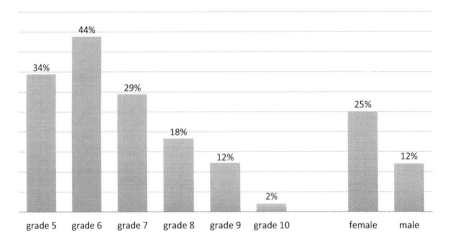

Figure 5.1 Proportional participation according to grade in school and gender.

presentations. Each class seemed to have its individual affective characteristics, perhaps depending on the current lesson and teacher, the time of day, or day of the week. However, the younger classes clearly responded in the most intense way to our presentation. They were ready to laugh, posed many questions, and provided examples of what they wanted to photograph. When we asked them in the end if they would like to participate, almost all raised their hand without much hesitation. In contrast, the students from the lower and higher classes responded with much more restraint, however, for different reasons as it appeared. While the youngest ones often seemed to be a bit intimidated and sometimes also disinterested, the oldest often appeared to be bored, skeptical, or even annoyed. When we asked them if they would like to participate, they often reacted slowly and looked around, as if wanting to make sure that they are not the only ones taking interest in it. Thus, the peak around grade six may be explained by two age-dependent dynamics with reverse effects: (1) an increasing interest in reflecting on oneself and one's feelings, which might influence the initial increase in participation; and (2) the subsequent rise of a skeptical attitude towards a project offered by adults, which might outweigh the first tendency at the onset of adolescence.[7]

Furthermore, the registrations are characterized by a clear gender imbalance: while one-quarter of the female students registered (25%), less than one-eighth of the male students did so (12%). This unequal distribution runs through all of the classes. It might be connected, in part, to the task of reflecting on one's feelings, which may conform better with female gender roles prevalent in the particular social milieu of the study. When asked which feature of the project (feeling, photography, research project, other) was most important for their decision to participate, 41% of the females and 21% of the males chose feelings. For the other features, which were secondary to the task, the gender distribution was reversed.

Next to age and gender, the origin of the students' parents also had an influence on the decision to participate. According to information provided by the school, roughly 74% of the students' parents were born in Germany, 15% in Vietnam, and 11% in other countries, mainly Russia. The proportions of these three groups in our final sample of actual participants differed clearly. While the proportion of the German-German participants remained similar (74 → 70%), the German-Vietnamese participants were underrepresented (15 →10%), and the students with parents from Russia and other countries were overrepresented (11 → 20%).

Basically, there are two ways to analyze this huge body of verbal and visual material. First, the social parameters of the participants can be used either as primary categories or to construct subsamples. It may be examined, for example, which features of the material depend in which way on the age of the participants. How does an emotionally charged environment change with age? Which emotions become prevalent at what age? How does the emotion vocabulary unfold while one is growing up? These and many other questions can also be posed in regard to gender. According to the impressions from the interviews, most female participants used a much more elaborate vocabulary than their male classmates did. They also gave hints about possible conditions that may foster such a fluency. For instance, many presented a picture of their "BFF" (best friend forever) and characterized them as a person with whom they can freely talk about all their feelings, even the most intimate ones. The male participants hardly presented anyone as a friend, let alone a best friend forever, as defined through emotional intimacy. Instead, most preferred to talk about buddies with whom they have fun.

Another way to analyze the huge data corpus is to choose a specific *theme* that became prominent during the interview process or the subsequent familiarization with the data, and to create a sample based on who addressed the respective theme. Subsequently, the subsample may be contextualized by describing the social characteristics of its members. Three examples of salient themes may suffice to provide an impression of the data material and possible interpretations. We shall describe the first two examples rather briefly in order to discuss the last example in more detail, as it is highly relevant from an affect-theoretical point of view.

One of the most persistent themes across gender and all age groups were pets. This prevalence may be explained, partly, by the convenience of photographing pets as compared to other family members. However, in many cases the participants described pets as being crucial for their emotional lives in multiple ways. One participant elucidated that the tomcat she represented helps her to relax and forget her worries whenever he jumps on her lap, since the pet does not spare a thought about his past or future. Another participant, who presented a picture of the family dog, explained that this companion was an important source of comfort since he, in contrast to all other family members, was reliably excited to see her after school. A third participant presented a picture of the place where two rabbits had been buried (see Figure 5.2). While looking at the picture and referring to her experience of her first real loss and grief, she struggled to maintain her composure.

Another theme that came to our attention were objects that not only elicited emotions as a given part of the students lifeworld, but that were specifically designed, treasured, or arranged in a way to store, reproduce, or remind one of certain feelings. Some of these objects referred to a particular emotional event in the past, for example, a medal obtained in celebration of an achievement, a treasured admission ticket to a national park where the student had experienced some happy moments, or a dress the participant had worn during a moving farewell party at the end of primary school. Other objects, such as pictures or cuddle toys, were used to sustain or recollect the bond with and feelings towards an absent but significant other. Finally, a number of pictures, such as photo albums (see Figure 5.3), were described as representing the feel of a particular period in life.

A third topic, that already turned out to be highly relevant during the interview process, is relaxation. For several reasons, this was particularly noticeable. First, the way our participants described experiences and practices of relaxation reminded us of knowledge workers in a highly competitive environment who struggle to maintain their work-life balance. Second, it emerged frequently as a topic (roughly 50 cases), even though it did not neatly align with what we considered as a feeling or with what we believed we had asked for. Indeed, in the process of analyzing the material, it became evident that relaxation is closer to affectivity than to particular emotions or feelings. In cultural studies, affectivity

Well, this is in the back of our garden, kind of in the corner. And I used to have two rabbits once and well, we buried them and yeah. The feeling is grief because I very, very, very much . . . oh no. Um yeah . . . well, they do lie very close to my heart.[8]

Figure 5.2 FeelingPicture and description of a girl from grade 9.

is often described as something that is inherently difficult to grasp and calls for new methodological approaches (see Slaby & Röttger-Rössler, 2018). Therefore, it may be particularly interesting to depict the theme of relaxation as a particular form of affectivity in some more detail.

Several features of relaxation that were repeatedly pointed at during the photo-interviews match with and specify some of the general attributes commonly ascribed to affectivity: forces acting upon bodies, marginal cognitive involvement, and situated relationality (see Seigworth & Gregg, 2010). First, the vocabulary of relaxation – that is, the words used to describe this phenomenon – mostly refers to forces or energies that pull or push on bodies. However, these forces are not described as intensifying but rather as subsiding. The term *relaxation* ("Entspannung, locker werden") refers literally to a subsiding pull on the body. Relaxation is usually contrasted with tension ("Anspannung, Verspannung") or stress ("Stress"), both of which refer to a drawing or pulling force. Another set of terms alludes more to a pushing force when, for example, relaxation is described as decreasing

Um, yeah, old memories. So the photo album in the middle, the small one, well, it is from my former best friend. In our elementary school years, we were out together very, very, very, very, very, very often and we experienced so much together. Um, she is also on this school now but we have drifted apart but we still get on well. But I think with this I just have again, um, well, I just make myself aware of what a good friend I used to have or still have, over again. And yeah, just to keep it in my memory.[9]

Figure 5.3 FeelingPicture and description of a girl from grade 9.

pressure ("Druck") or the removal of a burden ("Last, Belastung"). To counteract that pressure or to carry ("(er-)tragen") the burden is exhausting. To get rid of it is, at least temporarily, "lightening" ("erleichternd"), liberating ("befreind"), or relieving ("entlastend"). In the abstract language of affect theory, the vocabulary of relaxation may be translated as a transition from dissonance to consonance.

Second, relaxation is often described as a mode that involves little cognitive activity, reflection, or intentionality. In fact, it is often depicted as if such processes are being suspended. "Abschalten" (to "log off" or to "turn off"), for example, was a commonly used metaphor to articulate the cognitive side of relaxation. With this notion, the image of a device that is disconnected and stopped from operating is transferred to the brain, mind, or head. Other more descriptive attempts to convey the experience of relaxation included that one stops thinking or forgets, for instance, about a stressful aspect. Interestingly, the contrasting experience of tension or stress was not only characterized by a high cognitive activity and a clear directionality, such as thoughts about a pending exam, but also by a range of discrete emotions, such as fear, worry, or anger. By contrast, relaxation was hardly described as being accompanied by particular emotions. At best, it was circumscribed as a pleasant or comfortable experience.

Third, relaxation was depicted as relying on an ongoing relation between the actor and a particular object or environment that bears a relaxing potency. Relaxation does not commence before the actor gets in touch with his or her bed or hammock (see Figure 5.4), enters a certain environment such as a forest, sinks into the chair to read a fantasy novel, or feeds his/her goldfish. Thus, relaxation is clearly based on an ongoing affective relation between co-present actors. Most participants described, in one way or another, how establishing a new affective relation

B: I wanted to present my hanging chair. And I'm just very happy in there. I got it for my birthday and I'm there very often and I also read in there. And my mother always says that I shouldn't go in there, all the time.

I: *Why?*

B: Well, because then I'm in there too deep inside it. When I'm supposed to do something I'm in there anyway.

I: *What are you doing in there?*

B: Reading. And sometimes sleeping.[10]

Figure 5.4 FeelingPicture and description of a girl from grade 5.

is relaxing because it replaces or supersedes the former stressful thoughts and negative feelings that were directed at something they had experienced in the past or were expecting in the future. Thus, a dissonant, directional relation linking the actor to different places and tenses is replaced by a relation in the here and now that induces relaxation.

Another feature often ascribed by theorists to affectivity is its opposition to conceptualization, conscious experience, or reflection. Affectivity either evades any attempt at conceptualization or, if eventually captured, ceases to be affectivity. According to some of the most influential theories, affect would be transformed into emotion in the moment it is 'captured' (see Massumi, 2002). This feature, however, pertains only in part to the affectivity of relaxation. As is already indicated in the previous paragraphs, the participants depicted relaxation mostly in terms of what it is not, what is removed or what is replaced. They mostly talked about stress, the lack of time, the pressure to perform at school, the negative thoughts and emotions involved in it and the desire to get rid of it, or at least to forget about all this and thus, to relax. When asked what relaxation itself feels like, the students used rather broad expressions pointing to a positive experience, such as "it feels good", "it makes me feel better", or "it is nice". As some expressed explicitly, it is hard to say anything more about it: "Yes, it always makes me a bit happy and I feel, when I do it, I don't know . . . no idea". However, the empirical material suggests that the conscious experience and conceptualization of affectivity is, in the case of relaxation, constitutively derived from the contrasting experiences of stress, pressure, fear, and anger. Thus, relaxation is conceived in part through prior emotions that refer to stressful tasks, expectations, and the demands of others. If this horizon of stress disappears, relaxation may easily pass into other forms of affect, such as boredom, with an orientation towards intensification. Thus, while relaxation as such is indeed distant from conscious experience, it may become an object of experience, reflection, and conceptualization through its embeddedness in and contrast with an overwhelming daily routine.

The question of when and how, in the course of childhood, relaxation becomes an issue of reflection might shed more light on the conditions of its conceptualization. As the socio-demographic data indicates, the theme of relaxation increases with age. Several participants hinted to possible reasons. For instance, thinking back on how relaxation became relevant, a girl described a point in her past when the growing amount of homework threatened to eat up all the rest of her leisure time that was not yet occupied by school or other predetermined activities such as piano lessons or club sports. Others added that relaxation became important when graduation and the future career came into view, and they felt that they always could learn more. From this, it may be inferred that the awareness of relaxation is largely connected to the felt collapse of daily periods of unoccupied time. One participant, presenting a picture of a park, addressed this directly. Several afternoons per week, she spent half an hour waiting there for her mother, who worked close by. This was the only time in her daily routines, she explained, that she felt no pressure or urge to do anything other than walking or sitting around. Thus, from the perspective of the stressed actor, relaxation comes into awareness as something desired or intended that is paradoxically characterized by "switching off the head".

Relaxation adds an important perspective to the notion of affective *intensity* (or energy, force, etc.), which is a hallmark of affect studies. Studies in affect usually understand intensity as *high* intensity, or intensification, and, correspondingly, tend to emphasize moments of social dynamics and transformation. However, if affective intensity can increase and reach a climax, the opposite must be possible as well: decreasing or low intensity. Relaxation may serve as an example of low intensity affect.

Reflection

At first, we will consider the photovoice technique with regard to the example of relaxation, and afterwards we will carry on with a more general discussion of this method. When designing the photovoice examination, none of us expected that relaxation would be a major theme for the participants. Its prevailing thematization came rather as a surprise, as it did not fit our preconceptions about the affective lives of our juvenile study participants, whom we assumed were not yet confronted with the "serious side of life". Relaxation, as described by the students, can be considered as a prime example of the kind of everyday affectivity that has emerged in recent decades as a focal concern of middle classes, preoccupied with issues of wellbeing, work-life balance, or resilience. Nevertheless, we do not know of any study focusing on this phenomenon from the perspective of affect theory.

The fact that our participants pointed this example out to us may be ascribed to the specific participatory nature of this method and to the inclusion of pictures. By letting the participants explore their environment with a camera for two weeks, they were far enough removed from us and our expectations to be able to deal with the task in a highly independent manner. More importantly, the procedure of starting with visuals instead of words may have primed them to focus on the material or social side of their emotional life. That is, they were not urged to categorize their feelings, but could just scan their lifeworld for something of relevance for their feelings. Thus, many turned to the places, animals, objects, activities, and media practices that allowed them to relax, and took pictures of it.

When presenting the pictures, many participants did not yet seem to have a fixed idea about how to verbalize it. And, as demonstrated earlier, most ended up saying much more about what relaxation is contrasted against or how it is embedded in their stressful lives than describing relaxation directly. This may be due to the fact that relaxation itself is primarily a bodily mode of resonating with the immediate environment, helping to "turn off the head". However, having the image of a relaxing counterpart present during the process of verbalization enabled both the interviewee and the interviewer to stay focused on a kind of affectivity that is rather ineffable in itself. This made it possible to literally circumscribe the phenomenon in a jointly manner and to encircle it without furnishing it with undue conceptual clarity.

Also, on a more general level, it turned out to be extremely effective to talk with children about their feelings and emotionality based on photos taken by them for this purpose. It appears that the forethought that motivated the participants to take a particular photo was much easier to communicate in relation to a concrete picture than in an abstract manner. The subject of the photo was partially constructed in the viewing process, in the sensual reference to the image. Most of the participants could easily put into words what they wanted to represent with the picture, that is, an emotionally evoking aspect of their lifeworld. But many of the students, especially the younger ones, were obviously searching for words when trying to describe the feelings emerging in relation to it. On the contrary, they skated around their idea, they searched long for the right articulations and often involved the interviewer in this process by asking her or him what would possibly be the proper word in the respective case. Although the older participants in general displayed a greater repertoire for verbalizing their feelings, the gap between what they tried to express and what they actually said was still palpable.

Thus, based on the difference between visuals and words, the method of photovoice systematically renders visible a gap between a particular affective relation and verbalized feelings. A purely verbal interview about emotions or feeling tends to depend much more on preexisting emotion concepts, so that difficulties to verbalize aspects are often omitted. By contrast, the affecting relation is the starting point of verbalization in our method, since the task is to focus first on something in the environment that *makes* one feel or that is of particular relevance to one's feelings, to visually capture this something in a photograph, and to relate to it again during the interview. While looking at the image and trying to verbalize it, the interviewee (and to some degree the interviewer as well) imagines or, in part, even reestablishes the affecting relation between him/her and the chosen object or the picture representing it.

The complex constellation consisting of the interviewee, the interviewer, and the picture or its subject brings about rich material but also difficulties for its interpretation. For example, should the affective relation be interpreted as a relation between the interviewee and the picture or between the participant and the subject represented in the photograph? We believe that, to some degree, both relations are relevant. On the one hand, it has to be taken into account that photographs themselves have a polysemantic, emblematic, and sensual nature. A photo never represents just one fixed motive or meaning, but enables multiple and flexible insights and decodings. A photo thus has the capacity to evoke memories and associations that the photographer had not had in mind when taking the picture, and which might be grounded in his or her current situation. Moreover, as visual stimuli, photos provide an immediate, sensual relating to the world, beyond all words. On the other hand, it was obvious that the participants focused their description on the subject they had chosen to photograph. In fact, as we were primarily interested in the latter, we took several measures to deploy the pictures as a means to facilitate conversation about emotional and affective relations with the environment rather than to examine the affective potency of pictures as such. The participants were asked and given the opportunity to first attend to aspects of their environment in their everyday life and then to take a picture of it. To reduce the agency of the photographing technique, we emphasized that we were not interested in the aesthetic quality of the picture. Furthermore, the initial interview question, "What did you want to represent with this picture?", was directed at the subject that was chosen, not at the content of the present picture (which could have been brought into focus with a picture provided by the researcher and a question like: "What do you see in the picture?").

The experience of interviewing provided many hints that most participants actually followed the path we suggested. In response to the initial question, the interviewees usually directed the interviewers' attention to a very particular aspect of the picture. What the interviewees pointed out to the interviewer was sometimes surprising. The picture reproduced in Figure 5.2), for example, appeared to represent simply a piece of meadow or garden, until the interviewee explained that a rabbit had been buried there. She used the picture as an anchor to verbally unfold her affective relationship to this animal. Furthermore, the participants were usually quite clear about what in the picture was intended and what was accidental. When asked about an aspect of the picture they had not yet talked about, they often responded by saying something like, "this just happened to be there" or, "I didn't mean to photograph this". The cases in which a picture was described that was absent during the interview are insightful, too. This happened in response to the guideline question at the end of the interview, asking whether the participant had intended to take a certain picture but for some reason was not able to realize it. In principle, they would talk about it in a quite similar fashion as when the picture was present. However, the corresponding narratives were much shorter and rather shallow. Since the anchoring function of the picture was missing for both the interviewee and the interviewer, it was much more difficult to stay focused on the affective relation for some time, which would be necessary to verbalize and circumscribe it in some detail.

Conclusion

In our research with its particular focus on children's affective relations and formation of feelings in the urban setting of Berlin, photovoice has turned out to be highly productive in generating new insights. From our own experience with this method, the major advantages of photovoice, which have already been highlighted by others, can be substantiated. Compared to conventional interviews in which the interviewer is endowed with considerable authority, photovoice conveys more power to the participants. Although a general task is predetermined by the researcher – in our case to document personally affecting environments – the participants have the time to observe and choose what they consider relevant, and to communicate their choices by means of the pictures, which serve as starting points for the interview. In the interview situation, the pictures act as a third party, and thus dissolve the dyadic situation of a conventional interview, which may be intimidating for the interviewee. These participatory characteristics are particularly relevant in studies where the researcher and the researched do not belong to the same group in terms of age and cultural or social background, as was the case in our study. In fact, the participants generated a vast number of unexpected and sometimes surprising insights that we, drawing from our particular horizon of experience and knowledge, would not have asked for in a conventional interview.

To some degree, the method of photovoice may substitute the classical anthropological method of participant observation with its aim to take part in the lifeworld of the researched group in order to triangulate interviews and other forms of conversation. The difference is, however, that with photovoice, the observing role is primarily assumed by the participant (in our case in the form of self-observation), while the researcher co-observes by the means of the picture. Ideally, of course, photovoice would be combined with participant observation. However, it would hardly have been possible in the urban setting of Berlin to follow the students through their daily life.

Taken together, these characteristics make photovoice a suitable method for empirically studying emotions and affective relations. This is mainly due to the fact that photovoice binds the researcher and the research participants into a common relational sensual activity: to look at something means to situate oneself *in relation* to it. "We never look just at one thing" Berger (1972, 9) states, "we are always looking at the relation between things and ourselves". Through their photographs, the children enabled us *to see how they see things*, how they relate to their lifeworlds. However, through verbalizing their visualized affective relations in dialogue with the interviewer, the school students started to describe or circumscribe their implicit feelings and thus made them narratable. The relaxation example given in Figure 5.4 clearly demonstrates this point. By stating that her mother dislikes her laying in the hammock "because then I'm in there too deep inside it" ("weil ich dann zu drin da drin bin"), the girl who took this picture imposingly depicts her bodily and mental withdrawal from all the demanding forces of her environment in order to relax. What she describes here so vividly through the photograph and her wordings, but without using any emotion terms, are affective relations. These affective relations become traceable via the picture-narrations or *photovoices* elicited through this method. Our empirical material is full of such speaking cases.

In cultural studies, affect is usually described as being opposed to conceptualization, categorization, meaning, and conscious experience, and thus difficult or even impossible to be studied empirically, especially from the perspective of research participants. However, our adaption of the photovoice method appeared as a promising way out of this dilemma. It enables the participants to point at their affective relations by themselves, and to articulate the feelings connected to it. This is facilitated by the procedure of letting them first observe their environment for particularly affecting aspects, to photograph these, and to later use the pictures as anchors for articulating their experiences during the interview. The photos are of crucial importance within this process. They cause the participants to *look at* their environment by setting themselves in relation to the social and material elements of their everyday life. They do so first during the process of taking the photographs, but also later during the interview process. Through the act of *looking at* them again, the participants engage anew in the affective relations represented by the photos. The sharing and explaining of these affective reengagements with the interviewer, who also looks at the pictures, makes this method a highly collaborative research instrument.

Notes

1 See Röttger-Rössler et al. (2015) and Scheidecker (2017) for methodological approaches we deployed in the research on emotion socialization in small rural communities.
2 Next to the authors, the research team consisted of Felix Freigang, Sarah Richter, Franziska Seise and Trang Tran Thu. We thank them all warmly for their contributions to this work-intensive study. We further thank Yael Ponizovsky-Bergelson, who is an expert in photovoice, for her highly valuable advice.
3 For an overview, see Harper, 2002, 15; Banks, 2001.
4 Many interesting examples of sociological photo elicitation studies can be found in the journal *Visual Sociology*.
5 Students from grades 11 and 12 were addressed collectively at an event. Due to the particular conditions of introducing our project to them and their marginal participation, we do not take them further into account when discussing the composition of the sample.
6 The interviews were conducted at school during lesson hours, which the students were allowed to skip for the time of the interview.
7 This might also point to the fact that 'staying cool' becomes increasingly important among adolescents.
8 Original quote: "Es ist halt hinten bei uns im Garten, es ist so in der Ecke. Und ich hatte mal zwei Kaninchen und ja, die haben wir begraben und ja. Das Gefühl Trauer, weil ich halt . . . sehr, sehr, sehr viel . . . oh nein. Ähm ja . . . also liegen mir schon sehr am Herzen".
9 Original quote: "Ahm, ja alte Erinnerungen. Also das Fotoalbum dort in der Mitte, das kleine, ist halt von meiner ehemaligen besten Freundin. Wir waren in der Grundschulzeit sehr, sehr, sehr, sehr, sehr, sehr viel miteinander unterwegs und haben so viel zusammen erlebt. Ähm die ist jetzt auch auf der Schule, aber wir haben uns auseinandergelebt, aber wir verstehen uns trotzdem noch gut. Aber denk damit hab' ich mir halt nochmal so, ähm also mach ich mir halt jedes Mal nochmal bewusst, was ich für 'ne gute Freundin hatte oder immer noch habe. Und ja, dass es halt in meiner Erinnerung bleibt".
10 Original quotes: B: "Ich wollte meinen Hängesessel darstellen. Und ich bin halt sehr glücklich da drin. Ich habe ihn zum Geburtstag bekommen und dort bin ich auch oft und lese auch dort drin. [. . .] Ich bin schon sehr oft da drin. Und meine Mutter

sagt auch immer, dass ich da nicht reingehen soll, ständig". I: *"Wieso?"*, B: "Ja, weil ich dann zu drin da drin bin. Wenn ich was machen soll, dann bin ich trotzdem da drin". I: *"Was machst du denn da drin alles so?"*, B: "Lesen. Oder auch mal schlafen".

References

Abel, T & Deppner, MR 2012, 'Undisziplinierte Bilder. Fotografie als dialogische Struktur. Skizze eines gemeinsamen Denkraums', in T Abel & MR Deppner (eds.), *Undisziplinierte Bilder. Fotografie als dialogische Struktur*, pp. 9–28, Transcript Verlag, Bielefeld.

Banks, M 2001, *Visual Method in Social Research*, Sage Publications, Thousand Oaks.

Berger, J 1972, *Ways of Seeing*, Penguin Books, London.

Clark, CD 1999, 'The autodriven interview: A photographic viewfinder into children's experiences', *Visual Sociology*, vol. 14, no. 1, pp. 39–50.

Clark-Ibáñez, M 2004, 'Framing the social world with photo-elicitation interviews', *American Behavioral Scientist*, vol. 47, no. 12, pp. 1507–1527.

Collier, J Jr 1957, 'Photography in anthropology: A report on two experiments', *American Anthropologist*, vol. 59, no. 5, pp. 843–859.

Collier, J Jr 1967, *Visual Anthropology: Photography as a Research Method*, Holt, Rinehart and Winston, New York.

Collier, J Jr 1987, 'Visual anthropology's contributions to the field of anthropology', *Visual Anthropology*, vol. 1, no. 1, pp. 37–46.

Collier, J Jr & Collier, M 1986, *Visual Anthropology: Photography as a Research Method*, University of New Mexico Press, Albuquerque.

Epstein, I, Bonnie, S, McKeever, P & Baruchel, S 2006, 'Photo Elicitation Interview (PIE): Using photos to elicit children's perspectives', *International Journal of Qualitative Methods*, vol. 5, no. 3, pp. 1–11.

Harper, D 2002, 'Talking about pictures: A case for photo elicitation', *Visual Studies*, vol. 17, no. 1, pp. 13–26.

Lal, S, Jarus, T & Suto, MJ 2012, 'A Scoping review of photovoice method: Implications for occupational research', *Canadian Journal of Occupational Therapy*, vol. 79, no. 3, pp. 181–190.

Massumi, B 2002, *Parables for the Virtual: Movement, Affect, Sensation*, Duke University Press, Durham, London.

Röttger-Rössler, B, Scheidecker, G, Funk, L & Holodynski, M 2015, 'Learning (by) feeling: A cross-cultural comparison of the socialization and development of emotions', *Ethos*, vol. 43, no. 2, pp. 187–220.

Samuels, J 2004, 'Breaking the ethnographer's frames: Reflections on the use of photo elicitation in understanding Sri Lankan monastic culture', *American Behavioural Scientist*, vol. 47, no. 12, pp. 1528–1550.

Scheidecker, G 2017, *Kindheit, Kultur und moralische Emotionen: Zur Sozialisation von Furcht und Wut im ländlichen Madagaskar [Childhood, Culture, and Moral Emotions. On the Socialization of Fear and Anger in Rural Madagascar]*, Transcript Verlag, Bielefeld.

Schratz, M 1993, *Qualitative Voices in Educational Research*, Falmer Press, London.

Siegel, DJ 2006, 'Entwicklungspsychologische, interpersonelle und neurobiologische Dimensionen des Gedächtnisses. Ein Überblick', in H Welzer & HJ Markowitsch (eds.),

Warum Menschen sich erinnern können. Fortschritte der interdisziplinären Gedächtnis-forschung, pp. 19–49, Klett-Cotta, Stuttgart.

Seigworth, GJ & Gregg, M 2010, 'An inventory of shimmers', in idem. (eds.), *The affect theory reader*, pp. 1–25, Duke University Press, Durham, London.

Slaby, J & Röttger-Rössler, B 2018, 'Introduction: Affect in relation', in idem. (eds.), *Affect in Relation. Families, Places, Technologies*, pp. 1–29, Routledge, Abingdon, New York.

Wahle, N, Ponizovsky-Bergelson, Y, Dayan, Y, Erlichman, O & Roer-Strier, D 2017, 'On the margins of racism and war: Perspectives on risk and protection of young children of Ethiopian origin in Israel', *European Early Childhood Education Journal*, vol. 25, no. 2, pp. 305–320.

Wang, C & Burris, MA 1997, 'Photovoice: Concept, methodology, and use for participatory needs assessment', *Health, Education & Behavior*, vol. 24, no. 3, pp. 369–387.

Wang, CC & Redwood-Jones, YA 2001, 'Photovoice ethics: Perspectives from flint photovoice', *Health Education & Behavior*, vol. 28, no. 5, pp. 560–572.

Part II

Audiovisualities

Chapter 6

Images that move

Analyzing affect with Aby Warburg

Kerstin Schankweiler and Philipp Wüschner

I. Introduction

In contemporary societies of mass communication, the rising dominance of images has gained increasing traction as a trope, in both public life and scientific discourse. Visuality and 'the visual' are thus increasingly critical to understanding the role of affects and emotions that resonate within any given society. Of course, analyzing this role is not the exclusive domain of art history. There are, for instance, a diverse array of empirical methods for analyzing the current flood of images, including neuroscientific approaches and algorithms[1] that sort and classify images according to similarities in form, content, or style. However, art history as a philosophical discipline is less interested in statistical analysis than in hermeneutical methodologies, which demand an interpretation of singular and concrete cases. As such, art history hones a deeply embodied set of techniques and practices of interpretation that have long fostered what might be considered an embodied expertise. Art-historical practice is thus highly relevant to research on affectivity, particularly where affect is understood as a relational concept. If affect entails the capacity to affect and to be affected, then it follows that this capacity can be trained and refined. Likewise, the disposition art historians have come to know as "expertise" entails an affective relation between a researcher and her objects. We believe that an understanding of "the way art historians work"[2] can help extrapolate this affective relation, making it accessible to a broader research community and contributing to the field of affect theory at large.

This essay champions Aby Warburg (1866–1929) as an especially relevant resource for understanding affectivity in a visual context. Warburg is better known for his unorthodox style than for his methodological rigor. Yet as we shall seek to show, Warburg's particular approach can facilitate the methodological analysis of images as they pertain to affects, from an art-historical point of view. In this essay, we will test this approach not on an example from the canon of art history but on one from modern media. Warburg is appropriate for this task for two reasons. First, Warburg is considered a pioneer of 'image science'. His unfinished project of the *Mnemosyne Atlas* is recognized as an early and radical extension of art history and can be seen as visual culture studies *avant la lettre*. His work and methods are therefore especially valuable for any attempts to extend art-historical approaches beyond the discipline. Second, and even more importantly, what makes him especially interesting for our purposes here is that he is also the most prominent representative of the discipline dealing with the questions of affectivity and its visual mediation. His concept of *pathos formula* ("Pathosformel") offers not only an insightful account of how affectivity is formalized and 'stored' in works of art, but also provides fragments of a theory of affect in its own right.

Most methods of art history are descriptive in nature. They seek to link what can be seen with the socio-cultural, historical, or philosophical contexts and conditions of production and reception. Methods, in this sense, can concern the construction of a history or evolution of styles, formal elements, artistic mannerisms, symbols, and the particular semiotics of genres, as well as their categorization and comparison. They are often combined with theoretical perspectives tailored to particular research interests, such as gender or race. Within a hermeneutical framework, one particular arrangement of these tools is the iconographic-iconological method of image analysis, which is closely associated with Warburg's colleague Erwin Panofsky. Even within the safe bounds of hermeneutics, Aby Warburg remains, to this day, a kind of wild card, as is reflected in the differing attitudes of many of his contemporaries and successors. Ernst Cassirer, for instance, famously said that Warburg's archive either left the scholar running away screaming or compelled her to stay there for a lifetime (Saxl, 1949, 48). Meanwhile, Georges Didi-Huberman accused Warburg's successors, Ernst Gombrich and Erwin Panofsky, of trying to contain Warburg's vision within the limited confines of their own scholarly discipline (Didi-Huberman, 2003; see also Becker, 2013). In what follows, we will reverse this 'hedging in' of Warburg's approach. Taking Panofsky's systematized version of iconography and iconology as our starting point, we then move on to fuse these elements together again through Warburg's rather idiosyncratic approach, in order to hone in on the question of affect. Rather than hoping to emulate Warburg's peculiar frame of mind, we propose that an affective approach to images can benefit from closely attending to his seemingly mad methodology of arranging and rearranging his objects. His approach, we argue, not only exemplifies the art historian's habitualized method, but is also highly instructive for understanding the intellectual predicaments of affective analysis more broadly.

2. Iconology and image description

While Aby Warburg is often addressed as a pioneer of iconological practice (Becker, 2013, 1–3), the name of German art historian Erwin Panofsky is more profoundly associated with iconology as a genuinely art-historical *method*.[3] For this reason, Panofsky's methodological efforts are intimately bound to the birth of art history as an independent, methodologically founded discipline of the humanities. For the purpose of this volume, it will be useful to move backwards and start with Panofsky before approaching Warburg.

The two scholars met for the first time in 1912 at a conference in Rome. After Panofsky moved to Hamburg in 1921, their personal and professional relationship deepened. Panofsky's work was, until his emigration to the United States after the rise of Hitler, closely connected to the *Kulturwissenschaftliche Bibliothek Warburg* (Warburg's library in Hamburg). He developed an advanced and applicable model for the interpretation of art, drawing on Warburg's focus on the *meaning* of works of art, later known as the *Hamburg School of Art History*. This change of focus was a paradigmatic shift within the discipline, which was until then predominantly concerned with questions of style and chronological classification.

Panofsky himself compared the relationship between iconography and iconology with that between ethnography and ethnology (Panofsky, 1955). Accordingly, iconography is concerned with description and identification of depicted or the pictorial themes, while iconology aims at a more comprehensive interpretation of the content of an artwork. Based on this difference between iconography and iconology, Panofsky divided his method into three ideal-typical steps or stages of interpretation. These are (1) a pre-iconographic description of the object, (2) an iconographic analysis of the meaning of what is represented, and (3) an iconological interpretation, which contextualizes the object in its cultural and intellectual history. These steps are not usually applied one-to-one in the practice of art history today. They inform many art-historical analyses, but the stages of analyses inevitably merge.

Although it appears to be the most basic aspect of Panofsky's method, the relevance of image description remains highly influential. Writing about images and objects from an art-historical perspective is predominantly based on an ostensive description. Students learn and practice this essential technique at the very beginning of their studies, particularly in a German tradition. To do so, they are encouraged to look closely at original works of art and to describe them through conscious viewing. A description comprises various elements, including the image's composition – the direction of movement, spatial structure, etc. – as well as its surface, that is, its materiality, fracture, color, and the disposition of its surface areas and depicted bodies. But description also includes a reflexive understanding of the connection to the beholder, as well as the narrative structure and the time structure. Moreover, describing is a demonstrative act that already characterizes the image or object by highlighting certain aspects of the work and neglecting others. Thus, describing is always connected to the act of indicating and showing something, and is based on the art historian's own perception, observation, and reflection. Hence, it is objective not in the sense of a neutral truth, but in the sense that the art historian gives a plausible and traceable account of her being affected. Such an account does not necessarily seek to expose an introspective knowledge of one's feelings, but rather, to elucidate the interplay of the image's visible elements with their description.[4]

In his book *Patterns of Intention: On the Historical Explanation of Pictures* (1985), Michael Baxandall has famously commented on the relation between a picture, its explanation, and the practice of description:

> We do not explain pictures: we explain remarks about pictures – or rather, we explain pictures only in so far as we have considered them under some verbal description or specifications. . . . But though "description" and "explanation"

interpenetrate each other, this should not distract us from the fact that description is the mediating object of explanation.

(p. 1)

For Baxandall, a description of a picture is "a representation of thinking about a
picture more than a representation of a picture" (p. 5). To describe a picture, we
must rely on concepts. Baxandall points out that words and concepts are not used
absolutely or informatively but demonstratively. Descriptions are not given so that
the reader knows what the picture looks like enough to accurately sketch it, for
instance. Rather, descriptions work "in tandem with the object" (p. 8). Describing
is, above all, expressing one's interest in the picture. This then leads to a deeper
analysis and interpretation, while both description and interpretation impact one
another. As an expression of how we are affected by an image, a description is
already relational in nature.

In this sense, image description raises methodological questions of relevance
for anyone seeking to analyze affect from an art historian's point of view. How
can we describe affective qualities of movement or intensities, as what they are
and in what they do? In turn, this question raises several others: How is affect
materialized or encoded in images and pictures? What is the role of reiterating formal elements that constitute a series of images? How, finally, can an art-historical
perspective inform our descriptions of affective dynamics within and between
images, as well as between an image and its beholder?

Staying true to the demonstrative method of art history, let us look at an example. The following is an object of research in the project "Affective Dynamics
of Images in the Era of Social Media" at the CRC *Affective Societies* that investigates, among other things, 'viral images' from the 2011 Egyptian Revolution
(Figure 6.1).

This photograph was taken on 17 December 2011, in Cairo on Tahrir Square,
which was the site of political demonstrations during the Egyptian Revolution.
It depicts the brutal abuse of a woman by a group of military men. While two
men are dragging the woman along the ground, her upper body is bared and her
blue bra is exposed. Yet her face remains covered by her *abaya*. The pain that
the woman must have felt remains strangely abstract because her face is not visible, but the violence against her body is drastic and concrete. Both of her arms
are straight in the air above her head, creating a posture that seems not to be the
result of her movement, but rather of the men acting upon her. One man is poised
to kick her in the stomach: his left leg and arm are raised, his body leaned back
in the action. One can see the dynamic of the men's movements and body tension
around the woman they encircle, grabbing, dragging, and kicking her body, leaning forwards and backwards, with truncheons pointing into different directions.
These movements stand in stark contrast to the seemingly lifeless body of the victim, who appears to be unconscious and therefore defenseless. The violent action
of the scene in the center also stands out against the man to the right, who appears
somewhat resigned, as though taking a rest, not looking at what is happening

Figure 6.1 Egyptian army soldiers arrest a female protester during clashes at Tahrir Square in Cairo on 17 December 2011.

Source: REUTERS/Stringer.

beside him. The gray asphalt of the street and the soldiers' dark uniforms contrast against the only colorful spots on the image: the bright blue of the jeans and, above all, of the blue bra. The pavement around the scene is scattered with clutter, small stones, and pieces of paper. As leftovers, they bear witness to the demonstrations on Tahrir that were still going on at that moment.

This example of an image description follows some conventions: It starts by designating the image (photograph taken on 17 December 2011 in Cairo on Tahrir Square) and naming its theme (Egyptian Revolution, shows the brutal abuse of a woman by a group of military men). This provides some orientation for the reader or viewer, who might not otherwise know what they are looking at. The description in general takes the form of a narrative that guides its reader through the image, starting with the more important parts in the center, and then exploring the other parts, not necessarily mentioning each and every detail, but pointing out what is interesting from the point of view of the art historian describing the image. This narrative follows the action of the figures and their relation to each other. Apart from these very basic indications, a description will always take its cues from the object itself; if there are no figures, for example, we cannot follow their action. Because every art historian's description is grounded in his or her being affected, no two art historians' descriptions of an object will ever be exactly the same. Yet they can all claim a form of objectivity, because they point to formal elements of the image – such as color, light, or composition – that are accessible to all viewers. We contend that the ability to identify these elements is bound to the capacity of being affected and of becoming what Warburg called a "very sensitive seismograph" for formalized and mediatized motion and affect (cit. Gombrich, 1970, 254). This "seismographic" capacity can be refined through repeated encounters with bodies of art.

Even from this short description, it becomes evident that image description almost inadvertently transcends itself, moving from the very first steps of making sense of an image towards a broader iconographic and iconological analysis. The brightness of the skin cannot be separated from the violence of the scene. The visible contrast between the blue bra and the military uniforms, between exposure and armor, cannot be isolated from the conceptual contrasts between power and powerlessness or between notions of masculinity and femininity. In short, the affectivity of the visible cannot be seen separately from the discursive. Already within the first steps of describing it, both dimensions inescapably merge on a symbolic field, evoking and carrying forward a whole iconography of violence, war, vulnerability, and resistance. Therefore, to achieve a sufficient level of understanding, art history needs to be thought of as "allgemeine Kulturwissenschaft als Lehre vom bewegten Menschen" or *the study of culture as the study of the moved human being* (our translation; Warburg, 1924, cit. after Raulff, 1997, 42). This understanding is precisely how we define the study of *affective societies*. Indeed, in describing an image alone, the art historian will always already have to express and reflect upon her own cultural, historic, and affective entanglement, so that an element of idiosyncrasy can never be fully avoided. Part of the methodological effort of the iconologist lies in the attempt to be affected by an image in a productive, plausible, and perceptive way. The example of Aby Warburg may shed some light on what this could entail.

3. Aby Warburg's pathos formula

3.1 Pathos and its expression

Aby Warburg's concept of *pathos formula* ("Pathosformel") is often cited among practitioners of cultural studies ("Kulturwissenschaften") as one of their key concepts. Definitions of what a pathos formula is or does, however, vary heavily or remain absent altogether, mostly because Warburg himself never elaborated the notion further. With "Pathosformel" Warburg tries to address the depiction of expressive gestures, specifically those which are found in works of Renaissance art, echoing antique portrayals of almost archetypal affect ("Pathos"). Warburg was interested in the migration and circulation of images across time and space. He coined terms like *migration of images* ("Bilderwanderung") and *image vehicles* ("Bilderfahrzeuge") that indicate the transgressive nature of images. However, his approach was not universalistic, and he was not looking for universal pathos formulas that would occur in all cultures (Krois, 2002). Warburg also acknowledged that not every pathos would necessarily become a formula (ibid., 302). Rather, what Warburg wanted to describe with the concept of the pathos formula is the result of a transformation: something that is individual and refers to a specific event (pathos) becomes something generic and permanent (a formula). This formulaic character enables circulation and reiteration, in contrast to bodily expressions that are situational and ephemeral (ibid., 295).

Examples that Warburg uses are – above all – dancing female figures like nymphs, gestures of death and the dying, such as Orpheus, or scenes of erotic pursuits, such as Zephyr and Flora. However, pathos formulas are *not* studies of facial expressions of emotion as we find them, for example, in the French artist Charles Le Brun, whose *Méthode pour apprendre à dessiner les passions* (1702) advised artists and actors in the ways of portraying certain emotions. Warburg's interest lies not in the individual actualization of a general or basic emotion – like fear, anger, or desire – but in the generic reproduction of an expressive, affective formula that can serve many different purposes.

Under the impression of Charles Darwin's *The Expression of the Emotions in Men and Animals* (1890), Warburg understood pathos as inseparable from its expression, though without being identical to or causally related to it. Therefore, he did not follow the path of physiognomy, which understood expression as a mere effect of underlying mechanical occurrences in the soul. Drawing on Darwin, he understood expression as the result of conflicting forces between various elements. One such element is *affect intensity*, which comprises will- and habit-independent, biologically necessary 'direct actions' of a nervous system that is being affected. Another, *association*, can trigger the same expressive reaction without biological necessity, and through habit, bridges the gap between natural reaction and will-ful communication. Finally, the *principle of antithesis* indicates how forms of expressions are invented not by biological necessity but by an inversion of already established movements. This includes the creation of forms of expression that stay immanent to communication without biological necessity, such as shrugging one's shoulders to invert aggressive behavior (Didi-Huberman, 2016, ch. 3).

The principles of association and antithesis allowed Warburg to look for affect beyond its biological, embodied, or otherwise causal necessity. His focus on formulas as non-human agents does not mean that embodiment and experience, which have been emphasized in affect theory, have less relevance. However they, too, need to be flanked by formal qualities and their affective dynamics. In the end, bodies also have forms and can be read in this way. Building on the notion that affects have forms, Eugene Brinkema, in her book *The Forms of the Affects* (2014), outlines 'reading for form' as a methodological strategy:

> Reading affects as having forms involves de-privileging models of expressivity and interiority in favor of treating affects as structures that work through formal means, as consisting in their formal dimensions (as line, light, color, rhythm, and so on) of passionate structures.
>
> (Brinkema, 2014, 37)

Warburg's concept of pathos formula fits well into such a 'formalistic' account on affectivity, and can in turn help to elaborate it further.

For if there is no affect without expression, and if every expression that is not entirely necessitated by the physical demands of a body will, by force of association or antithesis, reenact an expressive habit or its inversion, then these personal or collective habits will determine the nature of affect itself. If, therefore, one could *store* these habits in the form of a repertoire or cultural memory,[5] one could also store the possibility of their affective reenactment, and thus, of affect or pathos itself. If this seems indeed to be part of Aby Warburg's program, in what sense precisely then can we say affect is 'stored' in its formalized or materialized state?

3.2 Formulaic iteration

Warburg used the word "Pathosformel" publicly for the first time in 1905 in a talk about *Dürer und die italienische Antike* (or *Dürer and the Italian Antiquity*), where he describes the defensive, protective gesture of Orpheus, who is about to be slain, as a "Pathosformel" (Warburg, 1905, 447).

Warburg then claims an expressive or 'gestural' genealogy that connects Dürer's depiction of the *Death of Orpheus* (Figure 6.2) to other, similar representations. Finally, through Angelo Polizianos' play *Fabula di Orpheo* and the writings of Ovid, Warburg also connects Dürer's depiction to the expressive repertoire or *formal vocabulary* ("Formensprache") of antique art. Warburg is *not* interested in an evolution of styles as understood by Giovanni Morelli, who had made them a point of scholarly interest in the 19th century. Rather, he is concerned with the formal iteration of expressions of pathos that constitute a memetic series within cultural memory, and which he calls *afterlife* ("Nachleben"). He claims that some of the affective intensity belonging to the *Death of Orpheus*, or the *War against the Amazons* of the Amazon Frieze from the Mausoleum at Halicarnassus, has survived a number of changes. These include *changes in time* (lying latent during medieval times in its varying forms of expression), *geographic changes* (from antique Rome, to Renaissance Florence, to Dürer's Nuremberg), and *changes in its cultural context* (from paganism to Christianity). Afterlife is not a theory of the evolution of emotional expression, wherein an original image is simply copied and slowly changes over time until reaching its current form – as pictograms, for instance, develop into letters. Instead of an evolutionary model, the notion of afterlife follows a psychoanalytical model of a symbolic relation between singular or collective experiences and symptomatic reiterations (Didi-Huberman, 2003). In this context, the image of Orpheus' death, for example, could be a formula for all affects concerning death, murder, loss, or mourning.

Warburg claims that some affective quality or pathos always survives – or finds an afterlife – when different representations of the same formula are reiterated over time – as in Orpheus' crouching back, falling, being dragged, or lifting one hand for protection. To explain what he means, Warburg draws an analogy

Figure 6.2 Albrecht Dürer, *Death of Orpheus*, 1494, ink sketch.

Source: bpk, Hamburger Kunsthalle, Christoph Irrgang.

between his theory and Hermann Osthoff's linguistic theory of intensification. In Osthoff's theory, the Latin word *bonus* ("good") changes to suppletive forms (*bonus, melior, optimus*) – just like some infinitives do when conjugated ("to be – am – is – are"). However, the sense of what is *expressed* by these words *survives* the semantic changes, remaining the same, only different (Warburg, 1929, 631). This means that what is 'stored' in pathos formulas is not the encoded *meaning* of a certain emotion – as Panofsky would likely see it – but its primal *intensity*.[6] In this sense, intensity becomes form, while form is dynamized by intensity.

The concept of intensity plays a pivotal role in the philosophy of Gilles Deleuze, whose works are foundational for affect theory. Some intensities, like temperature, are very common. Unlike extensive qualities such as length or volume, intensities of temperature cannot be divided. In order to "halve" a temperature, you have to reduce it continuously, and thereby change the nature of the body in general. In this process, according to Deleuze, intensities hit thresholds. Thresholds are singularities, like freezing points or boiling points, where the whole system undergoes a phase transition. In this moment, the 'pure intensity' can no longer be attributed to a body of ice *or* water *or* steam, but has to be thought of as belonging to all of them and none of them at the same time (Deleuze, 1995). Though less empirical in nature, Warburg's ideas about pathos fit neatly into this framework. They, too, describe qualitative changes of a body, and they, too, can reach singular thresholds that generate "extremes of physiognomic expression in the moment of highest excitement" (cit. Gombrich, 1970, 178). In these moments of intensity, which are captured in pathos formulas, the affect no longer belongs to one fixed emotional regime such as fear, agony, or lust, but instead marks the point of their possible transition. This allows Warburg to trace pathos formulas independently of their emotional contexts.

He goes so far as to claim that the emotional, cultural, and religious contexts of a pathos formula, and therefore its meaning, may completely invert into its opposite over the course of history. The desire of pursuit might transform into the fear felt in escape, while the agony of death might invert into the ecstasy of lust. He calls this shift *energetic inversion* ("energetische Inversion") to express the dynamism and ambivalence of tension-filled movement. Evil demoness or avenger angel, fighter or dancer – both are developed with the help of the same pathos formula. Warburg is interested in a generic and formulaic rendition of affective dynamics, rather than in individual expressions of emotion. His own example, Botticelli's *Birth of Venus* (Figure 6.3), may help to make this point clearer (Warburg, 1893).

For Warburg, the most basic formula for any intensity is motion or movement. In his dissertation on Botticelli, Warburg does pay special attention to the external and ornamental movement of things like drapes or hair in the wind. Although they add little on the level of content, these ornamental motions, which Warburg began to call *dynamograms* ("Dynamogramme"), intensify the image. Warburg claims that the reason they so fascinate and *affect* us is because they create the illusion of movement and liveliness in something that stands still. In a similar manner, the term *pathos formula* itself binds together the event of affecting and

Figure 6.3 Sandro Botticelli, The Birth of Venus, ca. 1480, Tempera on panel.
Source: Photographic Department of the Uffizi Galleries, Florence.

being affected (pathos) with the timeless, motionless idea of a formula. Take, for example, the allegory of Spring in which a dancing nymph welcomes Venus on the shores. We miss the point if we take her dancing only as dancing, when the dance actually works as an *intensifier* to the whole scene. Warburg does not locate the affective intensity, or pathos, in the faces of the goddess or any of the other three depicted figures. Rather, he sees it in the wave of Venus' hair, in the joyful tumbling of the flower petals in the wind (allegorized by the two figures on the left), and in the dance movements of the welcoming nymph on the right. These moving elements – fluttering garments, flying hair, drapes etc. – act like accessories that Warburg calls "bewegtes Beiwerk" (*moving accessories*), and can be traced through time and through artistic genres alike. So according to Warburg, if an artist wanted to add affective intensity to an image, she could *accessorize* them with formulaic props that reach back to antiquity, and that worked independently of facial emotional expression.

3.3 Pathos formulas as intensifiers

If we try to adapt these ideas to our analysis of the picture of the "woman with the blue bra", it becomes striking how little of its affective quality is actually carried by means of facial emotional expression. Only two of the faces on the picture can be seen clearly: those of the soldier on the left and the soldier on the right, who looks distantly away from the scene. The affective intensity of the face of the former must first be described in its formal qualities, as grimacing or twisting with his teeth barred. Only then, from an iconographic perspective, it could be interpreted as a distorted grin, and as an expression of exertion and violent ecstasy. More striking for an analysis of affect, however, is the intensity of the *dragged* body, the *falling abaya*, the *swung* truncheons, and the *dropped* clutter on the street. Darwin's principles of association and antithesis allowed Warburg to locate the true affective intensities of Botticelli's Venus *not* on her rather emotionless face, but in the "bewegtes Beiwerk" that accessorize her. In the same vein, the lifting of his helmet's visor by the soldier on the right and the lowering of his truncheon can be seen as prompting a movement that is antithetical to the violent scene in its center. And although it happens simultaneously with the beating of the woman, this pathos formula of exhaustion already anticipates the moment when the violence is over, as do the pieces of garbage that already prefigure the motionless remnants they are about to become. This temporary translatory movement is an integral part of pathos formula itself, a frozen moment in time that always already transcends the formulaic. This paradoxical *formulaic movement* is exactly how affectivity is *stored*. It is especially the suggested movement that approaches the observer actively and in an activating way.

In order to understand all these affective undercurrents, Warburg would encourage the researcher to try to connect this image to the pathos formula of Dürer's dying Orpheus, or even further back in time to the aforementioned fragment of the Amazon Frieze depicting a fight between the Greeks and the Amazons (Figures 6.4 and 6.5).

Suddenly, the scene can be read as the moment after the last strength of resistance, which was still palpable in the depiction of the Amazon, has been spent. A relationship of iteration and differentiation between the two images has been established. But apart from vague similarities, what would reconcile such seemingly random juxtapositions? Clearly, the photographer did not have Dürer or antique Amazons in mind when he took the shot. Yet, these associations only seem arbitrary and forced when they are misunderstood as an interpretation of the intentions of the artist, or of what the image represents. They become plausible precisely *as* associations. That is to say, they are only plausible when understood as the actualization of a repertoire that precedes all interpretation, and which allows associations. To view the 'blue bra' picture as a formulaic reiteration of the 'same but different' pathos of experiencing violence throughout history, means regarding the image's representational nature as secondary to its affective genealogy. Obviously, this is not the only possible way to look at it, nor is it inconsistent with a mere representational reading.

It cannot be denied that Warburg developed his idea of the pathos formula with reference to the human body. He was exclusively looking at figurative art

Figure 6.4 Amazon Frieze, Mausoleum of Halicarnassus (detail), ca. 350 BC, marble.

Source: Trustees of the British Museum.

Figure 6.5 Egyptian army soldiers arrest a female protester during clashes at Tahrir Square in Cairo on 17 December 2011.

Source: REUTERS/Stringer.

and was especially interested in the depiction of human bodies and of *human* affectivity that certainly affect the beholder in a particular and very direct manner. However, we deem it important to stress the fact that pathos formulas are *not* conceptually bound to the human figure, just as being affected by an image cannot be reduced to feeling empathy towards who or what is represented. In Warburg's efforts to address what he calls *moving accessories*, we can already see a trajectory that leads beyond the human body, despite the fact that Warburg identifies elements that are bound to the human body and its excited motion, like the aforementioned flying hair or draping. We would suggest expanding the scope of Warburg's idea toward *moving accessories* that are detached from the human body (like the pieces of garbage on Tahrir Square). A painting or photograph of a dark sky shrouded in clouds above a turbulent sea, for example, could also be described as an affecting formulaic movement, or even as pathos. Moreover, even art or images that are not figurative at all could potentially be read along these lines. Think, for instance, of abstract painting like the scribbled, calligraphic elements in Cy Twombly's work or Jackson Pollock's abstract expressionism. The literal meaning of *pathos* in the term *pathos formula* might be strained by such examples. Yet we would still suggest a conceptual continuity between pathos formulas in the narrow sense and these formulaic arrangements of things with non-representational elements. This continuity is, for us, best expressed in Warburg's own words as *dynamograms*.

As we have seen, the semantic framing of a pathos formula within an image is not essential to its affective intensity. The content or subject of the image and its affective intensity might, therefore, drift apart from each other. This can create tilting effects between pain and lust, for example, or between serene calmness and chilling lifelessness. So, when it comes to analyzing affects via an image description, attention must be paid to the internal resonances and possible dissonances between the context of the picture and the intensity of its affective qualities – akin to Roland Barthes' theorization of the *studium* or *punctum* in photography (Barthes, 1981). A pathos formula does not have a fixed meaning of its own. Rather, it helps to *generate* meaning by arranging the affective dynamics within an image.[7] In other words, a pathos formula does not illustrate a specific content, but almost literally "moves" or arranges the elements of an image, thereby also moving and arranging the affective relation between the image and the viewer. Warburg understood these two conjoined processes, affectively arranging the elements of an image and by that arranging the relationship between image and viewer, as "storing" and releasing or reenacting affective intensity in a certain dynamic 'gestalt'. It is precisely this mutual affective relationship to which the art-historical description of artifacts and images testifies. No analysis of any image can step outside this affective relation. Hence, Warburg's idea of a pathos formula is of value not only for art historians but also for every researcher of affectivity who finds herself affectively entangled in the very objects she studies.[8] Before we elucidate this more general methodological point further, we want to summarize in a few points what has been said so far:

a   The description of an image as the first step of its analysis is at the same time an expression of the affective dynamics between object and beholder. It makes this dynamic comprehensible and accessible to others by relating it back to the elements of the image.

b   As the analysis proceeds to explain the nature, effects, and sources of the relationship, its scope will widen to include, among other things, the iconographic and iconological interpretation of the elements of the image (contents, composition, symbolism, codes etc.).

c   According to Warburg, however, an analysis of content does not suffice. Instead, it is crucial to find and analyze those elements that intensify and thereby arrange the other elements. They will always (at least in a strict reading of Warburg) be an expression of some kind of motion, ranging from deathlike stillness to moments of ecstasy.

d   Some of these intensifiers, Warburg claims, are formulaic and generic in nature. These pathos formulas survived stored in artifacts that constitute the material, collective cultural memory. These pathos formulas link the image to a series of others that are not necessarily constituted by the represented content.

e   Lastly, contrary to what this list of bullet points might suggest, the analysis and interpretation of images does not work as a linear step-by-step program, but as a hermeneutically circular process of interpretation. This, we believe, is inevitable for any attempt to be true to the essential relationality of affective dynamics.

4. Learning from Warburg

In the last years of his life, Warburg worked on the extensive project of the *Mnemosyne Atlas* (Figure 6.6) in cooperation with his staff members and colleagues, above all Gertrud Bing and Fritz Saxl. The Atlas, named after the goddess of memory in Greek mythology, is his attempt at a cartography of pathos formulas. By the end of Warburg's life, the Atlas consisted of 63 boards wrapped in heavy black cloth covered with photographs of artwork, illustrations from books or albums, newspaper clippings, and other media. As such, the Atlas offers insights into the methodological challenges of analyzing affect in images.

Warburg tried to give an instant, synoptic impression of the cultural, historical, anthropological, and philosophical interrelations of different pathos formulas by opening up the *thought-space* ("Denkraum") in which they appear. His genealogies, which informed the *Mnemosyne Atlas*, were not restricted to a succession of artworks. In this way, Warburg's approach – always cognizant of the ruptures and

Figure 6.6 Aby Warburg, The Botticelli Panel (No. 39), *Mnemosyne Atlas*.
Source: The Warburg Institute.

discontinuities of history – poses a challenge to an evolutionary model. Warburg suggests a form of *presence* of antiquity not only in Renaissance art but throughout European history at large.

One cannot determine, in a general way, how affective intensity can be identified within an image, since not all affective qualities appear neatly as formulas. It is important to clarify where and how affect materializes in the image and to specify the exact qualities that need to be the focus of the image description. Finding the affective qualities will always require the expertise and sensibility of the researcher. Nevertheless, we can very often identify formal reiterations in the materialization of affects over an extensive period of time and with wide geographical range. And this fact highlights the role these formulas play in constituting communities and their collective cultural memory.

It is vital to understand that the cartography Warburg developed in the *Mnemosyne Atlas* was a work in progress, and it also entailed performative methods like *showing* similarities and connections by rearranging media on his black boards when giving a talk. Therefore, it could be said that the context formed by the media was performatively *created* by Warburg and his colleagues *in situ*, rather than deduced.

This leads directly to the greatest challenge in any attempt to follow a Warburgian method. How can it be proven that the links someone claims to see between different occurrences of a pathos formula exist outside their subjective association? How, on the other hand, can the existence of these links be denied, when according to Warburg all these relations are based exactly *on* associations stored in a collective cultural memory? According to Georges Didi-Huberman, the role of the researcher as a *seismograph* (Warburg) for the affects encoded in all sorts of media is a form of *embodied methodology*, where the knowledge, expertise, and sensitivity of the researcher remain vitally important (Didi-Huberman, 2003). This sensitivity can be exercised, but it cannot necessarily be explicated. As the example of Warburg's own, often idiosyncratic, research makes clear, an art historian's *method* can only be made explicit to a certain point. Hartmut Böhme once called Warburg a "theorist without theory" and "an extremely detailed research practitioner" who developed his "theoretical consciousness" from working with his research objects themselves, without necessarily objectifying this consciousness (Böhme, 1997, 9, our translation from German). An art historian's method remains, first and foremost, a habituated ability to be affected by images in a productive way.

5. Epilogue

Looking at Warburg's non-linear compilation of images today, one cannot help but feel reminded of image clusters on screens, of the internet's image world and visual memory, and of social media, although there are obviously many differences. His cross-cultural concept of images as migratory vehicles seems all the more relevant in today's context of globally circulating digital images. We seem to live in an era where the globalized world is itself a kind of digital *Mnemosyne Atlas*.

Warburg's method might be described as *thinking* with and through images, an approach that very aptly characterizes cultural practice today. The rise of more recent social media platforms like Instagram, Snapchat, and the like demonstrates that social communication is continually becoming more focused on the exchange of images. Social media shapes and has shaped a whole set of cultural practices surrounding images, such as sharing, liking, commenting, etc. These are interactive and affect-based processes of exchange between images and humans. As such, they emphasize even further the centrality of images in the circulation of affects. Images *move* users, who take action with images. But images also *move* other images that continually build and renew relations, which then appear in Clusters and Memes.[9] The affective dynamics that facilitate and even *constitute* these relationships can be understood as pathos formulas and analyzed as such. As we have shown, Warburg thought the afterlife of primal experiences of pathos came about through formulaic reiterations. In conclusion then, we want to stress that, within the realm of social media, this very same process must be understood as a means of instantly *spreading*, *distributing*, and *producing* affects. What we propose here is a Warburgian way of dealing with and describing affective dynamics of images in times of social media.

Notes

1 For example, the research carried out at the MPI for Empirical Aesthetics at Frankfurt a.M. For efforts from the new field of digital humanities with special regard to Warburg, see Impett and Moretti (2017).
2 Obviously, *the* art historian is a figment of the euro-centric mind, and we are well aware that German *Kunstgeschichte*, the perspective from where we speak, is not even paradigmatic for the broader discipline of academic art history, let alone for all other dealings with images or art in general.
3 Panofsky articulated this method for the first time in a lecture he gave in 1931, and then in different publications, finally in Panofsky (1955).
4 Lorraine Daston and Peter Galison show in their history of the concept of objectivity that a reduction of objectivity to neural facts has only surfaced in the mid-nineteenth century as a key paradigm for scientific research (Daston & Galison, 2007).
5 We prefer the term *repertoire* to the concept of a collective or cultural memory, for it is less appropriating regarding the diverse and subaltern strands of a society or community, and because it grants greater agency to those who reenact it. However, it is clear that for Warburg the term *memory*, which is alluded at in his *Mnemosyne Atlas*, is more appropriate.
6 Warburg himself has used the notion of 'intensity' with regard to pathos formulas; see Warburg, 1929, 631.
7 For a similar idea concerning concepts, see Slaby, Mühlhoff and Wüschner in this volume.
8 For a similar approach, see Stewart (2007).
9 The German art historian Wolfgang Ullrich has put Warburg's pathos formulas and Internet memes into context (Ullrich, 2015).

References

Barthes, R 1981, *Camera Lucida*, Hill and Wang, New York.
Baxandall, M 1985, *Patterns of Intention: On the Historical Explanation of Pictures*, Yale University Press, New Haven, London.

Becker, C 2013, 'Aby Warburg's Pathosformel as methodological paradigm', *Journal of Art Historiography*, no. 9, pp. 1–25. Available from: http://arthistoriography.files.word press.com/2013/12/becker.pdf. [27 September 2017].

Böhme, H 1997, 'Aby M. Warburg (1866–1929)', in A Michaels (ed.), *Klassiker der Religionswissenschaft. Von Friedrich Schleichermacher bis Mircea Eliade*, pp. 133–157, C.H. Beck, Munich.

Brinkema, E 2014, *The Forms of Affect*, Duke University Press, Durham, London.

Darwin, C 1890, *The Expression of the Emotions in Men and Animals*, Murray, London.

Daston, L & Galison, P 2007, *Objectivity*, Zone Books, New York.

Didi-Huberman, G 2003, 'Artistic survival: Panofsky vs. Warburg and the exorcism of impure time', *Common Knowledge*, vol. 9, no. 2, pp. 273–285.

Didi-Huberman, G 2016 [2002], *The Surviving Image. Phantoms of Time and Time of Phantoms: Aby Warburg's History of Art*, Pennsylvania State University Press.

Deleuze, G 1995 [1968], *Difference and Repetition*, Columbia University Press, New York.

Gombrich, E 1970, *Aby Warburg. An Intellectual Biography*, The Warburg Institute, London.

Impett, L & Moretti, F 2017, 'Totentanz. Operationalizing Aby Warburg's Pathosformeln', *New Left Review*, no. 107, pp. 68–97.

Krois, JM 2002, 'Die Universalität der Pathosformeln. Der Leib als Symbolmedium', in H Belting, D Kamper & M Schulz (eds.), *Quel Corps? Eine Frage der Repräsentation*, pp. 295–307, Wilhelm Fink, Munich.

Le Brun, C 1702, *Méthode pour apprendre à dessiner les passions. Proposée dans une conference sur d l'expression générale et particulière*, Chez François van-der Plaats, Marchand Libraire, dans le Gapersteeg, Amsterdam.

Panofsky, E 1955, 'Iconography and Iconology. An Introduction to the Study of Renaissance', in idem., *Meaning in the Visual Arts*, pp. 26–41, Doubleday & Company, New York.

Raulff, U 1997, 'Von der Privatbibliothek des Gelehrten zum Forschungsinstitut: Aby Warburg, Ernst Cassirer und die neue Kulturwissenschaft', *Geschichte und Gesellschaft*, vol. 23, no. 1, pp. 28–43.

Saxl, F 1949, 'Ernst Cassirer', in PA Schilpp (ed.), *The Philosophy of Ernst Cassirer*, pp. 47–51, Evanston, New York.

Stewart, K 2007, *Ordinary Affects*, Duke University Press, Durham, London.

Ullrich, W 2015, 'Inverse Pathosformeln. Über Internet-Meme', *Pop-Zeitschrift*. Available from: www.pop-zeitschrift.de/2015/10/15/social-media-oktobervon-wolfgang-ullrich15-10-2015/. [15 October 2015].

Warburg, A 1905, 'Dürer und die heidnische Antike', in A Warburg, 1998, *Die Erneuerung der heidnischen Antike. Kulturwissenschaftliche Beiträge zur Geschichte der europäischen Renaissance*, G Bing (ed.), 1932, reprint 1998, H Bredekamp & M Diers (eds.), pp. 443–448, Akademie Verlag, Berlin.

Warburg, A 2010 [1893], 'Sandro Botticellis „Geburt der Venus" und „Frühling". Eine Untersuchung über die Vorstellung von der Antike in der italienischen Frührenaissance', in M Treml, S Weigel & P Ladwig (eds.), *Aby Warburg, Werke in einem Band*, pp. 39–123, Suhrkamp, Berlin.

Warburg, A 2010 [1929], 'Mnemosyne Einleitung', in M Treml, S Weigel & P Ladwig (eds.), *Aby Warburg. Werke in einem Band*, pp. 629–639, Suhrkamp, Berlin.

Chapter 7

The temporal composition of affects in audiovisual media

Hermann Kappelhoff and Hauke Lehmann

To describe the temporal composition of affects in audiovisual media, we use the term 'audiovisual dramaturgy of affect'. This term designates a theoretical model which helps us to analyze the structures of audiovisual movement-images in regard to affectively engaging spectators.[1] The model ensures an empirical analysis that can, in principle, be reproduced among different researchers and connected to ever new specific research questions. It enables a comparative and system-based analysis for researching large corpora of audiovisual images ranging from fiction films to TV news footage and web videos. The method corresponding to this approach is called *eMAEX* (electronically based media analysis of expressive-movement-images). It was developed in the context of researching classical Hollywood war films (see Kappelhoff, 2016) and has since then been continuously refined.[2] The particular genre of the war film was chosen because it serves as a prime example for the strategic use of audiovisual media to mobilize affective engagement. Here, a highly developed knowledge about poetic strategies producing certain feelings converges with an explicit political intention to do so. This is why it is comparatively easy to systematically describe, analyze, and demonstrate these strategies of mobilizing affectivity.

We will first provide a short overview of the practical application of the model before elaborating on its theoretical background. After that, we will carefully describe every step of the process in detail before discussing possibilities of adapting the method to different subjects of study.

Overview

In principle, the method distinguishes between two levels of analysis: a micro and a macro level. The former results from a subdivision of the audiovisual material (fiction film, episode from a TV series, etc.) into scenic units which are the basis for identifying and describing so-called *pathos scenes* (see Kappelhoff, 2016, 135–144, and below). These scenic units represent a first step in structuring the audiovisual material according to what is perceived as meaningful compositional segments. These segments are not identified arbitrarily, but through a comparative integration of the segmentations of several analytically experienced researchers. In a next step, these researchers ascribe a heuristically defined marker to each scene – in the case of the war film, for example, 'sacrifice/victim' or 'injustice/humiliation/self-assertion'. These markers designate an approximate realm of affective qualities. They have been developed in a long preliminary phase of bottom up-analysis of single films, which predated this standardized process of categorization and also involved the development of research questions and hypotheses, themselves based on theoretical premises and historical findings. Over the course of the research period, these markers were tested repeatedly for validity (weighing comprehensiveness and exactitude against each other), thereby becoming more precise and more clearly distinguished from one another.

This subdivision enables us to now describe the film (or video or episode) on a macro level as a succession of pathos scenes, as what we call a *dramaturgy of affect* – a dramatic course of affective intensities each spectator goes through when watching a film. But back to the micro level: After having assigned markers to individual scenes, we proceed with analyzing the compositional structure of each scene. In order to describe this structure as the basis for the affective engagement of spectators, we have adapted the theoretical concept of *expressive movement* (see "Theoretical background") into a model of expressive movement units (EMUs). Each EMU traces the course of affective intensities along such expressive registers as music, acting, or camera movement. Such intensities can refer, for example, to the dynamic quality of a gesture, to a change in color temperature, or to the rhythmicality of a montage sequence. Depending on the scene, different registers may dominate.

Afterwards, the completed analyses are fed into a database, together with the respective film clips. There, they can be accessed and compared according to a range of different filter options: Depending on the specific research question, these filters make it possible to link the scenes and their expressive registers to different variables, such as specific motifs, plot constellations, narrative patterns, formal techniques, etc. In this way, with the help of the macro-dramaturgies as well as the pathos scenes, it becomes possible to make visible a broad spectrum of poetological connections and distinctions between films and other audiovisual formats – phenomena which often remain hidden when it comes to approaches that concentrate solely on plot and narrative, for example.

Theoretical background: the concept of expressive movement

The central theoretical concept for the method roughly outlined here is that of expressive movement. It has been elaborated in research on the melodramatic mode in theatre and film (see Kappelhoff, 2004) and proceeds from the hypothesis that media and art forms employ aesthetic techniques and poetics of affect which aim at activating and engaging the feelings of a diverse and anonymous public.

Although the goals connected to these cultural practices of generating affective involvement differ, as well as their use of media, artistic techniques, and material, the history of popular art can be described as a history of patterns that aim at modulating the feelings of an audience through media. One of the most important principles regarding this history is the configuration of time and movement as a specific form of expressivity: expressive movement. As far as historical conceptions of mass art are concerned, these movements do not just intentionally 'express' moods, atmospheres, and feelings, but can also evoke these feelings in spectators as an affective, bodily response in the first place.

Following Spinoza, Gilles Deleuze defines this kind of affective relationality in the following way: "Affectio is a mixture of two bodies, one body which is said to act on another, and the other receives the trace of the first. Every mixture of bodies will be termed an affection" (Deleuze, 1978). If we thus conceptualize affect, with Spinoza via Deleuze, as the capacity of bodies to affect and be affected ("affectio"), then expression should precisely not be understood as an outward movement articulating internal feelings, that is, as an intrasubjective relation. Instead, the concept of expression foregrounds the relationality of affects, or affect as relationality itself. The theoretical framework for such consideration is built, on the one hand, from psychological, linguistic, and anthropological theories of expressive movement, dating back to the second half of the 19th and the first half of the 20th century and connected especially to Wilhelm Wundt (1902), Karl Bühler (1933), and Helmuth Plessner (1982 [1925]). On the other hand, one can mention the aesthetic, philosophical, and art-theoretical concepts of expressive movement in Georg Simmel (1995 [1905]) and Konrad Fiedler (1991 [1887]).

In this context, expressive movement has to be understood as a category of interaffectivity: Rather than referring back to a feeling, it instead *generates* a feeling through and within the affective resonance of bodies interacting with each other. Plessner has formulated such an understanding succinctly. For him, expressive movement is not a distinct *type* of movement, but rather a specific *dimension* of it, based on the perception of a temporal *gestalt*:

> Wherever movements appear in the organic realm, they proceed according to a uniform rhythm; they show a dynamic gestalt that might be verifiable experimentally. They do not proceed bit by bit, as if their succession was assembled from individual elements, they do not constitute a mosaic of time; rather, a certain wholeness is given, in which the individual trajectories of movement can vary.
>
> (1925, 77, our translation)

The main characteristic of expressive movement lies in its temporal *gestalt* ("a certain wholeness"), realizing itself at every instance of its unfolding. However, the temporal form does not refer to the feelings of an intentionally directed body; rather, it expresses the capacity of this body to affect others by giving pictorial character to the movement – making it appear to others like an image. When describing the switch from intentional action to this image-like character, Plessner speaks of "movement-images" (p. 77). These movement-images do not exist for themselves but only take form within the affective resonance of a perceiving body. In this perspective, feeling appears to be linked to a temporal, even dramatic structure capturing the affecting and the affected body.

Hence, expressive movement describes the potentiality of an affective constellation, understood from one point of view (that of the perceived, affecting body) as an intentionally directed movement, from the other (that of the perceiving, affected body) as *a feeling for the feeling* of another. In a certain sense, it describes the transition from one configuration of affectively linked bodies to another, without existing in its own right at any point of this transition. This peculiar ontological status of expressive movement corresponds to what C.S. Peirce (1868), in his semiotic theory, classifies as "firstness" – taking, among others, the perception of color as an example. Firstness concerns quality, possibility, or potential as such, regardless of its actualization – for example, the "red" that is equally present in the sentence "this is red" and in the sentence "this is not red" (see Deleuze, 1986, 98). This understanding of firstness corresponds to Gilles Deleuze's influential conception of affects as "quality-powers" (p. 99). For Plessner, this ontological status is best grasped in laughing and crying, insofar as laughing or crying bodies can be understood as movement-images. As images, they express something to the same degree to which they make visible their own body in its affective entanglement with other bodies as well as with the surrounding world.

Following and extending these ideas, the concept of expressive movement has become a central point of reference for classical as well as modern film theory. It has influenced thinkers as diverse as Sergei Eisenstein (2010), Béla Balázs (2010), or Hugo Münsterberg (1916). As psychological, linguistic, and aesthetic approaches, film theory likewise proceeds from gesture and facial expression as paradigmatic forms of movement. However, it includes all aspects of cinematic staging as elements of a dynamic expressive figuration: color, light, space, music, montage, etc. The cinematic image itself, in its temporal dynamics, is understood in analogy to physical (micro-) movements. Correspondingly, expressive movement produces a site of subjectivity in which the perceptual activity of the audience's lived-bodies is inextricably linked to the expressive activity of the technological apparatus. Many protagonists of modern film theory followed up on this idea, the most prominent ones being Gilles Deleuze with his concepts of the affection-image (1986) and the time-image (1989), and Vivian Sobchack and her theories about embodiment and immersion (1992). On the whole, all these positions subscribe to the idea that the specificity of the cinematic mode of experience is constituted by the connection of technologically generated movement-images and affective dynamics.

The temporal basis of embodiment

Cinematic expressive movement has to be understood as an 'audiovisual rhythm' that includes all levels of staging. With regard to the position of the spectator, which we understand as a function of the temporal composition of movement-images, this rhythm appears as a force that affects bodies and constantly changes in its intensity. By branching out into the bodies of sensing, feeling, and thinking spectators, this 'cinematic affect' then creates the film's image-space in the medium of those spectators' sensations: a space of experiencing another way of "being-in-the-world" (Merleau-Ponty, 2002, 90–100). This is why we cannot distinguish between style and narrative function: the manner of arrangement and composition always and in each and every detail refers to the temporal form of a cinematic world becoming visible and audible over the course of perceiving a film. One could say that this process consists of a stylization of the spectators' seeing and hearing according to the manner in which this world unfolds itself. Narration is only one aspect of this process of unfolding.

The temporal patterns which are created in this process correspond to subjective experiences that can be recognized as dynamic feeling qualities: remaining in tense anticipation or waiting in boredom, waking up and dropping off to sleep, focusing on something or getting distracted are some examples of such experiences of subjectively felt time. But these patterns are neither present as sensations of filmic characters nor can they be described through those characters' actions. They rather evolve in the constant modulations of the cinematic image-space – that is, they are realized as the feeling of an awakening or tiring, widening or narrowing body of perception dependent on the corporeal presence of spectators. From their perspective, the temporal arrangement, the rhythm of an image-space which becomes visible and audible, which appears and changes, is transformed into a sensation that belongs to another self: the cinematic body carrying out acts of perception and expression (see Sobchack, 1992). Thus, each act of understanding a film is always already grounded in the audiovisual rhythm which entangles the cinematic image and the perceiving bodies of spectators.

How to get from theory to method: preconditions for a model

How can we adapt these considerations methodically? Our model is based on the idea that the compositional *gestalt* of audiovisual movement-images structures the temporal matrix for the perceptual and affective processes of watching films. Spectators realize the cinematic act of perception (i.e. the interplay between framing, camera movement, montage, and mise en scène) as a bodily sensation while simultaneously making sense of these sensations as a way of 'being-in-the-world'. There is thus a twofold relation between screen and audience: On the one hand, spectators experience a succession of affective intensities (colors, sounds, movement). On the other hand, they take this experience as a whole (*gestalt*) and reflexively refer to it as a feeling.

Based on this, we proceed from the methodological assumption that cinematic movement-images in their compositional structure and arrangement can be grasped in temporal units. These units are identical to what John Dewey (2005) postulates as "elements" constituting the unity of aesthetic experience (p. 121). Such temporal figurations lay the groundwork for a complex affective experience that is based on the aesthetic organization of the cinematic image itself. In its reflexive form as a unified experience, the process of affecting spectators has to be qualitatively distinguished from individual emotional reactions through which spectators answer to the form or content of a representation. The temporal dynamic of aesthetically modeled affects arranged over the course of a film is more than the sum of its parts. As a temporal form, it grounds the rhythms and tempi of an emerging, unfolding, and evolving *spectator feeling* (see Bakels & Kappelhoff, 2011): the reflexive act of perceiving the cinematic image and simultaneously being affected by it.

Thus, we consider neither the feelings of spectators nor the cinematic modalities of expression accidental in the sense of a stylistic, aesthetic, or formal surplus to a narrative or a representation given in and by itself. Quite the contrary: We regard them as primary, preceding any embodied constitution of audiovisual meaning as a mode of experience.

We are convinced that it is not possible to separate the processes of meaning-making from the affective power of cinematic forms of expression. Analyses which directly refer to represented actions, characters, or plot ignore the temporal structures of film-viewing without which there would be no representation in the first place. They ignore the unfolding of an image-space in which things, bodies, and forces relate to and interact with each other in a way that is fundamentally distinct from what we regard as a commonly shared everyday world (thereby establishing its own laws of movement and perception – potentially with each new shot). Every representation and graspable meaning is based on a feeling for the world that is produced in the encounter between screen and audience and allows spectators to make sense of what they see and hear. This becomes obvious when we think about how in genre cinema the aesthetic pleasure of the audience (thrill, amusement, horror, melancholy) depends on the specific temporality of different dramaturgies of affect. Furthermore, a comparative analysis focusing on the employment of specific temporal arrangements in different films can open a window into the historical development of a long-standing genre like the war film. Thus, one of the first steps in our overall approach is to identify, compare, and distinguish between such basic modes of affectively involving spectators.

Based on these theoretical considerations, *we understand the cinematic image as a dynamic unfolding, arrangement, and rhythmic modulation of a spectator feeling, which can be described as a compositional unity of movement-images realized on different levels of expressive modalities*. Hence, what we attempt with our comparative analyses is a reconstruction of these compositional structures by describing them as a specific succession and configuration of audiovisual movement patterns.

Outlining the procedure

As outlined in this section, we examine the films in a step-by-step process by systematically looking at ever smaller temporal segments: from scenic units to EMUs (expressive movement units). We also inspect their interaction with one another with regard to how this interaction constitutes a dramaturgy of affect. This allows for a qualitative description. Scenes are the building blocks for the films' dramaturgy of affect while EMUs shape the dynamic form of each scene. The EMUs are finally produced by the interplay between compositional elements such as camera movement, sound, character movement, montage, etc.

To implement and use this method, it was necessary to develop a computerized system of analysis. Whether in regard to the detailed analysis, its documentation or presentation, the systematic examination of expressive movement necessitates the ability to integrate audiovisual research data into a multimedia platform. For us, qualitative-descriptive empiricism is a method through which every film analytical statement can be verified and understood by looking at the audiovisual image itself and does not depend on individual intuition. However, it does draw upon the development of theoretical assumptions as well as knowledge about historical contexts. But as far as those premises, in turn, can be demonstrated through analysis, they too are open to falsification or verification. In this way, analysis as empiricism feeds back into the drafting of theoretical and historical conclusions.

The basis for identifying individual pathos scenes is the determination of the core conflict of a given genre, its pathos: the antagonism of intensities which provides the matrix of its dramaturgy of affect. In the case of the classical Hollywood war film, this pathos is produced, to put it somewhat schematically, by the unresolvable, affectively charged dilemma between the necessity of sacrifice for the greater good and the overwhelming factuality of physical suffering (see Kappelhoff, 2016, 1–8). This paradigmatic pathos formula of the war film can be in turn fleshed out by identifying pathos scenes which rework and reformulate this conflict in various ways. In this sense, our analysis starts with a movement that might well be described as a hermeneutic circle in the sense of Gadamer (2006):

> The circle, then, is not formal in nature. It is neither subjective nor objective, but describes understanding as the interplay of the movement of tradition and the movement of the interpreter. The anticipation of meaning that governs our understanding of a text is not an act of subjectivity, but proceeds from the commonality that binds us to the tradition. But this commonality is constantly being formed in our relation to tradition. Tradition is not simply a permanent precondition; rather, we produce it ourselves inasmuch as we understand, participate in the evolution of tradition, and hence further determine it ourselves. Thus the circle of understanding is not a "methodological" circle, but describes an element of the ontological structure of understanding.
>
> (pp. 293–294)

If we relate this broader statement to the specific problems of film theory, our initial engagement with a genre or comparable object of study can never be separated from the circulation of images connecting it to our own way of making sense of the world through the images we consume (this way of sense-making is precisely not identical to idiosyncratic intuition). Developing a thesis is not possible without defining one's own position with regard to the object of study. The act of identifying pathos scenes relies on acknowledging this interplay. Once we have established such a foothold with regard to our corpus, however, the analysis is held to the strict standard of being reproducible intersubjectively.

This implies that it is generally possible to adapt our model to studies on audio-visual media in other fields of research – such as social sciences, psychology, or linguistics, given a certain amount of genre theoretical and film historical input to provide a starting point. In order to accomplish this goal of adaptability, we needed to develop multimedia tools of presentation and description as well as an advanced computer database.

Let us now turn to the procedure itself, as it has been applied and developed throughout research projects concerning the Hollywood war film. First, we examine the standard narratives and stereotypical scenes of the films in question, taking a specific poetics of affect in the war film genre into consideration. As this step makes clear, the model is not implemented on a clean slate, but necessarily builds on expectations which are themselves based on a first, more or less extended encounter with the material. Following the results of our preliminary study, the main heuristic assumptions about a poetics of affect in Hollywood war films can be determined as follows:

1   The genre of classical war films can be described through a certain number of stereotypical narrative patterns and character constellations (standard scenes).
2   These standard scenes are strongly connected to aesthetic strategies of affectively engaging spectators.
3   It is possible to assign the standard scenes to distinguishable realms of affect, for example, mourning, fear, and rage.
4   Therefore, these standard scenes can be defined as *pathos scenes*.

Following a first phase of analyzing film examples, we went on to define our hypothetical assumptions more precisely: On the one hand, the distinct realms of affect are determined through recurring plot constellations (for example: fear and pugnacity correspond primarily to fighting scenes, mourning to the scenes of dying, the heroic act may imply rage). On the other hand, scenes are characterized by specific compositions of cinematic forms of expression that result in a particular mood (like gesture, color and lighting, spatial and acoustic patterns, montage). The audiovisual composition of a single scene is structured as an arrangement of temporal segments. These temporal segments unfold in a distinctive, most often three-step pattern (initiation, progression, closure). We define them as EMUs. Together and in their specific relation towards each other, they make up a scene as a whole. This relation constitutes the micro level of our analysis. The temporal arrangement of pathos scenes within the film's dramaturgy of affect – their order in time – is the basic structure of the process of producing and modulating feelings. The ever-specific compositional patterns of changing, contrasting, and merging qualities of feeling designate the level where the audience's affective involvement refers to a commonly shared spectator feeling. We can understand this dimension of the spectator feeling as the macro level of the poetics of affect in the war film genre. What follows now is a more detailed description of our standardized procedure.

The eMAEX system – a: set-up

This diagram (Figure 7.1) outlines the standardized procedure according to eMAEX (electronically based media analysis of expressive-movement-images).

The horizontal levels show the main steps in developing and applying this method.

1   The **set-up of methodological proceedings** defines the systematic application of our heuristic assumptions.
2   The **process of analysis** itself, where we identify, evaluate, and analyze pathos scenes according to the proceedings defined during the set-up-phase.
3   And finally, the **output management**, in which all the different media files and documents created during analysis are brought together to provide the basis for comparative studies.

The vertical levels of the diagram represent the stages in our work process according to the three-stage model mentioned earlier. On the set-up level, we proceed in the following way:

	Stage 1	Stage 2	Stage 3
A: Set-up of Proceedings			
B: Process of Analysis			
C: Managing Output			

Figure 7.1 Stages of the standardized eMAEX procedure.

	Stage 1	Stage 2	Stage 3
A: Set-up of Proceedings	Procedure of identifying pathos scenes		

Figure 7.2 A, Stage 1.

Stage 1: We generate a first set of categories of pathos scenes, which is then evaluated in a number of test case analyses. Based on the results of these test runs, the initial set of pathos scenes is refined into a typology of basic categories. In the case of the war film genre, a set of eight different types of pathos scenes could be identified, such as "Formation of a group body (corps)", "Homeland, woman, home", etc. These types could be identified because they were 1) seen often enough across the corpus, 2) relevant enough in terms of dramaturgical composition, and 3) distinctive enough to be recognized in different constellations. After these eight types proved operable in another run of test case analyses, we designed a manual. This manual describes the detailed features of the eight types of pathos scenes and their relation to distinct realms of affect.

One example would be the category "battle and nature". In the pathos scenes associated with this category, the battle against nature replaces the battle against the enemy and acts as a form of experiencing this battle. They develop from constellations offered by army formations and the natural hurdles which provide cover for the enemy and need to be overcome repeatedly, as well as from signs of exhaustion and death that nature inscribes on the individual body. Therefore, spaces of tension emerge within the cinematic composition: On the one hand, the individual soldiers who move forward and must maintain a clear view appear to be in an alliance against nature. This alliance aims at both trying to control/organize and to destroy nature. On the other hand, nature is portrayed as an agent of chaos, both in relation to the perception and orientation of each individual as well as to the efforts of the corps to maintain the necessary order to remain in action. The audiovisual amplification of this chaotic power is, paradoxically, the event of exploding nature, its destruction by the military's weapons.

The fundamental ambivalence of this relationship becomes very clear when we look at the fact that the soldiers' bodies blend into the natural scenery for protection and camouflage, on the one hand, but this process of blurring the margins of physical entities becomes the center of audiovisually staged threat, vulnerability, and exhaustion, on the other hand. The affective dimension of the pathos scene "battle and nature" stems from a cinematic concept occurring in classical horror films: the eerie uncertainty about something which one sees or hears, the fear of being abandoned, of losing one's bodily self and one's identity in chaos. The concrete temporal realization and unfolding of these general poetic principles is elaborated in the respective scene analyses (for an example, see Figure 7.8).

Stage 2: After the categories have been set, we regularly review their empirical validity – with regard to distribution, frequency, and consistency across the genre, precision of labeling and clarity of distinction against other categories. In this manner, we devised guidelines for evaluating the process of identifying pathos scenes: They should not be restricted to only a small portion of the corpus (although they do not have to appear in every film); they should reoccur more than once in individual films; they should be labeled precisely enough, but not too specifically; and they should immediately be distinguishable from other categories so that there is no danger of confusion.

	Stage 1	Stage 2	Stage 3
A: Set-up of Proceedings	Procedure of identifying pathos scenes	Procedure of evaluating pathos scenes	

Figure 7.3 A, Stage 2.

	Stage 1	Stage 2	Stage 3
A: Set-up of Proceedings	Procedure of identifying pathos scenes	Procedure of evaluating pathos scenes	Procedure of analyzing scenic composition

Figure 7.4 A, Stage 3.

Stage 3: In order to examine the compositional microstructure of a scene, the model of EMUs has been developed throughout an extended phase of theoretical and methodological debate. The results of parallel test runs were evaluated and brought together in a distinct model of film analysis. We implemented this model into a second manual, in which one can find details about the principles and procedures of analyzing expressive movement (see Figure 7.8). The mentioned manuals and guidelines are the basis of all further analytical operations. Their central objective is to guarantee a systematic and intersubjectively reproducible form of description provided by predetermined analytical steps.

The eMAEX system – B: analysis

We can now turn to the main operation of the workflow: the actual analysis. As delineated in the manuals, the different stages of our process of analysis consist of identifying, evaluating, and describing the pathos scenes.

Stage 1 is the identification of pathos scenes. At first, scenes are determined as temporal segments within the film. These segments are then classified as manifestations of pathos scenes. The classification is guided by the manual with regard to plot constellations and forms of cinematic expression.

Stage 2 consists in the evaluation of pathos scenes as a poetics of affect. After three to four scholars have individually identified and classified the pathos scenes of a film, we evaluate how their findings match each other. In order to achieve this, each scholar produces time-code-based scene logs. These logs are checked for consistency of temporal segmentation and categorical differentiation and get adjusted if necessary. The individual logs are then merged into a master log comprising the aligned data from the individual logs.

	Stage 1	Stage 2	Stage 3
B: Process of Analysis	Identification of pathos scenes		

Figure 7.5 B, Stage 1.

	Stage 1	Stage 2	Stage 3
B: Process of Analysis	Identification of pathos scenes	Evaluation of pathos scenes: poetics of affect	

Figure 7.6 B, Stage 2.

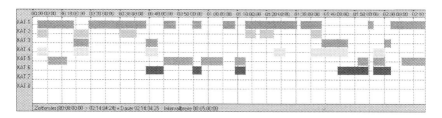

Figure 7.7 Diagram of the affect dramaturgy of a single film.

The master log is then transcribed into a diagram (see Figure 7.7). It represents the macro level of a single film's poetics of affect. To be read from left to right, the diagram visualizes the temporal arrangement of all pathos scenes constituting an affect dramaturgy over the course of the film. The colored boxes indicate the temporal progression of the scenes as well as the categories (1–8) and the respective domains of affect assigned to them. By comparing the diagrams, we can recognize reoccurring or diverging patterns. The degree of variance between such patterns indicates, among other things, the historical variations throughout the war film genre. This can be beneficial in two ways: on the one hand, one is able to make meaningful comparisons between individual films based on the development of a specific research question providing a productive perspective on the material. On the other hand, the material itself can help to generate questions guiding future research.

Stage 3: analysis of pathos scenes

In a third step, we describe the scenic composition and each of the EMUs. As defined in the second manual, we thereby focus on the dynamic patterns and expressive movement.

Here, the first task is to identify the distinctive dynamic pattern of a pathos scene (e.g., releasing or building tension, creating a hectic rush, boredom, or a feeling of constriction). The next step is to describe this dynamic pattern as a composition of expressive movements. Then, we divide the scene into EMUs: temporal segments unfolding in a distinctive pattern (initiation, progression, closure). The fourth step is to describe the EMUs with regard to different levels of audiovisual composition. After that, we proceed to qualify the affective realm of the scene which, according to our assumptions, is activated by the expressive movement. The following exemplary analysis refers to a scene marked as a "battle and nature" pathos scene in the film *Bataan* (Tay Garnett, USA 1943):

> After its establishment within a space of horror, a dynamic of fearful anticipation is transformed into an increasing tension that suddenly changes into the ecstasy and excitement of battle. The battle itself proceeds in stages: from the triumphant dissolution of boundaries to flowing movements and finally to the difficulties of individual, inert bodies that are forced to fight. This dynamic is shaped primarily by the scene's rhythm and montage, and can also be clearly retraced in the developments on the sound track.
>
> In the previous scenes, the group of the film's protagonists, American soldiers left to defend an isolated outpost in the Philippines against the Japanese, started one final offense. Then, they took a break during which the expectation of a Japanese attack was discussed. Now, in this scene, the attack actually happens. At first, two separate spatial and framing principles are established, one in regard to the group and one in regard to the enemy. The rhythm of editing creates the expectation that these two spaces will collide. This spatial antagonism can be found in the horror-like image of the jungle as a rather flat space hiding the enemy as well as in close-up shots of the group in which the rising expectation is mirrored. On the sound track we listen to horror-like music, which is opposed to the Sergeant's orders – the tension then culminates in a moment of sudden silence (>EMU 1).
>
> The first phase of the battle develops as a collision that ends in a fusion of the antagonistic spaces. In this unit, the completed constitution of the military

	Stage 1	*Stage 2*	*Stage 3*
B: Process of Analysis	Identification of pathos scenes	Evaluation of pathos scenes: poetics of affect	Analysis of pathos scenes

Figure 7.8 B, Stage 3.

group coincides with the ecstatic audiovisual dissolution and overpowering through the gunfire and noise of battle, as well as with the power of the explosions that destroy nature and the enemy. This dissolution also inscribes itself in the close-ups of the soldiers' faces (>EMU 2).

The second phase of the battle is the collapse of the space of action taking place after the two spaces have merged. A flow-like connection of movements ends up in the spatial separation of fighting individuals and the loss of a cohesive overview, therefore creating an environment in which the enemy is seemingly everywhere. The fusion of spaces is repeated as the fusion of bodies – as the fear of being killed, the pleasure and excitement of killing and of physical exhaustion. The play with timing and visibility enacted in the first third of the scene on a spatial level is repeated on a level of corporeality. The dense and multilayered soundscape is reduced step by step, and only individual, irregular gunshots remain (>EMU 3).

(Grotkopp n.d.)

The eMAEX system – C: managing output

Each of the three stages – identifying, evaluating, and analyzing the pathos scenes – generates a specific output, which we integrate in a database. Let us remember our heuristic assumptions once again: The war film genre can be described through a certain number of standard scenes which are assigned to distinguishable realms of affect by narrative patterns and by aesthetic strategies. In order to manage the output of our descriptions in a way which provides a basis for comparative analysis, these assumptions have to be implemented and illustrated properly. Within the user interface of our database, the films are embedded and organized as sets of pathos scenes. Here, you can see the film *Bataan* as an example (fig. 7.9):

It is possible to browse through all the films in regard to each type of pathos scene, making the war film genre, represented by our group of films, analytically accessible according to our heuristic assumptions.

On every page of a specific pathos scene, the scene is integrated as a clip (see fig. 7.11). In this way, it is possible to directly relate the audiovisual object of study to the analytical text which describes the composition of the scene and can be found directly underneath. By this means, we make the pathos scenes recognizable in a comprehensible way, in terms of their forms of cinematic expression. Links in the texts and at the bottom of the page redirect to the EMUs each scene consists of. So just as the film is organized as a set of pathos scenes on the macro level, the single scene is organized as a set of EMUs on the micro level. The pages of the EMUs are designed accordingly: A film clip is accompanied by analytical text, links, and space for additional material (like a diagram for example). The description of dynamic patterns and audiovisual composition always goes along with the actual moving image. With this, the standardized process of analysis is completed.

After identifying, evaluating, and analyzing pathos scenes, one can proceed with advanced studies based on the database (see Kappelhoff, 2010). In the case of the

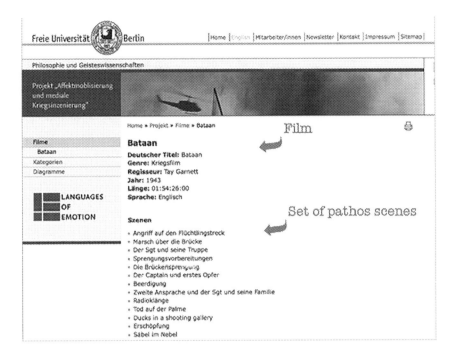

Figure 7.9 The individual film, divided into pathos scenes.

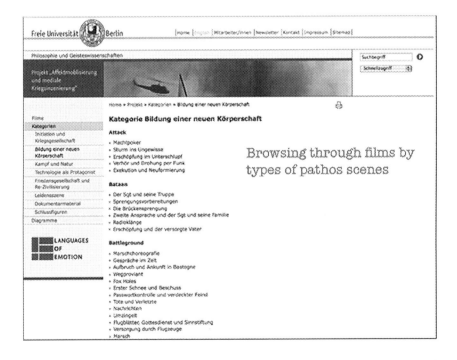

Figure 7.10 The page of each pathos scene shows its description and all the film scenes classified in accordance with it.

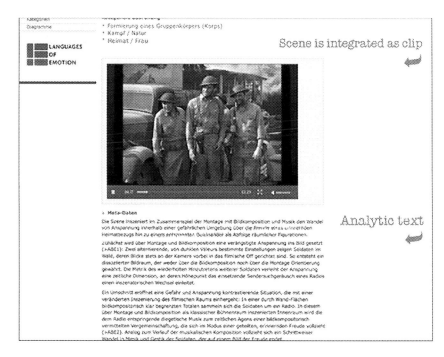

Figure 7.11 Integration of audiovisual scene and written analysis.

	Stage 1	Stage 2	Stage 3
A: Set-up of Proceedings	Procedure of identifying pathos scenes	Procedure of evaluating pathos scenes	Procedure of analyzing scenic composition
B: Process of Analysis	Identification of pathos scenes	Evaluation of pathos scenes: poetics of affect	Analysis of pathos scenes
C: Managing Output	Film as set of pathos scenes	Diagram of macro level	Scene as set of EMUs; Diagram of micro level

Figure 7.12 The completed diagram of the systematic analysis.

war film genre, these studies explore historical changes by focusing on variations of pathos scenes, their dramatic function as well as their dramaturgical arrangement. They result in a media history of affect by comparing audiovisual forms of expression in the Hollywood war film (cf. Kappelhoff, Gaertner & Pogodda 2013, Kappelhoff & Grotkopp 2012, Pogodda & Gronmaier 2015). The database functions as a research tool for such studies and is made accessible through our internet platform, which also facilitates multimedia-based publications resulting from the advanced studies (cf. Grotkopp, Rositzka & Scherer 2016); these latter publications have been made available not directly on the platform, but through an online journal.

Conclusion: adapting the model to a specific research question

The eMAEX method was developed in the course of a research project exploring the shaping of feelings in classical Hollywood war films. The method is supposed to allow us to reconstruct the specific forms of orchestrating moving images in order to trigger and modulate such feelings. It enables us to (1) explore the specific realms of affect that become relevant in regard to these forms and (2) study not only their concrete realization within individual scenes but also their (synchronic as well as diachronic) distribution across different films. In this respect, the war film genre is a special and privileged case: here, the analysis of dramaturgies of affect can always refer to a more or less clearly formulated intention of affectively mobilizing spectators and to a more or less clearly delineated generic formation through which this intention takes shape – within and across different historical contexts.

At least one question arises immediately: In which way do we have to adapt this model when turning to a totally different corpus of films – for example, a corpus we are concerned about in our current research on the so-called 'Turkish-German cinema' (see Lehmann, 2017)? This corpus differs in several important regards from the war film: First, there is no long genre history – in fact, the corpus might not even constitute a genre in the conventional (i.e. classical) sense. Instead, Turkish-German cinema draws on a whole range of different genres, such as road movies, coming of age, or gangster film, as well as on different modes of affectivity, such as melodrama, thriller, or comedy. While the war film certainly inserted itself into the existing genre system as well, it did so by integrating those diverse elements into a commonly shared manner of 'being-in-the-world', a 'logic' of the war film which was based on a clear political intention of mobilizing affective engagement in favor of the war effort of the United States. However, the films assembled under the label of 'Turkish-German cinema' do not follow such a common poetic logic. They do not integrate diverse elements into a new whole, but remain in a state of diversity instead: the culture clash comedy co-existing with a maternal melodrama or a gangster film. Correspondingly, it seems hard to identify an overarching political agenda to which these films refer, be it by affirming or by contradicting it. This implies furthermore that there are no instantly recognizable and stable plot patterns or standard scenes.

As one of the first results, our research question regarding this cinema will not, at first, be focused on historical transformation. We are rather confronted with the problem of determining which films do belong to the corpus in the first place and on what grounds. As it turns out, this question of defining a corpus is of some importance also theoretically: Up to now, 'Turkish-German cinema' has been defined in terms of the ethnic background of either the people being involved in the production of the films or the fictional characters portrayed in them. Such a definition runs the risk of reinforcing potentially racist stereotypes, or at least prescribing norms of identity. An alternative approach is clearly necessary – one that turns away from questions of (accurate) representation and instead focuses on the affective entanglement between screen and audience.

What this demonstrates is that the problem of defining a corpus is not a politically innocent one. Hence, in a first step, we begin to look at what has been defined as a corpus previously, asking whether there is some commonality to legitimize a compound of these films under one label. Following our hypothesis that we can determine a generic context on the basis of common poetic strategies, we again start by analyzing individual films – looking for, comparing, and tentatively defining types of pathos scenes. These pathos scenes will have to be gradually re-defined and rendered more precise as we go along, but they also always have to be broad enough to remain adaptable to the standardized procedure of analysis. At the same time, the methodological function of the pathos scenes will change and become more flexible, taking into account the broad variety of genres relevant for the corpus. Consequently, our research will focus less on stereotypical narrative patterns, but rather on the interlocking of different modes of affectivity: a type of pathos scene we called "Encountering the unknown" (see Lehmann, 2017) will turn out differently if realized in a melodramatic mode or in a comedic mode. In addition, analyzing pathos scenes in a generic context that is far less stable has turned our attention to the possibility that the theoretical status of the pathos scenes may be far more complex than originally envisioned: They do not only organize a spectator feeling in the sense of a dramaturgy of affect, and they do not only provide a basis for comprising EMUs into an expressive figuration of aesthetic experience; they also make visible the political area of conflict in which the production of audiovisual images takes place. In the case of the so-called 'Turkish-German cinema', there is considerable discursive pressure towards standardization: The existing clichés and stereotypes (ideas about how migrants from Turkey live in Germany, what their problems are, how these problems should be resolved, etc.) manifest themselves in guidelines and restrictions formulated by the editorial departments of public German TV stations, which are the main source of funding for feature films. These editorial departments translate the discourse about migration and integration into aesthetic and narrative conventions and expectations – how should such films look? How should characters develop psychologically? What kinds of conflict are possible? – that must be met in order to receive funding. Of course, such ideas are not only propagated by bureaucratic authorities but are also present due to the strong influence of Hollywood cinema and other frames of reference. When making a film, filmmakers are faced with these already existing images and have to find a way of dealing with them – of appropriating narrative and aesthetic patterns in order to create something that speaks to their own desires. Pathos scenes serve as points of crystallization, where these tensions can be perceived and analyzed on the level of concrete audio-visual staging. This allows us to gain insights into the aesthetic politics involved in the emergence of a genre. By unlocking the corpus of 'Turkish-German cinema' through the analysis of pathos scenes in individual films, we have already undertaken first steps in this direction (see Kilerci & Lehmann, 2018).

While a conclusive judgment has yet to be pronounced with regard to the generic status of Turkish-German cinema, it is intriguing to watch a model which was developed for a classical genre interact with a much more unstable and less homogeneous entity. This interaction challenges both our conception of Turkish-German cinema as well as the model itself. While the latter has been devised for standardized analysis, it has already revealed (some of) its critical potential, opening up new research perspectives and forcing us to answer new questions. This diagnosis seems to confirm at least one traditional conviction in the humanities: that there is no method independent from the object of study it is applied to.

Acknowledgments

Many thanks to Danny Gronmaier for his input and suggestions to improve this text! Thank you also to Antje Kahl and the other colleagues engaged in the review process at the CRC *Affective Societies* for their help and support!

This presentation is largely based on material compiled under Empirical Media Aesthetics, available from www.empirische-medienaesthetik.fu-berlin.de/en/ emaex-system/index.html [15 March 2018]. As not all colleagues who contributed to this work could be listed as co-authors of this chapter, we include them here: Jan-Hendrik Bakels, Hye-Jeung Chung, David Gaertner, Sarah Greifenstein, Matthias Grotkopp, Michael Lück, Christian Pischel, Cilli Pogodda, Franziska Seewald, Christina Schmitt, Anna Steininger. This chapter would not have been possible without their work.

Notes

1 For the purposes of this chapter, the terms *spectators*, *audience*, and *public* will be used more or less synonymously.
2 see www.empirische-medienaesthetik.fu-berlin.de/en/index.html. For a detailed description of this method, see Kappelhoff et al.: *eMAEX – Ansätze und Potentiale einer systematisierten Methode zur Untersuchung filmischer Ausdrucksqualitäten*. Available from www.empirische-medienaesthetik.fu-berlin.de/media/emaex_methode_deutsch/ eMAEX-_-Ansaetze-und-Potentiale-einer-systematisierten-Methode-zur-Untersu chung-filmischer-Ausdrucksqualitaeten.pdf?1401464494 [15 March 2018].
    You can find the respective analyses under www.empirische-medienaesthetik.fu-berlin.de/en/emaex-system/affektdatenmatrix/index.html [15 March 2018].

References

Bakels, JH & Kappelhoff, H 2011, 'Das Zuschauergefühl. Möglichkeiten qualitativer Medienanalyse', *Zeitschrift für Medienwissenschaft*, no. 5, pp. 78–95.
Balázs, B 2010, *Early Film Theory: Visible Man and the Spirit of Film*, ed. E Carter, Berghahn Books, New York, Oxford.
Bühler, K 1933, *Ausdruckstheorie: Das System an der Geschichte aufgezeigt*, Gustav Fischer, Jena.

Deleuze, G 1978, 'Cours Vincennes', *Les Cours de Gilles Deleuze*, 24 January. Available from: www.webdeleuze.com/textes/14 [20 June 2018].

Deleuze, G 1986, *Cinema 1: The Movement-Image*, University of Minnesota Press, Minneapolis.

Deleuze, G 1989, *Cinema 2: The Time-Image*, University of Minnesota Press, Minneapolis.

Dewey, J 2005, *Art as Experience*, Penguin Books, London.

Eisenstein, S 2010, *Selected Works: Volume 2: Towards a Theory of Montage*, ed. M Glenny & R Taylor, I.B. Tauris, London, New York.

Fiedler, K 1991 [1887], 'Über den Ursprung der künstlerischen Tätigkeit', in idem. (ed.), *Schriften zur Kunst I*, pp. 112–220, Bild und Text, München

Gadamer, HG 2006, *Truth and Method*, Continuum, London, New York.

Grotkopp, M n.d., *Analysis for the Scene "Close Combat"*. Available from www. empirische-medienaesthetik.fu-berlin.de/en/emaex-system/affektdatenmatrix/filme/bataan/23_nahkampf/index.html [15 March 2018].

Grotkopp, M, Rositzka, E & Scherer, T (eds.), 2016, *Mediaesthetics*, no. 1. Available from: www.mediaesthetics.org/index.php/mae/issue/view/5/showToc [15 March 2018].

Kappelhoff, H 2004, *Matrix der Gefühle: Das Kino, das Melodrama und das Theater der Empfindsamkeit*, Vorwerk 8, Berlin.

Kappelhoff, H 2010, *Kriegerische Mobilisierung: Die mediale Organisation des Gemeinsinns*. Available from: www.empirische-medienaesthetik.fu-berlin.de/multimediale_publikationen/kriegerische-mobilisierung [15 March 2018].

Kappelhoff, H 2016, *Genre und Gemeinsinn: Hollywood zwischen Krieg und Demokratie*, De Gruyter Mouton, Berlin.

Kappelhoff, H, Gaertner, D & Pogodda, C (eds.), 2013, *Mobilisierung der Sinne. Der Hollywood Kriegsfilm zwischen Genrekino und Historie*, Vorwerk 8, Berlin.

Kappelhoff, H & Grotkopp, M 2012, 'Film Genre and Modality: The Incestuous Nature of Genre Exemplified by the War Film', in S Lefait & P Ortoli (eds.), *In Praise of Cinematic Bastardy*, pp. 29–39, Cambridge Scholars Publishing, Newcastle upon Tyne.

Kilerci, N & Lehmann, H 2018, 'Beyond Turkish-German cinema: Affective experience and generic relationality', in B Röttger-Rössler & J Slaby (eds.), *Affect in Relation: Families, Places, Technologies*, pp. 259–280, Routledge, New York.

Lehmann, H 2017, 'How does arriving feel? Modulating a cinematic sense of commonality', Transit, vol. 11, no. 1. Available from: http://transit.berkeley.edu/2017/lehmann/ [15 July 2018].

Merleau-Ponty, M 2002, *Phenomenology of Perception*, Routledge, London, New York.

Münsterberg, H 1916, *The Photoplay: A Psychological Study*, D. Appleton, New York, London.

Peirce, CS 1868, 'On a new list of categories', *Proceedings of the American Academy of Arts and Sciences*, no. 7, pp. 287–298.

Plessner, H 1982 [1925], 'Die Deutung des mimischen Ausdrucks: Ein Beitrag zur Lehre vom Bewußtsein des anderen Ichs', in idem., *Gesammelte Schriften VII: Ausdruck und menschliche Natur*, pp. 67–130, Suhrkamp, Frankfurt am Main.

Pogodda, C & Gronmaier, D 2015, '*The War Tapes* and the poetics of affect of the Hollywood war film genre', *Frames Cinema Journal*, no. 7. Available from: http://framescinemajournal.com/article/the-war-tapes-and-the-poetics-of-affect-of-the-hollywood-war-film-genre/, [15 March 2018].

Simmel, G 1995 [1905], 'Aesthetik des Porträts', in idem., *Aufsätze und Abhandlungen 1901–1908*, pp. 321–332, Suhrkamp, Frankfurt am Main.

Sobchack, V 1992, *The Address of the Eye: A Phenomenology of Film Experience*, Princeton University Press, Princeton.

Wundt, W 1902, *Grundzüge der physiologischen Psychologie*, Wilhelm Engelmann Verlag, Leipzig.

Chapter 8

Analyzing affective media practices by the use of video analysis

Margreth Lünenborg and Tanja Maier

I. Introduction

One core argument of affect theory refers to the capacity of affects to spill over from one body to another, from human to non-human bodies and vice versa (Angerer, 2017; Gregg & Seigworth, 2010). If we take this argument not just metaphorically, but want to understand more precisely *how affect works*, we need to look empirically at situations where affects cross borders and become visible in bodies of different kinds. As we are interested in the affecting dynamics of media, we want to apply affect studies to audience research. Understanding media as a relevant "affect generator" (Reckwitz, 2017), we want to analyze how these dynamics become relevant for media audiences. To do so, we use video analysis, watching people while watching television. In this chapter, we will give insights into our work with video material and its potential to shed light on the affective dynamics of media audiences.

Before going into empirical details, we will first give some background on the research context in which our work with video data has been developed. In a next step, we flesh out basic understandings of media audience and its relation to affects and emotions. As we refer to an understanding of affect based in practice theory, we will explore in more details how audiences and their media practices are conceptualized in practice theory approaches (Part 3). The empirical steps working with video analysis follow in Part 4, including the collection of video data, the contextualization of video material worked out with situational maps, and methodological considerations towards different tools available for in-depth analyses of the digital video material. Finally, we reflect on the potential of video analysis and its limitations, discussing especially the changing contexts of media use with digital and mobile devices and its relevance for grasping the affective practices of media audiences (Part 5).

2. Affect theory as research context in audience studies

While affect studies has been focusing quite intensively on the analysis of media texts (e.g. Breger, 2014; Coleman, 2013; Fahlenbrach, 2010), work on the affective dynamics of the audience is still scarce. On the other hand, considerations about the audience within affect studies is mostly based on theoretical conceptualizations of the audience while empirical approaches are missing (Gibbs, 2011). Thus, affect theory delivers complex theoretical understandings of affects as driving forces moving people to engage with media, but little is known about how affects become observable, how they are acted out or how the relational character of affect becomes relevant during the process of media reception and appropriation.

Our approach to the analysis of affective practices of the audience is part of a research project on *Transcultural Emotional Repertoires in and by Reality TV*. Analyzing reality TV as a global media format, we are interested in the affective dynamics produced in and by these shows. We understand reality TV formats as regulating forces organizing acceptable and privileged expressions and performances of emotions, while others are marked as undesirable. These socially and culturally formed emotions are not primarily part of discourse and meaning production in these formats, but are mostly affectively produced as relational intensities between human bodies and media technology. Above all, we are interested in the relational character of affect and want to capture it with our empirical analysis. Understanding affect as a dynamic, processual and fluid capacity coming up in the relational interaction *between* actors, artifacts, temporal and spatial contexts (Blackman & Venn, 2010; Clough, 2000, 2007; Slaby, Mühlhoff, & Wüschner, 2016).

We ask how affective dynamics emerge through globally distributed popular media formats like talent shows, both on the level of production and broadcasting and among culturally diverse audiences. Central to this analysis are thus the affect-based dynamic-relational processes of reception and appropriation of reality TV. The performative construction of emotional border situations, their affective shifts, and their provoked transgressions are essential ingredients of such TV shows. At their center are seemingly universal emotional concepts, such as success/failure or pride/shame, which are locally transformed and adopted to successfully reach local audiences (Grüne, 2016; Kraidy & Sender, 2011). The format itself thus regulates the performance of emotions. An ensemble of such repetitive, socially rooted and regulated verbal and non-verbal emotional forms of expression and behavior can be described as an emotional repertoire. Emotions are ordered, evaluated and circulated through such emotional repertoires. Media products can be understood as a repository, carrier, mediator as well as a context for the production and negotiation of emotional repertoires. Social norms and values of the appropriateness of emotions are displayed and performed in audiovisual media. In reality TV, protagonists representing preferably contrastive lifestyles and culturally diverse backgrounds embody these emotional repertoires in a complex interaction of performed personal articulations and dramaturgically staged conflictive settings. The contrastive casting of protagonists ensures conflictive dynamics in the show and enables a diversity of viewers to be involved emotionally. The concepts, symbols and enactments of emotions and affects communicated by these shows address a culturally diverse audience. We inquire into the potential for these shows to offer affective belonging to their audiences. Since the focus in reality TV is less on substantial discursive meaning production than on affectively based provocation, indignation or enthusiasm, we are interested in the effects of these very affections. We are especially interested in understanding the affective dynamics of negotiating modes of belonging in and by these popular TV formats. These belongings may refer to the cultural background as well as to social, gendered or sexual affiliations. Thus, we are looking for such forms of negotiation in the TV format itself as well as on the side of the audience.

With our research interest, we add a new focus to this field of research. Scholars like Kavka (2008, 2014) and Bratich (2007, 2010) have offered an analysis of affect *in* reality TV. Yet less has been written on its potential for the analysis of audiences. Skeggs and Wood (2012) have conducted research on the audience of reality TV focusing on the affective dynamics pertaining to the social and cultural backgrounds of audience members. They used interviews, focus group discussions and audio recordings of reception settings called "text-in-action-viewing sessions" (Wood, 2007) and "text-in-action-method" (Wood, 2009, 100–117) – to scrutinize reactions of the audience to the program shown. We build on this work, but add with video analysis another empirical approach to an understanding of the affective practices.

To explain in more detail how affect can be implemented in the analysis of audiences, we start by introducing theories of practice as a theoretical conceptualization in audience research. Understanding activities of the audience as routinized parts of everyday life helps us to formulate watching television as a social activity performed in specific settings characterized by social as well as spatial contexts and constraints. However, focusing on practices enables us not just to understand routines, but ruptures as well, as they are based on shifts in elements of practice allowing for change. These considerations about audience activities as social practices are carried forward by a more detailed elaboration of affect grounded in practice theory.

3. Understanding affect with practice theory

Practice theory represents an interdisciplinary body of scholarship at the intersection of sociology (Bourdieu, 1977), media anthropology (Postill & Bräuchler, 2010) and cultural studies (Hall, 1997). An important strand of practice theory can also be traced back to pragmatist philosophy and the sociology of knowledge (Schatzki, 1996; Schatzki, Knorr-Cetina, & von Savigny, 2001). Given the great variety of practice-based approaches, it is common to speak of theories of practice as an 'argument' about the mutual constitution of social structures and human agency (Ortner, 1996, 2). Theories of practice reject both methodological individualism and holism as causes of sociality (Hillebrandt, 2014, 27), and foreground that neither agents nor structures alone explain the continuity of social relations. Practices, in contrast, are conceived as routines where structures and actors encounter and impact each other. With a marked focus on the "'everyday' and 'life-world'", practice theories are centered on the "shared knowledge" that actors use in the "symbolic organization of reality" (Reckwitz, 2002b, 244–246; see also Garfinkel, 1967; Lefebvre, 2014). Understanding the everyday as a "particular material setting" of social life, quotidian practices account for the "organization generating its ordinary features, its orders and disorders, its contingencies and conditions" (Smith, 1987, 99). The quotidian can thus not be reduced to a complacent or monotonous routine of action, but describes a negotiation in practice between "relations of enablement and constraint" (Schatzki, 2002, 99).

The incorporated (and often implicit) knowledge deployed in practice is embodied – that is, learned in "bodily mental routines" (Reckwitz, 2003, 256). However, it is also performed, and is recognized by others as a legitimate course of action or conduct in a given situation (Reckwitz, 2002a). Due to this strong emphasis on incorporation of knowledge, practice theories can be seen as "a body of work about the work of the body" (Postill & Bräuchler, 2010, 11).

In media and communication studies, practice theories have been taken up especially in the field of audience and reception studies (Postill & Bräuchler, 2010) and in research about the 'domestication' of new technologies focusing especially on the routinized patterns of everyday interaction with media (Bakardjieva, 2005; Couldry, Livingstone, & Markham, 2007; Hartmann, 2013; Röser, Thomas, & Peil, 2010). Couldry's landmark article "Theorising Media as Practice" (2004) became a strategic statement that advocated placing "media studies firmly within a broader sociology of action and knowledge" (Couldry, 2004, 117) and regarded the multiple embeddedness of media in everyday life – rather than only their texts, their socio-political or economic structures – as a primary research interest. Thus, practice theory follows an approach designated as "non-media-centric media studies" (Krajina, Moores, & Morley, 2014). As Couldry (2012, 43) pointed out: "The value of practice theory is to ask open questions about what people are doing in relation to media. . . . A practice approach also brings into view the wider articulations of practices in systems of power". In this light, our focus on the affective dimension of social practices with media presumes that "*every* social order as a set of practices is a specific order of affects" (Reckwitz, 2017, 116, italics by the author).

In audience research, rare concepts do exist that describe and theorize the relation between media practices and affects. As Gibbs (2011, 251) writes: "To date, affect has been a category that has made more impact in media theory than in audience studies – in fact, affect theory has not yet been seriously adopted at all by audience research". For our analysis, we use an approach that combines elements of media practice theory with affect theory for the study of audiences. This gives us the opportunity to achieve two goals: to systematically describe and conceptualize the "affected body" of members of the audience in media communication, and to analyze in depth the potential of affective belongings that reality TV shows offer to their audiences. Thus, a special emphasis will be placed on exploring structures of difference and power in relation to affective dynamics. For this reason, we would like to open up the discussion to "affective practices" (Reckwitz, 2017; Wetherell, 2012, 2015). As Wetherell (2015) suggests:

> A practice approach positions affect as a dynamic process, emergent from a polyphony of intersections and feedbacks, working across body states, registrations and categorizations, entangled with cultural meaning-making, and integrated with material and natural processes, social situations and social relationships.
>
> (p. 139)

Following Wetherell, we understand affective media practices as relational actions, which connect bodies (human and non-human, like technologies) and media text in specific mediated situations and emphasize bodily aspects of media practices in particular. As Wetherell (2012) has summarized:

> An affective practice is a figuration where body possibilities and routines become recruited or entangled together with meaning-making and with other social and material figurations. It is an organic complex in which all parts relationally constitute each other.
>
> (p. 19)

Relying on the understanding of relational affectivity as a concept of affect and emotion (e.g. von Scheve, 2017), we elaborate on the bodily dimension between media text and viewers as well as between members of the media audience. Our considerations will be exemplified by the case of television. In this view, affective practices of media consumption have the potential to bind individuals and collectives together or delineate them from one another. Such a practice "*orients the body in some ways rather than others*" (Ahmed, 2010, 247, italics by the author). This might refer to the sense of belonging to a (sub)culture or to imagined communities constituted by gender, sexuality or cultural background. We outline some preliminary thoughts about the relevance of affects for the production of belonging by and through popular media texts.

But how can we carry out such affect media studies in practice? In this chapter, we argue that (digital) video analysis and some tools based in situational analysis (Clarke, 2005) can help to analyze affective practices in television culture.

4. Video analysis and audience research

Our empirical approach combines textual television analysis and digital video analysis. The empirical basis is the 11th season of *Germany's Next Topmodel* from 2016. Our audience research, among other materials, used digital video data for the analysis of affective media practices. By video analysis, we mean mainly the audiovisual recordings that are created by the researchers for *reception and audience studies* – not recordings produced by other actors, may it be professional TV shows or clips shared on video-sharing websites (Knoblauch, 2012, 253). This, however, does not exclude the possibility of using further video recordings (of TV shows for instance) in the analysis. We will return to this topic further in the chapter.

In order to understand media practices, audience studies of television have usually used interviews as data or ethnographic approaches (e.g. Rose, 2006, 202–215). Video analysis as method and methodology is rarely found in relevant introductory literature and handbooks of qualitative research methods in communication and media studies (Gjedde & Ingemann, 2008; Schünzel & Knoblauch, 2017). In ethnographic and social science research, by contrast, there is a range of literature on video analysis and videography for the study of social interaction (e.g. Heath, Hindmarsh, & Luff, 2010; Kissmann, 2009; Knoblauch, Schnettler, & Tuma, 2014; Pink, 2001, 2006). Among other reasons, epistemological and methodological considerations are important reasons why researchers increasingly choose video analytical methods:

> Compared to observations made by the naked human eye, video recordings appear more detailed, more complete and more accurate. In a technical sense, they are more reliable since they allow data analysis independent of the person who collected the data.
>
> (Knoblauch, Schnettler, & Raab, 2006, 10)

The growing use of video recording in research practice is also related to the alternative offered by digital video technology that has improved the quality of the recording techniques and brought upon new possibilities of video analysis that span data collection, processing and the analysis process (e.g. Irion, 2002; Dinkelaker & Herrle, 2009).

Collecting and post-production of audiovisual data with video material

Lightweight, easy-to-use and mobile digital cameras open up possibilities for collecting audiovisual material in everyday situations of media consumption with increased flexibility, spontaneity and under limited burden. Digital technology has also optimized the possibilities of recording in poorly lit settings or without artificial light. Thus, it is now possible to obtain some useable image quality in suboptimal recording settings with limited strain, for instance, while watching TV in the evening at home. In our project, we recorded living rooms at home using two digital cameras installed on tripods to the left and right of the couch. Since we are interested in the process of affectively based belonging while watching TV, we have analyzed groups as well as couples in their everyday settings.

For our study, we record the reception process in front of the TV in the private living rooms as well as the TV show on the screen. Based on our theoretical approach, we assume that affection arises between media text and technologies and the body of the viewers. Therefore, it is necessary to develop an approach that circumvents the dualism of text research on the one hand and reception analysis on the other. As our aim is to analyze the bodily relation between the medium and the person watching, we used split-screen videos as a tool. Thus, using video editing software, one can synchronize the footage of the social situation in front of the TV with the TV show running at that moment. The split-screen is an excellent tool for analyzing what the bodies of the watching participants react to. For further detailed analysis of the material, we used other tools such as slow motion, time lapse, zooms, stills as well as the 'subtitling' of the footage with transcripts made with video editing software.

Mapping approach and relational analysis

Since there is little or no prior knowledge of this subject, we have sought a methodical approach that allows for an inductive procedure. For this reason, we decided to use tools drawn from the *grounded theory methodology* (GTM) More precisely, we use the mapping approach developed by Clarke (2005) in her situational analysis. The situational analysis is theoretically and methodologically in line with constructivist modes of GTM that aim for partial analysis and theory building (Clarke, 2005; Charmaz, 2006). Clarke argues for an understanding of context not as something that surrounds a situation, but as constitutive in itself. She points out:

> *The conditions of the situation are **in** the situation.* There is no such thing as "context". The conditional elements of the situation need to be specified in the analysis of the situation itself as *they are constitutive of it*, not merely surrounding it or frame it or contributing to it. They *are* it. Regardless of whether some might construe them as local or global, internal or external, close-in or far away or whatever, the fundamental question is "*How do these conditions make themselves felt as consequential – **inside** the empirical situation under examination?*" At least some answers to that question can be found through doing situational analysis.
>
> (Clarke, 2005, 71–72, her emphasis)

Her understanding of situations as constitutive directly relates to our relational understanding of affect. In the following, we consider elements of this approach in order to analyze the effects of affection during joint watching of television programs. Of the tools mentioned by Clarke, however, we only used the so-called 'situational maps', which make it possible to examine relevant elements of a situation and its relations to another:

> **Situational maps** . . . lay out the major human, nonhuman, discursive, and other elements in the research situation of inquiry and provoke analysis of relations among them.
>
> (Clarke, 2005, xxii, her emphasis)

The goal is to analyze this complexity and relationality of the affecting viewer relations and to identify the elements that matter in a specific situation. Affect theory considers the ability of both human and non-human bodies to affect and to be affected. Media texts, technology and indeed any artifacts and materialities, can all affect. Yet the question remains as to which specific elements matter in a particular situation. It is therefore necessary to observe the immediate situation of reception. Thus, we used *messy situational maps* to look at what elements exist and matter in media-related affective settings. According to Clarke, the key questions of situational analyses are "Who and what are in this situation? Who and what matters in this situation? What elements 'make a difference' in the situation?" (Clarke, 2005, 87). In addition, Knudsen and Stage suggested some important and useful research strategies for tracing and characterizing affective dynamics in their book *Affective Methodologies*:

1   formal or stylistic characteristics of communication in affect (e.g. outburst, broken language, hyperbole, redundancy).
2.   the intense building of assemblages (consisting of, for example, texts, actions, images, bodies and technologies).
3.   non-verbal language and gestures of affected bodies.
4.   communicative content about experienced or attributed affect (made by, for example, informants, the researcher him-/herself or in existing texts).
5.   the rhythmic intensification, entertainment (through a common pulse) or destabilization of affective energy in relation to specific spaces and (online) sites (Knudsen & Stage, 2015, 9).

In the following, the mentioned questions and procedures will be applied to the specific problems of affect-related media research.

Doing relational analysis with situational maps

To create the situational maps, we initially used the classic open coding strategies of GTM. On the level of open coding, some codes are assigned to the audiovisual material, and initial loose concepts are built without linking them together or comparing them at this stage. Charmaz (2006, 43) defines coding as follows: "Coding means naming segments of data with a label that simultaneously categorizes, summarizes and accounts for each piece of data". The labels she mentions are named codes and are consolidated into concepts during the research (Gibbs, 2007, 39). Concepts are, in this context, a more abstract form of codes. In our definition, we then differentiate the situational concepts that are linked to the specific and empirically analyzed reception situation from the more abstract concepts that are part of the theory and model building. There are fluid transitions between codes – which are more descriptive – and situational and abstract concepts, which are more analytical.

Because we primarily want to identify affective media practices as a phenomenon within reception processes, we coded the entirety of the collected data.

The analysis took place in sequences, although we also followed the units of action of the TV show. To achieve this, we made protocols of the sequences of the analyzed episodes of GNTM that we used as units for the analysis of the video footage. The sequence protocols function as a way of making visible the relation between the affective practices happening in front of the TV screen and the action units of the TV show themselves.

Thus, we watched our audiovisual material several times and then started to create open codes and concepts that summarize what we see happening. Shown as follows is a short transcription of a sequence and an open coding case (see Table 8.1).

Relevant elements of the affective dynamics can be identified through this first step of open coding of the video footage. For instance, the sequence protocol can help pinpoint at what moments of the action specific affective media practices arise. This can then be compared to other cases. The split-screen analysis allows us to investigate the relational character of embodiment between the bodies of the audience and the audiovisual media text at this early stage of data analysis.

Using the codes and concepts, we then created *messy situational maps*. Situational maps capture all relevant elements in the reception situation "in a rough and dirty way in order to represent the field's messiness" (Mathar, 2008). The next question is how these elements are related to each other. Following Clarke, we conducted a relational analysis with situational maps:

> The procedure here is to first make a bunch of photocopies of your best version to date of the situational map. Then you take each element in turn and think about it in relation to each other element on the map. Literally center on one element and draw lines between it and the others and *specify the nature of the relationship by describing the nature of that line*. One does this systematically, one at a time, from every element on the map to every other. Use as many maps as seems useful to diagram yourself through this analytic exercise. This to me is the major work one does with the situational map once it is constructed.
>
> (2005, 102, author's emphasis)

In order to incorporate the bodily relation of people into the media text and media technologies, we then conducted a relational analysis of the affective dynamics at play. To illustrate our qualitative media analysis with situational maps, we have chosen a specific form of affective media practice from our research. In Figure 8.1, we take the concept of "sharing the excitement" as our primary object for a relational analysis with messy situational maps. Figure 8.1 shows, however, only a reduced version of a situational map.

It is important to underline here that the maps are not depictions but tools of analysis. Such maps can be created by hand or using software (we used Microsoft PowerPoint here). Their sole purpose is to illustrate our method of analysis. Figure 8.1 visualizes a relational analysis using a messy situational map, including

Table 8.1 Open Coding Case. Focus on "sharing the excitement".

Timecode	TV	Audience	Codes	Concept
01:28:30		A: looks to the left, probably at her cat. Suddenly gets up (and leaves the image). Says: "Check out what she's doing" (talking about her cat in the living room). Comes back after more or less 15 seconds and sits down on the sofa again. Plays with her hair.	glance	affective disengagement
01:30:55	"[...] you were always my champion [...]"	A: reaction to TV: "Whaaatt??" and looks at B	response-cries	"sharing the excitement" on both sides of the screen
		B: Sitting quietly and watching what's happening. Doesn't react to A.	gaze	
		A: Bows forward. Watches in a concentrated way, grabs the last piece of food on the plate near her.	Lean-forward eating	
	"[...] you are in the final [...]"	B: Gives a loud round of applause, bows forward and laughs	acclamation, lean-forward	
		A: Reacts to her mum and also starts clapping. The candidate rejoices and places her hands on her face. Claps once.	acclamation,	
		B: "She definitely deserved it. She looks like a model".	evaluation	
	"[...] she is in the final [...]"	A: Picks up Klum's "final" and starts singing: "Finale, oh oh oh". Lays her arm around B. B: Joins the singing, both sing: "Finale, oh oh oh oh".	acclamation, fan chant	

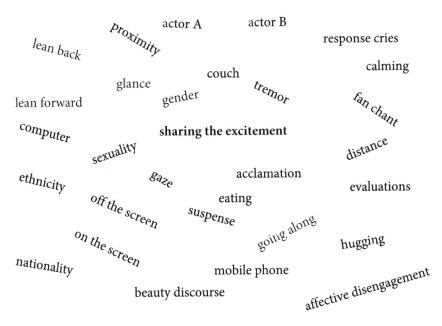

Figure 8.1 Relational analysis using messy situational map. Focus on "sharing the excitement" (working version).

some relevant codes and first concepts (simplified visualization). During the research and by engaging with the data we could further nuance and conceptualize the codes and concepts. Figure 8.2 shows a further situational map that we have made. It builds on concepts that are more abstract and includes the visualization of spatial and social structures of the reception situation.

A finding about relational analysis that was made possible by using the situational maps is that 'sharing the excitement' as an affective media practice is relevant *on both sides of the TV screen.* A relational analysis of the affective dynamics while watching TV shows how the viewers are involved in the TV show on an affective bodily level. When TV content is meant to arouse suspense, it addresses the bodies of the audience, which translates into affections like focused glance, body tension (e.g., lean-forward position), happy embraces, applause or fan chants. An affective media practice such as 'sharing the excitement' is linked to a cognitive assessment of the suspenseful media content. The discourses underlying those assessments are primarily related to (female) beauty and success. Frequently, while watching TV together, 'enlightened resistance' against the objectification of female bodies is less likely to be observed as disdainful remarks and insults: "What? She doesn't look like a model at all!", "She's way too fat to be a model", "She's so annoying with all her posturing", or "She's moving so

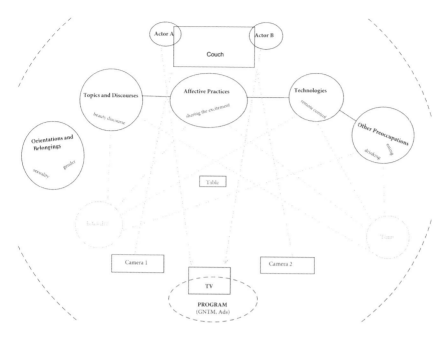

Figure 8.2 Relational analysis using abstract situational map.

ungracefully" are only some examples given here. Ludic contempt, insult and denigration are also visible in bodily reactions: one example here would be the bodily imitation of the model's performance, while denigrating her moves in the collective conversation. In this case, the relational analysis demonstrates how affective practices and discourse are closely related. The audience enjoys forms of judgment and devaluation of the candidates through the jury and partly takes a jury position itself by playfully 'sharing the excitement'. Thus, the evaluation of female bodies is adopted and performed as an affective practice through the reception process.

Our relational analysis shows that the creation of the affect is reinforced by further elements. For instance, it could be observed that the homely context and the position of the body on the sofa influence shared bodily excitement in an important way. The more the body of viewers 'melts' into the sofa to unwind, the more the activity potential and reaction capacity decreases. When the body disentangles itself from the sofa, slides to the edge and becomes more tense, the activity potential and reaction capacity increases. A relational analysis can thus demonstrate the importance of often neglected factors and make visible the constitutive character they have for the analysis of media practices. Furthermore, the relational analysis does not only show where connections are created but also where none emerge.

The shared excitement is not disturbed by other communication technologies (second screen, phone). Other media technologies are used repeatedly, but not in the moments of 'sharing the excitement'. It is therefore striking that viewers act out exactly this affective media practice without taking the mobile phone in their hands and being distracted by it. Thus, the relational analysis allows not only to show the existing relations between single elements, but also to make visible the constitutive role of what is *not done* for affection.

All in all, the relational analysis of the video material has made visible that the affection that occurs when people watch TV together develops relationally. These elements include the relation between the TV content, the TV device and the audience. In addition, the social interactions of the audience among themselves, the spatial organization with its artifacts and the practices linked to them (especially the use of second screens, the sofa, eating, drinking) as well as the discourses and socio-cultural positioning updated in the very moment of reception.

Our results show that viewers continuously negotiate the affective practices offered by the show they watch. For these considerations, we refer to Stuart Hall's (1980) encoding-decoding concept used to analyze the negotiation of meaning by the audience. However, here we do not refer solely to meanings and interpretations, but also to *affective practices* on the side of the audience. Being affected, however, is not a question of personal affiliation, but situational. Simple affective media practices range from laughing and singing all the way to hugging someone and crying out on both sides of the screen. A more complex and longer-lasting affective media practice is performed as 'sharing the excitement'. Overall, we found two different *forms* of affective media practices within our material with a special emphasis on bodily practices. With *practices of affective resonance* the affective registers offered by the media are being taken up physically and reenacted. By contrast, *practices of affective dissonance* show defense responses and activities of distancing oneself from the "commodity bodies" of the candidates as offered by the media.

Affective constructions/building of belonging

The situational maps alone cannot yet let us read how a sense of belonging is created by media practices. A higher level of theoretical abstraction is needed to achieve such an interpretation of the data. This can be accomplished by a simultaneous detailed analysis of some chosen sequences.

Based on our theoretical frame, three central levels of constructions of belonging can be identified: 1) locally situated communitization, 2) translocal mediated communitization and 3) symbolic communitization (by class, gender, ethnicity etc.). Following up on this, we switch to the analytic level, looking for the effects of affects. We want to briefly introduce our analysis discussing the role of affective media practices in the building of belonging. As a theoretical and heuristic concept to identify different levels of belonging, we apply the term of *orientation*. Following Ahmed, affects make us follow specific orientations when we come into contact with bodies:

> What matters is itself an effect of proximities: we are touched by what comes near, just as what comes near is affected by directions we have already taken. Orientations are how the world acquires a certain shape through contact between bodies that are not in relation of exteriority.
>
> (2010, 234)

According to Ahmed, affects move human bodies towards other human bodies as well as towards things, technologies and places, but also away from them – following the logic of attraction and rejection. This process constructs objects as familiar or alien. Such affective orientations do not only come into consideration for material objects, but also when it comes to ideas and evaluations (Allhutter & Hofmann, 2014, 63). It becomes clear that affects and discourses cannot be considered separately. If we understand affects as a social-relational practice in media reception processes, it is possible to grasp empirically orientations and belongings.

At the first level, reception analysis raises the question of how on-site consumers of the TV show create, emphasize or break out of types of belongings (i.e. as couple, family or fans) in a bodily affective way. We understand the social setting of watching TV together as a *locally situated form of communitization*. The practice of joint watching organizes social relations as parents and children, friends or partners. The participants negotiate joint viewing preferences (within the family or as a couple) and organize rituals of joint viewing habits (e.g. the 'girls' TV evening'). These forms of belonging are affectively produced within the audiovisual material and embodied through performance on the side of the audience. In this context, the viewers do not just imitate the affective practices seen on the screen – for instance, hugging when they see a hug on TV – but in fact anticipate such practices before they have occurred on screen, and continually repeat such practices after seeing them. In other words, we see forms of re-enactment as well as pre-enactment as part of habitual affective media practice (e.g., Silverman, 1996, 126ff.; Grusin, 2010). Alkemeyer (2006) has shown how fans at football games perform motions and bodily practices that not only *reenact* what happens on the field but frequently also *anticipate* it. In this regard it can be shown that fans update 'pre-existing' poses (Silverman, 1996, 202) and affective practices that connect them not only with the on-screen characters but also with other bodies in front of the screen. Figures 8.3 and 8.4 show that the viewers not only imitate the affective practices of excessive hugging, but also anticipate these practices. This becomes clear when we look at the timecode: both women hug each other, *before* it is shown on screen and at the same time they repeat affective practices that were staged several times.

Figure 8.3 Watching GNTM, Timecode: 02:10:44.

Figure 8.4 Screenshot GNTM, Timecode: 02:10:41.

Being together with friends and family offers opportunities for practices of *affective resonance* – a feeling of coziness on the audience side. Looking in more detail at these concepts of 'home', we suggest that the cultural proximity of these 'settings of home' – in terms of gender, class or cultural/ethnic background – regulates the intensities of affects on the audience's side. Thus, while offering coziness as a 'good feeling' in the living room, the power of reality TV lies in the patterns of distinction and exclusion along the lines of gender, class, culture, ethnicity that are acted out in affective practices.

On a second level, an affective media practice like "sharing the excitement" can be read as a *form of affective participation* in the show. In particular, the 'final decision' at the end of each episode provokes a definitive positioning as fan or critic of a certain character, as we showed earlier. We argue that taking part in watching a reality TV show embodies the participation in certain ways of life and everyday culture, which connects us with others. Based on habitual media consumption and knowledge about the genre and its promises, only those members of the audience who are familiar with these forms of consumption and culture and who find their preferences and values as part of this culture will eventually be able to participate (Alkemeyer, 2006). Affective media practices are only performed by those human bodies that are affected by this specific way of life. The affective participation and the pleasure created by the show become clearly visible in the orientation of the bodies (e.g. focused gaze, hugging), and they can also be expressed through linguistic expressions (e.g. response cries) or by verbal communicating (e.g. "that moved me"). Affective practices are then understood as the connecting force between the bodies of viewers and television, whether as technology, representation, staging or genre. Thus, the belonging to an (imagined) *translocally constituted community of other viewers* becomes visible.

The third level – that can be made visible using the video footage – is centered around the problem of how the audience's affective practices create and change national, gendered, ethnic, sexual or other kinds of belonging based on *modes of symbolic communitization*. By doing so, affective practices can be analyzed as a means of constructing and negotiating belonging that is created following the logics of linking or separating through action (i.e. doing ethnicity, othering, doing gender). It becomes clear that the viewers often show defense responses and that they are distancing themselves from the 'commodity bodies' of the candidates offered in the TV show. This is what we call *practices of affective dissonance*. We would like to illustrate this with one last example. Figure 8.5 shows a screenshot of GTNM during a "Cosmopolitan shooting". For this occasion, all candidates are trained to perform specific standardized body postures. In this way, the individual bodies of the protagonists are incorporated into a gendered and consumable 'commodity body'. Figure 8.6 shows a screenshot of a girl watching the show together with friends in front of her TV set. She notices these performative body representations and comments on the way one of the candidates performs her commodified body ("What the hell is she doing?") while imitating her body language. This way, a verbal dissociation with the commodity bodies takes place,

Figure 8.5 Screenshot GNTM.

Figure 8.6 Watching GNTM.

while the offered bodily expressions are being imitated physically. This can be characterized as simultaneity of verbal distancing, bodily imitation and playful staging. A video analysis can show how recipients repeat or negotiate affectively grounded gender norms and conventions through media-oriented practices. This also sheds light on the fact that affects and gender norms do not arise out of the bodies of the individual actors but come up relationally through interactions with publicly circulating gender representations.

5. Evaluation

Focusing on affective media practices requires visualization methods to investigate the temporality, relativity and intensity of the social-relational phenomena. Forms of video analysis are particularly suited to capturing the affective dynamics of media practices. Video analysis makes it possible to include undefined and volatile phenomena such as affects within a detailed analysis. The implementation of digital recording formats has dramatically widened the opportunities to use and analyze video footage. These opportunities include recording everyday reception practices with mobile phone cameras, for instance, or editing video footage through the synchronization of different footage, as well as the availability of certain tools of analysis, such as split-screen analysis or using special software created for the analysis of video footage.[1]

However, a basic constraint of video analysis lies in the construction of the visual through the lens of a camera. Mostly, researchers can only see an extract of the world through the footage. Video footage can never be "natural data", but are always already representations, excerpts and evaluations of social worlds. They cannot reflect reality because they are a social practice themselves, producing an academic view on everyday practices. The video camera in a living room is never a 'fly on the wall' but produces a specific type of observation material that is constrained by its positioning, the perspective of the camera and the camera motion, light or colors. Social reality itself is never directly empirically accessible – neither by tools of observation nor by surveys or video analysis. These fundamental epistemological assumptions of constructivism need to be taken into account. However, the respective co-constructions can be identified, reflected upon and debated (Charmaz, 2006).

Further limitations of video analysis of everyday media reception are also linked to the recruitment of candidates. Limits are set to what happens when a camera is set up in a private space. As already pointed out, not only does the researcher make a selection, but the research participants as well take part in an "auto-selection": what kind of person is willing to be filmed while watching TV in their everyday life at home or in other places? As we were interested in the social and cultural diversity of audience members, we need to take into account the limitations arising from social regulations about the willingness or reluctance to produce visible representation of the private home.

Video material allows for an analysis of multimodal communication including verbal and non-verbal articulation, body movements and social and environmental settings in its relational character (see Knudsen & Stage, 2015). All these elements become visible and applicable for analysis *in its temporal structure*. It is especially this opportunity to rely on the rhythm – here especially consisting of periods of calmness and boredom – alternating with periods of high intensity and intensive involvement.

With regard to the analysis of affects, the following conclusions can be drawn for video analysis: The situationally bound, relational affective occurrence is in no case directly accessible. Video recordings enable a specific detection and reproduction of a singular event. The benefit is undoubtedly the ability to sequentially reconstruct the complex, relational setting in its temporal dynamics.

However, there is no doubt that an independent analytic formation of the event is already taking place. The selection of participants, as well as the empirical access to the field via the camera, constitutes interventions in an everyday event. Just as affect research is constantly shaped by the researchers' own affections *vis-a-vis* the empirical material they collect, so too must the conditions of data collection always be understood as constitutive of affective events.

Affect research must consider this invasive characteristic in at least two ways. On the one hand – as we have sought to explain here – these very conditions of data collection and analysis are to be included transparently and reflexively in the evaluation process. On the other hand, multi-method approaches can correct this invasive character of the analysis. In addition to forms of video analysis, forms of questioning, memory work or media diaries can also be used to include self-descriptions of the spectators' affective experience.

The increasingly complex conditions of media reception – wherein audiovisual media are watched on different and increasingly mobile platforms – demand ever more complex research settings. While watching TV at home has been theorized in terms of globalization (Morley, 2005), the mobile availability and the diverse, fluid and less stable settings of media use need to be worked out profoundly in terms of their affective dynamics. We could observe members of the audience using a second screen, such as a smartphone or tablet, while watching television, thus divvying their attention between different media attractions. Current mobile forms of using audiovisual media, however, are changing these dynamics profoundly, as users engage in such media on public transport, during any kind of break, or even as entertainment in the schoolyard. Using audiovisual media here becomes part of other social practices of sharing, inscribed into mediated environments. Analyzing affective media practices in these mobile, digitalized contexts demands new research settings. But at the same time the relational character of affect *as part of social practices* here becomes even more apparent.

Note

1 As a software for the transcription and analysis of video data, the following programs are offered: InqScribe, Transana, Feldpartitur SaaS Micro, Nvivio, MAXQDA, Dedoose, Digital Replay System (DRS).

References

Ahmed, S 2010, 'Orientations Matter', in D Coole & S Frost (eds.), *New Materialism*, pp. 234–257, Duke University Press, Durham.

Alkemeyer, T 2006, 'Rhythmen, Resonanzen und Missklänge. Über die Körperlichkeit der Produktion des Sozialen im Spiel', in R Gugutzer (ed.), *Body Turn. Perspektiven der Soziologie des Körpers und des Sports*, pp. 265–296, Transcript Verlag, Bielefeld.

Allhutter, D & Hofmann, R 2014, 'Affektive Materialitäten in Geschlechter-Technikverhältnissen. Handlungs- und theoriepolitische Implikationen einer antikat-egorialen Geschlechteranalyse', *Freiburger Zeitschrift für Geschlechterstudien*, vol. 20, no. 2, pp. 59–78.

Angerer, ML 2017, *Ecology of Affect: Intensive Milieus and Contingent Encounters*, Meson Press, Lüneburg.

Bakardjieva, M 2005, *Internet Society: The Internet in Everyday Life*, Sage Publications, Los Angeles.

Blackman, L & Venn, C 2010, 'Affect', *Body & Society*, vol. 16, no. 1, pp. 7–28. Available from: https://doi.org/10.1177/1357034X09354769 [1 August 2018].

Bourdieu, P 1977, *Outline of a Theory of Practice*, Cambridge, Cambridge University Press.

Bratich, J 2007, 'Programming reality: Control societies, new subjects and the power of transformation', in D Heller (ed.), *Makeover Television. Realities Remodeled*, pp. 6–22, I.B. Tauris, London, New York.

Bratich, J 2010, 'Affective convergence in reality television. A case study in divergence culture', in M Kackman, M Binfield, MT Payne, A Perlman & B Sebok (eds.), *Flow TV: Essays on a Convergent Medium*, pp. 55–74, Routledge, London.

Breger, C 2014, 'Configuring affect: Complex world making in fatih Akın's Auf der anderen Seite (The Edge of Heaven)', *Cinema Journal*, vol. 54, no. 1, pp. 65–87.

Charmaz, K 2006, *Constructing Grounded Theory: A Practical Guide Through Qualitative Analysis*, Sage Publications, London.

Clarke, AE 2005, *Situational Analysis: Grounded Theory After the Postmodern Turn*, Sage Publications, Thousand Oaks.

Clough, PT 2000, *Autoaffection: Unconscious Thought in the Age of Technology*, University of Minnesota Press, Minneapolis.

Clough, PT 2007, 'Introduction', in PT Clough & J Halley (eds.), *The Affective Turn: Theorizing the Social*, pp. 1–33, Duke University Press, Durham, London.

Coleman, R 2013, *Transforming Images. Screens, Affect, Futures*, Routledge, Chapman & Hall, London.

Couldry, N 2004, 'Theorising media as practice', *Social Semiotics*, vol. 14, pp. 115–132.

Couldry, N 2012, *Media, Society, World: Social Theory and Digital Media Practice*, Polity Press, Cambridge.

Couldry, N, Livingstone, S & Markham, T 2007, *Media Consumption and Public Engagement: Beyond the Presumption of Attention*, Palgrave Macmillan, Basingstoke.

Dinkelaker, J & Herrle, M 2009, *Erziehungswissenschaftliche Videographie: Eine Einführung*, VS, Wiesbaden.

Fahlenbrach, K 2010, *Audiovisuelle Metaphern. Zur Körper- und Affektästhetik in Film und Fernsehen*, Schüren Verlag, Marburg.

Garfinkel, H 1967, 'Studies of the routine grounds of everyday activities', in idem., *Studies in Ethnomethodology*, pp. 35–75, Prentice Hall, Englewood Cliffs.

Gibbs, A 2011, 'Affect theory and audience', in V Nightingale (ed.), *The Handbook of Media Audiences*, pp. 251–266, Wiley-Blackwell, West Sussex.

Gibbs, GR 2007, *Analyzing Qualitative Data*, Sage Publications, London.

Gjedde, L & Ingemann, B 2008, *Researching Experiences; Exploring Processual and Experimental Methods in Cultural Analsysis*, Cambridge Scholars Publishing, Newcastle.

Gregg, M & Seigworth, G (eds.), 2010, *The Affect Theory Reader*, Duke University Press, Durham, London.

Grüne, A 2016, *Formatierte Weltkultur? Zur Theorie und Praxis globalen Unterhaltungsfernsehens*, Transcript Verlag, Bielefeld.

Grusin, RA 2010, *Premediation: Affect and Mediality After 9/11*, Palgrave Macmillan, Basingstoke, New York.

Hall, S 1980, 'Encoding/decoding', in Centre for Contemporary Cultural Studies (ed.), *Culture, Media, Language: Working Papers in Cultural Studies, 1972–79*, pp. 128–138, Hutchinson, London.

Hall, S 1997, *Representation: Cultural Representations and Signifying Practices*, Sage Publications, London.

Hartmann, M 2013, 'From domestication to mediated mobilism', *Mobile Media & Communication*, vol. 1, pp. 42–49.

Heath, C, Hindmarsh, J & Luff, P 2010, *Video in Qualitative Research: Analysing Social Interaction in Everyday Life*, Sage Publications, London.

Hillebrandt, F 2014, *Soziologische Praxistheorien. Eine Einführung*, Springer VS, Wiesbaden.

Irion, T 2002, 'Einsatz von Digitaltechnologien bei der Erhebung, Aufbereitung und Analyse multicodaler Daten', *Forum Qualitative Sozialforschung/Forum: Qualitative Social Research*, vol. 3, no. 2. Available from: www.qualitative-research.net/index.php/fqs/article/view/855 [1 August 2018].

Kavka, M 2008, *Reality Television, Affect and Intimacy: Reality Matters*, Palgrave Macmillan, Houndmills.

Kavka, M 2014, 'A matter of feeling: Mediated affect in reality television', in L Ouellette (ed.), *A Companion to Reality Television*, pp. 459–477, Wiley, Malden, Oxford, Sussex.

Kissmann, U (ed.), 2009, *Video Interaction Analysis*, Peter Lang, Frankfurt am Main.

Knoblauch, H 2012, 'Introduction to the special issue of qualitative research: Video-analysis and videography', *Qualitative Research*, vol. 12, no. 3, pp. 251–254.

Knoblauch, H, Schnettler, B & Raab, J 2006, 'Video-analysis: Methodological aspects of interpretive audio visual analysis in social research', in H Knoblauch, B Schnettler, J Raab & HG Soeffner (eds.), *Video Analysis. Methodology and Methods. Qualitative Audiovisual Data Analysis in Sociology*, pp. 9–28, Peter Lang, Frankfurt am Main.

Knoblauch, H, Schnettler, B & Tuma, R 2014, *Videography. Introduction to Interpretive Videoanalysis of Social Situations*, Peter Lang, Frankfurt am Main, Bern.

Knudsen, B & Stage, C 2015, 'Introduction: Affective methodologies', in idem., *Affective Methodologies. Developing Cultural Resarch Strategies for the Study of Affect*, pp. 1–24, Palgrave Macmillan, Houndsmill.

Kraidy, M & Sender, K (eds.), 2011, *The Politics of Reality Television. Global Perspectives*, Routledge, New York.

Krajina, Z, Moores, S & Morley, D 2014, 'Non-media-centric media studies: A cross-generational conversation', *European Journal of Cultural Studies*, vol. 17, pp. 682–700.

Lefebvre, H 2014, *Critique of Everyday Life*, Verso, London.

Mathar, T 2008, 'Making a mess with situational analysis? Review essay', *FQS*, vol. 9, no. 2.

Morley, D 2005, *Home Territories: Media, Mobility and Identity*, Routledge, London.

Ortner, SB 1996, 'Making gender: Toward a feminist, minority, postcolonial, subaltern, etc. Theory of practice', in SB Ortner (ed.), *Making Gender: The Politics and Erotics of Culture*, pp. 1–20, Beacon Press, Boston.

Pink, S 2001, *Doing Ethnography: Images, Media and Representation in Research*, Sage Publications, London.

Pink, S 2006, *The Future of Visual Anthropology: Engaging the Senses*, Routledge, London.

Postill, J & Bräuchler, B 2010, *Theorising Media and Practice*, Berghahn Books, New York.

Reckwitz, A 2002a, 'The status of the "Material" in theories of culture: From "Social Structure" to "Artefacts"', *Journal for the Theory of Social Behaviour*, vol. 32, pp. 195–217.

Reckwitz, A 2002b, 'Toward a theory of social practices: A development in culturalist theorizing', *European Journal of Social Theory*, vol. 5, pp. 243–263.

Reckwitz, A 2003, 'Grundelemente einer Theorie sozialer Praktiken: Eine sozialtheoretische Perspektive', *Zeitschrift für Soziologie*, vol. 32, no. 4, pp. 282–301.

Reckwitz, A 2017, 'Practices and their affects', in A Hui, T Schatzki & E Shove (eds.), *The Nexus of Practices*, pp. 114–125, Routledge, Milton Park.

Rose, G 2006, *Visual Methodologies. An Introduction to the Interpretation of Visual Materials*, Routledge, London.

Röser, J, Thomas, T & Peil, C 2010, *Alltag in den Medien – Medien im Alltag*, VS Verlag für Sozialwissenschaften, Wiesbaden.

Schatzki, TR 1996, *Social Practices: A Wittgensteinian Approach to Human Activity and the Social*, Cambridge University Press, Cambridge.

Schatzki, TR 2002, *The Site of the Social: A Philosophical Account of the Constitution of Social Life and Change*, Pennsylvania State University Press, University Park.

Schatzki, TR, Knorr-Cetina, K & von Savigny, E 2001, *The Practice Turn in Contemporary Theory*, Routledge, London.

Schünzel, A & Knoblauch, H 2017, 'Videographie und videoanalyse', in C Wegener & L Mikos (eds.), *Qualitative Medienanalyse. Ein Handbuch*, UTB, Stuttgart.

Silverman, K 1996, *The Threshold of the Visible World*, Routledge, New York.

Skeggs, B & Wood, K 2012, *Reacting to Reality Television: Performance, Audience and Value*, Routledge, New York.

Slaby, J, Mühlhoff, R & Wüschner, P 2016, 'Affektive Relationalität. Umrisse eines philosophischen Forschungsprogramms', in U Eberlein (ed.), *Zwischenleiblichkeit – Intercorporeity, Movement and Tacit Knowledge*, pp. 69–108, Transcript Verlag, Bielefeld.

Smith, DE 1987, *The Everyday World as Problematic. A Feminist Sociology*, Northeastern University Press, Athens.

von Scheve, C 2017, 'A social relational account of affect', *European Journal of Social Theory*, vol. 1, no. 21, pp. 39–59.

Wetherell, M 2012, *Affect and Emotion: A New Social Science Understanding*, Sage Publications, Los Angeles, London.

Wetherell, M 2015, 'Trends in the turn to affect: A social psychological critique', *Body & Society*, vol. 21, no. 2, pp. 139–166.

Wood, H 2007, 'The mediated conversational floor: An interactive approach to audience reception analysis', *Media, Culture & Society*, vol. 29, no. 1, pp. 75–103.

Wood, H 2009, *Talking with Television. Women, Talk Shows, and Modern Self-Reflexivity*, University of Illinois Press, Urbana.

Chapter 9

Videography of emotions and affectivity in social situations

Hubert Knoblauch, Michael Wetzels
and Meike Haken

Summary

Videography is a method for the analysis of social situations that combines ethnography with video analysis. Scholars have taken interest in the methodological advantages of this approach (Tuma, Schnettler, & Knoblauch, 2013). Yet less has been written about the specific applications of videography to the study of affective social life. In this chapter, therefore, we explore some of the ways this method can be usefully applied to the social scientific analysis of emotions and affectivity, drawing on 'jubilation' as a prime example.

Our analysis shall proceed in several parts. In a first part, we sketch the development of videography as a method and outline its major traits (1). A second part delineates our understanding of emotions and affectivity in audiovisual studies more broadly (2). In a third, larger part, we then turn our attention to illustrating our argument through the paradigmatic audiovisual example of jubilation at a sports match (3). To set the stage for our analysis of jubilation as an emotional expression, we begin by explaining how to select data and make a transcription (a). We then discuss the degree to which this expression is communicative and relational rather than 'in' the body, since it arises in the context of an audience and a game (b). Then, in the next step of our sequential analysis (c), we will argue that the meaning of this emotion needs to be understood as an affective dynamic unfolding temporally in the course of a performance. In a fourth part, we turn our attention to the institutional context through a comparison to religion (4). Here, we shall indicate how and to what degree the observable emotional quality of jubilation can be explained by the affective dramaturgy of football as an aleatory game, by the affective arrangements of football as an agonal game and by affective frames. Finally, in a fifth part, we shall ask how we can generalize from single cases as they have been analyzed here (5).

Development and major features of videography

Since the very beginnings of the social sciences, film and video have been used as data for the qualitative analysis of social life (Reichert, 2007). However, only in recent decades has a specific methodology been developed and shared internationally. Thus, Goodwin (1980) has analyzed video-recorded interaction in everyday encounters, Erickson and Shultz (1982) employed video for school counsellor interviews, and Heath (1986) has undertaken video analysis of medical encounters. Methodological reflection began in the 1980s (Erickson, 1982; Heath, 1997; Lomax & Casey, 1998) and is now documented in various edited volumes (Kissmann, 2009; Knoblauch, 2006). It is elaborated in general methodology books (Heath, Hindmarsh, & Luff, 2010; Knoblauch, Tuma, & Schnettler, 2014) as well as with reference to specialized fields, such as the learning sciences (Goldman et al., 2007) and religious studies (Knoblauch, 2011a).

As opposed to the multitude of standardized and quantitative studies of audiovisual data in the social sciences, these studies are decidedly interpretive.[1] Their basic assumption is that actions and interactions are guided by meanings that must be understood by the researchers and need to be explicated in analysis in order to be scientific (Schutz, 1962). Moreover, all these studies share a basic ethnographic orientation. Video data focus on what is situationally "happening in the social world", and are then interpreted and analyzed as data outside of the field setting by means of the data (Knudsen & Stage, 2015, 2). Because it combines *video* analysis and focused ethno*graphy*, we refer to this method as *videography* (Knoblauch, 2006). To avoid the assumption that audiovisual recordings directly 'represent' the processes observed, videographers need to have been participating in the situations recorded in order to access their participants' points of view.[2] This way videographers can use videos as media for their observations. Their participation prior to the recordings should enable them to assess their reactivity to the situation, while their ethnographic knowledge should enable them to account for the typical actors' knowledge in the situations recorded.

The method of videography has been portrayed in books and handbook articles in quite some detail (e.g. Knoblauch, 2011b; Tuma, Schnettler, & Knoblauch, 2013). It consists in the collection of video data by the ethnographer in the field, a preliminary coding of the data according to the research question, and a fine-grained analysis of the data selected. This fine-grained analysis has to be accomplished by means of a sequential 'video analysis' of the courses of action and interaction recorded and by an interpretation of the video's visual content by means of hermeneutics, semiotics and ethnography. This way, specific forms, patterns and genres of action are identified as typical for those aspects of the field addressed by the research. By linking the institutionalized structures with the situated actions and the actor's knowledge, videography helps explain the communicative construction of these aspects of the field.

In this paper, we do not want to repeat the existing literature's portrayal of videography as a method. However, we shall briefly review those methodological aspects which are relevant to our perspective on the study of affectivity and emotions. Videography is characterized by a triple focus with regard to fields:

a   on *the field:* videography requires preliminary ethnography, which allows researchers to identify the focus of observations as well as ethnographical

methods and serve to collect appropriate information about the context of
what is recorded;

b   on *the social situations:* videography typically focuses on certain actions,
interactions and practices within a certain setting or across setting. Videography is, as Erickson (2005, 1198) has remarked, characterized by a "focus"
on the "particulars of situated performance as it occurs naturally in everyday
social interaction";

c   on what *the camera* records: this may range from a large crowd in a stadium
covered by a 360-degree camera to a fixed camera focusing on interacting
bodies, or to the mobile camera focusing on moving hands or heads mounted
on actors in motion.

With respect to what the camera records, technology plays quite an important role.
Video is a technology for recording communicative, socially observable actions
with a level of detail not even accessible to the actors themselves. It allows for
the permanent use, re-use and re-focusing of audiovisual data for the sake of validation and comparison by a range of technical options: playing and repeating,
slow motion and zooming are among the most important techniques from which
researchers profit when doing video analysis. Videographic data is therefore characterized, first, by the mimetic character of video. Video represents not only sound
and voice but also bodies, objects and visualized space. This way, video data
provide an enormously rich and immensely dense data corpus objectified in a way
which makes it accessible to other researchers' interpretations and analyses. As
a visual medium, video also allows one to analyze various aspects of a situation
simultaneously, which may be grasped even by someone who has witnessed the
situation only on closer scrutiny afterwards. As opposed to photography, video is
thus a temporal medium, which allows the researcher to analyze the *sequentiality*
of actions, interactions and other social processes.

Video, emotion and affectivity

Audiovisual studies of emotions draw on a long and often popular history of
research. Initially based on the visual classifications of major emotions from Le
Brun to Darwin, they are currently also developed by research based on recording
people in laboratory settings. In much of this research, emotions are identified as
forms of behavior that can be coded independently of the actors. Emotions are
assumed to be 'expressing' internal bodily states deemed to depend on physiological and neurological processes often considered as causes. In particular, the study
of human and animal facial expressions led to an approach whose popularity
goes far beyond scientific research and is massively influenced by Ekman (1972).
Based on video recordings and stills of individual faces, the research methodology is guided by direct measurement and by the judgment of observers who are
assumed to assign codes not influenced by their cultural, professional or contextual knowledge.

As popular as this standardized approach has become, it remains paradigmatic for research that considers emotions not only as an 'expressive' phenomenon but also as an individual one occurring within a person's body. Therefore, the focus of emotions is typically on facial expression, gestures or postures of isolated, individual persons, whose physiological processes can be measured. However, over the last decades, this approach has been criticized severely within the social sciences and humanities.[3] As a result, a range of studies has demonstrated how deeply emotions are dependent on cultural meaning, rules, language and communication (e.g. Harré, 1986; Hochschild, 1979; Lutz & White, 1986). In addition, research is moving from regarding emotions as passive and individual to focusing on their active social role, such that "facial displays in dialogue are symbolic acts selected to convey meaning to a recipient" (Bavelas & Chovil, 1997, 337). Based on video recordings of everyday conversations Peräkylä (2012), i.e., studied emotions in interactions between interlocutors, and Marjorie Goodwin and Charles Goodwin (2000) show how "emotion is organized as an interactive process" (Goodwin & Goodwin, 2000, 255).

These studies indicate an approach that differs significantly from the psychological study of emotions sketched above. As this approach guides our following analysis, it is worth delineating it here. Emotions, as we understand them, are not just an expression of some interior physiological processes but are also communicative. There is no doubt that emotions are always a form of self-communication, referring to social knowledge about emotions as well as to subjective feelings. Emotion is "publicly accessible" in Erving Goffman's (1956) sense, particularly, but not exclusively in public settings, such as the one of audience. In fact, we can observe and videotape them because of their communicative character. As affect theory leads to the "prioritization of communication" in audience research (Gibbs, 2011, 252), emotions should not just be seen as naturalized processes *in* the body, but also as processes communicated *by* the body. What and how the body communicates can be understood as emotion by oneself as well as by others. That understanding is possible because the body provides a certain "gestalt" for emotions or, including facial expression as well as gestures or postures. Although much research from Darwin to Ekman assumes a kind of biological determination of these gestalts, the meaning of bodily communication may be understood in some cases as 'emblems' or forms. Most of it is semantically much less specified than linguistic signs. However, these forms are dependent on and affected by their relation to the contexts that we shall address here. In this respect, it is also relevant that emotional communication can be mediated beyond the local situation.

Because of their communicative dimension, emotions are relational in character. They are not restricted to the 'interior' world or the correlation of bodily expression and physiology. Rather, the relation of the body to someone or something allows us to grasp the meaning of emotions. Certainly, the meaning of emotions depends on some 'stimulus' or some 'exciting fact', such as James' famous "bear" (James, 1890). Emotions, of course, are linked to the embodied awareness of physiological changes and the corresponding subjective feelings. But, instead of being mere 'reactions', emotions depend on a meaningful understanding of what they relate to. It is because of this relational meaning to something else that we understand emotions to be affected by the embodied action of someone else.[4] By focusing on observation, understanding and analysis of audiovisually recorded communicative actions, we want to avoid the quite common methodological fallacy of presupposing affectivity. Instead, we want to demonstrate the analytical usefulness of these categories in the cursory sketch of an empirical analysis.

Analyzing jubilating

In order to demonstrate the relationality of emotion, we shall start our analysis by turning to an assumedly 'clear case' of an emotion: a jubilating gesture in a football game. Later on, we will suggest that the specific jubilating 'gesture' itself can be understood as a sequence of events forming a ritual of what may be called 'joy'. But, how can we assess whether 'jubilation' means joy more generally? If we ask the persons involved, we risk retrospectively reconstructing their subjective feelings and the corresponding rules. If we focus on audiovisual data, however, our focus is on the embodied performance in the context of the audience, the stadium and the game.[5]

Selecting data and transcription

Before we turn to the data, we shall first indicate how it was retrieved. Videographic data, such as video recordings, documents, interviews and notes, constitute the data corpus from which fragments are selected according to their relevance to the disciplinary field and to the research question. In a first step, the corpus has been coded with respect to this question, which in our case is 'audience emotion'. Coding here means to ascribe a preliminary category to a larger segment of data, mostly video and annotations. These then may become subject to a fine-grained analysis, refining or correcting the code.[6] In the fine-grained analysis, what is ascribed to a code becomes subject to detailed interpretation and sequential analysis.

If they contain verbal elements, the fragments need some more or less detailed transcription before they can be subject to fine-grained sequential analysis. Many more or less sophisticated transcription systems are available, some of them useful for transcribing video data (Knoblauch, Tuma, & Schnettler, 2014). Most of these are oriented by the system suggested by Jefferson (2004). The granularity of transcription, however, depends on the data itself. If speech figures importantly in religious sermons, for instance, literal transcriptions of the text may be necessary. In conversations among seated actors, transcriptions must include paralinguistic features. If communicative action is mainly performed by bodies, it may be necessary to use notation systems for visual aspects, as represented by gaze, bodily posture or material aspects of the spatial setting.

Although our project addresses the research of collective emotions in different kinds of audiences (religion and professional football), in this paper we want to start with a similar perspective like much of the described perspectives of emotion studies and select data in which the camera focuses on and foregrounds an individual actor.[7]

Simultaneity

In the first step, we are trying to understand what is in the focus of the camera on the level of *simultaneity*. By interpretation we mean to draw on ethnographic knowledge from within the scene (where are we?), on semiotic knowledge of what is visually represented (e.g. the shirt's colors) and on general cultural knowledge about the situation, such as the knowledge of football, football audiences or stadiums.[8]

In the still selected from the chosen fragment, we see a man in the middle wearing a blue t-shirt and lifting his arms halfway towards his own body by clenching his fists and stretching them away towards the front (see Figure 9.1). We shall call him Peter, and the gesture is what we have been coding as jubilating.[9]

By trying to reconstruct why the fragment has been coded as jubilating, we realized that we drew on everyday knowledge. On closer consideration there is not just 'one gesture' at play, but rather a multimodal bodily *gestalt*. There is a gesture realized by the arms, but the man has also been erecting his body while the audio channel emits a loud "yes". And if we look from a different perspective, we can also see a smiling face. We have interpreted this multimodal *gestalt*

Figure 9.1 Peter jubilating in a football stadium.

of the body as 'jubilating' when coding (Müller et al., 2013). Obviously, we drew on very general cultural knowledge, not knowing, however, if the *gestalt* can be understood differently in other settings.[10] Thus, in the field of religion, the two arms raised signify humility and devotion, although they differ slightly from the triumphant gesture exemplified here.

When trying to substantiate this interpretation semiotically, however, we found few systematic studies based on audiovisual data on the embodied forms of jubilating, and even less on jubilating in football. In one of the few studies on the topic, Morris (1981, 168) identifies the multimodal gestalt as the "arms aloft gesture". Morris claims that this is the most common of all triumph displays, as it enlarges those who are gesturing, making them feel 'taller'. Morris stresses the ethnological function of that feeling, explaining that "in animal terms, by scoring the goal he has instantly raised his status in his group" (ibid., 168). The gesture can thus be considered a 'universal' one, as it expresses the emotion of triumph or "triumph displays".

Morris' interpretation is popular, yet quite a typical example for an approach which regards emotions in isolation as expressions of some interior processes. In addition, in gesture studies, aspects of the body often are considered in isolation, and their meaning is ascribed to them by the observer as if it were determined by a universal 'body language'. If we only extend our perspective slightly on the same still, we may detect how easily such a universalistic assumption may be falsified. For even among the people standing close to Peter who are represented with large parts of their bodies on the still, no one else exhibits the exact same body 'gesture' as him. The woman next to him, for example, does not stand up, but lifts both of her arms up to the front of her face, forming a triangle by clapping both of her hands together. The man to the left of Peter is stretching his left arm, jumping up while his hand is clenched to a fist in a manner reminiscent of leftist worker movements. This one we would call an emblematic gesture, which is also used in other non-political fields, such as pop music or in populist performative styles of sermons in New Pentecostal congregations.

The fact that the *gestalt* or the gesture varies even in the same context, and with the same 'stimulus', contradicts the universality claim. Moreover, it challenges the thesis of "affect contagion" as a corporeally based form of mimetic communication (Gibbs, 2011, 259). As we show later, Peter does not mimic the audience or the player scoring. Rather than imitation, we see differences in gestures, postures and facial expressions that communicate different emotions. These differences become particularly visible if we scrutinize the background: here we see the local fans who not only jubilate visibly in an even more extended way, jumping up with arms aloft, but also hear them shouting in loud unison, in a way not imitated by anyone on the still. Instead of claiming a premature universality of the "triumphant gesture" (Morris, 1981), we should rather explain the obvious differences in posture, gesture and facial expression. If we take their bodies to communicate emotions, we assume that these differences can be accounted for by what Goffman (2010) has called *involvement*. A person who jubilates 'like a fan' clearly shows how much she relates to the team scoring, to the fans and to the rest of the audience. She not only jubilates but also demonstrates her emotion visibly and audibly in the way she performs them for herself and others. Standing up resembles the posture of the fans, so that Peter can make widely visible that he is as cheerful about the goal as they are – and much more so than the woman next to him. Yet, by not shouting loud and singing like them, he displays a different kind of involvement. Involvement, in this sense is a category that becomes observable through comparisons between different types of actors, and which can be taken as an indication of the intensity of subjective feeling (Goffman, 1966). Involvement is indicated by materialized symbols, such as the team's emblems, shirts or scarfs (Collins, 2004, 81–83). However, it is also performed in a way that indicates the audience members' "differential participation status" (Goffman, 1981). Just as there is not one kind of emotion, there is not one kind of audience, since significant differences exist in the way audience members perform. These differences may be seen as 'emotional displays', demonstrating to whom they belong and with whom they respectively share solidarity. We should not, however, reduce their performance merely 'displaying emotion' to others. As the sequential analysis will show, they are also tuned in with what is happening on the field in such a way that we can say they are affected by them.

Sequential analysis

Up to this point, we have been focusing on the simultaneous aspects of the visual still. Video, however, is a temporal medium, and this temporality is accounted for by *sequential analysis*. Sequential analysis looks at how the meaning of communicative action is constituted in time. That is, it considers how actions are reflexively designed in the course of their performance so that they are understood by others and, consequently, by themselves. In order to reconstruct the order that is unfolding sequentially, we can use the specific qualities of the video and reconstruct it through repetitious watching, so long as we also have some understanding of the participants' knowledge. This understanding is typically retrieved through ethnography. The sequentiality has a great advantage for the interpreters of allowing for the validation of interpretations. Interpretations of first turns or moves are used to project next turns, while the empirical form of next turns or moves allows interpreters to decide which interpretation of the first turns by the actors has been chosen and is therefore valid.[11]

Sequential analysis refers to communicative action 'turns', such as bodily positions, movements, vocalizations or other objectivations performed or produced, which demonstrate what the bodies are oriented towards and by what they are oriented. In the case of Peter, this is quite obvious. Although he stands in the audience and orients in a rather differential way toward the audience's action, his face as well as his body are clearly orienting toward something else: the pitch, the game and the players (see Figure 9.2). We can account for this relation by inserting a second slide representing the scene he is looking at in the moment: the player raising his right hand in a way that indicates he scored the goal.

Figure 9.2 Peter's jubilation relates to the scorer on the pitch.

Peter's gesture does not just parallel the scorer's gesture but also 'reacts' to the goal scored just before. The behavioristic association of 'reaction', however, is quite misleading. First, as we have seen previously, Peter 'interprets' the goal with his distinct manner of jubilating. Secondly, as we have shown, jubilation is one gesture in a sequence of moves. To clarify what we mean by sequence, it may be helpful to indicate its major move sets in a rough sketch of a transcript as seen here (see Figure 9.3):

We have subdivided jubilation into four sequences (1–4), which are referred to by three kinds of representations: the conduct of Peter and the audience on the still, the course of events on the playground (A-D), and the scorer's location, toward which Peter is bodily orienting.

The sequence sets in as the goal is shot (A). Immediately afterwards, Peter's mouth opens, presumably taking part in the unison shouting of "Yes!" which we can hear throughout the entire video fragment. Simultaneously Peter raises his body almost in synchrony with the other people around him (1). While the scorer turns away from the goal and raises his right hand with his head slightly lowered (B), Peter stretches both arms forward, fists clenched in a standing position, still focusing the pitch where the goal was scored, while the person in front of him already turns his body to the right (2). Then, we see Peter turning his upper body halfway to the right, his fists open and his hands starting to clap. As another player joins the scorers' celebration by putting his right arm around his shoulder (C),

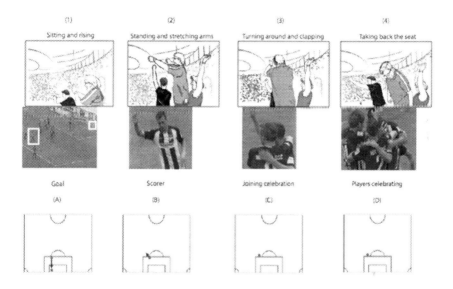

Figure 9.3 Sequential order of jubilating the scored goal.

Peter also turns his focus away from the playing field to the right, where we see other audience members standing and applauding while the fan block celebrates in the background. Returning to his initial position (4), Peter stops clapping as the players continue celebrating the goal on the pitch (D).

Leaving a series of minor moves aside, we can broadly distinguish four kinds of body positions through the sequence of jubilating: sitting and rising (1), standing and stretching arms (2), turning around and clapping (3) and taking back the seat (4).

The sequence demonstrates quite clearly that jubilating is not one gesture; rather, it is a series of moves which exhibit not only an 'inner emotion' but also a relation to something else. Doing so, it not only 'reacts' to the goal but acts in ways that resemble and differ from what other audience members do. As other members in the audience, he does respond to the actions on the field *and* the other audience members (Goffman, 1981) in a way, which takes on a certain form. Its beginning is bounded from the course of motionless sitting; it has a hesitant beginning; its first climax is the jubilation and finishes by an appreciative applause. If one looks at his body movements in space and time, the sequence follows the three-partite pattern suggested by van Gennep (1986) as a ritual: it starts by leaving the ordinary, reaches a climax in the extraordinary and then returns to the ordinary once again. By ritual we mean here a pattern of communicative action without assuming that it is standardized and endowed with "emotional energy" (Collins, 2004). Rather, emotionality itself is gradual and performed by an involvement and alignment with others. Moreover, the most decisive aspects of the emotion depend on the context. It is because actors are observing the first goal of the football game that the gesture is triggered and its meaning defined. We will now turn to these contextual factors by discussing the notion of affective arrangements and affective dramaturgy.

Aleatory, agonality and affective frames

Despite its structural similarity to other rituals, the processual sequence of Peter jubilating exhibits an affective dynamic. This affective dynamic is strongly related to the specificity of football in three specific ways.

First, we have to consider that one of the basic features of football is that it is an "aleatory" game (Caillois, 1958). In other words, it is decided contingently by goals. While in many settings, ritual sequences are conventionalized, jubilation is characterized by a kind of eruptive spontaneity quite typical of this game. Although one can expect goals, the moments when goals are scored are usually unexpected. As much as Peter's short hesitation accounts for the decisive role of emotional knowledge, the spontaneity of his and the others' jubilation are also affected by the unexpectedness of the goal.[12] This thesis may seem daring. However, it could be tested by comparing jubilation with other games in which goals can be expected with much more frequency, such as handball.

In order to gauge the intensity of emotion, and the audience's different kinds of involvement, we must consider more than the 'local' momentary situation. The sequence we have been considering occurs when Peter's home team scores a goal. Dramaturgically, it is relevant that this is not just any goal, but the first goal of the game, scored quite late in the match (second half around the 68th minute). This temporal background is quite relevant to the performance of emotion. For example, while the first three goals in the match between Germany and Brazil during the 2014 World Championship had been frenetically applauded by the German fans, the sixth and seventh received more reserved reactions, even by the German players and fans who 'felt', as public discourse had it later, embarrassed for the Brazilians.[13] In the case of football, the sequence of goals enacts a dramaturgy that affects the audience in a rather typical way. The dramaturgy of winning a football game 4–3 after a 0–3 down is quite different from a game won after an early lead. For this reason, we might talk about an *affective dramaturgy*. Note that this temporal order is independent of the formal order of the game, such as its division into two halves.[14] Rather, the order of those events that are ritualized the most, such as goals, are what accounts for the dramaturgy.

Second, due to their numbered order, one might be tempted to produce a game-theoretical model of such an affective dramaturgy, easing the tension and catharsis in football according to the potential scores. In order to assess its affective dynamics, however, one would need to consider an even more extended temporal order. The affective dramaturgy of the score is embedded in the knowledge about the relevance of the game, and about the teams and their relation to one another, their history and their future (i.e. promotion or relegation as a result of the game). Affective dramaturgy is also embedded in the particular discourse history or 'narrative' of the game in question, for instance, 'the classic', the 'scandalous team' and so forth. This knowledge may differ among audience members in a way that is related to their differences in involvement. Yet, because it affects the performance of their respective emotions, we would suggest the notion of affective *frames*.[15] 'Decisive' games such as 'finals', or 'prestige' games against the historical competitor in the same region, for instance, affect the audience quite differently than routine league games do. These affective frames depend on the audience's subjective knowledge, their internal communication and, of course, on public discourses or formalized systems of order by which this knowledge is mediated (e.g., standings and standardized rules of the game in sports; the liturgical year or commandments and interdictions in religion).

Finally, our analysis of jubilation has also indicated the relevance of sociospatial categories. Thus, the plurality of forms of jubilation is typically located in the mixed area in the stadium and differs from terraces of the 'ultras', for instance. Football stadiums and stands, in fact, exhibit a spatial order typical of most agonal games.[16] There is much more at stake than two teams competing against one another for victory. In addition to this, the audience members relate to this order spatially through symbols, emblems and direct involvement. The agonality (Caillois, 1958) is clearly expressed in the spatial distribution of the pitch of one team against another, and as a feature of the audience itself. By means of their bodies, symbols and communicative acts they split up into two opposed parts, often located opposite one another. In addition, the spatial order leaves a rather large part of the audience positioned in between. To the degree that the audience members demonstrate their ritual involvement, the emotional performance tends toward a dual order: while a goal summons jubilation on the part of the winning team's audience, it simultaneously results in very different or even opposite emotional performances on the part of the other team's audience. This, again, is dependent on the dramaturgy at play: whether 'we' have lost the game, whether there is still hope, and so forth.[17]

This agonality plays a most decisive role for the emotional performance. In fact, the ritual involvement of Peter could not be understood if he would not take sides in the agonal order. It affects him so much that he would have performed in a most different way if he had been a fan of the other team. It seems we can suspect a general pattern of the agonal arrangement that affects the audience who follows this order by 'opposing' sets of emotions (Goffman, 1977; Slaby, Mühlhoff, & Wüschner, 2017). Of course, this split is mediated by the referees and by large segments of the audience who may withhold clear signs of ritual involvement, including those who may merely be 'spectators'. In this way, they are demonstrating that involvement is not just a psychological category, but also one of the multifold ways of how to perform as a member of an audience.

Conclusion

For the sake of brevity, we must refrain from an exhaustive review of current debates in video analysis scholarship, and from exploring the impact of recent technological innovations on videographic methods (see (1)). Instead, by way of conclusion, we shall focus our attention on one pending question elicited by our case study: how can we arrive at general findings through videography? As is well known, qualitative research does not aim at generalization by quantifying standardized items. Instead, it consists in specifying, qualifying and typifying. Ordinarily this is often done by the means of words. In audiovisual analysis, however, the items by which phenomena like emotions are specified are themselves either audiovisual or transcriptions of audiovisual content. In this chapter, we have sought to identify some communicative aspects of emotions, using an exemplary audiovisual data of jubilation as our case study. We have substantiated the argument that jubilating can be understood by its relatedness to other audiences, players and the game. The specific form or gestalt depends on the kind of involvement with the audience, the sequential coordination to the agonal event (affective arrangement) as well as on the affective dramaturgy of the aleatory game and the affective framing.

This chapter analyzes audiovisual data collected ethnographically. The analysis focused on the ongoing bodily performance of actors and audiences, which has been analyzed sequentially. Interpreting these simultaneous aspects also entails some ethnographic knowledge of football, of the game and of the stadium – factors we have used to discuss affective dramaturgy and arrangement in this chapter. In order to describe the method with respect to the audiovisuality of the data, we have left out the subjective dimension of emotions, which can only be reconstructed through interviews, autoethnography and phenomenology. In order to focus on the communicative aspect of emotion addressed in the research question sketched here, we also omitted the specific public discourses that are relevant to this game. For an encompassing analysis of affectivity, we would certainly need to account methodically for all three levels: the subjective meaning, the communicative performance and the institutionalized order.

Moreover, we have to concede that all concepts suggested are only based on a single case. Therefore, they are hypothetical concepts in the sense of theoretical sampling in Grounded Theory (Charmaz, 2006). However, the hypotheses we have proposed can be supported, corrected or falsified on the basis of the audiovisual and ethnographic data collected. Furthermore, the data we collected opens pathways to further questions for research. Such research could include, for example, investigating how emotions differ within the same audience, or comparing the effects of different spatial arrangements in the stadium or of different levels of dispersion and concentration among fans. Further research on this question could also consider how fans are affected by different narrative dramaturgies or background knowledge about football, the league or the team.

It is quite clear that the sample of data plays a decisive role for the questions we ask and answer. These questions depend on the focus: for instance, whether we have recordings of the faces, the bodies or collective body formations. They also depend on the extent and quantity of footage recorded, coded and analyzed on our video data sample. Finally, they also depend on the content of the ethnographic sample: are we talking about the audience of one team or are the collected data typical for professional football of some period, area or type? Generalization is not only based on comparisons of the same type, but also on minimal or maximal contrasts. Given the thesis of eruptivity in the affective dramaturgy of football, it might be worth looking for an adequate comparison, such as handball, which sometimes has more than 100 goals per game. The ethnographic sampling strategies we suggest could also allow for questions of a larger scale. In our project, for example, we collected data in audiences of a series of professional football games. We also collected data of religious audiences in similar or sometimes even the same setting. Audiovisual data is a powerful tool for comparative social science research in this regard. It allows one to assess the differences and similarities between the emotional repertoires of religion and sports, for instance, within the very same spatial setting, such as a stadium. Videography of this sort allows us not just to tell but also to 'show' what is meant by religion, sports, audience or emotion in a comparative perspective. Such comparisons may yield promising avenues of research into the broader question of large social fields like sports or religion relate to one another.

Acknowledgments

For comments on the text, we express our gratitude to Margret Lünenburg, Tanja Maier, Kerstin Schankweiler, Hauke Lehmann, Antje Kahl and René Tuma.

Notes

1 Standardized forms of video analysis apply linguistic or numeric codes to more or less large segments of videos, derived from (more or less explicit) theoretical assumptions that follow the deductive-nomothetic model. In recent years, it may even be automatized by means of audiovisual software (Koch & Zumbach, 2002).
2 In addition, videography may use photo and video-elicitation, i.e. interviewing the actors recorded by showing them video recordings of their conduct.
3 Scherer (1994, 27) stresses that there is no evidence "of basic or fundamental emotions as independent or integral biological or psychological categories".
4 The relational understanding of affect shared in this volume as reciprocal transformation of a body in relation to another body in a physical and meaningful (imaginary,

symbolic) way (Seyfert, 2012) is implied in our notion of communication as recipro-
cally embodied performance (Knoblauch, 2017), which is the starting point of our
empirical analysis.

5   It is this embodied performance that we call communicative action (Knoblauch, 2017).
As a form of action, we would also need to consider the subjective meanings which
could be assessed by interviews, autoethnography etc. For the sake of brevity, here we
focus on the video analysis.

6   Sophisticated software (such as Dartfish) increasingly allow one to create visual code-
books with video samples, and to simply insert drawings and highlight relevant movements directly in the video. NVivo, ATLAS.ti, HyperRESEARCH and Transana allow
one to code video 'on the fly'.

7   The popularity of this perspective is quite obvious in mass media, in which the emotionality of large audiences is regularly identified with close-up shots of individual
bodies or faces (Adelmann, Keilbach, & Stauff, 2001).

8   The three sources of knowledge correspond to three methods, which are favored in
different methodologies: hermeneutics, semiotics and ethnography (Knoblauch &
Schnettler, 2012).

9   The video was recorded on 28 August 2016 during a game between Hertha BSC and
SC Freiburg. Michael, who has been participating in the audience, recorded it.

10 After his election, Pope Benedict XVI initiated the first sequences of this sign of triumph
on the balcony of the Apostolic Palace, which he, however, quickly smoothed down.

11 Moves correspond to the 'turn' in conversation analysis, but refer to visible instead of
only acoustic phenomena. On the methodology of sequential analysis see Knoblauch,
Tuma and Schnettler (2014, 91–93ff.).

12 Expectations towards the game are, of course, dependent on knowledge about the
game. As Michael has observed, members of the audience, which do not share knowledge of the game, do not only find it much less "dramatic". They will not be affected by
it and will find it boring, even if they shared some emotional knowledge. On emotional
knowledge, see Knoblauch and Herbrik, 2014.

13 Compared to the field of religion, the like of such an important dramaturgical 'non-
local' background was observed at the papal visit in Berlin in 2011. The fact that Pope
Benedict XVI was the first German pope in 600 years amplified the medial discourses
of "Wir sind Papst" and therefore the celebritization of "Ratze", which affected the
frenetic jubilation at his arrival in the Olympic Stadium of Berlin.

14 One can compare this affectivity to the dramaturgy in films, where suspense, for example, can intensify emotions. Emotions in film audiences, in sports, are much more
invisible and disciplined, as their emotions are subjected to feelings (Kappelhoff &
Bakels, 2011).

15 We draw here on Goffman (1974).

16 In religious events it is remarkable that the typical spatial order of churches is reproduced in other settings, as for example stadiums.

17 Fans may counter the expected displays of emotion by 'strategic' performances which
are typically routinized or conventionalized by parts of the audience, e.g. cheering for
the loosing team 'in order' to motivate them, or sarcastic jubilation for the scoring team.

References

Adelmann, R, Keilbach, J & Stauff, M 2001, ' "Soviel Gefühle kann's nicht geben!": Typ-
isierung des Feierns und Jubelns im Fernsehsport', *Montage AV*, vol. 10, no. 2, pp. 43–57.
Bavelas, J & Chovil, N 1997, 'Faces in dialogue', in JA Russel & JM Fernandez-Dols
(eds.), *The Psychology of Facial Expression*, pp. 334–346, Cambridge University Press,
Cambridge.

Caillois, R 1958, *Les jeux et les hommes*, Librairie Gallimard, Paris.

Charmaz, K 2006, *Constructing Grounded Theory: A Practical Guide Through Qualitative Analysis*, Sage Publications, London.

Collins, R 2004, *Interaction Ritual Chains*, Princeton University Press, Princeton.

Ekman, P 1972, *Emotion in the Human Face. Guidelines for Research and Integration of Findings*, Pergamon, New York.

Erickson, F 1982, 'Classroom discourse as improvisation: Relationships between academic task structure and social participation structure in lessons', in LC Wilkinson (ed.), *Communicating in the Classroom*, pp. 153–181, Academic Press, New York.

Erickson, F 2005, 'Ethnographic description', in U von Ammon, N Dittmar, KJ Mattheier & P Trudgill (eds.), *Sociolinguistics. An International Handbook of the Science of Language and Society*, vol. 2, pp. 1197–1212, De Gruyter Mouton, Berlin, New York.

Erickson, F & Shultz, J 1982, *The Counselor as Gatekeeper: Social Interaction in Interviews*, Academic Press, New York.

Gibbs, A 2011, 'Affect theory and audience', in V Nightingale (ed.), *The Handbook of Media Studies*, pp. 251–266, Wiley-Blackwell, London.

Gottman, E 1956, *The Presentation of Self in Everyday Life*, unpublished dissertation. University of Edinburgh.

Goffman, E 1966, *Behavior in Public Places*, The Free Press, New York.

Goffman, E 1974, *Frame Analysis. An Essay on the Organization of Experience*, Northeastern University Press, Boston.

Goffman, E 1977, 'The arrangement between the sexes', *Theory and Society*, vol. 4, no. 3, pp. 301–331.

Goffman, E 1981, 'Footing', in ibid. (ed.), *Forms of Talk*, pp. 124–159, University of Pennsylvania Press, Philadelphia.

Goffman, E 2010, *Relations in Public. Microstudies of the Public Order*, Transaction Publishers, New Brunswick, London.

Goldman, R, Pea, R, Barron, B & Derry, SJ 2007, *Video Research in the Learning Sciences*, Routledge, New York.

Goodwin, C 1980, 'Restarts, pauses, and the achievement of a state of Mutual Gaze at turn-beginning', *Sociological Inquiry*, vol. 50, no. 3–4, pp. 272–302.

Goodwin, MH & Goodwin, C 2000, 'Emotion within situated activity', in A Duranti (ed.), *Linguistic Anthropology: A Reader*, pp. 239–257, Wiley-Blackwell, Malden, MA.

Harré, R 1986, *The Social Construction of Emotions*, Basil Blackwell, Oxford.

Heath, C 1986, *Body Movement and Speech in Medical Interaction*, Cambridge University Press, Cambridge.

Heath, C 1997, 'Video and sociology: The material and interactional organization of social action in naturally occurring settings', *Champs Visuels*, vol. 6, pp. 37–46.

Heath, C, Hindmarsh, J & Luff, P 2010, *Video in Qualitative Research*, Sage Publications, London.

Hochschild, AR 1979, 'Emotion work, feeling rules, and social structure', *American Journal of Sociology*, vol. 85, no. 3, pp. 551–575.

James, W 1890, *The Principles of Psychology*, Henry Holt, New York.

Jefferson, G 2004, 'Glossary of Transcript symbols with an introduction', in CH Lemer (ed.), *Conversation Analysis: Studies from the First-Generation*, pp. 13–23, John Benjamins, Philadelphia.

Kappelhoff, H & Bakels, JH 2011, 'Das Zuschauergefühl – Möglichkeiten qualitativer Medien-analyse', *Zeitschrift für Medienwissenschaft*, vol. 5, no. 2, pp. 78–96.

Kissmann, UT 2009, *Video Interaction Analysis: Methods and Methodology*, Peter Lang, Frankfurt am Main.

Knoblauch, H 2006, 'Videography. Focused ethnography and video analysis', in H Knoblauch, B Schnettler, J Raab & HG Soeffner (eds.), *Video Analysis: Methodology and Methods. Qualitative audiovisual Data Analysis in Sociology*, pp. 35–50, Peter Lang, Frankfurt am Main.

Knoblauch, H 2011a, 'Videography', in M Stausberg & S Engler (eds.), *The Routledge Handbook of Research Methods in the Study of Religion*, pp. 433–444, Routledge, London.

Knoblauch, H 2011b, 'Videoanalyse, Videointeraktionsanalyse und Videographie – zur Klärung einiger Missverständnisse', *Sozialer Sinn*, vol. 12, no. 1, pp. 139–145.

Knoblauch, H 2017, *Die kommunikative Konstruktion der Wirklichkeit*, Springer VS, Wiesbaden.

Knoblauch, H & Schnettler, B 2012, 'Videography: Analyzing video data as a "Focused" ethnographic and hermeneutical exercise', *Qualitative Research*, vol. 12, no. 3, pp. 334–356.

Knoblauch, H & Herbrik, R 2014, 'Emotional knowledge, emotional styles and knowledge', in C von Scheve & M Salmela (eds.), *Collective Emotions*, pp. 356–371, Oxford University Press, Oxford.

Knoblauch, H, Tuma, R & Schnettler, B 2014, *Videography. Introduction to Interpretive Video-analysis of Social Interactions*, Peter Lang, Frankfurt am Main, Bern, Bruxelles, New York, Oxford, Warszawa, Wien.

Knudsen, BT & Stage, C 2015, 'Introduction: Affective methodologies', in BT Knudsen & C Stage (eds.), *Affective Methodologies. Developing Cultural Research Strategies for the Study of Affect*, pp. 1–21, Palgrave Macmillan, Hampshire, New York.

Koch, SC & Zumbach, J 2002, 'The use of video analysis software in behavior observation research: Interaction patterns of task-oriented small groups', *Forum Qualitative Sozialforschung*, vol. 3, no. 2, Art. 18. Available from: http://dx.doi.org/10.17169/fqs-3.2.857. [20 July 2018].

Lomax, H & Casey, N 1998, 'Recording social life: Reflexivity and video methodology', *Sociological Research Online*, vol. 3, no. 2. Available from: www.socresonline.org.uk/3/2/1.html [24 July 2018].

Lutz, C & White, GM 1986, 'The anthropology of emotions', *Annual Review of Anthropology*, vol. 15, pp. 405–436.

Morris, D 1981, *The Soccer Tribe*, Jonathan Cape, London.

Müller, C, Cienki, A, Fricke, E, Ladewig, SH, McNeill, D & Teßendorf, S 2013, *Body – Language – Communication. An International Handbook on Multimodality in Human Interaction*, vol. 1, De Gruyter Mouton, Berlin, Boston.

Peräkylä, A 2012, 'Epilogue: What does the study of interaction offer to emotion research?' in A Peräkylä & ML Sorjonen (eds.), *Emotion in Interaction*, pp. 274–289, Oxford University Press, Oxford.

Reichert, R 2007, *Im Kino der Humanwissenschaften. Studien zur Medialisierung wissenschaftlichen Wissens*, Transcript Verlag, Bielefeld.

Scherer, KR 1994, 'Toward a concept of "Modal Emotions"', in P Ekman & RJ Davidson (eds.), *The Nature of Emotion. Fundamental Questions*, pp. 25–31, Oxford University Press, New York.

Schutz, A 1962, 'Common sense and scientific interpretation of human action', in A Schutz (ed.), *Collected Papers*, pp. 3–47, I. Nijhoff, The Hague.

Seyfert, R 2012, 'Beyond personal feelings and collective emotions: A theory of social affect', *Theory, Culture & Society*, vol. 29, no. 6, pp. 27–46.

Slaby, J, Mühlhoff, R & Wüschner, P 2017, 'Affective arrangements', *Emotion Review*. Available from: https://doi.org/10.1177/1754073917722214. [20 July 2018].

Tuma, R, Schnettler, B & Knoblauch, H 2013, *Videographie: Einführung in die interpretative Videoanalyse sozialer Situationen*, Springer VS, Wiesbaden.

van Gennep, A 1986, Übergangsriten (*Les rites de passage*), Campus Verlag, Frankfurt am Main, New York.

Part III

Performativities

Chapter 10

Investigating affective media practices in a transnational setting

Ingrid Kummels and Thomas John

Introduction to the setting: a transnational indigenous community between Mexico and the US

This case study explores the affective media practices of people who live in the Zapotec village of Yalálag in Mexico, and of those who migrated from Yalálag to Los Angeles, California. Taking a media anthropology perspective, we propose that the mediatization of social relations and its affective dimensions are key for processes of transnational community building.[1] We contend that actors living in Mexico and the US rely on affective media practices to create a 'home' that connects them physically or virtually to multiple places, among them the Mexican community of origin.[2] That certain groups of migrants engage in community building on both sides of the international border is by no means a given process. Our project therefore strives for insight into the ways media practices enable Zapotec people to fashion a relationship to several places of belonging simultaneously, when experiencing or provoking affects related to joy, pride, envy, or hate that they associate with the places in question. It also examines their ability to generate what media scholars call a "co-presence" by connecting people living at various localities, and the extent to which such practices foster their integration into their new country of residence in terms of political participation, social protection, and citizenship.

Yalaltecs who immigrated since 9/11 do not have permanent resident status in the United States, and their risk of being deported has increased under the Trump administration. For these illegalized immigrants, the use of digital media is critical to staying in touch with their relatives and friends in the Mexican village of origin, and they resort to patron saint fiestas as a primary means of fostering transnational social relations. Such fiestas in honor of a Catholic saint have been celebrated in Yalálag since the Colonial era. Starting in the mid-1980s, migrants also began to host these fiestas (called *kermesses*) in Los Angeles, which include performance of Zapotec dances to raise funds for the village of origin. Professional mediamakers who operate commercial video enterprises regularly document the fiestas either in Yalálag or Los Angeles. They often focus on recording Zapotec dances like *La danza de los Negritos* in their fiesta videos, especially when there are innovative aspects to the performances. In addition, Facebook has become the most popular forum for the transnational villagers to socialize with relatives and friends living far away. Ordinary persons therefore engage in taking photographs – whether with a mobile phone or professional single-lens camera – recording digital video, posting images, and commenting on social media like Facebook and YouTube (see Kummels, 2017a). When such users document highlights of their life and work on personal Facebook pages, they often use pictures depicting themselves and relatives engaging in fiestas as community affairs. An important dimension of exchanging and reproducing Zapotec culture in a transcultural setting therefore unfolds through these diverse media practices that become sites of relational affective dynamics.

Affective media practices as a methodological approach

To explore the emotive aspects of socializing and exchanging Zapotec culture while carrying out ethnographic research in this transnational setting, we conceptualized our object of investigation as affective media practices. We began as a two-person team in 2016 in Yalálag, and later one of us followed up in Los Angeles.[3] We were able to build on current theories of media practices as well as of affective practices. When asking ourselves how sites of affective dynamics should be discerned and which criteria should be used to make those decisions, we paid attention to media practices, that is, to "what people do and say in relation to media" (Couldry, 2004). We conceive such practices as encompassing a broad range of communicative devices, beginning with engagement in the corporeal medium of dance and leading up to interactive social media practices. For the sphere of indigenous people's media, these practices are particularly relevant. Despite their marginalized position, these indigenous actors have opened up new media spaces in a geographical, practice-oriented, and imagined sense, for the most part on their own initiative and with great vitality (Kummels, 2017a, 7). The concept of affects, on the other hand, refers to experiences of intensity when perceiving new differences in contrast to what existed before. Affects are distinguished from emotions as culturally shaped conceptualizations systemized in emotion repertoires (SFB Affective Societies, 2016, 3–5). Yet affective dynamics are often hard to recognize during their evolution, and actors' subsequent interpretations proved crucial in deciphering them. In conversations, our interlocutors emphasized how they experienced Zapotec dance practices and their dissemination via video and social media as a communicative space in which they often 'get into a bigger conversation'. They then experience acutely how they and other persons are 'affected' in the course of interaction.

Combining the concepts of practice and affect has the advantage of allowing for the identification of a broad range of affective phenomena, beginning with those involved in actors' routines, affects which cannot be controlled, and extending to affects that are strategically provoked by actors with the aim of "doing affects" when engaging in media communication (Kummels, 2017b, 135).[4] In other words, affects then emerge from intentional acts of management. Many of our interlocutors reflected on such affective media practices intensively and shaped them consciously because their routines in the United States had been disrupted as a result of their former mobility and present immobility with regard to Mexico. They described affects in terms of place, of a newly perceived intensity of 'being here' and 'not being able to be there' and therefore engaging in efforts of bridging geographical distance by using digital media for generating a form of 'co-presence' (see Madianou, 2016). Many of their media practices were geared toward generating affects to create a sense of being at home in various places, such as their community of origin, their current place of residence, and some other place they had left behind (see Moores, 2012, 54). Moods in general are selectively managed by choosing emblematic spaces and consuming music and photographs to this end (Scheer, 2012, 209). Rooms, buildings, and objects can be explicitly conceptualized to provoke feelings such as reverence or admiration, and therefore become "affect generators" (Reckwitz, 2015, 41–45). We transferred these ideas to the performative practices of Zapotec dance on-site, and its current mediatization and transnational circulation through video and social media.

The actors in the present case study availed themselves of existing and novel media to create a form of 'co-presence' with the dancers' undocumented parents in Los Angeles who were unable to travel to the Zapotec dance performance in the Mexican village of Yalálag. Media actors – ranging from ordinary persons who engage in media to professional mediamakers – often establish social relationships by sharing an important event taking place at the location they are currently visiting with people physically far away. Zapotec interlocutors called these practices of generating 'co-presence' through digital means of communication in both countries "*armar la historia*", that is, to "piece together a story" or produce a narrative through media.[5] Such practitioners concentrate at "media stations" (Postill, 2010, 12) at which many media practices intersect, and where affective dynamics might therefore intensify. In our case study (see the next section), the venues of the Los Angeles female dance group Nueva Generación Krus Yonn turned out to be media stations. At these stations, we were able to identify key actors "doing affects" as they recorded the dancers audiovisually and/or commented on them to position themselves with the ensuing transnational debates.

At a theoretical level, we needed to consider that the increasing management of social relations via new communication technology also transforms the quality of affects themselves. In our case study, the immobilization caused by restrictive US immigration policy meant that migrants relied on medialization to create a 'co-presence' with family and friends. Actors in general adapt their "feeling rules" and emotions to mediatize these forms of social interaction (Berg, 2015, 123; Madianou, 2016, 196–198). Media scholars suggest that the ubiquity and speed of current networked technology may be modifying the temporality ascribed to emotions. For example, emojis have emerged as a means of communicating and

performing emotions digitally, since their catchy presentations and facile circulation allow global networked communities to rapidly share and react to them (see
contributions in Prieto-Blanco & Schreiber, 2016). In the transnational migration setting, nostalgia has acquired a new "digital" or "productive" quality geared
toward shaping the future (Mejía Estevez, 2009; Kummels, 2017b). With regard
to the present case study, we ask why actors seek to anchor interrelational affects
to multiple places. We propose that they may be resignifying existing emotions
and transculturalizing emotion repertoires when mediatizing Zapotec dances and
culture via video and social media.

An event-centered case study: mediatizing Zapotec dance culture and "Doing Affects" between Oaxaca and California

In July 2016, we concentrated on pursuing our research questions with regard to
the annual patron saint fiesta in honor of Santiago El Mayor Apóstol in Yalálag.
Here, as usual, traditional dances were performed all day long on two consecutive Sundays. However, at this fiesta a controversial premiere took place that
was anything but typical. The female dance group Nueva Generación Krus Yonn
had arrived from Los Angeles only a few days before. For the first time, young
women between 13 and 19 years old publicly performed the sacred *La danza de
los Negritos* – traditionally reserved for men – in front of the Santiago chapel.
The young dancers were born in Los Angeles. Their parents are Yalaltecs who, for
years, have been living in the California mega-city, most of them without documents. Their performance triggered discussions at multiple fora on-site in Yalálag
and Los Angeles, and within a transnational media space between Mexico and
the US. As part of these debates, images and videos of the young women and
their pioneer dance performance were recorded and posted online. In face-to-face
conversations in Yalálag and Los Angeles, as well as in phone calls or chats on
social media like Facebook, the following issues were debated: Should young
women be doing this dance, especially young women who were not born in their
parents' village of origin? What was the quality of their performance? Was this
version 'authentically Zapotec'? Should it be assessed positively or negatively by
the transnational community of Yalálag, and what indeed should Zapotec culture
consist of in the future?

During the first week of the patron saint fiesta, we sought to identify which
actors were participating in the dance performance, what media practices they
were applying, and what the results might be for transnational community building. Relying on George Marcus' (1995) mobile ethnographic approach, we first
'followed' the appearance and the respective debate it triggered. Our first insights
were based on participant observation and conversation on-site. Nevertheless, we
had to apply several methodological layers, sometimes simultaneously, to be able
to trace the affective dynamics from the perspective of different actors in two
countries implementing diverse media practices. This is illustrated in the following chart (see Table 10.1).

Table 10.1 Methodological layers of investigating affective media practices.

	Ethnographic research method	Techniques of recording and empirical material	Analysis method	Problems, restrictions
First layer	Conducting participant observation of affective media practices; informal "go along" conversations about these practices at media stations	Memory minutes	Reconstructing and detailing to obtain a "thick description" (Geertz, 1973) on the one hand and formulation of argumentative nuclei on the other hand (Elwert, 2002)	Recognizing practices actors consider relevant requires acquiring enough everyday contextual knowledge (Orientierungswissen; Elwert, 2002)
Second layer	Studying audiences' reception and viewing actors' videos, i.e., patron saint fiesta videos and individual Facebook pages	Memory minutes, recording interviews and acquisition of audiovisual material from the actors; collection of downloads and screenshots from Facebook and YouTube	Media anthropological audience studies; analysis of contents and aesthetics based on audiovisual material	Attaining access to "natural situations" of audiences viewing actors' videos and to the producers' and viewers' exegesis of them
Third layer	Producing and viewing researchers' videos	Making one's own recordings with a camcorder or single-lens camera	Analysis of contents and aesthetics of researchers' videos based on images and texts	The researchers' presence and act of recording influence the discussion and the affective dynamics produced
Fourth layer	Conducting eliciting interviews about affective media practices in Yalálag and Los Angeles via the interviewee's exegesis of his or her Facebook page	Recording interviews with audio equipment (camcorder or single-lens camera), for example, recording an interviewee using his or her Facebook page	Coding and textual analysis of the transcribed interviews based on grounded theory (Glaser & Strauss, 1967)	Adopting multilingual access (Zapotec, Spanish, English) toward affective phenomena; using a Zapotec language consultant

First layer

Let us start off with the first layer. A vital dimension of ethnographic research consisted in acquiring everyday contextual knowledge (called *Orientierungswissen* in German) of the Yalaltec transnational community. This knowledge guides action and encompasses affective dimensions such as "hopes and fears" as Georg Elwert emphasized (2002, 5, footnote 3). First insights came from 'go along' conversations, that is, accompanying particular persons who, for different reasons, are interested in the dances during the fiesta. As a result of these insights, during this research period we realized that dance events and the medium of Zapotec dances are important dimensions of (re)creating community and Zapotec culture. In this field, affects are negotiated as they unfold, and existing emotion repertoires are reproduced, challenged, or altered. To summarize our findings, Yalaltecs charge sacred dances (*danzas sagradas*) affectively when describing them as part of the patrimony of their village of origin since time immemorial, and in expressing fears that their dances could be copied and distorted.[6] Emotions (*sentimientos*) are intentionally embodied in Zapotec dances. Parodic dances, called *danzas chuscas*, make fun of (*burlarse, parodiar, ridiculizar*) neighboring ethnic groups (see also Cruz-Manjarrez, 2013, 153–189).[7] In addition, dancers parody the deviations of certain members of the Yalaltec community from existing norms – for example, in attire, morality, marital status, or business practices. Research in Los Angeles showed that transcultural migrants have recently enacted their realities and aspirational dreams by embodying US superhero figures like Spider-Man (see also Peña, 2017). Zapotec dances therefore can be conceptualized as "affect generators" that oscillate between vilification and utopian fantasy. This further underscores the traditional and ongoing role of dance groups as traditional instruments of politics. In the village of origin, four neighborhoods compete by upholding their own patron saints, brass bands, and dance groups with the goal of attracting the largest audience and of collecting funds for specific community projects. The Los Angeles satellite community has also adopted this pattern of neighborhood organization, including its form of competition and brisk culture of factional debate. Yalaltecs consider the basic affective approach of their transnationalized community as "being forthcoming" (*"somos comunicativos"*). This has both positive and negative connotations, since at times the debate around community issues has turned aggressive. Yalaltec actors differ according to age, education, media use, media literacy, social class, migration generation, place of residence, and immigration status even within the family. Dissent is negotiated face-to-face and screen-to-screen, particularly between Yalálag and Los Angeles.

Conducting participant observation initially allowed us to develop a sense of awareness that the dance group's performance evolved in the midst of great tension. To calm the spirits, no mention of Krus Yonn's appearance was made in the circuit of self-fashioned media at first. In subsequent conversations, the degree of acceptance we heard about the premiere depended on varying intersections of age, gender, education, migration experience, place of residence, occupation, and political orientation. While some male *maestros de danza* in Yalálag assessed the women's performance as a deliberate provocation and even as an offensive parody, female supporters of the dance group celebrated it as a renewal of Zapotec culture within a transnationalized Oaxacalifornia.[8]

We then purposely focused participant observation on the appearance of the dance group in Yalálag. This allowed us to identify how key media actors clustered at two media stations. The first consisted of the village's main street and its town hall. This media station was noteworthy for its orderly, almost routine course of events. The female dance group was welcomed by an official representative of the village. After parading down the street, the dancers entered the town hall, where the mayor received them and delivered a speech in their honor. This type of reception, which was formerly reserved for delegations from neighboring villages, has become routine nowadays whenever brass bands and dance groups come to visit from Yalálag's own satellite communities. The arrival message of one of the dancers and the reception speeches of Yalálag's officials were all delivered in a serious, respectful, and ceremonial manner. The reception ceremony was also systematically recorded on video – a routine procedure at comparable events. The local videographer Pancho Limeta has specialized in such recordings with his business Pancho Video. As a pioneer videographer in Yalálag, he is a key media actor. While engaged in the left-wing Grupo Comunitario movement in the 1980s, he appropriated film for political purposes. But in the course of migrating to the US, Yalaltec viewers began shifting their interests and resources to religious fiestas, also financed by migrants.[9] Their urge to disseminate their own cultural manifestations within the transnational audience motivated villagers to appropriate video as a media technology in the first place. At media station 1, we realized that Pancho's mere presence recording the reception lent the female dance group the recognition it had sought.

Media station 2 was the dance venue in front of the chapel of Santiago. On Sunday of the so-called Octava[10] of the patron saint fiesta, more than a dozen of those present diligently recorded the many dances, either with mobile phones or with professional single-lens cameras. In this case, film practices added to the tension. During informal conversations on-site, we learned that these recordings were controversial within the community, since many fear that particular dances might be copied and 'stolen'. Lisvelia, the dance group leader, engaged in an innovative media practice. She may have been the first to transmit a performance in Yalálag via iPhone using FaceTime, an application that transmits live video conference-style. By using the wireless LAN of the nearby hospital, she created a transnational screen-to-screen forum. During the 20-minute transmission, the newness of the method as well as the novelty of the performance itself were commented on, particularly by the mothers, aunts, and godmothers of the dancers – that is, mainly by women. We captured these text comments in one of our researchers' videos. In addition, they are documented on Lisvelia's Facebook page. The users thanked Lisvelia and the dance instructor. They congratulated the dancers, expressing pride in their female protagonism ("A proud moment for us women!!"). They expressed "joy" (*alegría*) at being able to view their daughters dancing. The affective mini-icons of emojis were also applied, especially clapping hands. Through these media practices and "doing affects" at this precise moment, Yalaltec women of two generations created a co-presence with regard to the dance performance, which intentionally had been anchored in the village of origin to enhance its authenticity within Zapotec culture.

Second layer

Later we analyzed how videographer Pancho's images of the reception ceremony and the performance constructed these events as integral to the patron saint fiesta of the village of origin. They appeared in the main video, documenting the patron saint fiesta, which consequently circulated through on-site sales of the DVD, parcel service to the United States, and on his business Facebook page. Both media forms have become an essential part of the transnational village's 'official' representation. In addition, the dance group leader had specifically asked Pancho to record a DVD, which she promised would be financially rewarding since each dancer would buy one. The almost two-hour-long video he produced, "Los Negritos dance performed by young ladies living in Los Ángeles California", captures the normative emotion repertoire of "the ceremonious" (*lo ceremonioso*). A film aesthetic and content analysis, as well as an interview with Pancho and his clients, provided initial information as to how the Yalaltecs conceptualize these videos as a village film genre. As Pancho explained, he caters to clients who "do not want a documentary".[11] They expect videos to virtually represent 'reality' – that is, the viewer's perception of reality – and to do so in real time to the extent possible, therefore with little editing. Since a sacred character is attributed to *La danza de los Negritos*, clients expect both a performance and an audiovisual representation that conveys these qualities. In turn, these characteristics are associated with emotions such as the joy of life experienced when dancing. Pancho focused on capturing all eight dancers with a rigid camera perspective – never foregrounding a particular dancer – since the consumer's main desire is to be able to assess the quality of the dance as if on-site. Specifically, viewers want to evaluate the execution of the quadrille-like dance choreography and the precision of hopping steps called *puntillas*. On the emotive level, their appraisal requires the representation of the dancer's entire body within the larger choreography to be able to assess the joy and energy that a dance is thought to produce. The dances are fashioned via the rigid camera perspective, the camera angle, the length of the recordings, as well as the interplay of dance and music to an overall narrative of "the ceremonial". In this regard, dance and sentiment are conceptualized as closely connected to place. According to Zapotec religious beliefs, the earth is the prime natural force, and the dancer's relation to the earth is crucial to receiving this energy.[12] Female incursion into the former male-dominated realm therefore means that women acquire a right "to feel and live by dancing".[13] Pancho designed the visual language of the video around this emotion repertoire and its expressions, which the Yalaltecs look for and judge in dance performances on-site and in their digital media forms.

Photographs and film clips were circulated during and after the event on the Facebook pages of the dance group leader and the mothers of the dancers. These Facebook photos and video clips differed from Pancho's inclusive and harmonious portrayal of the Los Angeles female dance group participation. Instead, they conveyed a picture of a group of young women who need to surmount obstacles – even within their own transnational community – to achieve gender empowerment. The mothers of the dancers – including the leader, whose own daughter is a member of the group – created family-style albums on their Facebook pages, which they filled with photographs of their daughters performing. In their comments, most wrote that their daughter's participation was a way to empower women. One mother stressed that her daughter should not let anything hold her back. At the same time, these media actors also anchored the dancers to place, both to the village of origin and to Los Angeles. For example, the dance group leader combined two photos of her daughter as a dancer and a musician with a genealogy that ties her to her grandparents in Yalalag. In the accompanying text she underscores that her daughter is a second-generation Yalalteca in Los Angeles who is also proud of her roots in the village of Yalálag.[14] Through the generational gap addressed indirectly in this comment and the obstacles mentioned by other mothers, the dance is not only reinterpreted with regard to gender hierarchies in the home village, but is also resignified in the context of the specific affective meanings attributed to race and ethnicity in Los Angeles. The descendants of the migrants from Oaxaca began to consider performing "indigenous dances", as one youth called them, as a source of pride only 10 or 15 years ago.[15] Zapotec dance representations on Facebook pages are used to express intimate dimensions of human experience such as affects related to pride versus shame. Meanwhile, these affects are enmeshed within larger economic and political processes. Along with other scholars, we therefore conceptualize them as part of an "affective economy" (see Ahmed, 2004; Berg, 2015, 137). The circulation of Zapotec dances through video and social media both produces and reflects this entanglement of affect, economy, and politics. The affective media practices concerning the dances at fiestas and *kermesses*, for example, intersect with the school education of children and youth and the occupations of adults, as we will see in the following section. The ability to navigate these interconnected areas with the help of digital communication has become crucial for actors' cultural, social, and economic life in a transnational setting.

Third layer

Let us briefly proceed to the third methodological layer, which concerns researchers recording events and interviews with a camera. Engaging in this kind of media practice always entails influencing decisively the actors and environment being investigated. It is therefore not a simple means of documentation, but instead triggers a new 'filmic reality'. This may sometimes be desirable, for example, when researchers want to collaborate with subjects more closely. In this case, the leader of the dance group and several other parents enthusiastically accepted our request for an interview and permission to film, as they were keen on promoting the event. The leader then chose the setting where she and the eight dancers would be interviewed as a group. Nevertheless, to everybody's surprise, our researchers' video generated an unexpected insight into the affects aroused by the performance. In this group interview, the young dancers only briefly commented on their female pioneer role and the need to overcome the reservations of the 'patriarchal' society of origin.[16] They suddenly seemed overwhelmed by feelings of frustration as a result of their parents' inability to attend the performance because of their immigration status. Some of the young women began to cry. At the same time, they alluded to the intergenerational frictions they experience at home in Los Angeles. Telling their stories before our camera and to us – an audience outside their community – therefore triggered these kinds of uncontrolled affects.

Fourth layer

The last methodological layer of eliciting interviews on affective media practices face-to-face in Yalálag and Los Angeles offered further insights into the complexity of the affective media dynamics involved with the dance performance. These offline narratives transcend and complement the discourse that dominated social media. They thus constructed the dance performance as an act of gender empowerment vis-à-vis the community of origin's 'outdated' gender structure and as a moment of triumph and joy. In these interviews, we systematically traced the motivations, intentions, and development of media practices from actors' divergent perspectives. After transcription, they were analyzed on the basis of Grounded Theory (Glaser & Strauss, 1967). We applied theoretically informed qualitative coding to identify and interpret actors' implicit and explicit emic concepts regarding affectivity.[17] Their multilingual skills posed a particular challenge for our interpretations. Yalaltec people who do not speak but understand the Zapotec language may nevertheless refer to emotions coded in that language. Emic concepts expressed in Spanish and English therefore require profound knowledge of Zapotec culture and language. We regularly consulted a local expert with regard to these language skills that we lacked.[18]

An example relevant to the following interview analysis is our consultant's explanation of the word "heart". The term "heart", or *lhall* in Zapotec, refers to what Zapotec people consider the source and generator of all kinds of affects. Zapotec actors usually describe the heart as an agent and a trigger for an array of feelings, referring, for example, to a heart that 'shrinks' and provokes sadness, or one that 'opens itself' and generates joy.[19] In Zapotec thought, volition requires close coordination of heart and mind to be able to make a good decision. We therefore converted emic concepts such as those coded as "the heart" into researchers' concepts, such as those concerning practices of "doing affects" in the transnational community. As a result of this analysis, we determined that social status and political power do not only depend on age, education, migration experience, social class, or indigenous ethnicity, but also – and quite importantly – on savviness with respect to affective media practices. Integrative community initiatives in a transnational setting and their effectiveness require this kind of expertise.

The perspectives of parents of the female dancers were juxtaposed and compared with those of the dance group leader. The former share an illegalized status and a working-class background as employees in restaurants and housekeepers. Interviews revealed how they urged their children to practice Zapotec dances as an educational strategy that ties them both to the Mexican village of origin and to Los Angeles, in order to get ahead in the United States ("*salir adelante*").[20] The parents of a 19-year-old dancer promote their children's participation in Zapotec dance groups to socialize them according to values they attribute to the village of origin, but which they have in fact reformulated in the US setting. These values are negotiated against the backdrop of a generational gap within their family, which has a mixed immigration status. The relationship between immigrant parents and children who have been socialized in the US is affected by the racial hierarchy of their new country. The parents commented on how during adolescence their US-born daughter distanced herself from them by discriminating against their village of origin, referring to it as "your (backward) *rancho*", and questioning their authority. Yet the parents unexpectedly triggered a turn from shame to pride when they sent their then 14-year-old daughter to Yalálag during her vacation as punishment.[21] To their great surprise she returned with new admiration for Yalaltec culture. The parents then supported her participation in Zapotec dance, since it is promoted by the US school system as an extracurricular sport and therefore conducive to a career and social ascent.

As for the dance group leader, she was born in Los Angeles and is a first-generation[22] Yalaltec-American with a high school education who works in an office. In an interview, Lisvelia talked about the dance initiative as a project with a political dimension that was also intended as a form of modernizing Yalaltec culture in a transnational setting. Accordingly, she planned Nueva Generación Krus Yonn's first appearance very strategically, focusing on making an impression on the village of origin and its 'outdated' gender structure. She followed up on other initiatives involving female appropriation of formerly all-male dances. Such initiatives are booming in the context of transnational community building. Since 2014, girls whose parents migrated from villages neighboring Yalálag and formed satellite communities in Los Angeles, have been performing all-female versions of *La danza de los Negritos*. The dancers from Yalaltec families were also keen on proving that this is not solely a "man's *danza*". Therefore, the name of the dance was feminized and renamed *La danza de las Negritas* in the program of events.[23] According to Lisvelia, this triggered a machista revolt prior to the performance. Some Zapotec men in Los Angeles scoffed that women performing ritual dances would move the wrong part of their bodies: their "boobs". The women were just as harsh, chiding that dancing would impair the girls' reproductive capacity.[24] Meanwhile, there were obstacles to be tackled in Los Angeles, beginning with finding a Zapotec dance instructor willing to teach the men's dance to girls. Nevertheless, she persevered. The dance group was created and began training for this one appearance in Yalálag. Performing in Los Angeles was considered a secondary goal.

Interviewing Lisvelia while she was engrossed in her affective media practices proved to be particularly illuminating about her strategies. Our conversation took place at her PC while she was logged onto her Facebook page.[25] We did not merely speak about the events represented in images, film clips, and commentaries archived there. Instead, these materials elicited Lisvelia's explanations of how and why she had deliberately used media practices to advance political initiatives through Zapotec culture, negotiating the future of this culture for a transnationalized community. Since 2009, the dance group leader has maintained a personal Facebook page, where she has uploaded more than 1,000 video clips that have been seen by as many as 2,000 users at a time. Since she first began posting, Lisvelia has perfected her skills to fashion an attractive Facebook page, including novelties such as FaceTime and Facebook Live transmissions. Based on her practices, the time invested in them, and the expertise acquired by executing and improving their effectiveness, she can be characterized as an "ethnic influencer" (Kummels, n.d.).[26]

During Ingrid's interview with her, some of Lisvelia's Facebook practices pointed to a number of ambivalent affects that were triggered by the co-presence between people participating in the dance performance and their relatives living in Los Angeles. Lisvelia would open the photo albums and videos and click on those she particularly cherished, such as the live transmission from the female dance performance in Yalálag. She lamented, "it broke my heart" that none of the other dancers' mothers were able to be present. Yet this feeling inspired her to record a fun greeting from the girls, dressed in their dance costumes. She transmitted the greeting live to the girls' parents in an effort to ease the tension caused by geographical distance. Her representation of the dance performance therefore deviates from the perspective of the videographer Pancho, who concentrates exclusively on its ceremonial aspects. Yet what was intended as a fun greeting also caused a moment of intense strain. In an interview, the mother of one of the female dancers declared how the live transmission from Yalálag had been both exciting and painful for her.[27] It had given her an unexpected sense of the place she had left 12 years ago. At the same time the transmitted images conveyed quite plainly to her the fact of 'not being there' physically and not being able to assist her daughter in her village of origin. The pain she experienced on the inside because of her lack of mobility contrasted with the joy, encouragement, and pride she and the other mothers expressed on the FaceTime forum while watching the performance on their mobile phones.

Through her choice of Facebook entries and comments during the interview, Lisvelia demonstrated how she, as a first-generation Los Angeles Yalalteca, actively constructs a transcultural identity by discussing the nature of Zapotec culture and its authenticity. Since they are presumed to be "less Zapotec", people like her who were born in the US are sometimes belittled as *yalaltecos gringos* in the village of origin. At the same time, they now thoroughly shuffle up the

Zapotec culture scene with a view to reinforcing transnational community ties. In the interview, she related how she counteracted allegations in Yalálag that the female dance performance had been a deliberate attempt at mocking the dance. On the one hand, she responded with a counterargument widely disseminated in Los Angeles: "Nothing in this world is the original, nothing".[28] On the other hand, Lisvelia took care to legitimize the new, creative dance performance initiatives with narratives and images connecting them to the 'original' village and place-based sentiments indexing authenticity. On several of her Facebook pages, she employed genealogical motifs in images and text to connect the young dancers to grandparents living in Yalálag. During the interview she revealed that her own grandfather told her daughter, during a visit to Yalálag in 2006, to "take over" the dance. The girl had asked him why only men performed *La danza de los Negritos*, and he had answered: "My granddaughter, whatever you want to dance, whatever is born of your heart, go for it".[29] In this anecdote, Lisvelia interestingly refers to the traditional Zapotec unity of heart and head, according to which sentiments and intellect must coincide for volition, to conceptualize a central moment of female empowerment in the transnational setting. She also uses this concept on her Facebook page. After the female dance group appeared at four other Zapotec *kermesses* in Los Angeles, Lisvelia posted the following message along with a smiley emoji next to a portrait of the eight dancers: "Whatever you set your heart and mind to, it can and will be done. Feeling proud". Gender empowerment is promoted through images and text conveying affects as an indispensable component of the unity of heart and mind. "Doing affects" allows young women to surmount obstacles such as men who "hate" this female appropriation of dance. As one female visitor to the page comments: "I gone through all that hate for dancing what they say is a 'mans' Danzas but that never stop me from doing so".

Conclusion

The present case study examined how actors separated physically by a strictly enforced international border between Mexico and the United States use affective media practices. Such practices turned out to be the site where affects connected to the sense of control or impotence, and where the sense of movement or immo-bilization was experienced, communicated, withheld or internalized by the actors. Identifying affective media dynamics in itself was at first no easy task. But our multi-layered methodological approach, which combines findings of practice and affect theory, paved the way. This approach is complex and somewhat time con-suming, but nevertheless feasible, efficient, and promising. In particular, actors' reflexivity with respect to their routine and their strategic engagement in affects ("doing affects") proved to be a key for our analysis. On the whole designing this decidedly actor-centered approach allowed us to discern multiple perspectives and ways of "doing affects" and how they may enhance transnational community building, even when people sharply dissent. The actors we worked with all expe-rience varying degrees of socioeconomic and gender inequality, as well as racial discrimination implied in and augmented by increasingly restrictive migration policies. Nevertheless, our research results indicate that, despite these obstacles, the diverse actors in question adeptly use affective media practices strategically for establishing a home in multiple places when erecting a transnational community. The approach presented here thus merits further development. In particular, it suggests the need to adapt the established anthropological toolkit to the changing social relations, affectivities, and "feeling rules" at stake during this era of ever-tightened national borders and digital interconnectedness.

Notes

1 Transnational communities are constituted by inhabitants of two or more localities who connect them to a joint field of social relations and communicative space (Kummels, 2013). A notable aspect of indigenous Mexican migration, in particular from Oaxaca, has been its transference of local governance system from the Mexican village to diaspora settlements in the United States for the ends of transnational community building.

2 'Home' is conceptualized from a researcher's perspective as enacted in culturally varying practices of either displacement or rootedness to which affectivity and emotionality are key. Emic terms for 'home' in Spanish include the expressions *mi pueblo* (my village or my people) and *mi comunidad* (my community).

3 Ingrid Kummels and Thomas John jointly initiated field research in Yalálag at the end of May 2016. The senior researcher (IK) regularly instructed the junior researcher (TJ) in the methodology of field work during the two-month period ending in July. She conducted the research in Los Angeles in 2017.

4 Research in another transnational Ayuujk community had shown that in the course of producing and consuming video images of the hometown and its fiesta, migrant actors often intentionally charge them with affects that target fondness and love for the locale and the people living there (Kummels, 2017b).

5 Interview with Cecilia Mestas, Yalálag, 26 July 2016 (IK).

6 According to the Zapotec community's self-image, it is "the 'Cradle' of Dance", and its inhabitants are well-known for their mastery of elaborate dance patterns. They claim the 'copyright' to dances like *Los Huenches* and *Los Negritos,* among others.

7 This is the case of *la Danza de los Mixes. La danza de los Negritos* portrays 'Others' too, in this case Yalaltec merchants on a pilgrimage to Guatemala observed *negros* dancing and copied them.

8 Oaxacalifornia is a term coined by the anthropologist Michael Kearney that since the 1990s has been widely used by Mexican indigenous organizations based in the US. The dance normally requires putting on a mask, which the female group did not wear, creating an interesting controversy, which cannot be dealt with here due to space constraints.

9 Interview with Francisco "Pancho" Limeta, Yalálag, 25 May 2016 (IK).

10 The Octava is a prolonging of the same fiesta into the following weekend.

11 Interview with Francisco "Pancho" Limeta, Yalálag, 5 May 2016 (IK).

12 Interview with Cecilia Mestas, Yalálag, 26 July 2016 (IK).

13 Informal conversation with Jaime Morales, Yalálag, 15 April 2017 (IK).

14 The terminology adapts to the Zapotec interlocutors who refer to migrants' children born in the US as the 'first generation'. In contrast, 'second generation' is the term that is mainly used in scholarship for this social group.

15 This positive reappraisal can be ascribed among others to the celebration of *kermesses* and initiatives of Oaxacan indigenous organizations, among them the Organización

Regional de Oaxaca (ORO), which hosts the dance festival of the Los Angeles Guelaguetza since 1987.

16 Group interview with eight dancers. Yalálag, 24 July 2016 (TJ; IK).

17 For a similar approach on the basis of grounded theory with regard to linguistic terms and practices of emotion, see Eksner (2015).

18 Juana Vásquez Váquez was one of the native speakers and Zapotec linguistic experts consulted.

19 Juana Vásquez Váquez, memory minutes, Yalálag, 15 April 2017 (IK).

20 Interview with the parents of a 19-year-old dancer, Los Angeles, 27 February 2017 (IK).

21 The parents conceived of this as punishment due to the poverty of Yalálag compared to the conditions of relative affluence to which their daughter was accustomed in the US.

22 See footnote 14.

23 The other satellite communities in Los Angeles originate from Zoochina, Yatzachi el Alto, Zoogocho and Xochixtepec in the Oaxacan Sierra Norte. The female dance group from the Zoogocho community in Los Angeles was the first to rename the dance *Lu danza de las Negritas*.

24 Interview with Lisvelia, Los Angeles, 23 February 2017 (IK).

25 Interview with Lisvelia, Los Angeles, 1 August 2017 (IK).

26 "Influencer" is used to designate individuals with a strong presence and reputation in social media who exert power on consumer behavior. The term "ethnic influencer", Ingrid Kummmels (n.d.) likewise refers to individuals with a strong presence and reputation in social media, but who use these narrative skills to influence people in terms of cultural expressions and ideals considered to be characteristic of an ethnic group.

27 Interview with a mother of one of the dancers, Los Angeles, 28 February 2017 (IK).

28 Interview with Lisvelia, Los Angeles, 23 February 2017 (IK).

29 Interview with Lisvelia, Los Angeles, 23 February 2017 (IK).

References

Ahmed, S 2004, 'Affective economies', *Social Text*, vol. 22, 79, no. 2, pp. 117–139.

Berg, U 2015, *Mobile Selves. Race, Migration, and Belonging in Peru and the U.S*, New York University Press, New York.

Couldry, N 2004, 'Theorising media as practice', *Social Semiotics*, vol. 14, no. 2, pp. 115–132.

Cruz-Manjarrez, A 2013, *Zapotecs on the Move: Cultural, Social, and Political Processes in Transnational Perspective*, Rutgers University Press, New York.

Eksner, J 2015, 'Indexing anger and aggression. From language ideologies to linguistic affects', in H Flam & J Kleres (eds.), *Methods of Exploring Emotions*, pp. 193–205, Routledge, London.

Elwert, G 2002, 'Feldforschung. Orientierungswissen und kreuzperspektivische Analyse', *Sozialanthropologisches Arbeitspapier*, no. 1. FU Berlin, Berlin.

Geertz, C 1973, *The Interpretation of Cultures*, Basic Books, New York.

Glaser, B & Strauss, A 1967, *The Discovery of Grounded Theory. Strategies for Qualitative Research*, Aldine Transaction, Chicago.

Kummels, I 2013, 'Transnationale Gemeinden', in S Hensel & B Potthast (eds.), *Das Lateinamerika-Lexikon*, pp. 315–316, Peter Hammer Verlag, Wuppertal.

Kummels, I 2017a, *Transborder Media Spaces: Ayuujk Videomaking Between Mexico and the US*, Berghahn Books, Oxford, New York.

Kummels, I 2017b, 'Fiesta videos: "Home" and productive nostalgia between Oaxaca and California', in S Schütze (ed.), *Dossier: New Spaces of Belonging Between Mexico and the United States*, in *Sociologus*, vol. 67, no. 2, pp. 131–150.

Kummels, I n.d, 'Archivar aspiraciones entre México y EE.UU.: *Influencers* étnicos y el archivo dancístico zapoteco online', in G Cánepa Koch & I Kummels (eds.), *Antropología y archivos en la era digital: usos emergentes de lo audiovisual*. IDE/PUCP, Lima.

Madianou, M 2016, 'Ambient co-presence: Transnational family practices in polymedia environment', *Global Networks*, vol. 16, no. 2, pp. 183–201.

Marcus, G 1995, 'Ethnography in/of the world system: The emergence of multi-sited ethnography', *Annual Review of Anthropology*, vol. 24, pp. 95–117.

Mejía Estévez, S 2009, 'Is nostalgia becoming digital? Ecuadorian diaspora in the age of global capitalism', *Social Identities*, vol. 15, pp. 393–410.

Moores, S 2012, *Media, Place & Mobility*, Palgrave Macmillan, London.

Peña, L 2017, 'Danza de los Superhéroes. Zapotec immigrant tradition in transnational transfer', *Boom California*, 17 July. Available from: https://boomcalifornia.com/2017/07/17/danza-de-los-superheroes-zapotec-immigrant-tradition-in-transnational-transfer/ [10 February 2018].

Postill, J 2010, 'Introduction: Theorizing media and practice', in B Bräuchler & J Postill (eds.), *Theorizing Media and Practice*, pp. 1–32, Berghahn Books, Oxford, New York.

Reckwitz, A 2015. 'Praktiken und ihre Affekte', *Mittelweg*, vol. 36, pp. 27–45.

Prieto-Blanco, P & Schreiber, M (eds.), 2016, 'Networking knowledge, special issue: Together while apart?' *Mediating Relationships and Intimacy*, vol. 9, no. 6.

Scheer, M 2012, 'Are emotions a kind of practice (and is that what makes them have a history)? A Bourdieuan approach to understanding emotion', *History and Theory*, vol. 51, pp. 193–220.

SFB Affective Societies 2016, *A Glossary. Register of Central Working Concepts*. Working Paper SFB 1171 Affective Societies, 16 January.

Chapter 11

The ethnography of affect in discourse practice

Performing sentiment in the time machine

Jonas Bens

Introduction

This chapter proposes an ethnographic approach to discourse practice as it is embedded in affective dynamics. At the heart of such ethnographies is the observation of discourse practice events – most broadly defined as a specific place in the world and a specific moment in time in which people communicate in order to be heard by a public. Such events have usually been investigated with a focus on language and speech. Without abandoning the analysis of talk, I make the argument that it is crucial to strive for an ethnographic investigation that captures quite broadly the affective dimension of the events in which such talk takes place. To that end, I will first lay out what I mean by an ethnography of discourse practice and then argue two points on methodology. First, discourse practice events should be understood and described as affective arrangements. Second, discourse practice events can be described as time machines in which sentiments become manifest, are enacted, invoked, mobilized, shaped and transformed.

Writing about discourse practice events

An ethnography of discourse practice is basically a writing project to produce an analytically dense account of how discourse is practiced. The data basis for this writing project is gathered first and foremost by observing events (Bernard, 2011, 256–290). A "thick description" (Geertz, 1973, 3–32) of the event will often be at the center of such an ethnographic text. Other bodies of data regularly complement such observations: data derived from narrative interviews of participants' perceptions and experiences before, during and after an event (see Harders & Ayata in this volume), as well as systematic investigations of the researcher's personal experiences during the research process (see Stodulka; Dilger, Kasmani & Mattes in this volume). In this text, however, I will focus on data derived from ethnographic observation as the center of an ethnography of discourse practice. It is therefore necessary to introduce the four relevant conceptual terms in this endeavor: ethnography, discourse, practice and event.

Ethnography, from the Ancient Greek ἔθνος for "group of people" and γράφειν for "to write", signifies the process of writing about people. It is revealing that the term is used both for the mode of research that is done by anthropologists (and sometimes also by representatives of other disciplines engaging in qualitative social scientific research) as well as for the product of such research – the book, the article or the research report. When the famous Bronislaw Malinowski investigated the Trobriand Islanders he was conducting ethnography, and his book *Argonauts of the Western Pacific* (1922) is likewise called an ethnography. As the term simultaneously describes a research practice, a writing style and a literary genre, "ethnography is, from beginning to end, enmeshed in writing" (Clifford, 1986, 25), bringing about such different texts as research proposals, field diaries, codes, memos, books and journal articles.[1] The ethnographic practice in the field has therefore been rightly characterized as a mode of "participating-in-order-to-write" (Emerson, Fretz, & Shaw, 2011, 23). To a certain degree, the ethnographic endeavor defies the ideal separation of the research process into several consecutive steps: (1) formulating a research question, (2) collecting data, (3) analyzing that data and (4) writing up and publishing the findings. Instead, all of these steps are constantly conflated: data collection and data analysis happen simultaneously, the research question is constantly reformulated, and all of this happens in the process of writing all kinds of texts.

The word *discourse* comes from the Latin *discursus*, the past participle of the verb *discurrere*, which can be translated as roaming and wandering. The idea of discourse means that linguistic utterances, once brought into the world by human communication, harden into complexes of meaning that wander around in the world and have a life of their own.[2] A dialectic is characteristic for the concept of discourse. On the one hand, discourses are produced, maintained and transformed by human communication. On the other hand, discourses precede human communication and also regulate what people can say in the first place. Michel Foucault (1972), whose works on discourse have widely influenced social science thinking, argues that discourses regulate who can say what, when and in what way. That is why people both wield power with discourses and strive for power over discourses. In the Foucauldian sense, the investigation of discourses means investigating how knowledge, power and truth are produced, shaped, transformed, instituted and challenged.

The project of investigating discourses is often called discourse analysis. In discourse analysis, materials are investigated that both produce and represent discourses, for example, fictional or non-fictional texts, images, or transcripts from interviews or everyday communication.[3] The discourses themselves, however, are abstract phenomena that exist beyond and independent of these materials, but discourses crystallize in them and in the institutions that bring them about. An ethnographic approach to discourse goes beyond the examination of texts and images, it "must always go beyond literary traces, beyond explicit narrative, exegesis, even argument. For the poetics . . . [of discourse] lie also in the mute meanings transacted through goods and practices, through icons and images dispersed in the landscape of the everyday" (Comaroff & Comaroff, 1992, 35).[4] In other words, the ethnography of discourses is about observing practices.[5]

The term *practice* describes people's actions in real-life situations in which human actors and material environments are co-present. When people act, they are, in one way or the other, subject to structural constraints. Practice theory, as it has been put forward by Pierre Bourdieu (1972), Michel de Certeau (1980) and others, aims at coming to terms with this dialectic of structure and agency. Actors are determined by structural forces which precede their existence, but which are also the precondition for their action. When people act, they reproduce the structure they are embedded in, but also have limited agency to shape and transform structure. Linguistic anthropologists have talked about discursive practice theory (McElhinny & Muehlmann, 2006) and argue that people also practice discourse in a spectrum of structure and agency. To what extent actors are dependent on structure and how much they are able to maneuver cannot be decided on the theoretical level. It is an empirical question that depends on the concrete discursive situation, changing with place and time (Bens, 2018c, 260–263).

The ethnographer encounters discourse practice in what I call *discourse practice events* – most broadly defined as a specific place in the world and a specific moment in time in which people communicate in order to be heard by a public. Actors participate in a discourse practice event with the explicit purpose to engage in communicative action. They speak to participate in discourses, often to challenge some discourses and to stabilize or mobilize others. Actors attend these events as speakers and listeners. Ideal types of such discourse practice events are typically investigated in political and legal settings: court hearings, sessions in parliament, public demonstrations, political manifestations, election campaign events, etc.[6]

The discourse practice event is a *speech event*, as the term is used in linguistic anthropology (Hymes, 1972),[7] and a *performance event* in the sense of those anthropologists from folklore studies who have focused on the ethnography of oral narratives (Bauman, 1977).[8] Firmly based on this established methodological ground, I will argue in this chapter that the discourse practice event can also be described as an affective arrangement. To that end, I will first present a discourse practice event out of my own research as an example and then approach it with a focus on affective dynamics.

A discourse practice event in Northern Uganda

To exemplify my methodological propositions on an ethnography of discourse practice, I will draw from my own research on the International Criminal Court's outreach activities in Uganda (Bens, forthcoming.). The International Criminal Court (ICC) is an international organization based on the Rome Statute, an international treaty with 124 member states.[9] The ICC's purpose is to investigate "the most serious crimes of concern to the international community as a whole" (Rome Statute, art. 3, sec. 1). It conducts trials to punish the individuals responsible for those crimes (Schabas, 2011).

One of the cases before the ICC – still ongoing at the time of writing – was *The Prosecutor v. Dominic Ongwen*. Ongwen stood trial for the commission of war crimes and crimes against humanity in the course of the armed conflict between the Ugandan government and the rebel force Lord's Resistance Army (LRA) in Northern Uganda. Among other crimes, Ongwen was accused of being responsible for the conscription of child soldiers, forced marriage, sexual slavery and the killing of civilians by attacking Internally Displaced Persons' camps (IDP camps) in Northern Uganda between 2004 and 2005.

The trial was conducted at the ICC headquarters in The Hague, far removed from the crime scenes and the victims. With the explicit aim to bridge this divide between the victims and the trial, the ICC conducted several outreach activities. One prominent format were public screenings of key moments of the trial proceedings. These public events took place at different sites in Northern Uganda, in small urban centers such as Gulu, Kitgum or Lira as well as in small villages who were directly affected by the violence of the LRA when they served as locations for IDP camps in the early 2000s.

During my fieldwork in Northern Uganda, I observed several such events.[10] At these events, a television screen was put up and a large group of people attended to watch the trial proceedings in The Hague – among them former victims and their families, the interested public, representatives of the ICC and local politicians. The events were similarly structured. Before the broadcast began, a group of people assembled. Often a representative of the ICC or a local NGO connected to the ICC was present to organize the event. At the beginning, the ICC representative or another guest of special status (local politicians, cultural or religious leaders) delivered a short speech. Then followed the screening. During breaks and after the screenings had ended, experts or interpreters (in case the screening had not taken place in local languages) paraphrased what had transpired during the proceeding. The audience asked questions, and some communicated their opinions. I see these screenings as discourse practice events, because people attended these events as speakers and listeners. They wanted to familiarize themselves with – and sometimes even change and modify – the relevant discourses in and around the trial.

At one of these events which I observed during my fieldwork, a high-ranking ICC official was expected to attend an outreach event. In that instance, more than 2,000 villagers attended. They were seated on plastic chairs in very large tents, which had been provided under the auspices of the ICC outreach unit. Screens were put up, and the trial proceedings were broadcasted on television. After the ICC official had arrived, together with some members of the press, he gave a short speech in front of the crowd, the trial proceedings being shown on TV in the background. Many people looked interested and paid attention to the official, but most of them, not being fluent in English, could not understand the content of what he said. At one point he said: "In my fifteen years working for the ICC, I have never seen anything of this magnitude regarding community engagement in a proceeding". It took a little time for a translator to translate the ICC official's words into the local language. Then people applauded. After the official had ended his speech, he called for questions. One village official started by telling the ICC official that many in the community had not had the opportunity to fill out the forms necessary to formally participate in the trial. By that he referred to the fact that in a trial before the ICC, the victims of the accused can be legally represented as a group and thereby formally participate in the trial proceeding. These victim groups then serve as a third party besides the prosecution and the defense. The local official asked, in the local language, if it will still be possible for those who had not yet filled the form to participate in the trial. People applauded loudly – about as loud as before.

The ICC official answered in English. He replied that he could not do anything about the forms, as there had been a deadline before the start of the trial, which had already passed. But he wanted to reassure people that they could neverthe-less take part in the trial and see justice be done by participating in screening events like these, accompanied by discussions. This magnificent event would be an example of such victim participation. After his reply was translated, many vil-lagers started whispering conversations amongst each other. There was no audible applause.

At the time I had the strong impression that something significant had tran-spired here, although I was not yet sure what. Having listened closely to what people had said, I had already detected some kind of irritation. The local official had asked a question, and the ICC official had not answered in the affirmative without reservation. But it only became fully clear to me that this was a significant exchange when the collective mood seemed to shift after the ICC official's second statement. His second statement ("this magnificent event") was semantically not very different from his first statement ("I have never seen anything of this mag-nitude . . ."). But while his first statement was received with applause, his second statement evoked hesitation on the part of the villagers. Something had changed. Taking this scene and the moment of irritation as a starting point, I argue that in order to describe ethnographically what happened there, it is necessary to come to terms with affect and atmosphere in the ethnography of discourse practice events. Such an analysis that focuses on the idea of the discourse practice event as an affective arrangement brings together linguistic analysis and performance analy-sis by considering the affective dynamics that emerge during these events.

The discourse practice event as an affective arrangement

When one thinks of discourse practice, it seems to be evident that language is at the center of it. And, indeed, the analysis of what people say, how they phrase it, at what time during the event they are uttering it and to whom remains at the center of ethnographically analyzing discourse practices.[11]

From an ethnographic perspective, language always appears as a performance (Duranti, 1997, 14–17). This slimmest possible notion of performance has been proposed by linguist Noam Chomsky, who differentiates between competence (the capacity to use language) and performance (the actual use of language).[12] On the most basic level, this means that language comes to the fore as speech acts.

Language that is not uttered during the event remains inaccessible to participant observation.[13] In the outreach event described earlier, the ICC official says: "In my fifteen years working for the ICC, I have never seen anything of this magnitude regarding community engagement in a proceeding". Such an utterance can be the starting point for an ethnographic analysis.

Speech act theorists have insisted that speaking is basically an action like any other; it is "doing things with words" (Austin, 1962). The performative dimension of language refers to speaking as a practice with consequences. One can wield power through language (Derrida, 1989; Butler, 1997). When the ICC official referred to the size of the crowd, for example, an ethnographic account should capture what the speech act 'does' during the event. In this case, the ICC official's utterance praises the many villagers who took the trouble to attend the screening. It also praises the ICC official's own employees who organized the outreach event and mobilized so many participants. On a more general level, the utterance validates the efforts of international criminal institutions, especially of the International Criminal Court, to stay in contact with victims and let them participate.

These questions on what the speech act does already entail that the idea of people performing language always means that they do so vis-à-vis an audience, and that these audiences 'co-author' the speech act (Duranti, 1986). Speakers 'put up a show', and how they say things is evaluated by audiences according to aesthetic canons. This is most obvious in ritual (Conquergood, 1989; Turner, 1987; Bauman, 1977) and theatre (Fischer-Lichte, 2008; Schneider, 2011), but also everyday interactions have the quality of performances (Goffman, 1956). The ICC official performed in front of an audience of about 2,000 villagers, but there were also other audiences he spoke to: his own people in the ICC, the international community, the media representatives that are present and maybe others (see Bens, 2018a).

To assess the performative dimension of language as holistically as possible, the ethnographer should carefully investigate the affective dynamics that enfold during the event in the co-presence of bodies. On a most basic level, affect and emotion research remind ethnography to focus on what enfolds in the co-presence of bodies in space – in other words: the concrete event. Social science emotion research (Röttger-Rössler & Markowitsch, 2009; Burkitt, 2014) and affect theory from the humanities (Gregg & Seigworth, 2010; Clough & Halley, 2007), which form the theoretical basis for conceiving of society as fundamentally affective (see Kahl in this volume), are based on a critique of individualistic accounts of affect and emotion and makes a strong case for a social-relational approach (von Scheve, 2018). Affect and emotion manifest not only in people's perceptions but also in the concrete arrangements in which events take place. In other words, discourse practice events are about performing language embedded in multifarious affective dynamics. For the ethnographic endeavor, it is crucial to find a descriptive mode which enables the ethnographer to write about this affectivity of discourse practice. An analytic starting point can be the concept of affective arrangement that has been put forth by Jan Slaby and Rainer Mühlhoff in this volume. They understand affective arrangements as

> heterogeneous ensembles of diverse materials forming a local layout that operates as a dynamic formation, comprising persons, things, artefacts, spaces, discourses, behaviours, and expressions in a characteristic mode of composition and dynamic relatedness. [This] . . . approach facilitates micro-analyses of affective relationality as it furthers both an understanding of the entities that coalesce locally to engender relational affect, and also the overall "feel", affective tonality or atmosphere that prevails in such a locale.
>
> (Slaby, Mühlhoff, & Wüschner, 2017, 2)[14]

The task of ethnography is then to describe the affective arrangement by describing how the human and non-human, material and immaterial components are arranged, how they relate to other and what kind of dynamics take place in these relational interactions. The concept of affective arrangement allows us to include other performers beyond the speakers and listeners into the description of affective dynamics, such as "scenery and stage props" (Goffman, 1956, 13), voice, gesture, spatial arrangements, and visual regimes. Not only the speakers contribute to the affective dynamics in the ICC outreach events, but also the television sets broadcasting the trial in the background, the tents which protect people from the burning sun, the sound system transmitting the speakers' voices, the interpreters who translate the speakers' words into the local language, and many other human and non-human, material and immaterial bodies that can be assembled in the affective arrangement. How exactly these components of an affective arrangement affect the dynamics of a discourse practice event cannot be pre-decided on the level of methodology, but remains to be seen in the empirical research. From a methodological standpoint, an ethnography of discourse practice that is interested in exploring affective dynamics should, however, focus on a thick description of how the components of the arrangement perform together as a "team" (Goffman, 1956), establishing affective relations and curating atmospheres.

The speaker's utterances during the ICC outreach event are embedded in such relational dynamics. Already on the semantic level, the ICC official's first utterance ("In my fifteen years . . .") is only meaningful in relation to the co-present bodies – the 2,000 villagers. The praise that it contains affectively links the speaker to his multiple audiences. The language affects the villagers, the reporters who later write about the event and other audiences. It creates an affective dynamic between the speaker and the audience of the villagers that becomes manifest as an atmosphere.

Atmosphere describes the affective tonality, the overall 'feel' or mood that enfolds at a place in a specific moment. As such, affective arrangements always produce some kind of atmosphere. People experience it as something that is not (only) coming from inside, but also from the surroundings (Griffero, 2014;

Riedel, 2018). Atmospheres are experienced as liminal phenomena; people realize atmospheres in moments of change (Riedel, 2018). An ethnography of atmospheres has to focus on those moments of change and shift, when one atmosphere shifts into another. Ethnography should describe exactly those moments when the constellation of bodies changes in such a significant way that another 'overall feel' is being established. Moments when people focus toward the speaker, orient their bodies towards him or her and later burst into applause are such instances of atmospheric change.

After the ICC official's second statement, the atmosphere shifted into something else. Before, the bodies of the audience members were oriented towards the speaker, applauding; afterward, they were directed towards each other, discussing what had been said. The whole configuration of the affective arrangement changed, becoming manifest in a shift of atmosphere, which indicated that something had happened. The audience was affected, although it remained unclear in what way exactly. The speech acts and the description of the observed atmospheres alone do not seem to be enough to settle the question of what exactly happened, let alone why. I argue that in this moment, something was enacted that went beyond the scene and even beyond the whole event – a performance that related to sentiment.

Enacting sentiment in the time machine

Affective dynamics and atmospheres not only depend on the concrete performances of co-present bodies during the time of the event. As much as affect and emotion research points ethnography towards the event itself, discourse practice is embedded in a dialectic between micro-level interactions and structural constraints. In other words, by focusing on affectively interrelated co-present bodies alone, the workings of historically embedded macro-level processes of power might remain invisible.

This points to one of the main dilemmas of the ethnographic endeavor. Any ethnographic investigation must be conducted at a certain place at a certain time, while the ethnographer aspires to come to terms with processes that have a past and a future, often in other places. One could call this ethnography's event-and-process dilemma (see Scheffer, 2007). One famous methodological approach to this dilemma is the call for "extended case studies", put forward by the "Manchester school" in anthropology (Gluckman, 1973). Conducting such an extended case study basically means to try and observe a trouble case from its inception over its resolution until its aftermath. In other words, based on long-term ethnographic fieldwork.

It is undoubtedly important to strive for this ideal. In my ethnography of the Dominic Ongwen case before the ICC, I divided my fieldwork time of altogether 12 months into four phases, starting in The Hague, then traveling to Northern Uganda, then again conducting fieldwork in The Hague and finally researching in Northern Uganda again, covering a period of about two and a half years of the proceedings in total. Nevertheless, I was not able to cover the whole case proceedings in the time of the research project, not to speak of the aspirations of an extended case study. No matter how much one tries to observe cases over an extended period of time, the methodological problem remains how to account for process *inside* the event; in other words, how does one find process and structure in the observation data (see Bens, 2018b)?

I want to propose the metaphor of the *time machine* to methodologically approach this event-and-process dilemma in ethnography. As discourse is practiced as performances, I argue that these can be *re-enactments* of the past and *pre-enactments* of the future. Larger processes and the event's historical position in it do not influence how the discourse practice event can take place *per se*, but only as past and present materialize, in one form or the other, at the time of the event.[15]

In our exemplary event, one important example for re-enactment is the video screening in the ICC outreach event. The screen itself is a body inside the affective arrangement, and it re-enacts what happened in court in relation to other bodies present at the outreach event. As such, the trial, that is going on long-term and at another place, inscribes into the outreach event. Storytelling can have the character of re-enactment when participants give testimony of the past violence. Sometimes, during these events, participants raise demands of what should be done to pay reparations to victims or what other lessons should be learned from the past violence in the future. At these points, past and future materialize in the present. The way these materializations take place shape the event, and one should focus on the exact workings of such performative pre- and re-enactments.

In the question-and-answer session after the ICC official's speech, the local official referred to past as well as to future events. He spoke of the fact that a number of community members had not been able to fill out specific forms in the past, and he also expressed a wish for the future, that legal participation in the trial would still be possible. On the level of the affective and emotional perception of actors present in the event, storytelling in the form of pre- and re-enactment can elicit emotional responses when actors are reminded of feelings through narrative. Then pre- and re-enactments serve as frames inside of which actors normatively assess the present situation and form opinions about the event's legitimacy and relevance (Bens, 2017).

Through these re-enactments and pre-enactments – be they verbal or non-verbal – structural factors and long-term processes inscribe into the event. Larger discourses that go beyond the event influence what actors can say and how. From the perspective of the affectivity of discourse practice, these larger discourses enter the stage as *sentiments*. Sentiments are relatively stable evaluative regimes of meaning that are embedded in and colored by affective and emotional dynamics (Bens & Zenker, 2019).

In the question-and-answer session, the ICC official answered the question put to him by offering a notion of participation that differed from that of the local official. While the local official talked about legal participation of victim groups in the trial, the ICC official referred to a more informal participation of villagers attending public screenings of the trial. Inscribed into this exchange are differing sentiments of justice.

Although this exchange was seemingly about victim participation, a contextualization with other bodies of data collected during ethnographic fieldwork reveals that the local official not least referred to the issue of reparations. The villagers were concerned that only by formally participating in the trial proceedings would they become eligible for individual reparations through ICC's Trust Fund for Victims. The local official anticipated the time after the end of the trial. If Dominic Ongwen will have been convicted, the Trust Fund for Victims might give money to his victims.[16] Interviews I have conducted with grassroots victim organizations in Northern Uganda show that sentiments of restoration and reparation heavily influence people's perceptions of justice (Bens, 2017).

The ICC official did not react to this allusion, either deliberately or unwittingly. He instead pointed to the current event as an example of effective victim participation – implying that a formal participation in the trial was not necessary to see justice in action. By this he referred to a sentiment of retribution, in which the successful punishment of the perpetrator is to be desired as a just outcome.

These competing sentiments of justice are macro-phenomena and structure many different debates on transitional justice. In transitional justice scholarship, this is framed as the debate between retributive justice and restorative justice (see e.g. Clark, 2008). Retributive justice points to retribution and punishment of perpetrators in order to come to terms with large-scale violence. Restorative justice points to repair the damage done by this violence, be it in the form of monetary reparations or some other kind of healing broken social relationships.

These competing sentiments were inscribed into discourse practice events and were performed in the affective arrangement. Sentiments not only influenced the speech acts as such, but also the atmosphere in the event. The atmospheric irritation resulted to a large degree from partial incompatibilities between sentiments that were structurally and processually embedded rather than just produced during the event. The atmospheric irritation again re-inscribed these sentiments into the discourse and hence to some degree reproduced them.

Conclusion

An ethnography of discourse practice investigates the workings of discourse practice events through participant observation, writing about this as 'thickly' as possible. I have argued for conceiving of discourse practice events as affective arrangement in order to come to terms with the affective dynamics in which performative talk enfolds in the co-presence of bodies. Although performing talk is in the center of discourse practice, the focus on affect points ethnography to the concrete event in which such performances are embedded, and which can be captured through ethnographic writing.

This chapter makes a plea for putting observation data into the center of ethnographic research. Affective dynamics and shifting atmospheres point to moments of irritation and affection that can serve as starting points for further ethnographic research. A shift in atmosphere that seems somewhat puzzling, because it does not seem to be solely motivated by the course of the event itself, might indicate moments where structure and process inscribe into the event.

Since events are not only shaped by the inner workings of the event itself but also by larger structural forces and long-term processes, I have proposed to include an investigation of re-enactments and pre-enactments into an ethnography of discourse practice. As such, the discourse practice event appears as a time machine in which past and future emerge as performances. Discourse practice events produce sentiments that outlive the events in which they are invoked. Sentiments inscribe into the inner workings of discourse practice; they are debated, contended and sometimes even transformed.

Notes

1 Recently, there has been a debate in anthropology about using this multimodality of ethnography to make visible (through several media such as blogs) the ethnographic endeavor also before the publication of a finished and polished ethnographic book. This can be done by publishing texts and other media such as audio and video files while the research is still ongoing (Collins, Durington, & Gill, 2017; Powis, 2017).

2 Sometimes linguistic anthropologists use the term "discourse" to refer only to concrete human communicative interaction. Conley and O'Barr (2004, 6–9), for instance, differentiate between "micro-discourse" (people actually talking to each other in real-life situations) and "macro-discourse" (discourse in the Foucauldian sense). In this text, I use "discourse" in the Foucauldian sense and refer to "micro-discourse" by employing the terms "talk" and "speech".

3 For an example of discourse analysis of political discourses from my own research, see Duile and Bens (2017).

4 I tend to disagree with the Comaroffs, however, in that they seem to underestimate the event in time and place as an analytic object of historical ethnography. They rightly highlight social processes (Comaroff & Comaroff, 1992, 37–38), but to a degree where it becomes difficult to assess what this actually means for the ethnographic data collection.

5 This is not to say that an anthropological investigation of texts is not a worthwhile endeavor. I have argued elsewhere that an anthropological reading of legal texts is and should be an integral part of legal anthropology (Bens, 2013). Although such an approach draws from ethnography, it is not identical with it.

6 It is to be conceded that the concept of discourse practice event proposed here is quite broad and might describe many situations in very different ethnographic research projects – far beyond political or legal ethnography. It remains the ethnographer's decision if it makes sense to investigate certain settings and situations as discourse practice events, or in another fashion that seems more apt for being able to describe what is going on. If one conducts ethnography in a hospital ward, for instance, people talk all the time, but this talking is not always at the center of the event. When a doctor speaks with a patient to discuss the therapy, it would be a stretch to describe this situation as a discourse practice event. When the doctor speaks in a team meeting, maybe even discussing hospital guidelines, it might be more beneficial to investigate such a setting as a discourse practice event.

7 "Speech event analysis derives its empirical validity from the fact that . . . members of all societies recognize certain communicative routines which they view as distinct wholes, separate from other types of discourse, characterized by special rules of speech and non-verbal behaviour and often distinguishable by clearly recognizable opening and closing sequences" (Gumperz, 1972, 17).

8 "Oral performance, like all human activity, is situated, its form, meaning and functions rooted in culturally defined scenes or events – bounded segments of the flow of behaviour and experience that constitute meaningful contexts for action, interpretation and evaluation. In the ethnography of oral performance . . . the performance event direct[s] attention to the actual conduct of artistic verbal performance in social life" (Bauman, 1986).

9 For the current number of signatories, see the webpage of the Assembly of State Parties to the Rome Statute: https://asp.icc-cpi.int.

10 My fieldwork in Northern Uganda was part of a larger research project conducted under the auspices of the Collective Research Centre *Affective Societies* at Freie Universität Berlin. I also conducted ethnography of ICC proceedings in The Hague, mainly during the Dominic Ongwen trial. The workings of a courtroom can likewise be investigated with the ethnography of discourse practice I describe here. I have made some remarks on the specifics of courtroom ethnography elsewhere (Bens, 2018b).

11 The prime project of linguistic anthropology is to investigate the pragmatics of language, hence how people use language in actual social interaction and deploy the whole array of anthropological methods. These methods include participant observation, interviews, surveys and questionnaires, records of naturally occurred conversations, and written texts (Ahearn, 2017, 12, 55–62). The most important methodological directive from linguistic anthropology is to produce as many recordings of speech acts (in the form of audio or video recordings) as possible and to transcribe many hours of talk into written transcripts as a basis for analysis. If we think about the outreach event which I just introduced, it is clearly important to collect as much data as possible (and time-economically feasible) on what is actually said there and by whom. The content of the talk – ideally accessible in a word-for-word transcript (Bernard, 2011, 424–426), more often, however, transcribed from handwritten jottings (Emerson, Fretz, & Shaw, 2011, 21–44) – is the most important element of the discourse practice event.

12 Chomsky's differentiation parallels Ferdinand de Saussure's (1916) famous distinction between *langue* (language as an abstract system) and *parole* (language in use).

13 Often it will be of interest to focus an analysis on what was deliberately not said during a discourse practice event and why. Such data can be provided by asking people after the event about blank spaces or even 'elephants in the room' – topics which were not talked about, but were known by many of the participants.

14 Slaby, Mühlhoff and Wüschner see affective arrangements as concrete micro-settings that have a specific time and place. As examples, they list "a specific work environment, from an ordinary office to a stock market trading floor, a subcultural niche, an event space such as a concert hall or sport site, a protest movement on a public square, various public sites of interaction such as in public transportation, streets, commercial environments, interaction with administration and bureaucracy, online platforms and social media user interfaces, even ceremonial regimes such as Christmas or a funeral" (2017, p. 2).

15 Thomas Scheffer has made this point by arguing for a "trans-sequential analysis", which focuses on an "object-in-becoming" (*Objekt-im-Werden*) that reappears in several events in a sequence (Scheffer, 2015). This object also materializes both the past and the future. His proposition includes an approach to investigate "cases-in-becoming", which he has shown with his ethnography of court cases (Scheffer, 2010). Such an approach goes beyond what I am proposing here.

16 If reparations are actually connected to a formal participation in the trial, and of what nature such reparations might be in the future, is seen very differently by different actors. While the ICC personnel seems to aspire to collective reparations in the form of development projects, many villagers in Northern Uganda believe that they can expect individual reparations and that they need to 'get on the list' if they wish to be eligible for them (Bens forthcoming.).

References

Ahearn, L 2017, *Living Language: An Introduction to Linguistic Anthropology*, 2nd edn, Wiley-Blackwell, Malden.

Austin, JL 1962, *How to Do Things with Words: The William James Lectures Delivered at Harvard University in 1955*, Oxford University Press, New York.

Bauman, R 1977, *Verbal Art as Performance*, Newbury House, Rowley.

Bauman, R 1986, *Story, Performance and Event: Contextual Studies of Oral Narrative*, Cambridge University Press, Cambridge.

Bens, J 2013, *Ethnie als Rechtsbegriff: Kulturanthropologische Problembeschreibungen zum Allgemeinen Gleichbehandlungsgesetz*, Shaker, Aachen.

Bens, J 2017, 'Gerechtigkeitsgefühle und die Legitimität des Internationalen Strafgerichtshofs in Norduganda', in J Bens & O Zenker (eds.), *Gerechtigkeitsgefühle: Zur affektiven und emotionalen Legitimität von Normen*, pp. 215–241, Transcript Verlag, Bielefeld.

Bens, J 2018a, *Affective Transference and the Problem of Multiple Publics: What Is the Audience for Transitional Justice?* International Conference "Public Emotions: Affective Collectivity in Audiences", Berlin, Germany.

Bens, J 2018b, 'The courtroom as an affective arrangement: Analysing atmospheres courtroom ethnography', *Journal of Legal Pluralism and Unofficial Law*, vol. 50, no. 3.

Bens, J 2018c, 'When the Cherokee became indigenous: Cherokee Nation v Georgia and its paradoxical legalities', *Ethnohistory*, vol. 65, no. 2, pp. 247–267.

Bens, J forthcoming, 'Transitional justice atmospheres: The role of space and affect in the international criminal court's outreach efforts in Northern Uganda', in K Seidel & H Ellisie (eds.), *Normative Spaces in Africa*. Routledge, London.

Bens, J & Zenker, O 2019, 'Sentiment', in J Slaby & C V Scheve (eds.), *Affective Societies: Key Concepts*, pp. 96-106. Routledge, London.

Bernard, HR 2011, *Research Methods in Anthropology: Qualitative and Quantitative Approaches*, 5th edn, Altamira Press, Lanham.

Bourdieu, P 1972, *Esquisse d'une théorie de la pratique, prencédé de trois études d'ethnologie kabyle*, Librairie Droz, Geneva.

Burkitt, I 2014, *Emotions and Social Relations*, Sage Publications, London.

Butler, J 1997, *Excitable Speech: A Politics of the Performative*, Routledge, New York.

Clark, JN 2008, 'The three Rs: Retributive justice, restorative justice, and reconciliation', *Contemporary Justice Review*, vol. 11, no. 4, pp. 331–350.

Clifford, J 1986, *The Predicament of Culture: Twentieth-Century Ethnography, Literature, and Art*, Harvard University Press, Cambridge.

Clough, PT & Halley, J (eds.), 2007, *The Affective Turn: Theorizing the Social*, Duke University Press, Durham.

Collins, SG, Durington, M & Gill, H 2017, 'Multimodality: An invitation', *American Anthropologist*, vol. 119, no. 1, pp. 142–146.

Comaroff, J & Comaroff, J 1992, *Ethnography and the Historical Imagination*, Westview Press, Boulder.

Conley, JM & O'Barr, WM 2004, *Just Words: Law, Language, and Power*, 2nd edn, University of Chicago Press, Chicago.

Conquergood, D 1989, 'Poetics, play, process, and power: The performative turn in anthropology', *Text and Performance Quarterly*, vol. 9, no. 1, pp. 82–95.

de Certeau, M 1980, *L'Invention du quotidien: Arts de faire (vol. 1) et Habiter, cuisiner*, vol. 2, Gallimard, Paris.

Derrida, J 1989, 'Force de loi: Le fondement mystique de l'autorite/force of law: The mystical foundations of authority', *Cardozo Law Review*, vol. 11, no. 3, pp. 920–1045.

de Saussure, F 1916, *Cours de linguistique générale*, Payot & Rivage, Paris.

Duile, T & Bens, J 2017, 'Indonesia and the "Conflictual Consensus": A discursive perspective on Indonesian democracy', *Critical Asian Studies*, vol. 49, no. 2, pp. 139–162.

Duranti, A 1986, 'The audience as co-author: An introduction', *Text*, vol. 6, no. 3, pp. 239–247.

Duranti, A 1997, *Linguistic Anthropology*, Cambridge University Press, Cambridge.

Emerson, RM, Fretz, RI & Shaw, LL 2011, *Writing Ethnographic Fieldnotes*, 2nd edn, University of Chicago Press, Chicago, London.

Fischer-Lichte, E 2008, *The Transformative Power of Performance: A New Aesthetics*, Routledge, New York.

Foucault, M 1972, *L'ordre du discours*, Gallimard, Paris.

Geertz, C 1973, *The Interpretation of Cultures: Selected Essays*, Basic Books, New York.

Gluckman, M 1973, 'Limitations of the case-method in the study of tribal law', *Law and Society Review*, vol. 7, no. 4, pp. 611–641.

Goffman, E 1956, *The Presentation of Self in Everyday Life*, University of Edinburgh Social Science Reserach Centre, Edinburgh.

Gregg, M & Seigworth, GJ (eds.), 2010, *The Affect Theory Reader*, Duke University Press, Durham.

Griffero, T 2014, 'Atmospheres and lived space', *Studia Phenomenologica*, vol. 14, pp. 29–51.

Gumperz, JJ 1972, 'Introduction', in JJ Gumperz & D Hymes (eds.), *Directions in Sociolinguistics*, pp. 1–31, Holt, Rinehart and Winston, New York.

Hymes, D 1972, 'Models of the interaction of language and social life', in JJ Gumperz & D Hymes (eds.), *Directions in Sociolinguistics*, pp. 35–71, Holt, Rinehart and Winston, New York.

Malinowski, B 1922, *Argonauts of the Western Pacific: An Account of Native Enterprise and Adventure in the Archipelagoes of Melanesian New Guinea*, Routledge, London.

McElhinny, B & Muehlmann, S 2006, 'Discursive practice theory', in K Brown (ed.), *Encyclopedia of Language and Lingusitics*, vol. 3, 2nd edn, pp. 696–699, Elsevier, Oxford.

Powis, R 2017, 'Heartened by iconoclasm: A few preliminary thoughts about multimodality', *American Anthropologist*, vol. 119, no. 2, pp. 359–361.

Riedel, F 2018, 'Atmosphere', in J Slaby & C V Scheve (eds.), *Affective Societies: Key Concepts*, Routledge, London.

Röttger-Rössler, B & Markowitsch, HJ (eds.), 2009, *Emotions as Bio-Cultural Processes*, Springer, New York.

Schabas, WA (ed.), 2011, *An Introduction to the International Criminal Court*, 4th edn, Cambridge University Press, Cambridge.

Scheffer, T 2007, 'Event and process: An exercise in analytical ethnography', *Human Studies*, vol. 30, no. 3, pp. 167–197.

Scheffer, T 2010, *Adversarial Case-Making: An Ethnography of English Crown Court Procedures*, Brill, Leiden.

Scheffer, T 2015, 'Diskurspraxis in Recht und Politik: Trans-Sequentialität und die Analyse rechtsförmiger Verfahren', *Zeitschrift für Rechtssoziologie*, vol. 35, no. 2, pp. 223–244.

Schneider, R 2011, *Performing Remains: Art and War in Times of Theatrical Reenactment*, Routledge, London.

Slaby, J, Mühlhoff, R & Wüschner, P 2017, 'Affective arrangements', *Emotion Review*. Available from: https://journals.sagepub.com/doi/abs/10.1177/1754073917722214?jour nalCode=emra [27 July 2018].

Turner, V 1987, *The Anthropology of Performance*, PAJ Publications, New York.

von Scheve, C 2018, 'A social relational account of affect', *European Journal of Social Theory*, vol. 21, no. 1, pp. 39–59.

Chapter 12

Affective dynamics in the theatre

Towards a relational and poly-perspectival performance analysis

Doris Kolesch and Matthias Warstat

Performance analysis as method

Performance analysis is a research method developed in European and American Theatre and Performance Studies since the 1980s. In the European context, it followed on the heels of a Theatre Studies approach to communication theory, semiotics, and (post-)structuralism. In the USA, by contrast, its roots lie in the emergence of Performance Studies as an independent academic discipline. Performance analysis studies the forms, effects, and significance of cultural performances in general, and of theatre performances in particular.

Performances are understood here as events of showing and observing, for which actors and the audience gather together at the same place and time. A canonical definition of the performance provided by ethnologist Milton Singer can serve to distinguish these performances from other types of events. According to Singer, performances are characterized by "a definitely limited time span, or at least a beginning and an end, an organized program of activity, a set of performers, an audience, and a place and occasion of performance" (Singer, 1972, 71). However, performance analysis did not emerge from ethnography. Rather, it was developed with an eye toward artistic performances and professionalized theatrical forms. In performance analysis as it is practiced today, one can distinguish two major tendencies: a semiotic variant and a phenomenological one (Weiler & Roselt, 2017).

The semiotic variant seeks to understand how meaning is produced in performances. A performance is conceived of as an ensemble of heterogeneous signs that correspond to one another in a complex manner and must be decoded by the spectators. The aim of this approach is to capture precisely the signifying structure of the performance, in order to extract its mechanisms of meaning-making. As a result, the focus is placed on different semiotic systems of theatre (including spoken word, voice, sound, gesture, proximity, scenery, costume, makeup, lighting, and much more) and on recognizable units of meaning. The analyst attempts first to divide the performance into smaller units (sequences, scenes, or smaller entities) in order to then locate the dominant or determinant signifying structures and to interrogate their meaning. It is often useful to isolate particularly striking individual signs or signifying complexes and to examine these from multiple perspectives. Alongside authentic or 'concrete' meaning, connotations and associations are also of interest, allowing for nuances and individual variants of understanding to emerge (see among others Ubersfeld, 1977, Pavis, 1976, Elam, 1980, Fischer-Lichte, 1983).

The phenomenological variant of performance analysis is more interested in effects than meanings. Its focus is on what spectators experience in the course of a performance. This means it is imperative for the analyst to describe precisely his or her experience of the performance and reflect upon it. To facilitate this, a so-called "memory protocol" is typically completed shortly after the performance, in which the analyst describes those aspects or moments of the performance which had a particularly strong or lasting effect upon him or her. In reflecting on these "striking moments" (Roselt, 2013), the emphasis usually falls not on meanings but on experiences that can be understood though categories like sound, voice, rhythm, atmosphere, or presence (Fischer-Lichte, 2004). The subjective quality of the resulting descriptions is not taken to be a problem, particularly because the concept of phenomenon (i.e., the perceived or experienced thing) in the strict sense is such that the perceiver and the perceived are understood to be inextricably linked to one another (Merleau-Ponty, 1964). In a similar manner, entities like atmospheres are, from a phenomenological perspective, conceived of as an experience mutually constituted by the perceiver and the perceived (Böhme, 1995). Thus the analyst's writing is inspired by the phenomena.

Today, the two variants of performance analysis are typically combined. This is because contemporary theatre studies are generally interested in both the semiotic and the experiential dimensions of performances. A number of researchers place value on a distinction between performance analysis and analysis of the mise-en-scène (Balme, 1999): while, in the latter, the emphasis is on the broader idea behind what is shown on stage and developed through the rehearsal process, performance analysis tends toward a concern for experiences and interpretations of the here and now of an individual performance event. In point of fact, however, even these two perspectives can easily be combined with one another in analytic practice. The focal point of an analysis depends above all on the type of performance. For an artistic theatrical performance, the analyst's interest is typically in extracting the fundamental ideas behind the staging and providing a differentiated account of the aesthetic means employed to realize these ideas. When analyzing a cultural performance, by contrast (e.g., a festival, a ritual, or a political assembly), the researcher's primary concern may be the rules guiding action or the agency of individual actors. The cultural function of the performance can also serve as a point of departure for the analysis.

Some more recent trends within Theatre Studies place particular demands upon performance analysis, often in connection with newer theatre forms. For some time, Theatre Studies scholars have ceased to limit their studies to familiar theatre forms from their native regions. With the globalization of professional theatre, interculturality has become a widespread dimension of performances. This has led to a multiplication of experiences of non-comprehension, which are difficult to deal with in semiotic analyses: can one analyze semiotic processes when one is unfamiliar with the underlying codes? The tendency toward immersive and participative theatre forms also confronts the analyst with new challenges. For a performance that invites or sometimes even compels observers to play along or actively participate simultaneously, denies these same observers the sort of distance that the practice of analysis would seem to presuppose. The many emergent forms of embodiment or figuration present a further analytic difficulty: we are still lacking adequate and agreed-upon concepts for a number of forms of action and types of actors now widespread in contemporary theatre, such as acting spectators, performers portraying themselves or their own biographies, and the role of non-human objects (e.g., props) as actors.

Performance analysis and the question of emotion and affect

Joy, rage, worry, hate, mourning: the various theatre traditions of the world have each produced their own sign systems for representing culturally coded emotions like these. In particular, vocal, facial, and bodily signs are used by actors to portray individual emotions. Accordingly, performance analysis can study how the impression of a particular emotion was produced by an actor. The focus of the analysis is then on individual signs, which can be conceived of as the expression or index of an emotion. This type of semiotic analysis of emotions in performances can only function when the analyst is very familiar with the emotional repertoires of the culture in which the performance is situated. European dramatic theatre can draw upon a series of canonical textbooks in which the appropriate bodily signs for individual emotions are described with great precision (see, for example, Johann Jakob Engel's *Ideen zu einer Mimik*, 1785). When using such a semiotic method, it is important not to lose sight of the fundamental distinction between emotions and signs of emotions. One cannot infer, based on the external portrayal of certain emotional signs, that there is an actual, supposedly internal *feeling* of these emotions on the part of the actor. Denis Diderot's "paradox of the actor" (*Paradoxe sur le Comédien*, 1769–78, 1830) holds that the opposite is the case: the most accurate and convincing semiotic expression of a feeling is achieved by the one who does not actually feel the emotion in question at all. It is also important to recall here that signs of emotions are not to be sought exclusively among the human participants in a performance. Even the non-human elements of the performance – such as objects in the room, backgrounds or scenery, musical notes or sounds, and colors or lighting – can be understood as signs of emotions.

A phenomenologically oriented performance analysis is interested less in the reading of individual signs than in the holistic "corporeal feeling" (Waldenfels, 2000) of affectivity. The analyst must give an account of his or her own "state" during the performance. The so-called memory protocol is an important resource in this regard. The analyst uses such a protocol to record which events and experiences from the performance are, in retrospect, the subject of particularly intense memories. In so doing, he or she proceeds from the assumption that affectivity unfolds between the perceiver and the perceived. From the phenomenologist's perspective, a precise description of one's own perceptions is not to be characterized as "subjective" or criticized as "overly subjective", because it is precisely the task of such an approach to call into question the act of thinking in subject-object dichotomies. Affects, we would like to argue, neither arise exclusively in the subject nor strictly in the object. Instead, they are produced jointly by the subject and object of the perception. This reciprocal dynamic of affecting and being-affected can be described as affective relationality. The relation on stage, but especially the relational dynamics between stage and audience, is a prototype of affective relationality characteristic of social constellations more generally.

A good memory protocol is characterized by a detailed description of "striking moments" (Roselt) from the performance. The idea is not to produce a chronological or even a complete account of the theatrical event. Instead, more precisely and, from an affective perspective, more compellingly, the task of the memory protocol is to allow the author to focus on those details that were particularly memorable to him or her. Even in the explicit addressing of affectivity, memory protocols often reach very different degrees of precision and differentiation. It matters whether an affect is simply detected and named, or if one attempts to give a precise account of the specific scenic constellation that could have given rise to that affect. As such, it is worthwhile not only to determine that one was disgusted or euphoric, but also to ask which precise event or arrangement might have been responsible for the sensation of disgust or euphoria. The unique possibilities of an affect-oriented performance analysis become clear when one takes into account that affects are not individual, internal events, but instead manifest in situations and through actions. Indeed, directors use the proxemic dimension of performance – that is, the variable positioning of the different actors in space – in order to call attention to affective relationships between characters or figures (for example, closeness and distance, attraction and rejection). Spatial-visual and sonic atmospheres are often used as another important means of portraying diffuse, unclear, and often ambivalent affective dynamics. Instead of psychologizing or speculating about emotional states, performance analysis is thus meant to use the potential that lies in a precise description of situations and action forms: how, and in what mode, is a particular action – such as a simple walk across the stage – carried out? What sort of situation does an actor encounter when he or she walks onto the stage? How do actors address their audience from the stage? Can one describe a particular affective gesture [*Gestus*] in the turn toward the audience? The concept of the gesture can serve as a source of orientation for affect-centered analyses of this sort. It refers to 'stances' or 'comportments' of actors that are shown both corporeally and communicatively. A theatre theory informed by Brecht's account of the *Gestus* proceeds from the assumption that such comportments never have their sources simply in individual actors, but instead unfold between actors and are dependent on social contexts. Hence, statements on the gesture can begin with observations of individuals, but can also be extended to encompass entire situations or social relations. Ideally, at the end of such analyses, one does not find a catalogue of emotions that can be attributed to individual actors, but instead a differentiated description of a situational constellation that always also includes the analyst. The position of the analyst is always an aspect of the analysis, and should thus be laid out explicitly: what was my place or role in the performance described? Did the performance touch me or move me? What relations to other actors or things did the performance demand of me, or make possible?

Two case studies – challenges in postmigrant and immersive theatre

As we mentioned at the end of the first section, novel theatre forms pose unique challenges to that variant of performance analysis which is oriented towards affect and emotion. From the many possible examples, we have chosen to describe two of these in greater detail in the following. These forms are known as postmigrant and immersive theatre.

There are many reasons why it seems particularly important to focus on rela-tionality in analyses of postmigrant theatre productions. In performance analysis, phenomenological and semiotic analyses bump up against specific problems that can be meaningfully addressed through the lens of affect theory. The notion of 'postmigrant theatre' emerged in German-language theatre discourses approxi-mately 10 years ago. The first to use it was the small Berlin theatre called Ballhaus Naunynstraße, under the artistic direction of Shermin Langhoff. In this context, postmigrant theatre is understood to be a theatre form which is largely practiced by individuals who are second- or third-generation immigrants, but who do not wish to be identified exclusively with this migratory background. Instead, they prefer a kind of syncretism of identity constructions ("patch-work" or "hyphen-ated" identities). The *Ballhaus Naunynstraße* is located in Kreuzberg, a district of Berlin where many German-Turkish families have lived for decades. Shermin Langhoff began her work at the theatre in 2008. Under her direction, the theatre has successfully achieved a plan to include this long-established German-Turkish milieu in its theatre work, and in particular, the younger generation. It did so through projects involving youths from the neighborhood, or through a repertoire including many pieces and stagings by German-Turkish authors and directors.

Since 2015, the virulence surrounding "refugee politics" has caused massive changes in the theatre situation of a number of European countries. Today, it is difficult to highlight individual institutions as particular locales for a postmigrant theatre in the way that used to be possible with the Ballhaus Naunynstraße or, occasionally, with the Gorki Theatre. Now, the majority of the established theatre institutions do projects with refugees. For many theatres, these have been isolated and short-lived projects, resulting from cooperations with refugee initiatives and not infrequently with groups of refugees from homes for asylum seekers as well.

Many theatres have even founded permanent Exile Ensembles, in which refugees with professional theatre backgrounds create productions for the theatre's regular repertoire.

When engaging with stagings that emerge from the field of theatre and migration, performance analyses encounter two primary difficulties. On the one hand, this form of theatre takes a programmatic stance against unidirectional attributions by outsiders. Postmigrant theatre forms emerged as a form of critique of the self-certainty with which members of an ostensibly long-standing majority assigned attitudes, lifestyles, and feelings to people with migrant backgrounds. For this reason, it would be inappropriate for a performance analysis to then attempt – in the semiotic tradition – to assign individual meanings to the vocal, expressive, and bodily 'signs' offered by the actors. The first challenge thus consists in avoiding a reductive interpretation, in which individual signs are said to represent particular emotions. On the other hand, postmigrant theatre has a marked political thrust. This aspect can be easily overlooked when a work is viewed from a strictly phenomenological perspective, at least if this perspective limits itself to simply registering and describing one's own "corporeal feeling" in the course of the performance. For on what grounds could this feeling be given priority in the analysis over those of other participants in the performance? The second challenge for the analyst thus lies in the need to not universalize his or her own position and sensations with respect to the performance.

The answer to both challenges could be to concentrate, in the course of the analysis, on material relations and, in accord with this, to uncover the ways in which actors, objects, voices, languages, and their spatial relations affect one another. Affectivity can only be adequately described from a perspective that takes transindividual processes into account, and thus concerns itself not just with human actors (and their bodies and voices), but also with things, objects, movements, and material arrangements. In order to attain this perspective, it can be helpful to describe not concrete interactions between individuals, but instead to concentrate on the material transformation of individual elements. How, for example, is the text underlying the staging translated into different material registers? What relation does the highly differentiated linguistic material stand in to the other materials of the performances, and which movements and affective arrangements arise out of this? A staging of the *Hamletmaschine* by the Exile Ensemble of Berlin's Gorki-Theatre (Director: Sebastian Nübling, premiere on 24.2.2018) can serve as an example, allowing us to elaborate further on these questions and indicate some avenues of response.

Like many postmigrant theatre productions, the Gorki Theatre's *Hamletmaschine* is very language-centered: monologues, dialogues, and choral speech are at the forefront, suggesting that an analysis might take the textual dimension of the performance as its point of departure. *Hamletmaschine* is a 1977 piece by Heiner Müller, one of the East German playwright's most famous pieces. Formally, it is a fragmentary text. It anticipates later pieces by Elfriede Jelinek, if not in its brevity (approximately nine printed pages) then perhaps in its post-dramatic structure, which systematically transgresses the limits of dramatic figuration. The text begins with the memorable lines: "I was Hamlet. I stood on the coast and spoke with the surf Blah-Blah-Blah, at my back the ruins of Europe". Today, this beginning may recall the situation of the refugees at the borders of Europe, but otherwise Müller's piece does not seem to be predestined to serve as the future textual basis for a postmigrant staging. It is a meta-theatrical text that reflects on the traditions of classical European theatre, above all Shakespearean theatre (with Hamlet and other canonical figures) and classical Greek tragedy (along with its associated discourses on the futility of theatrical action). The fundamental idea of the Exile Ensemble's staging consists in creating a textual collage. The subject of Müller's text is a ruined world, violent and devoid of any future, and the role of the artist therein. Elements of this work are joined with recent texts from the Syrian theatre practitioner Ayham Majid Agha, who is himself a member of the Exile Ensemble and can be seen on stage as an actor. His texts are concerned with his own experiences in a Syria rocked by civil war. By inserting Agha's texts into the collage, the textual dimension of the performance acquires a multilingual structure, as the newly added text fragments from Agha have been left in Arabic or English, while the text from Müller is spoken primarily in German.

In order to attain a better analytic understanding of the performance's affective relations, we need to examine more closely two relationships that this staging of the *Hamletmaschine* enters into within its newly constituted theatre text: namely, the relationship between language and space on the one hand, and the relationship between language and the body on the other. The dominant directorial idea of this staging is to acoustically and visually spatialize the text spoken on stage, compiled of fragments from Müller and Agha. The seven actors move across the mostly empty stage, shaded black, behind a kind of gauze screen. The spoken German, Arabic, or English text is projected onto this screen with varying light intensities and different fonts. At the same time, one can see on the upper right and left extremities of the stage – as is customary in all performances at the Gorki Theatre – translations of the spoken text as supertitles. This constellation produces wide-ranging effects. Through the filigree projection technique, the written signs of three different languages appear to the viewer as inscriptions on the bodies of the actors. The interplay between moving bodies and the constantly changing, flowing projections of writing evokes an impression of great dynamic complexity. The spoken language does not just seem as if it were cast upon the bodies of the performers, but also as if it were set free of them, since the movement of the written characters appears to not be synchronized with that of the bodies. The multilingual text literally inserts itself between the actors and spectators as a luminous projection on the gauze screen. In this way, the potentially dividing character of language becomes manifest. At the same time, however, it also foregrounds the aesthetic beauty of differing types of written signs. Script and language affect the bodies of the actors and the perceptive activity of the spectators to the same extent, but in differing directions.

Of decisive importance for the nature of the projection is the fact that all of the actors on stage appear in colorful, clown-like full-body rubber masks (costumes: Eva-Maria Bauer). In addition, the actors' voices are transmitted indirectly through microphones and sometimes sound distorted, as if by laughing gas. The result is that the staging as a whole acquires a grotesque undertone. The composition of the Exile Ensemble has been the subject of frequent discussion in the press: it is made up of actors from Syria, Palestine, Afghanistan, and other Middle Eastern regions who fled to Germany. However, concealed by rubber masks and speaking with distorted voices, this aspect of the ensemble is simply no longer perceptible. The bodies seem to resist not only the attribution of nationalities and other identifying traits, but they are also no longer legible with respect to individually ascribable emotions. Along with the masking of the face, the form of the staging – as grotesque – makes it impossible to attribute specific emotions to individual actors or figures in earnest. It is also entirely unclear which cultural repertoire could serve as the basis for such an attribution of emotions. The gauze screen, textual projection, and clown costumes form a threefold barrier between the actors and the audience, highlighting the radical indirectness and inaccessibility of visible expression. At the same time, it is apparent that the rubber masks affect the performance in many ways: they are the decisive feature contributing to the undertone of the grotesque. They determine the possibilities afforded to the actors for facial and bodily expression. And they also shape the experiences of the spectators, for no matter how one reacts individually to aggressive clown grimaces and bodies bound up in rubber, these are in any case impressions that place an intense demand on the affective capacities of the perceiver throughout the entirety of the performance. The political potential of the performance results from just this sensory-spatial experience, i.e. that an artistic engagement with war, violence, and flight is only possible through complex linguistic-aesthetic mediation, and is thus extremely indirect, fragmented, and susceptible to all sorts of misunderstandings.

As we have only been able to indicate briefly here, such an analysis of the Exile Ensemble's *Hamletmaschine* would precisely *not* aim to attribute specific emotions to individual actors, or even to place the emotional dimension of the theatre in the foreground. Instead, the task lies in the attempt to inquire into the affective potential of the piece through a strictly *relational* view of what happens on stage. The performance's relational qualities are to be analyzed without being limited to personal interactions on the stage or the communication between the stage and the audience. The material arrangements are thus to be understood in a comprehensive and no longer anthropocentric sense. Performances are affective and, at the same time, affecting constellations, that find themselves in a state of constant motion. Through this motion, the positions of acting and observing are constantly redistributed. Thus, affect-oriented performance analysis is interested from the very beginning in attending to relations and constellations, instead of one's own, subjective responses. Evidently, one cannot simply separate one from the other.

But from a political perspective, it makes a difference whether one gives priority to one's own subjective experiences and individual standpoints, or whether one emphasizes relations and intensities that are always capable of destabilizing one's own position.

This type of destabilization can also be experienced in unique fashion in immersive theatrical forms. Immersive theatre forms have been developed since the 2000s by groups as diverse as Interrobang, Lundahl & Seitl, Ontroerend, Goed, Punchdrunk, Rimini Protokoll, SIGNA or Shunt, to name but a few. This relatively recent development in contemporary theatre hybridizes modes of reception and experiences of involvement. These modes are reminiscent of new media – such as video, computer games, and virtual reality – and of 'real-world' environments, including assessment centers, live role-plays, theme parks, murder-mystery weekends, and geocaching. And of course, they are also reminiscent of theatre, installation, and performance art. As such, immersive theatre presents a unique challenge for the performance-analytic study of affective dynamics.

Immersive theatre and immersive performances are often staged in urban spaces that have not been institutionalized as locations for art, such as empty factories or office buildings, vacant lots, subway tunnels, and the like. Thus, aspects of site-specific performance and installation art flow into these performance formats. In this way, they combine representational schemas from acting, performance art, and installation art with elements from pop culture (e.g., film, television, and the entertainment industry), as well as from the work world, the healthcare system, psychotechnics, jurisprudence and bureaucracy, or even sex work. They create elaborate, atmospherically dense spaces that evoke a holistic impression that is not only visual but also contains acoustic, olfactory, gustatory, and material relations to the objects, fabrics, and textures used. In this way, they produce parallel worlds in which participants frequently spend several hours interacting with the performers, with other participants in this world, and indeed with the artificial world itself.

Immersion derives from the Latin verb *immergere*, which originally meant the submersion of a body or object in a liquid. In a metaphorical sense, it meant sinking or submerging oneself into a given situation. Classical immersion experiences include Christian baptism or language acquisition, as when individuals are placed in a foreign-language environment in order to learn the language.

In recent years, discourses and theories of immersion were particularly virulent in the context of film, video, computer games, virtual reality, and other media-technological developments. However, it must be emphasized that immersion is by no means a hallmark of the recent present, nor solely a characteristic of media-technological achievements. Instead, it seems significant to distinguish between different forms and dimensions of immersion. In this way, the psychic-psychological immersion in an artistically and/or medially created world can be differentiated from a perceptual-physical experience of immersion (Dogramaci & Liptay, 2016, 11). One can distinguish a more mental-cognitive dimension of immersion from immersion experiences that are perceptual or that may even include the entire body: the former shapes aesthetic procedures of illusion and, as fictional immersion, is characterized by the fact that "the majority of the recipient's attention is directed away from the environment and toward the arte-fact" (Voss, 2008, 127). These perceptual and bodily experiences of immersion are frequently the product of immersive theatre, but they are also brought about in immersive professional, consumer, and experiential worlds, in which the par-ticipant represents an active and constitutive element of the environment in which he or she is located.

A concise account of the various forms and tendencies of immersive theatre can be given as follows: it mobilizes spectators in a comprehensive sense, and it does away with the stage as a clearly demarcated, particular space, indeed totalizes it. In so doing, immersive theatre interrogates the fundamental conditions of theatre as such, for example with reference to spatiality, the relationship between actors and audience, or the experience of community.

Among the countless challenges that immersive theatre poses for a performance-analytic study of affect and emotion, we would like to concentrate on a single aspect: namely, the problem of determining what the object of the performance analysis should be. Put differently, we are confronted here with the question of whether *a* performance in the singular still exists at all, let alone whether it could be analyzed. This question is raised in exemplary fashion by the Danish-Austrian artist group SIGNA's production *Sons & Sons* (premiered on 6 November 2015 in Hamburg). SIGNA has been developing performance installations for over a decade with great success, and has thus exercised a formative influence on one form of immersive theatre.

In *Sons & Sons*, approximately 50 performers interacted every evening with and for about 70 visitors. During the 6-hour performance installation, visitors were addressed as new employees of the firm Sons & Sons, although it remained unclear throughout what sort of firm Sons & Sons is, what they do, or what sort of business they practice. As new employees in the firm, the theatre attendees were required on their first day (or rather, evening) of work to complete an individual-ized route that moves them through different divisions of the firm. At precisely determined points in time, for example 7 minutes and 30 seconds past 7 o'clock, visitors had to be present in whichever section of the firm had been specifically des-ignated for them. (It should be noted that even orienting oneself in the expansive building that is the former Vocational School for Construction Workers is a chal-lenge.) These appointments produced ever-changing small groups of six to eight people, who then experienced a variety of different scenes and scenarios together. There was an "Office of Internal Laws", a "Central Department of Expansion- and Potential-Development", and a "Department of Resistance-Training". There was even a "Free Time Centre", a "Medical Bay", departments of "Childhood Affairs" and "Romantic Issues", as well as a "canteen" and the office of the firm's director.

As new employees, the visitors had to carry out different tasks in each depart-ment, tasks whose significance was typically obscure. In so doing, they were secretly tested and judged by the performers. These performers, who played long-standing employees of Sons & Sons, were each outfitted with a comprehensive work biography, a "son" name, and a personal history. The performers evaluated the behavior of each individual participant at every station through questionnaires distributed at the entrance, whose categories and evaluative scales also remained cryptic.

The spaces and atmospheres created seemed to recall a long-past era between the 1960s and 1980s, that could not be precisely dated. The yellowing, often dilapidated setting – combined with strict performers clad in beige and mouse-grey, and ill-fitting costumes – evoked a mixture of a socialist training ground, a religious cult, and a "Stasi" headquarter (the secret state police of the former German Democratic Republic). There were hardly any computers on the desks at the Sons & Sons firm, and when they were present, they seemed to have been taken straight from the Technology Museum. Instead, there were analogue telephones, old adding machines, slide rules, and other tools from a now-bygone world of work. Even the paper used everywhere was yellowed and dirty; it felt like a material greeting from an indeterminate past. In the "Department of Childhood Affairs", pastel tones in blue and pink dominated. Primitive, discarded children's beds made of iron – recalling images of Romanian orphanages shortly after the fall of the Berlin Wall – were piled high with mountains of old stuffed animals. The new employees had to sit in a circle with two resolute kindergarteners who made them each call their mothers on a toy telephone and tell her, in front of the entire group, what they had always wanted to tell her. In the "Free Time Centre", there were party hats, paper streamers, and cheap champagne; the "Medical Bay", which smelled distinctly like a hospital, contained beds in which participants had to lie and imagine their own deaths. It recalled less of a real, functioning hospital room than the rooms in Ilya Kabakov's " 'total' installation" *Treatment with Memories*.[1]

The various assignments that participants had to carry out in the different departments gave the impression of an assessment center, a therapy session, and a role-playing simulation at once. However, visitors also found themselves mere spectators in an opaque performance, again and again. They would observe obscure punishment rituals or a kind of marriage ceremony, but would also become witnesses – through sounds – to a scene of violence. Although individual elements or partial sequences from these situations seemed entirely familiar, it was never entirely clear to the visitors what or how something was being acted out here, and according to which rules. Throughout the performance installation, participants were continually confronted with the most diverse expectations regarding their roles and behavior – confronted not only with the expectations of the performers and other participants, but also with their own. And yet, these expectations remained entirely implicit. It was always unclear which behavioral or role expectations were being brought to bear concretely, and which of the countless, palimpsest-like layerings of possible frames or frameworks were valid in a given situation. Had one been the theatrical audience to a wedding performance, one guest at a wedding party, a neutral witness to a wedding, or none of the three – or even all three at once? Until the very end, what would happen next remained open and unpredictable. The only thing that was clear was that participation, behavior, answers, actions, or even refusals to act on the part of the participants were all an integral component of the event taking place, and that all present – performers and participants alike – would have to react to it. As one example, we offer an incident of strikingly strong affective dynamics that Doris Kolesch experienced during her visit to the performance, and that she recorded in her memory protocol as follows:

> In the "Office of Internal Laws", we encounter the firm's director, who intro-duces herself as Ronda Sohn. She is resolute, dictatorial, seems as if she would tolerate no dissent. After telling us some of the laws and rules of the firm, she asks the group of new arrivals: "Would you like something to drink? Mineral water, perhaps, with or without [mit oder ohne]?"[2] Two men in my group say: "Yes please, with!" A glass of water is extended to them, whose cloudy appearance and the granular substance at the bottom made suddenly and indubitably clear that the question "With or without?" did not refer to the expected carbonation, but instead to – salt. The two thirsty men refuse to drink the saltwater, and Ronda Sohn begins lecturing them about what an unacceptable waste it is, in light of the worldwide water shortage, to not drink the water. She does not accept any disagreement. A short dispute ensues between the performer and the visitors; blandishments, logical arguments, and pleas from the visitors have no effect on Ronda. On the contrary, she announces that the group – which includes, in addition to the two thirsty young men, a woman and me – cannot leave the Office of Internal Laws until they have drunk the water. She goes one step further and issues the threat that this delay might make the four of us late for our next appointment as well. For a time, nothing happens, and our little group stands indecisively in front of the small kitchen range in the office. Ronda Sohn holds the glass of salt water, arm extended, towards the men. They try over and over to explain why they don't want to drink the water. I register a mixture of confusion, curiosity, and discomfort in response to the situation. At the same time, I feel the impulse to intervene in the situation, but I hold back in order to see how the situation will develop further (or resolve itself). Finally, the woman standing next to me takes pity on the men and downs the glass of water with a stoic expression. Later, in the hallway, I ask her why she drank the water. She answers that she just wanted things to move forward.

It's unlikely, indeed probably impossible, that this situation repeated itself on other evenings in just this way. Perhaps it was never asked if anyone wanted something to drink, perhaps no one said yes, perhaps a different liquid was offered – a visitor to a different performance of *Sons & Sons* reported that she was meant to drink a glass of water with hairs in it.[3] It is not only the groups of visitors that are continually recombined in the different departments, for although the performers have learned the basic structures of the scenes and situations by rote, and how to integrate the actions and activities of visitors into them, even these are different with every performance.

The visitors' journeys through the different departments of Sons & Sons, which are handed out to them at the beginning of the event on a clipboard, are individualized such that no two visitors' experiences are ordered exactly the same way. After every station, the groups are dissolved and reconstituted; no one proceeds through all of the firm's departments, but instead passes by certain divisions that he or she cannot access. In addition, every situation changes not just on the basis of the unpredictable behavior of the new employees, but also because the performers continually select one or two guests to participate in so-called one-on-ones or one-on-twos. For these, the performers disappear with the chosen visitor(s) through a side door or into an adjoining room, where they carry out a sequence of events that remains concealed from the others. However, the selection of individual visitors for these private experiences remains visible to all.

A further degree of variation and complexity is introduced through the fact that repeated visits allow for further, entirely different experiences. Those who participated in *Sons & Sons* twice (or even more frequently) were integrated into the proceedings as performers and entrusted with small tasks. These people were addressed by their "son" name – assigned to them at the end of their first performance visit – and integrated into the fiction as new employees. This procedure is more or less unknown in theatre and performance contexts, but it appears comparable to the structure of video games in which skill, ability, and experience allow one to reach ever-higher levels of play, with different tasks and challenges.

This extended description of central aspects of *Sons & Sons* was necessary to demonstrate that there is in a radical sense no 'performance' here, and certainly not one in the singular. We are confronted with an extreme diversity of distinct performances, but the up to 70 different routes, narratives, and reception experiences that can be experienced every evening at *Sons & Sons* go far beyond the ever-present subjectivity of individual perception and sensibility that we must usually account for in artistic reception processes or perception experiences. In performance installations like *Sons & Sons*, we have instead art events that are deliberately structured in such a way as to diversify and individualize the object of perception. Instead of one performance in the evening, there is a vast series of performance versions that resemble one another in their structure and general character, but differ in significant ways at the level of their concrete unfolding. The multi- or poly-perspectivism necessary to grasp and then analyze the constitutive diversity of these performance versions and their associated affective dynamics tests the limits of established forms of semiotic and phenomenological performance analysis alike. Hence, immersive formats in modern art provoke questions like the following: How can one adequately describe and study both the structural seriality and the radical singularity of individual performance versions? What weight with respect to the artistic whole can be assigned to observations and reflections that result from the experience of an individual, concrete performance version? How can we scrutinize the claims of other participants that contradict our own experiences of the performance? Theatre Studies and neighboring disciplines must develop adequate methods, procedures, and descriptive techniques in order to answer these and similar questions. What may prove methodologically productive for such theatre forms is to extend the radically subjective perspective of performance analysis by interviewing other spectators, and also by integrating other materials like audience discussions, reports in online forums, and so forth. In this way, one could begin to approach a poly- or multiperspectival view on individually striking moments and situations.[4] Early explorations within the framework of the research project "Reenacting Emotions: Strategies and Politics of Immersive Theatre", part of the Collaborative Research Center *Affective Societies*, have shown that the knowledge acquired thereby can confirm many theoretical assumptions – for example, about the effects of theatre performances – but can also extend or correct these assumptions. In a manner resembling that of the woman in the salt-water scenario, who intervened in order to allow the performance to proceed, a number of those surveyed indicated that the performance, for all its analogies and points of comparison to structures, phenomena, and situations of everyday life, was still being perceived as a self-contained, independent ensemble. Attempts to interpret the performance situation as the unmediated and unproblematic embodiment of a social and political situation, as is frequently done not only in the press but also within Theatre Studies, thus appear problematic. At the same time, the surveys and interviews suggested that immersive theatre forms, which are frequently criticized for being manipulative or even rejected outright, hold significant potential for generating self-reflection on the part of spectators about their own embeddedness in social and societal structures.

Summary – relationality and poly-perspectivism

The two examples show two possible ways that a mode of performance analysis informed by affect theory could be developed further. Our assumption is that affectivity in theatre is a dynamic process that places different actors, objects, texts, and spaces in relation with one another in a variety of ways. Affects thus take place *between* actors and agents, and not *in* them. Affects are to be distinguished from emotions as individual psychic states through this relational character. In contrast to an emotion, a feeling, or a mood, an affect is primarily a transindividual event. For performance analysis, this means first that it cannot unproblematically universalize the individual view and subjective response of the analyst, as had often been the case in past treatments of performances within Theatre Studies. Nor should it invoke an auxiliary construction like "the spectator", to whom the most varied interpretations, perspectives, attitudes, and emotions can be attributed. Such speculative attributions only *seem* to account for the experiential dimension of a performance. In truth, neither the performance itself nor the experience of "a" spectator in the theatre can be had in the singular.

We see two opportunities for doing justice, analytically, to the plurality of performances and experiences of performances that become so apparent from an affect-theoretical perspective: on the one hand, the fundamental relationality of the performance event must be made the point of departure for the analysis. On the other hand, one must use the opportunity to confront one's own view on the performance with those of other participants (be they spectators, actors, or other producers). The poly-perspectivism of the performance should be reflected in a new polyphony of performance analysis, which must be developed in transdisciplinary exchange with the social sciences as well as the humanities. Interviews, focus-group conversations, and the discourse-analytic inclusion of diverse records of audience reception are not counter-models to performance analysis. Instead, they can be an integral component of an academic engagement with performative events, one that heeds the transindividuality of the affective.

Notes

1 See Kabakov, 1995; Weidemann, 1998.
2 TN. When offering guests water in Germany, it is common to ask if they want it "with or without", with the implied but unspoken object of the preposition being carbonation.
3 The anecdote concerning the water glass with the hairs in it was provided by FU Master's student Joanna Noga.
4 Within the framework of the research project "Reenacting Emotions: Strategies and Politics of Immersive Theatre", part of the Collaborative Research Center *Affective Societies*, Theresa Schütz carried out audience surveys and qualitative interviews, receiving many valuable insights into audience reactions and affective modalities. Further innovative approaches for the methodological development of Theatre Studies (including performance analysis) can be found in Reason and Sedgman (2015).

References

Balme, Ch 1999, *Einführung in die Theaterwissenschaft*, Erich Schmidt, Berlin.
Böhme, G 1995, *Atmosphäre*, Suhrkamp, Frankfurt am Main.
Dogramaci, B & Liptay, F (ed.), 2016, *Immersion in the Visual Arts and Media*, Brill Rodopi, Leiden.
Elam, K 1980, *The Semiotics of Theatre and Drama*, Methuen, London.
Fischer-Lichte, E 1983, *Semiotik des Theaters*, Gunter Narr, Tübingen.
Fischer-Lichte, E 2004, *Ästhetik des Performativen*, Suhrkamp, Frankfurt am Main.
Kabakov, I 1995, *Über die "totale" Installation*, Canz, Ostfildern.
Merleau-Ponty, M 1964, *Le Visible et l'invisible*, Gallimard, Paris.
Pavis, P 1976, *Problèmes de sémiologie théâtrale*, Presses de l'Université du Québec, Montréal.
Reason, M & Sedgman, K (eds.), 2015, 'Theatre audiences', *Special Issue of Participations*, vol. 12, no. 1.
Roselt, J 2013, *Phänomenologie des Theaters*, Wilhelm Fink, München.
Singer, M 1972, *When a Great Tradition Modernizes. An Anthropological Approach to Indian Civilization*, Pall Mall Press, London.
Ubersfeld, A 1977, *Lire le théâtre*, Éditions sociales, Paris.
Voss, Ch 2008, "Fiktionale Immersion", in G Koch & C Voss (eds.), *"Es ist, als ob": Fiktionalität in Philosophie, Film- und Medienwissenschaft*, pp. 127–138, Fink, München.

Waldenfels, B 2000, *Das leibliche Selbst. Vorlesungen zur Phänomenologie des Leibes*, Suhrkamp, Frankfurt am Main.

Weidemann, F (ed.), 1998, *Ilja Kabakov – Treatment with memories. Ausstellungskatalog*, Hamburger Bahnhof – Museum für Gegenwart, Berlin.

Weiler, C & Roselt, J 2017, *Aufführungsanalyse. Eine Einführung*, Francke, Tübingen.

Chapter 13

Shared and divided feelings in translingual texts of Emine Sevgi Özdamar

Performativity and affective relationality of language, writing and belonging

Anne Fleig

This chapter deals with the question of how to explore the affective dimensions of contemporary literature, especially in translingual writing, and how to search for possible ways to analyze these aspects. More than just a result of writing, affect is an integral part of the writing process itself. In light of this, I will examine the performativity of language in different types of texts by well-known German author Emine Sevgi Özdamar. Many of her texts deal intensively with questions of language, especially those of acquiring a new language and of moving within and between languages. These texts take part in a process that ultimately leads to shared and divided feelings of belonging to both the new language and the first language as a foreign one. These questions are inseparably linked to Özdamar's own way of life in Germany, where she worked as an actress and as a *Dramaturgin* before becoming an author. Therefore, her texts perform and reflect the difference between speaking and writing in a characteristic, theatrical manner. Word by word, they form a stage for translingualism and for the writing process itself. Özdamar's literary reflections demonstrate that moving between languages is driven by affect as an encounter between bodies and words, thus creating an affective relationality of language and between languages. Her work also shows that the affective and performative production of translingualism is closely linked to Özdamar's concept of authorship.

1. Introduction and theoretical background

What does 'Analyzing Affective Societies' mean to a Literary Critic? How could we think of literature in its affective entanglements? And what do we do when we try to analyze literary texts in regard to affect? Can we read for affect in terms of meaning represented in written texts? Or does affect rather inform writing in an affective process of transformation? And how can we deal with the specific movement between the process of writing and the written text as its product? These questions point directly to language in its dynamic relations to actors in everyday life, to concepts of authorship and the highly complex framework of the monolingually written literary tradition.

From the viewpoint of Literary Studies, we conceptualize language and textuality in a double perspective. First, we think of these concepts in terms of communication, discourse, and representation; second, we reflect on language as material that builds on itself, which then structures the written text and provides an affective register of rhythm, sound and figures of speech. In both perspectives, we have to be aware of the bodily dimension of language: rather than understanding it as an abstract entity, I would suggest conceptualizing language as an ongoing process that occurs in speaking and writing and combines performative presentation and representation in a movement within itself. In this sense, we do not only ask for language as a mode of affect, but also for affect building words and other utterances (Fleig, 2019).

Seen from a historical perspective, reflections on language and literary writing are closely intertwined. Furthermore, since the late 18th century, conceptions of writing and male authorship (Kittler, 2003) are almost inseparably linked with the emergence of monolingualism. Since this period of literary history, to think of language has meant to think of one or more countable entities of language and literature. Further, building on this idea, the reliance on language as an entity points to the notion of language as a kind of possession of the language user. This so-called monolingual paradigm (Yildiz, 2012) is still influential for today's conceptions of language in everyday life as well as in literary writing and the literary field.

The concept of monolingualism, and of having one natural mother tongue, is perhaps the most important backdrop to what we aim to explore within the CRC *Affective Societies* – "Geteilte Gefühle", which means shared *and* divided feelings. My project, "Shared and Divided Feelings. Narratives of Belonging in Contemporary Transcultural German-language Literature"[1] sets out to analyze German-language literary texts published after 1989 as privileged sites for the presentation and performative production of translingualism as an affective practice reflected in literary writing. These texts are not only understood to represent issues of belonging or migration, but also to bring about this belonging or non-belonging in an affective mode of performativity. This affective mode is thus related to the dynamics of language in speaking and writing and especially those of translingualism.

These dynamics articulate themselves as shared and divided feelings of belonging in contemporary transcultural German-language literature, in several respects. Firstly, the dual meaning of the German word "teilen" contains a communicative reference to community and the public. On the one hand, the term expresses the feelings of belonging that are communicated through the process of writing. Authors and readers, as well as narrators and characters, *share* these feelings with others and connect them to their cultural and social environment. Yet, these feelings are also *divided*, which is the second meaning of the German word. That is, they are subject to ambivalences and ruptures, experiencing and expressing a sense of difference vis-à-vis the status quo. Secondly, this difference often includes reflections on the so-called mother tongue. As every language is a learned language, there is no 'native' tongue (Prade, 2013, 2). In this sense, even the mother tongue remains another tongue, comprising "unknown words, unheard pronunciations, expressions and phrasings" (Prade, 2013, 2–3.) that not only high-light the difference between speaking and writing, but also articulate and point to different feelings of belonging. "Geteilte Gefühle" thus always encompass the issue of non-belonging. This aspect plays a particularly important role in cur-rent conceptualizations of translingualism and its resistance against the notion of belonging to one language and one nation only.

a. Methodology

The material, or – as sociologists might call this – the empirical basis of my pro-ject, are literary texts. These texts encompass different prose, genres, essays, short stories, novels, acceptance speeches and various kinds of poetic texts published in German after 1989 by authors who do not have German as their first language or who are bi-lingual. After reading and rereading these texts, the research team had to look for an approach that enabled us to document affective processes within these texts, since it is difficult to analyze literary writing in the making. This approach also included an overview of the state of research on affect-related pro-cesses in literary studies and on literature in affect studies.

As large parts of affect studies positioned themselves against the most influ-ential linguistic turn and the 'culture as text' paradigm, the relation of affect to language has not been on top of the agenda of affect studies. However, following Jacques Derrida and Judith Butler, there has been an intense discussion since the 1990s on the performativity of language and even of words. In this context, Eve Kosofsky Sedgwick argued "that the line between words and things or between linguistic and nonlinguistic phenomena is endlessly changing" (Sedgwick, 2003, 6), thus providing space for different kinds of meaning and language as a dynamic, always changing process. The next step towards a notion of affect pertaining to both language and literary texts, is to develop a concept of performativity that unfolds between speech and writing as a dialogic encounter between bodies and worlds.

While there is still little research on affect in literary studies (Berlant, 2011; Riley, 2004; Richardson, 2016), there is almost no research on affect stud-ies within German literary criticism, with the exception of research in Gender Studies (Zimmermann, 2017). Although there is increasingly more German studies research drawing on historical representations of emotions (Winko, 2003; Zumbusch, 2016), the circulation of affect and emotion (Ahmed, 2004) in analyz-ing literary texts remains a rarity in German studies.

Inquiring into the affective dimensions of contemporary literature means thinking of affect as a dynamic relationship between bodies. This includes the interweaving of bodily experiences and memories, words and world. In literary writing, affect unfolds between the writer's body and the written text. Referring to the concepts of Spinoza and Deleuze, this movement has to be regarded in a double way, as being formative of and transformative for the writer as well as the process itself (Fleig, 2019; Röttger-Rössler & Slaby, 2018).

Within this context, we decided to continue our research on two different paths. First, we looked for affect in literary theory and engaged in the intensive process of rereading the oeuvre of Mikhail Bakhtin. His works are well known in the field of postcolonial studies, and he also developed an innovative approach to language and literature in their entanglements with daily life. Second, we tried to find texts by contemporary translingual authors that explicitly reflect on literary writing and its affective impact. The aim was to raise questions concerning affect and literary texts by reading Bakhtin, and to get preliminary answers to those questions by rereading the material.

The Russian literary theorist Mikhail Bakhtin (1895–1975) developed the concept of the polyphonic modern novel and its 'heteroglossia'. The polyphonic novel is structured by dialogism and involves a pragmatic understanding of communication as the capacity to move between different words, voices, discourses ('heteroglossia') and, consequently, between different languages. In particular, his book *Problems of Dostoevsky's Poetics* (1984 [1929]) and his later essay *Discourse in the Novel* (1981 [1934]) carve out Bakhtin's concept of dialogism. Dialogism highlights literary language as a language in use and as a dynamic, ongoing process driven by different 'forces of encounter' (Deleuze), or as Bakhtin put it, by "languages of social groups, 'professional' and 'generic' languages, languages of generations and so forth" (1981, 272). In this view, even literary language "is only one of the heteroglot languages" (ibid.).

For Bakhtin, there is no unitary language. Because of this, there is no possession of language as there is no individual speaking in this unitary language either (ibid., 269). There is only the "authentic environment of an utterance, the environment in which it lives and takes shape" (ibid., 272), that builds on the dynamics of linguistic life. Bakhtin's concept of 'heteroglossia' is a productive starting point for thinking of differences between literary genres, between speech acts or between speech and writing (Acker, Fleig, & Lüthjohann, in preparation). Bakhtin's notion of dialogism is based on the bodily experience and performative capacity of language that shapes every utterance. It can be interpreted as affective relationality (see Röttger-Rössler & Slaby, 2018), unfolding between different speakers, languages or other environments. Following Bakhtin's research, words and different utterances resonate and affect each other in a process of questioning and answering, speaking and writing, that leads to a polyphonic ensemble of speech in the written text.

b. Mother tongue and other tongues

It is often found that translingualism is thought of as a 'new' quality of transcultural literature. However, it is important to be aware of the persistence of the monolingual framework as a genuinely modern phenomenon. As mentioned earlier, the emergence of monolingualism dates back to the late 18th century. It established "the idea that having one language was the natural norm, and that multiple languages constituted a threat to the cohesion of individuals and societies" (Yildiz, 2012, 6). In particular, German thinkers like Herder or Schleiermacher developed the concept of the mother tongue that stresses the unique and unchangeable origin of one's tongue. They related it to the modern nation-state, suggesting that the language of one's mother is also naturally the language of the state one "belongs to" (ibid., 9). Yildiz analyzes the relationship between language and nation with the mother tongue as its "affective knot" (ibid., 10). It does not consider meanings of individual speech acts, but rather structures the way in which language can be used by "supplying it with notions of maternal origin, affective and corporeal intimacy, and natural kinship" (ibid.).

The concept of the mother tongue affects not only practices of subjectivation but also practices of literary writing. As Yildiz points out, the uniqueness of language imagined as a mother tongue "lends it authority to an aesthetics of originality and authenticity" (ibid., 8). Looking back to literary discourse at the end of the 18th century, the historical formation of national languages is closely linked to modern literature and to the emergence of the modern author. Building off this context, it is most interesting that Özdamar refers to the German literary tradition of bourgeois drama and theatre in several of her texts. This is not only an intertextual reference but also a reference for the monolingual framework of speaking and writing on which she explicitly reflects in her acceptance speech for the *Chamisso Prize* (see Özdamar, 2001). What is important here is the difference between speech and monolingual literary writing. This difference helps to show that literary translingualism reflects on multiple voices that emerge from written text, reintroducing their bodily dimension in a dialogic interaction.

Regarding Bakhtin, the notion of dialogism allows us to differentiate between the discursive order of monolingualism and different practices of writing that are always characterized by a "plurality of possible expressions, and hence a different tongue for every speaker" (Prade, 2013, 3). Like affect, language is relational in the sense that it relies on individual bodily activities that are formed and informed by social norms and discourses. This holds true for both speaking and writing. The relationality of affect and language thus directly leads back to the argument that there is no "singular, homogenous language" (ibid.). Rather, spoken and written language as well as affect are to be conceptualized as dynamic and performative processes that we as humans are part of but that we cannot possess. Connecting to these processes, it might be helpful to remember that 'emotion' comes from the Latin *emovere*, meaning "to move" or to "move out" (Ahmed, 2004, 11). Affects and feelings move in a double sense: while circulating, they connect and disconnect us with other people, bodies or objects, leading to an instructive, dialogic relationship of movement and attachment (ibid.). They are not only situated in the human interior that is expressed or represented in literature, but they also take shape in language use and everyday life, thus creating the dialogism of translingual writing as an affective practice.

2. Example: translingual texts of Emine Sevgi Özdamar

To illustrate the previous theories, the German author Sevgi Emine Özdamar offers an example of the performativity and affective relationality among language, writing and belonging. Her writings comprise an important part of this research material and fulfill the criteria mentioned in section I.a. Özdamar was born in Malataya/Turkey in 1946, where she learned Turkish growing up in her family, as well as in school due to the language reform of Atatürk. In 1965, at the age of 18, she went to Germany for the first time. She did not know any German and worked as a so-called 'guest worker' in Berlin, earning money in order to go to an acting school in Istanbul. There she had her first appointments as an actress, but in 1971 she came back to Berlin because of the Turkish military coup. She had the opportunity to sit in productions at the *Volksbühne* under the direction of Benno Besson, and got her first theatre engagement at Bochum in the late 1970s. She became an actress and settled in Germany, where she also had acting roles in films. In the 1980s, she started writing with several theatre plays before turning to short stories and novels. As Ortrud Gutjahr has pointed out, Özdamar's writing is not only characterized by changing from Turkish into German, but also by changing from dramatic to rather epic forms (Gutjahr, 2016, 8). Özdamar herself reflects on the process of acquiring the German language as a new language as well as a literary language in many of her texts. Today, she is quite well known as one of the first German authors with a Turkish background. Özdamar's writings include theatre plays, short stories and three novels, which are known as the so-called *Berlin-Istanbul Trilogy*. She has won several important literary prizes, among them the *Ingeborg-Bachmann Prize*, the *Adelbert-von-Chamisso Prize* and the *Kleist Prize*. She was the first non-native author to win the *Ingeborg-Bachmann Prize*, the latter being an important signal of acknowledgment in the German literary field.

a. Belonging through language

In the translingual writings of Özdamar, we can explore feelings of belonging that move the first-person narrator between cities, countries and languages in a literal sense, as well as how these feelings shape language use in the double sense of moving. Due to their bodily experience, they are related to the German language in a very specific way. This relationship is not an issue of identity or identity politics, but of shared and divided feelings of belonging that emerge and articulate themselves through German. Moving from one language into another is not just a process of transformation driven by affect, but also of literary writing as an affective practice which allows us to reflect simultaneously on this process and on writing itself.

Most characteristic for Özdamar's poetics is the dissociation of speech and writing that she allows to unfold in almost all her works. This dissociation acts in a dialogic relation with her mother and her first language Turkish, which she compares to the German literary tradition, to theatre, and to different public communities of speech. Within this dissociation between terms, Bakhtin's notion of dialogism becomes clearer through examples in which every utterance is shaped by its environment. This holds true for the German language, which has opened promising perspectives for the author and her first-person narrator, as well as for the Turkish language, which has been affected by the violence of the military coup in the early 1970s and which left Özdamar with feelings of non-belonging and pain (Özdamar, 2005, 16).

In many of her texts, Özdamar explains her switch from using the Turkish language to using German in terms of affect. In her first publication from 1990 [2010], she reflects on the loss of her mother tongue and its consequences, especially regarding her relationship to her mother. Titled *Mutterzunge* (*Mother Tongue*, 1994), it demonstrates how she reflects on language and how she cares about every single word resonating with other words in the text, all while playing with their different sounds and meanings in Turkish and German, and in spoken and written language. This resonance is also evident in the title of Özdamar's first novel, *Das Leben ist eine Karawanserei hat zwei Türen aus einer kam ich rein aus der anderen ging ich raus*, 1992 (*Life is a Caravanserai has two Doors I came in one I went out the other*, 2000). It indicates and performs the dynamics of life itself, and especially those of migration, moving between two doors as well as moving between two languages.

As Özdamar learned German while she was a student, her literary writing tries to retell her life story in her new language. This new language of German, and her relation to it, can be highlighted in the title of her acceptance speech for the *Chamisso Prize, Meine deutschen Wörter haben keine Kindheit*, which clearly defines the relationship with the language. For Özdamar, German is significant because it is the language of her professional acting career, writing career and of her becoming an author. In this context, her belonging to German is part of a highly complex process of emancipation while acquiring not only a new language but also a literary tradition in which she tries to inscribe herself. In other words, to think of authorship in terms of affect enables us to rethink the whole literary tradition as a space of belonging based on movement and attachment. Reading and rereading Özdamar's texts several times, the argument that her dialogic translingual writing, her concept of authorship and belonging to the literary tradition as the main reasons why Özdamar deals so intensively with spoken and written language becomes more and more prevalent. All her texts are examples of how acquiring a new language and moving between languages are eminent questions of affective relationality.

In her acceptance speech for the *Kleist Prize* (2004), the author claimed: "Die Zunge hat keine Knochen. Wohin man sie dreht, dorthin bewegt sie sich. Ich drehte meine Zunge ins Deutsche und plötzlich war ich glücklich" (Özdamar, 2005, 17). In this statement, Özdamar explores the notion of one's language by emphasizing the body part, the tongue, as a highly flexible, anatomical instrument that has no bones, moving between inside and outside. Unlike in German, the word 'tongue' in Turkish – as well as in English – means language. Thus, Özdamar can use the tongue as the bodily basis for speaking and as a metaphor of movement and mobility between languages. This mobility is presented as a free choice, based on her own decision. Özdamar claims that she turned her tongue to German and became happy. It seems to be this moving of her tongue towards the German language that creates deep feelings of belonging and of finding a new home within the language through the flexibility of the tongue muscle, which is lacking any solid bone structure. This serves as an analogized version of how Özdamar found herself in a foreign culture and foreign language.

The poetic agenda Özdamar unfolds in this speech during her acceptance of the *Kleist Prize* can be understood as the dissociation of speaking and writing. She has developed this perspective on her literary practice in *Mother Tongue* (1994 [1990]) and later in her acceptance speeches. Both speeches tend to link her writing to the German literary tradition and the literary public. All these texts focus explicitly on belonging and translingualism, in which we can repeatedly find the quotation "Die Zunge hat keine Knochen" ("A tongue has no bones"). It thus presents and represents the center of her literary writing.

The reflection of different languages also marks the beginning of Özdamar's debut *Mutterzunge* (*Mother Tongue*):

> In my language, "tongue" means "language".
> A tongue has no bones: twist it in any direction and it will turn that way.
> I sat with my twisted tongue in this city, Berlin.[. . . If only I knew when I lost my mother tongue. My mother and I sometimes spoke in our mother tongue. My mother said to me, "You know what? You just keep on talking, you think you're saying everything, but suddenly you jump over unspoken words".
>
> (Özdamar, 1994, 9).

> In meiner Sprache heißt Zunge: Sprache.
> Zunge hat keine Knochen, wohin man sie dreht, dreht sie sich dorthin. Ich saß mit meiner gedrehten Zunge in dieser Stadt Berlin. . . . Wenn ich nur wüßte, wann ich meine Mutterzunge verloren habe. Ich und meine Mutter sprachen mal in unserer Mutterzunge. Meine Mutter sagte mir: "Weißt du, du sprichst so, du denkst, daß Du alles erzählst, aber plötzlich springst du über nichtgesagte Wörter".
>
> (Özdamar, 1990, 9).

The turn from Turkish to German is described as a move that involves the body. At first, speaking seems to be tightly linked to the mother. But, as the tongue has no bones, it is easy to turn it and to carry it away to another place. In *Mother Tongue* the first-person narrator reflects on the loss of her Turkish mother tongue. She claims that she does not know when this happened, but remembers her mother talking to her. Thus, the narrator stresses that Turkish has become part of her memory and of listening rather than speaking. During this process, the mother tongue appears as a "foreign language I know well" (Özdamar, 1994, 10) ("gut gelernte Fremdsprache" (Özdamar, 1990, 9)), while German obviously is the new language of daily life. Consequently, the narrator's mother remarks that her Turkish has changed. There are somehow disruptions in her talk, which underline the process of changing her language, going on word for word in each dialogue. This process is two-fold: it means changing from Turkish to German and, while doing so, changing the German language itself.

This transformation is already reflected in the title of her publication. As language and tongue are two different words in German, their combination in *Mother Tongue* hints at a new language that is based on translation and translingualism. In making her mother tongue a foreign language, Özdamar also alters her new language, which the title precisely indicates: "Mother Tongue" turns German into an "other" tongue (Prade, 2013, 6), while Turkish phrases and idioms are partly intertwined. The same process is reflected in the way the narrator makes small 'artificial mistakes'. If one strictly applied the rules of German grammar, the line "A tongue has no bones: twist it in any direction and it will turn that way" (Özdamar, 1994, 9) ("Zunge hat keine Knochen, wohin man sie dreht, dreht sie sich dorthin" (Özdamar, 1990, 9)) is not entirely correct. Its chiastic structure, however, resembles and reiterates the 'turning of the tongue' and performatively emphasizes a mimetic momentum of speech (Konuk, 2001, 96). While repeating the line "A tongue has no bones" ("Zunge hat keine Knochen") in different texts, it is slightly changed through this repetition, thus reflecting the affective relationality between daily life, feelings of belonging and the process of literary writing. Within this repetition, circulation and variation stress the affective dynamics of writing that language itself performatively produces in a continuous, double process of German language acquisition and belonging to it. Furthermore, this example demonstrates spoken and written language as a dynamic process of affective relationality that humans are part of, but cannot fully master.

b. Translingualism and authorship

The dialogism of speech and writing in Özdamar's texts leads to a second aspect regarding her 'other' tongue and her authorship. The author's tongue plays an important role within the framework of monolingualism. As those small mistakes refer to standardization in written language, they illustrate the transition from speaking to writing, and thus the development of Özdamar as an author. While she strategically uses small alterations in many of her literary texts (Konuk, 2001, 93), she builds a polyphonic, literary language for the first-person narrator that explicitly reflects on the difference between speech and writing. Within this difference, the new literary language undermines the notion of authenticity und uniqueness that is an important aspect of modern authorship. However, both of her acceptance speeches are without such 'mistakes'. In this sense these speeches that she gave without making the same literary mistakes demonstrate a mastery in writing. Both emphasize her belonging to German as the language of her literary work, for which she has gained recognition and praise as an author. While the affective relationality of Özdamar's new language undermines the notion of authenticity and authorship, her acceptance speeches both claim the authority of a typical German author by reflecting on the paradoxical nexus of spoken and written language as well as of monolingualism and translingualism.

In her acceptance speech for the *Chamisso Prize*, Özdamar reflects explicitly on the difference between speaking and writing:

> Seit zehn Jahren werde ich gefragt: "Warum schreiben Sie auf Deutsch?" Ich spiele seit zwanzig Jahren auf deutschen und französischen Bühnen Theater, und niemand dort hat mich gefragt: "Warum spielen Sie In Deutsch?" "Warum spielen Sie in Französisch?" Niemand hat gesagt: "Man kann doch nur in der Muttersprache die Gefühle richtig ausdrücken".
>
> (Özdamar, 2001, 130f.)

Obviously, her writing evokes these questions.

As I have already mentioned, national language and modern literature are closely intertwined. Since romanticism, this relationship has been based on notions of authenticity and originality, which authors express in their writing. They are supposed to be the master of their life story and, moreover, of the literary text. Özdamar refers to this ironically, and thus questions the monolingual framework in a double manner. By repeating several stories of her protagonist's life in her short stories as well as in her novels, she undermines the master narrative of one life story as well as the notion of possessing one language. In her view, the mother tongue is not necessary for expressing feelings in the 'right' way. In her acceptance speeches, however, she refers to the framework so directly that it affects the relation of monolingualism to authorship.

It is striking that the question of right or wrong appears in the context of feelings. While feelings imply a notion of authenticity, the question of right or wrong implies the suspicion that the author is not telling a true story. This suspicion is based on the notion of a true language and the concept of possessing one true language only. As one can see in discussions within the literary field, language proficiency might be the most important condition of being accepted as an author.

Contrary to this position, Özdamar claims her authority based on a dynamic understanding of language focusing on translingualism. This holds true for spoken and for written language. As she argues in the acceptance speech for the *Chamisso Prize*, the words are bodies themselves (Özdamar, 2001, 132). This is to say that they are embodied, lively and exuberant as well as cautious, hidden or masked, resonating with each other in different perspectives. Language is not only the basis of all communication, but is also dialogical. It thus has a theatrical character which opens a space of belonging that the speaker herself is part of. In this perspective, both words and languages reflect each other in a dialogic mode of belonging and non-belonging.

There is, however, a difference between speaking and writing. Spoken language appears as rather a kind of mimetic, playful communication. As Özdamar says in her acceptance speech, she can leave the words of theatre in the dressing room. There is quite another attachment to written literary language and to the concept of authorship based on monolingualism. Both point to a certain national literary tradition that could elicit feelings of belonging. In this sense, Özdamar reflects on the German literary tradition as well as on the German language itself. At the end of her acceptance speech for the *Chamisso Prize*, Özdamar quotes her publishing editor's remark upon the question of why she changes from Turkish to German in writing: "Vielleicht schreibst du in Deutsch, weil du in der deutschen Sprache glücklich geworden bist" (ibid.).

As Özdamar claims in both of her acceptance speeches, there are two reasons for the happiness which is from her point of view inherent to the German language. The first reason is the richness of the German literary tradition and its critical notion of changing the world encompassed by it. The second reason is closely linked to this kind of literary promise: the most decisive argument for turning from Turkish to German is the experience of violence when the military took over in 1971.

In her speeches, Özdamar focuses on the importance of the German literary tradition, especially in theatre. Names like Jakob Michael, Reinhold Lenz, Heinrich von Kleist, Georg Büchner and Bertolt Brecht highlight this importance in the tradition clearly. As part of the German literary tradition, they are part of her belonging to the German language, and particularly to the German literary language she has chosen and created. Regarding her understanding of language, it is crucial that she came in closer contact to German in a theatrical space. When she says she turned her tongue to German and was suddenly happy, she also adds in both of her acceptance speeches: "dort am Theater, wo die tragischen Stoffe einen berühren und zugleich eine Utopie versprechen" (Özdamar, 2001, 129, see also Özdamar, 2005). Clearly, her belonging to the German literary tradition is related to the promise of change.

The other reason for moving from Turkish into German in her writings lies in the changes in Turkish public life after the military coup. As a critical intellectual, Özdamar was in prison, she lost friends to police killings, and she witnessed an atmosphere of fear and restraint. In her poetological texts, she argues that this terrifying, political atmosphere strongly impacted the Turkish language, which ultimately has become ill.

Because of her bodily perspective on words and the double meaning of tongue and language, Özdamar is able to say that her mother tongue falls ill. Turning her tongue into German, therefore, can be understood as a means of healing, while her Turkish is changed into a 'foreign' language keeping distance due to the political circumstances. Additionally, the affective practice of translingualism first gives her the sense of belonging to a literary tradition that opens up a space of healing and becoming happy again. Second, the privilege of translingualism is to change the German language and to create new concepts of authorship.

c. Translingual performativity in the Berlin-Istanbul Trilogy

These poetic reflections, based especially on the title of Özdamar's first publication and on her acceptance speeches, now lead me to her rather literary writings, and especially to her "Berlin-Istanbul Trilogy". The trilogy consists of the novels *Das Leben ist eine Karawanserei hat zwei Türen aus einer ging ich rein aus einer kam ich raus* (*Life is a Caravanserai Has two doors I came in one I went out the other*); *Die Brücke vom goldenen Horn*, 1998 (*The Bridge of the Golden Horn*, 2007) and *Seltsame Sterne starren zur Erde. Wedding Pankow 1976/1977* (2003, no English translation yet). All of these deal with questions of language and of the performative production of translingualism in novelistic narratives. When pulling Bakhtin into the research, we can think of them in terms of dialogism and different speech genres. In Özdamar's literary texts, acquiring the German language happens through communication in everyday life, like in the workplace or in the streets, and through the German literary tradition of theatre. It is, therefore, also attached to an imaginary public as a part of dialogism and affective relationality, that is at the same time reflected as a possibility of speech and of belonging to a speech community in writing.

The *Berlin-Istanbul Trilogy* tells the story of a young girl growing up in different cities in Turkey during the 1950s, and finally leaving her family to work as a migrant in Germany. The novels chronicle her frequent travel between Germany, Turkey and other countries, her work and political engagement within the student movement in Berlin and in Istanbul as well as her life in both East and West Berlin in the late 1970s while working "in the Brechtian Tradition at the *Volksbühne* theater" (Yildiz, 2012, 146). They are retrospective, first-person narratives based on Özdamar's own experiences. As "fictional autobiographies[,] they mix invention and history" (Boa, 2006, 526). They also blend child and adult perspectives (Maguire, 2013) as they mix languages in translation from Turkish to German and from speaking to writing. In her third novel, covering the years 1976 and 1977, Özdamar also mixes different types of texts. She works passages of her actual diary from the 1970s into the text of the novel, further emphasizing its autobiographical character. In these novels, it is difficult to distinguish between author and first-person narrator. The interplay of fact and fiction in Özdamar's novels dealing with her own life story is inseparably linked to her concept of dialogism and translingualism as an affective practice. While this process is happening, the mixture undermines the notion of authenticity that is one important aspect of modern authorship.

When Özdamar first came to Berlin, she worked in a factory with other Turkish women. In her second novel, the narrator describes the difficulties of trying to learn German, since she and the fellow workers did not learn any German while working. Instead, they tried to eavesdrop on it on the streets, making the sound of language part of a creative translation strategy. The spoken German language as well as street life became a kind of theatre play, her own acting a kind of onomatopoetical pantomime:

> Groceries were on the top floor of Hertie. We were three girls, wanted to buy sugar, salt, eggs, toilet paper and toothpaste at Hertie. We didn't know the words. Sugar, salt. In order to describe sugar, we mimed coffee-drinking to a sales assistant, then we said: shak shak. In order to describe salt, we spat on Hertie's floor and said: "Eeeh". In order to describe eggs, we turned our backs to the assistant, wiggled our backsides and said: "Clack, clack, clack". We got sugar, salt and eggs, but it didn't work with toothpaste. . . , So my first German words were shak shak, eeeh, clack clack clack.
>
> (Özdamar, 2007, 9)

> Bei Hertie im letzten Stock gab es Lebensmittel. Wir waren drei Mädchen, wollten bei Hertie Zucker, Salz, Eier, Toilettenpapier und Zahnpasta kaufen. Wir kannten die Wörter nicht. Zucker, Salz.
> Um Zucker zu beschreiben, machten wir vor einer Verkäuferin Kaffeetrinken nach, dann sagten wir Schak Schak. Um Salz zu beschreiben, spuckten wir auf Herties Boden, streckten unsere Zungen raus und sagten: "eeee". Um Eier zu beschreiben, drehten wir unsere Rücken zu der Verkäuferin, wackelten mit unseren Hintern und sagten: "Gak gak gak". Wir bekamen Zucker, Salz und Eier, bei Zahnpasta klappte es aber nicht. . . . So waren meine ersten deutschen Wörter Schak Schak, eeee, gak, gak, gak.
>
> (Özdamar, 1998, 18)

This citation demonstrates the performative production of spoken language and of mimetically acquiring the new language as well as of ironically altering it into a foreign language.

Moreover, the protagonist tries to get a feeling for German by reading newspaper headlines in big letters and spelling the words without knowing their meaning. This way of learning is a rather mimetic one, too, combining reading and acting in an onomatopoeic manner. The frequent appearance of onomatopoeia, especially at the beginning of the novel, stresses the importance of speech and the narrator's creativity in translation. Her semantically 'incorrect' translations show "how the acquisition of foreign language is at once resistive and a creative process" (Gutjahr, 2009, 124). Regarding affect, we can clearly find shared and divided feelings of belonging within this process of acquisition.

Again, language becomes part of a theatre play. The protagonist practices German like an actress. Her approach is word for word, keeping distance and establishing a theatrical relationship with the language, which enables her to take a critical perspective on it, as for example in the discussion of the newspaper headlines. The narrator's approach of learning German word for word underlines the dialogism of utterances in daily communication and different speech genres. Her theatrical translation strategy stresses the relationality of words affecting and resonating with each other.

Later, the narrator begins seriously learning German at a language school in Istanbul. At this school, Bertolt Brecht is regarded as one of the most esteemed authors in a tradition of German theatre as a critical practice that seeks to change society. Already during her first stay in Berlin, the Turkish head of her residence had provided the eager protagonist with Brecht's texts, and had taken her with him to *Volksbühne* in East Berlin. Like in Goethe's novel *Wilhelm Meister's Apprenticeship*, the theatre serves as a central medium of education for the main protagonist, who wants to become an actor, too. Both characters are convinced of their theatrical mission and both want to live a poetic life (Gutjahr, 2009, 126).

These references to theatre and to the modern novel trace a historical transformation that allows Özdamar to tightly interlink the German language with German literature. Her acquisition of the German language and her literary education, or *Bildung* in German, go hand in hand. From her point of view, both theatre and novels make a promise to the future and lead to her becoming an actor and later an author. This process has at least two consequences. First, the protagonist's newly established belonging to the 'world of literature' leads to a dissociation from her family, and especially from her mother and grandmother. While the protagonist leaves childhood and her mother tongue as a foreign language, she enters German as a literary language. The second consequence is that the familiar tradition of speech continues in the performative dimension of theatre. Both lead to a new language that makes the Turkish tongue a memory, but also alter the German language by introducing spoken language into writing through meanings created by bodily experiences. This bodily dimension is part of the affective relationality that structures both spoken and written language. It is the basis of dialogism (Bakhtin, 1981) and of shared and divided feelings ("Geteilte Gefühle") within Özdamar's writing. Finally, it builds her affective practice of translingualism that changes the monolingual framework.

3. Methodological conclusion

This chapter began with the questions: what does 'Analyzing Affective Societies' mean to a literary critic? And how could we think of literature in its affective entanglements? Through my reading of different texts by Emine Sevgi Özdamar, this chapter sought to show that Özdamar's translingual writing leads to a new language that emerges through, and at the same time reflects on, shared and divided feelings of belonging and non-belonging. While inscribing herself in the German literary tradition, Özdamar's work contributes to changes in the German language and to the literary system, while opening it for 'other' voices and different tongues. Her writing is driven by a dynamic and transformative mode of belonging to a public speech community that shapes speaking and writing within 'Affective Societies'.

Relating to this context, I suggest that investigating affect and affective relationality in literary texts leads to several new theoretical perspectives for affect as well as for literary studies. First, introducing Bakhtin and his concept of dialogism and the heteroglot novel allows researchers to rethink the relation between affect and language in its performativity. It also helps researchers to link this performativity to the writing process, to the practice of translingualism, and finally, to a dialogic concept of authorship. This holds true for both the material of writing and representations of affect and feelings. Regarding the 'culture as text' paradigm, it is important to be fully aware that there is no text without an author and that bodily experiences in relation to a language matter. However, concepts of authorship are themselves informed by different notions of language, especially those of the monolingual framework and its norms and discourses, such as the authenticity of feelings.

I have analyzed the development of Özdamar's literary language as a movement between, and characteristic attachment to, Turkish and German, by highlighting the dissociation between speaking and writing. I have read different types of her texts to analyze the differences in her reflections on acquiring a new language and feelings of belonging. Without the author's rather poetological reflections in her acceptance speeches, it would probably have been much more difficult to emphasize her writing process. Nevertheless, this would not be impossible, since we can find the development of Özdamar's translingual practice in her *Berlin-Istanbul Trilogy*, too. Almost all her works are characterized by creative translations between her life story and fiction, and between languages and words that resonate with each other. Analyzing the affective aspects of her writing has highlighted the development and the performativity of her translingual writing. It also foregrounds her writing's strong ties to theatre and to the German literary tradition, in a dialogic interaction of speech and writing. There is no standard procedure for analyzing literary texts. However, affect creates a more sensitive environment for language and all its utterances. Analyzing affect in translingual writing means analyzing the dynamics of language and belonging within a social process of transformation.

Note

1 The project is funded by the German Research Foundation (DFG). Part of the research team are currently Marion Acker and Matthias Lüthjohann.

References

Acker, M, Fleig, A & Lüthjohann, M 2019, 'Affect and accent. Public spheres of dissonance in the writings of Yoko Tawada', in A Fleig & C von Scheve (eds.), *Public Spheres of Resonance. Constellations of Language and Affect*, Routledge, New York.

Ahmed, S 2004, *The Cultural Politics of Emotion*, Edinburgh University Press, Edinburgh.

Bakhtin, M 1981, 'Discourse in the novel', in M Holquist (ed.), *Michail Bakhtin: The Dialogic Imagination. Four Essays*, trans. C Emerson & M Holquist, pp. 259–422, University of Texas Press, Austin, London.

Bakhtin, M 1984, *Problems of Dostoevsky's Poetics*, ed. and trans. C Emerson, University of Minnesota Press, Minneapolis.

Berlant, L 2011, *Cruel Optimism*, Duke University Press, Durham and London.

Boa, E 2006, 'Özdamar's autobiographical fictions: Trans-national identity and literary form', *German Life and Letters*, vol. 59, pp. 526–539.

Fleig, A 2019, 'Writing affect', in J Slaby & C von Scheve (eds.), *Affective Societies – Key Concepts*, Routledge, New York.

Gutjahr, O 2009, 'Integration through education: The new intercultural bildungsroman and the example of Sevgi Özdamar's *The Bridge of the Golden Horn*', in U Garde & A-R Meyer (eds.), *Belonging and Exclusion: Case Studies in Recent Australian and German Literature, Film and Theatre*, pp. 114–132, Cambridge Scholars Publishing, Newcastle upon Tyne.

Gutjahr, O 2016, 'Inszenierungen eines Rollen-Ich. Emine Sevgi Özdamars theatrales Erzählverfahren', in Y Dayıoglu-Yücel & O Gutjahr (eds.), *Emine Sevgi Özdamar*, pp. 8–18, edition text und kritik, München.

Kittler, FA 2003, *Aufschreibesysteme 1800–1900*, Fink, München.

Konuk, K 2001, *Identitäten im Prozeß. Literatur von Autorinnen aus und in der Türkei in deutscher, englischer und türkischer Sprache*, Verlag Die blaue Eule, Essen.

Maguire, N 2013, 'Reading and writing the child's voice in Emine Sevgi Özdamar's *Das Leben ist eine Karawanserei hat zwei Türen aus einer kam ich rein aus der anderen ging ich raus*', *Forum for Modern Language Studies*, vol. 49, pp. 213–220.

Özdamar, ES 1992, *Das Leben ist eine Karawanserei hat zwei Türen aus einer kam ich rein aus der anderen ging ich raus*, Kiepenheuer & Witsch, Köln.

Özdamar, ES 1994, *Mother Tongue*, trans. C Thomas, Coach House Press, Toronto.

Özdamar, ES 1998, *Die Brücke vom Goldenen Horn*, Kiepenheuer & Witsch, Köln.

Özdamar, ES 2000, *Life Is a Caravanserai Has Two Doors I Came in One I Went Out the Other*, trans. L V Flotow-Evans, Middlesex University Press, London.

Özdamar, ES 2001, 'Meine deutschen Wörter haben keine Kindheit. Eine Dankrede', in idem., *Der Hof im Spiegel. Erzählungen*, pp. 125–132, Kiepenheuer & Witsch, Köln.

Özdamar, ES 2003, *Seltsame Sterne starren zur Erde. Wedding Pankow 1976/1977*, Kiepenheuer & Witsch, Köln.

Özdamar, ES 2005, 'Kleist-Preis-Rede', *Kleist-Jahrbuch*, pp. 13–18.

Özdamar, ES 2007, *The Bridge of the Golden Horn*, trans. M Chalmers, Serpent's Tail, London.

Özdamar, ES 2010 [1990], *Mutterzunge. Erzählungen*, Rotbuch, Berlin.

Prade, J 2013, '(M)other tongues: On tracking a precise uncertainty', in idem. (ed.), *(M)other Tongues: Literary Reflexions on a Difficult Distinction*, pp. 1–21, Cambridge Scholars Publishing, Newcastle.

Richardson, M 2016, *Gestures of Testimony. Torture Trauma and Affect in Literature*, Bloomsbury, New York, London, Oxford, New Delhi, Sydney.

Riley, D 2004, *Impersonal Passion: Language as Affect*, Duke University Press, Durham.

Röttger-Rössler, B & Slaby, J (eds.), 2018, *Affect in Relation. Families, Places, Technologies*, Routledge, New York.

Sedgwick, EK 2003, *Touching Feeling. Affect, Pedagogy, Performativity*, Duke University Press, Durham and London.

Winko, S 2003, *Kodierte Gefühle. Zu einer Poetik der Emotion in lyrischen und poetologischen Texten um 1900*, Erich Schmidt Verlag, Berlin.

Yildiz, Y 2012, *Beyond the Mother Tongue. The Postmonolingual Condition*, Fordham University Press, New York.

Zimmermann, AM 2017, *Kritik der Geschlechterordnung. Selbst-, Liebes- und Familienverhältnisse im Theater der Gegenwart*, Transcript Verlag, Bielefeld.

Zumbusch, C 2016, *Handbuch Literatur und Emotion*, De Gruyter Mouton, Berlin.

Part IV

Reflexivities

Chapter 14

Researching affects in the clinic and beyond

Multi-perspectivity, ethnography, and mental health-care intervention

Edda Heyken, Anita von Poser, Eric Hahn, Thi Main Huong Nguyen, Jörg-Christian Lanca and Thi Minh Tam Ta

Introduction

During an early session of an innovative group therapy for Vietnamese patients, our interdisciplinary team observed a situation charged with affective resonance. For an emotion-evoking exercise, patients were asked to pick images that appealed to them from a stock of photographs and were encouraged to explain their decision. Many chose pictures relating sensually to Vietnam, such as landscapes and food. Two men selected images of urban scenes. Mr. Q, who reported feeling sad in the beginning, chose a cityscape in sepia. Mr. C's images depicted Berlin themes. Mr. Q explained that he went for the "western" city images because he thought they were beautiful. Mr. C, next to him, confirmed provocatively that it had to be beautiful, and that it showed Saigon before it fell into "communist" hands. He leaned back in his chair, crossed his legs, and added mockingly, "Mr. Q might rather know it as Ho Chi Minh City". Some other patients giggled about the implicit innuendo and the two men's different relations to Vietnam. Mr. Q, who up to this point was unaware of the content of the picture, reacted with irritation to the other's gaze. Earlier in this session, he had already been amended for his obtrusive temper in front of the group, which triggered bodily displays of unease. The two men started disputing vigorously now, lecturing one another about right and wrong perceptions of "their" city. Their voices grew louder and more agitated as the argument escalated. Amused, Mrs. L, a third patient, pointed out, "Now they are going to fight!", while others refrained from involvement. At this point, Dr. Thi Minh Tam Ta, the psychiatrist leading the group therapy session, intervened and ended the dispute. Mr. Q struggled to calm down. He stared at the floor while jittering his leg. Mr. C withheld any further dyadic involvement, turned away, and dropped his frown.

What does this example of a field situation showcase? What relevance to mental health do affects, migration, and patients' life-courses have? Is there an association between various migratory experiences and different affective states? How can understanding this nexus advance psychiatric assessment and care? And what is the benefit of analyzing this situation by means of multi-perspectivity? With our contribution, we aim to clarify how our presence as a team can foster both the ethnography of a "vulnerable" field and mental health-care intervention. This vignette describes heterogeneous feeling-rules and affects tied to a place which both men inhabited under different circumstances. The observation reveals information on migratory and biographical strains, emotional constitution, acquired patterns of conduct, illness narratives, socialization, estrangement, and gender roles. To capture this information as well as the multifaceted affective processes, different researchers' perspectives coalesce for comprehensive contextualization. This gain of knowledge is not just epistemic but may feed back into psychiatric/ psychotherapeutic interventions to engender a "person-centered medicine" (see Kirmayer, Lemelson, & Cummings, 2015).

In our contribution, we highlight the methodological importance of interdisciplinary and multi-perspectival research on affects in a heterogeneous field. Empirically, we relay data of elderly Vietnamese first-generation migrants in Berlin who visit a specialized outpatient clinic[1] to cope with long-term affective crises in their lives. Our team gained a deeper understanding of when and why affective crises turn into severe forms of distress and mental illness, and at which point in their lives actors[2] decide to access professional treatment. In recent years, medical and psychological anthropologists, psychiatrists, and psychologists have worked towards establishing cultural phenomenological and context-specific forms of medicine (Hollan, 1997; Kirmayer, Lemelson, & Cummings, 2015; Littlewood, 2010, 1980; Kleinman, 1980). These forms entail person-centered approaches to acknowledge the importance of patients' biographies and their situatedness in life in relation to various social, cultural, political, and economic circumstances. Taking this claim seriously, our team of two psychiatrists, one psychologist, and three anthropologists has been breaking new methodological ground while researching affects as part of *Affective Societies* in and beyond the clinic. Over two years, we accompanied elderly Vietnamese patients in Berlin within an innovative affect- and emotion-focused group therapy, developed by the team's psychiatrists and psychologist. Simultaneously, the anthropologists met the patients in different social, spatial, and structural environments outside the clinic. We aim to explain how joining our multiple methodological approaches and perspectives allowed us to build a more comprehensive frame for understanding the affective complexities in the lives, crises, and conducts of our interlocutors. In relaying the cases of four patients, we portray how we learned from each other in methodological, conceptual, and cross-disciplinary ways. We discuss the advantages and the potential hazards involved in the course of systematically entangling multi-perspectivity, ethnography, and mental health-care intervention.

Researching affects through multi-perspectivity

Our team members[3] have varying access to the two men from the first vignette, thus enabling us as a team to gain a holistic understanding of their respective affective crises. The psychiatrist, Tam, has a well-established therapeutic relationship with them and is, among other things, equipped with medical authority. The psychologist, Main Huong, documented their anamneses and knew them from individual therapy sessions as well. Each of the men was introduced to one of the anthropologists by Tam, facilitating a trustful relationship that engendered their agreement to an ethnographic observation of their individual therapy sessions and narrative interviews.[4] Previously, Tam and Eric, a second psychiatrist, had mediated the role of the three anthropologists, Edda, Lanca, and Anita, in clinical encounters with their patients. During individual and group therapy sessions, the anthropologists engaged in "silent participation" and adopted a decidedly neutral position. For instance, they tried not to interfere with the direction of their gaze or with their body posture.[5] In cases, for instance, in which patients involved the anthropologists too closely, which in therapeutic terms constituted a "distraction" strategy, the anthropologists would redirect the patient's focus back to the therapeutic process.

Mrs. L, for example, the woman mentioned earlier, showed ambivalent compliance behavior within the group therapy that all researchers observed. When entering the room – oftentimes late – she entered with a confident and casual body display, regularly checked her phone during sessions, mocked instructions, stretched or yawned expressively, or engaged in non-therapy-related conversations when the topics discussed affected her uncomfortably. Her exalted demeanor was usually noticed by the other patients and contributed to her particular position in the group. Sometimes her behavior elicited dissonance, while in later therapy sessions it was somewhat ignored. The anthropologists tried not to interact with this behavior but instead noted her expressions and displays of (non-)verbal and response behavior in connection with the temporal affective dramaturgy of relevant situations, gender dynamics, and power relations.

Mr. Q, Mr. C, and Mrs. L participated in a biweekly, two-hour-long emotion- and affect-focused group therapy, where Vietnamese patients over 50 years old and of diverse migratory histories established their respective roles in a clearly delineated, new, and consolidating circle of peers. During the situation described at the beginning of this essay, Tam primarily attended to maintaining patients' compliance with the exercises and fostering beneficial affective group dynamics, for example, by balancing out tensions or moderating a dissent between patients. Main Huong paid close attention to the actors' phrasing, relating their demeanor to her therapeutic experiences with them and their individual explanatory models of their perceived distress (see Kleinman, 1980). Two anthropologists informed on the patients' biographic background focused on their bodily displays and positionalities. While Edda had learned that Mr. C's memories of Saigon predate his escape to the Federal Republic of Germany in the early 1980s, Mr. Q had told Lanca how he moved to Ho Chi Minh City after 1975 and came to the German Democratic Republic as a contract worker. The two men represent two diverging but common migration experiences in the heterogeneous Vietnamese Berlin.[6]

The therapists conducted the therapy sessions in Vietnamese and drew on culturally informed metaphors, images, and themes about life and sociality in

Vietnam, resonating with the Confucian and Buddhist values that appealed to the patients. To avoid an essentializing gaze, however, we placed an important focus on the process of making meaning of transnational ways of life in Berlin, where most of our interlocutors have been longstanding residents. Our empirical findings prove that the acceptance of therapeutic programs increases through implementing patients' perspectives, which are molded culturally as well as subjectively (Ta et al., 2017; von Poser, Lanca, & Heyken, 2017). For example, the therapists worked with an imagination exercise in which the bamboo plant is used as a metaphor for flexibility and stability (Hinton & Kirmayer, 2017; Hinton et al., 2007). The participants accepted this exercise as it alluded to familiar symbolic, material, and sensory horizons. Whether an exercise appeared culturally apt or not was found out during time-slots in the therapy itself, in which perceived cultural differences or the impact of diverse social factors within the patients' lifeworlds were reflected and discussed. Addressing and negotiating conflicting norms and values paved a way to contextualize the perceived distress and promoted the unfolding of transcultural dynamics in a safe place that enabled participants to voice their anxieties (Nadig, 2006). The implementation of ethnographic methods fostered an inductive participatory approach to the therapeutic development. This approach consisted in including patients' re-creative as well as proactive references and responses. Indeed, it was only during such discussions that the anthropologists discontinued "silent participation" in order to respond when patients actively addressed them. This inductive participatory course of action differed from more rigidly framed, standardized psychotherapy manuals as it encouraged the patients to generate emic perspectives. The therapy was usually closed with an open half-hour slot, during which the participants casually conversed with each other, the therapists, and the anthropologists.

The case of Mr. N, another patient of the group, showcases how researchers' different perspectives and relations to one actor allow for more detailed insights into the emic understandings of affective crises (von Poser, Lanca, & Heyken, 2017). Edda gained these data in a long-term ethnographic involvement in and outside the clinic over a two-year period and in constant exchange with Tam, the psychiatrist in charge. When Mr. N was transferred to the outpatient clinic by a German psychiatrist about 28 months ago, he showed typical symptoms of depression: insomnia, loss of interest and appetite, weakness of concentration, headaches, forgetfulness, restlessness, avolition, rage, tinnitus, a reduced physical and mental resilience towards stress, and problems in interpersonal relations (Nguyen, TMH et al., 2017; Dreher et al., 2017). He linked the longstanding causes of his distress to situations of mobbing at work. Tam diagnosed a moderate depressive episode as part of a recurrent depressive disorder, grounded in PTSD from multiple war and refugee traumas. Mr. N had suffered in the war as a South Vietnamese Army soldier. After the war and the seizure of power of North over South Vietnam, he was imprisoned and humiliated before he fled the country. Back then, he had already been suffering from nightmares and episodes of intense distress, and the vivid war memories had since haunted his sleep, causing insomnia. Tam's first therapeutic intervention was to relieve Mr. N of his current work-related stressors. To mitigate the affective and sleeping disorders, she prescribed anti-depressive medication, offered individual psychotherapeutic sessions and helped him with psychosocial interventions. Later, he additionally joined the group therapy.

Tam introduced Edda to Mr. N in the light of his migratory history that corresponded with the project's outline,[7] while his PTSD-related symptoms did not stand in the foreground. Edda soon learned that her interlocutor was confronted with "aggressive emotions" that would emerge, for instance, when watching war-related scenes on television or seeing weapons; these would trigger flashbacks and make him smell the pungent scents of ammunition and death. Before meeting Mr. N outside the clinic, Tam instructed Edda on how to interrupt his negative and destructive thoughts in such situations, for instance: handing on contents of the therapy and jointly repeating mindfulness exercises with Mr. N.

After the first interview in the clinic in which Mr. N briefly outlined his war and refugee experience, he met Edda outside the hospital. Based on the suggestions by the therapists during team intervisions,[8] Edda applied a reactivating approach by instigating outdoor walks to modify his behavior of social isolation. The walks eventually turned into ethnographic *go-alongs* (Kusenbach, 2003) through Mr. N's neighborhood, several parks, and natural environments in Berlin during which he generated biographical narratives and re-evoked various memories of past experiences from Vietnam revealing affects in relation to past and present events. While sitting at a lake under a weeping willow, he talked about the need to accept death according to his experiences of war, persecution, and imprisonment, and his decision to risk his life and flee the country. Walking in a narrow grove, he self-confidently highlighted how, as a soldier, he had lived in the jungle for years and learned to survive with few resources and to navigate using the sun. During a visit to the Asian section in Berlin's Botanical Garden, he touched specific leaves and described their medicinal use. The sensory interaction with his environment and his ability to survive by relying on his senses and skills reverberates in his feelings until today. Through spatial immersion, he reactivated hidden memories that were blocked out by his recent crises. Interestingly, the go-alongs contributed to a stimulation of Mr. N's memories, and he said that he felt "relieved" after remembering.

Pursuing go-alongs was a time-consuming method, but they built a solid basis of trust. Asking Mr. N about emotions while moving reactivated memories as affective actualizations (see von Poser, 2018). He agreed to elaborate on topics from our go-alongs. Hence, thematically pre-sensitized, stationary, extended interviews with memory-evoking objects like photographs and maps became a methodological supplement. At home, he recalled how he regulated his emotions as a necessity to cope with the surrounding sorrow and hardships. While preparing Phở, a traditional soup, Mr. N narrated and combined his memories with oral histories from elderly acquaintances, voicing a relational mode of affective remembering. Alternatingly, Edda continued to meet Mr. N both in movement and in stationary meetings.

Mr. N's participation in the group therapy paved the way for the other researchers to observe his as well as other patients' interactions. For instance, in one session, positive memories were highlighted to counter acute affective burdens. Patients were asked about positive memories from the past to cope with acute distress. Mr. C recalled the taste of nước mắm (fish sauce), dropping his earlier frown and lighting up. Shortly after, his facial expression shifted again when he recalled memories of his hometown from which he had fled. Mr. N joined in, and both expressed their ambivalent feelings towards Vietnam. Apart from their statements, knowledge of their biographies and close observation by multiple researchers with different foci made it possible to single out specific affecting moments. We were thus able to connect these affecting moments with shared patient experiences of imprisonment after the war and an inflexible reaction pattern towards their past. Moreover, we observed that other participants in the group were relationally affected in different situations. For instance, as former contract workers, Mr. Q and Mrs. L could often empathize with one another when talking about affective burdens. They would avidly discuss issues like feeling pressured by the expectations of far-off family members. Their common separation from kin also impeded reliance on familiar *emotion repertoires* (von Poser et al., 2019) to solve problems through relational intervention with close relatives. Often, this led them to direct recurrent negative emotions towards themselves and others. During the group discussion, we observed that patients with a refugee history seemed somewhat detached from this topic. However, during group sessions, other positionalities, such as affective consonances or dissonances that were dynamically observed through multi-perspectivity, also structured interactional behavior.

Patients' reports on their well-being, their interactions with one another, and their compliance with the therapy exercises, their signs of progress and setbacks are best understood as parts of processes. Longitudinal observation was thus an important component of our approach to studying patterns of change. In the beginning, patients arrived at the clinic individually, mindful to maintain a reserved body posture and avoid interaction. After several weeks, however, Anita noticed an evolving mutual relatedness during waiting-room observations. Some patients now arrived carpooling, sat together, and chatted while waiting. The non-verbally expressed open attitude reflected an increasing acceptance of and engagement with the therapy process. In ethnographic encounters, Mr. N described to Edda how conversing with the other participants helped him soften his social isolation. He started to exchange messages with another patient on a regular basis. Also, during the session, the exchange between patients grew more vivid and open, even when dealing with sensitive topics. When patients were asked to commend each other in an exercise to confront Vietnamese and German conversation styles, Eric noted that the participants' depressive symptoms appeared remitted on account of their interaction behavior. The patients applied their knowledge of body posture from earlier sessions, referred to concrete actions, and related to one another. The flow of conversation was dynamic, their facial expressions attentive. Their attention to each other was heightened and gestures of care and empathy grew more common: when Mrs. L finally managed to arrive on time for a session, other participants commended her. Patients began inquiring about each other's well-being when someone showed displays of bodily discomfort, for instance, rubbing temples. Later in therapy, this relatedness increased: when patients would voice complaints about pain or conflicts, others reported what appeared helpful to them in similar situations.

After each session, when there was time for an informal exchange over tea and snacks, we observed both group dynamics and individual progress beyond the formalized therapeutic frame while diverse relations unfolded between researchers and patients. Multi-perspectivity had two benefits for our research. Firstly, the multilateral relationality and reciprocity between researchers and patients enabled us to reach a broader understanding of their lifeworlds, their affective and biographic experiences, and how they deal with mental suffering. Secondly, multi-perspectivity paved the way for a dynamic feedback with additional information for the therapy process, as we will illustrate in the following section. Hence, the therapists were able to adapt to patients' individual needs, address their emic illness experience, and offer a highly person-centered mental health-care.

Synthesizing and analyzing data from the clinic and beyond

As became apparent, our disciplinary knowledge and subjective positionalities create a web of approaches and perspectives that, once interlocked, help to thoroughly understand the affective complexities in the lives of elderly Vietnamese patients. We were better able to examine the causes of perceived distress through an analysis of human behavior, subjective and psychological experiences that, as Douglas Hollan (1997) points out, influence and are influenced by social and cultural processes. Multi-perspectivity comprises the holistic perspective of the actor and allows for person-centered forms of medicine by accompanying patients through various mental health-care processes. In therapy, voiced, hidden, or suppressed affective crises become contextualized by the relational embeddedness and by the interaction behaviors of the actors with their social or material environments. The anthropological input for the therapeutic outline consisted in implementing the emic perspectives we collected through conducting a person-centered ethnography (see Hollan, 1997). We contextualized the adherence of patients to contents or exercises by considering their situatedness. This close sensuous view of the patients from multiple perspectives elicited an affective dramaturgy of the individual sessions and of how this dramaturgy unfolded over the two-year period. To grasp the complexity of exactly how affects emerge in relations (Slaby & Röttger-Rössler, 2018), each researcher individually concentrated on how the patients reacted to the social, spatial, and material settings. Moreover, we paid attention to sensory impressions, regimes of (non-)verbal expression, and response behavior, as well as to gender and power relations. From a psychiatric and psychological perspective, we consider affects and emotions with regard to their verbal and embodied expression, intensity, and duration, as well as their cognitive perception. Moreover, we consider their influence on the therapists' own affects and emotions (see Whelton, 2004). One illustrative example is Tam's reflection after the group therapy. Whereas Tam experienced the therapy sessions on positive emotions as pleasant, the transition towards the sessions on negative emotions required greater effort to balance the patients' heterogeneous affects. While the patients learned to self-regulate the negative emotions, it became easier for the therapist to approach difficult emotions such as, for example, anger. The fact that Tam's affects and emotions to a certain degree mirrored the affective dynamics of the group became an essential source of therapeutic information and fueled our relational understanding of affects and emotions (for the methodological value of researchers' sensory and affective field experiences, see also Mattes, Kasmani, & Dilger, in this volume). This epistemic approach is based on the psychodynamic concept of transference and countertransference of the "unconscious dimensions of affective, felt and emotional experience" (Redman, 2009, 65). As Tam's emotional reactions were co-shaped in relation to group dynamics, she, in turn, actively regulated and impacted the group's affects. Hence, the therapist was both a participant-observer and an involved agent, rather than a detached, neutral, and dispassionate technician (Halpern, 2001; Gelso & Hayes, 2007).

In order to explore emotions with regard to their physical, expressive, and cognitive dimensions as outlined by Helena Flam (2015), the anthropologists examined how biographic or migratory experiences shape coping strategies. We found that the patients' coping mechanisms were influenced by, for example, experiences of displacement, harassment, and deprivation in the case of Mr. C and Mr. N, and by separation from or worry about the family in the case of Mr. Q and Mrs. L. Therefore, conditioned behavior, such as performing (non-)verbal displays of superiority, may serve the adherence to social norms. In this way, expressions of health problems were actively silenced. Distrust of biomedical approaches, the belittling of affective crises, and a fear of losing face were important factors in this regard. Such factors may well have impeded patients from going to the clinic and exacerbated their social isolation and feelings of harshness toward themselves, resulting in the kinds of contradictory feelings seen in the case of Mr. N. Over the course of the therapy cycle, we noticed a growing resonance in discussions with other patients about the function and consequences of worry. Although Mrs. L's non-verbal display (eyes and body posture turned away from the speaker) clearly contradicted her engagement in discussions, the intense behavior of refusal and distraction which she had displayed in the beginning of the group therapy eventually softened.

As the anthropologists accompanied the patients in their daily routines, they were able to investigate emotions and affects through observations of situated behavior. Furthermore, they were able to pay attention to non-verbal, implicit expressions and verbalizations, and to patients' movements within their material and social environments. Additionally, doing ethnography in the patients' respective communities enabled the anthropologists to detect how social and cultural processes influence the patients' subjective and psychological experiences and vice versa. In order to reveal obligatory feeling rules as well as moments of rupture, Edda asked Mr. N to narrate memories and give examples of felt (non-) belonging in different settings. She reflected the answers with the expectations he imposed on himself and his social surroundings as well as his behavior in social encounters. Through extended biographic interviews and the method of emotional free-listing, Edda also came closer to Mr. N's explanations of his past and present affective crises. During a mindfulness exercise which Edda practiced with Mr. N on one of their go-alongs to stop his destructive spiral of thoughts, she asked him to particularly pay attention to the materiality of the direct surroundings. In so doing, she rather unintentionally revealed another source of his affective distress which he had not brought up in therapy and which revealed the intricate connection between affects, the materiality of objects, and memory (Svašek, 2012). As he noticed different bolts on a bridge in front of them, he reacted vigorously and said that the screws reminded him of work-related stress in combination with physical tensions. Then he dropped his shoulders, exhaled heavily, and said that, since childhood, his mechanical skills had been a resource of self-empowerment and that, during his flight, when the motor of the boat broke down, he was the only one who could repair it. The affective dissonance revealed valuable details that supported Tam's valuation and improved the therapeutic process.

The ethnographic observations which feed the development of an ethnographically informed therapy manual contextualize the patients' everyday relational strategies of behavior in different places of Vietnamese Berlin, and thus complement insights gained in psychotherapeutic encounters. Our reflections and negotiations of critical situations through intra- and interdisciplinary intervisions and through "backtracking emotions" (Wettergren, 2015) allowed us to understand the relationally evoked emotions and affects that accompany specific actions and situations. To utilize the researchers' relationally evoked emotions as an analytical tool, Blix Bergman (2015) recommends "emotional participation" to precisely describe why and how the emotional experiences in the field were perceived (see also Stodulka, Dinkelaker, & Thajib, this volume). To do so, for example, we dialogically discussed the common research experience of failed attempts at interacting with interlocutors (see Mattes & Dinkelaker, 2019). In so doing, we were able to jointly reflect on the situatedness of both our interlocutors' and of our own affective navigations. In contrast to the majority of individually conducted anthropological research, we benefited from anthropological team research and intradisciplinary multi-perspectivity. The anthropologists systematically cooperated in the contextualization and interpretation of situations, especially if they were charged with uncomfortable affects. In combining those exchanges with the regular intervisions of the entire team, the anthropologists were able to contextualize both the patients' and their own affective resonances (Spencer & Davies, 2010; Stodulka, 2015; Slaby, 2016). It is critical for anthropologists to pay attention to processes of affective relationality in vulnerable fields for both epistemological and ethical reasons, since doing so increases the chance to responsibly assess difficult situations.

Our team interversions included several steps. In a first step, we shared our observations directly after a session, when we were still acutely affected by our impressions. In a second step, each of us wrote detailed minutes based on the notes taken during the session, which allowed us to shift the focus from an overall impression to a thick description of the patients' (non-)verbal expressions. In a third step, with some distance to affectively charged situations, we collated the written data with video material recorded during the therapy sessions. The psychiatrists evaluated a long-term impact as a positive process that became traceable through applied multi-perspectivity.

Typically, after a session, Tam shared her perception of the group dynamics and of the patients' development and involvement in relation to their courses of illness, while Main Huong added details based on her focus on the patients' verbalizations and modes of phrasing. The anthropologists paid attention to modes of interaction, individual demeanor towards the group, facial expressions, posture, and direction of view. Together, we discussed the patients' collective and individual responses to the session. In merging these observations with impressions and statements from several encounters, we were able to draw a broader picture of each patient's current status and of her or his involvement in the group and attitude towards others. For example, adding information about current socioeconomic burdens or frustrations in the life of Mrs. L helped us to contextualize why she made attempts to withdraw from the therapeutic process.

Our synthesized perspectives revealed insights into the relations between the patients and the therapist as well as into the dynamics of compliance, submissiveness, or avoidance of certain topics of conversation. The spatial immersion into an affective arrangement (Slaby, Mühlhoff, & Wüschner 2017), for example, was used to illustrate the influence of surroundings on subjectively perceived well-being. For an exercise, Tam led the group into different staged settings. We observed that, in a rather unpleasant setting, the patients moved closer together, raised their shoulders, and looked around attentively. In contrast, in a rather pleasant setting they assumed relaxed postures, smiled, and showed enhanced displays of ease. The affective dramaturgy evoked by Tam served as an intervention to show the patients how they may transform negative into positive emotions by frequenting a positively reverberating place. After the session, we jointly discerned the patients' negative and positive reactions during the exercise. In later sessions, the patients repeatedly referred to this impactful exercise, and their exchange of impressions triggered a discursive and cognitive development amongst them. Interestingly, this session also marked a salient moment of group consolidation within the therapy cycle.

We have been analyzing our extensive body of data in relation to the processuality and sequentiality of therapeutic contents and patients' individual as well as relational developments. Throughout the therapy, the patients showed different impacts of the interventions on their well-being. While two patients dropped out in the course of the therapy, others benefited significantly. The therapeutic frame allowed for the coexistence of unpredictable affective dynamics to negotiate conflicting and contradictory experiences. For instance, in the beginning of the therapy, Mr. Q and Mr. C, the protagonists of our first vignette, were clearly caught within an affective dissonance with one another, as each of them claimed a different sense of belonging to the same city while negating the legitimacy of the other's claim. Yet, they progressively found ways to negotiate these different senses of belonging in less offending ways. Our observations, for example, revealed a strong sense of belonging that became apparent during conversations about the preparation and consumption of food. The patients differentiated dishes according to regional South and North Vietnamese flavors. Discursively analyzing regional preparations and tastes of rice enabled them, at least in this situation, to talk about the country's differences without the pressure of having to reenact political animosities. Understanding affectivity as relational rather than individual (Slaby, 2016; Slaby & Röttger-Rössler, 2018) helped us make sense of this as well as other situations.

Conclusion: multi-perspectivity, ethnography, and mental health-care intervention

Our multi-perspectival approach enabled us to thoroughly grasp affects, emotions, and intra- as well as interpersonal coping strategies in relation to the affective efforts of migration among Vietnamese migrants in Berlin. We approached these efforts in transdisciplinary terms as psychosocial burdens, understanding them both from a psychiatric perspective as psychosomatic and psychiatric symptom, and from an anthropological perspective as emotional processes linked to a spatiotemporal and socio-biographic genesis. Our findings thus gave us insights into the affective relationality at work in our patients' lives and conducts. We were able to determine why Mr. C initially approached other patients who appeared to be "weaker" or less informed with gestures of dominance, under what circumstances Mr. Q would often grow belligerent when proven wrong, or why Mr. N could recount his crises more easily while moving through natural environments rather than staying put in confined, stationary settings. These findings helped to increase the compliance with the therapy and the patients' healing processes. Mr. Q, for instance, could resonate better with another patient in the group once both uncovered similarities in their affective challenges.

Apart from their epistemic value, our insights feed directly back into mental health-care intervention with various benefits for the patients. The interdisciplinary work facilitates a personalized and ethnographically informed therapy based on the patients' own emic and dynamic understandings. Furthermore, diverse relations and reciprocities with multiple researchers set a frame for informal exchange beyond the hierarchical therapist-patient dyad. Several patients also appreciated the opportunity to "talk themselves empty" in non-therapeutic contexts such as during extended ethnographic interviews. According to our interlocutors, talks about their condition outside the therapy setting with various researchers became another way of handling their felt distress. New and flexible perspectives countered stigmatization and advanced their sense of agency. During the therapy cycle, the patients no longer portrayed their condition as an essential flaw but as a treatable illness.

Of course, ethical dilemmas accompany interdisciplinary research and need to be accounted for methodologically and conceptually to contend with evolving tensions. Changing settings and the patients' contacts with different researchers with diverse competencies, needed to be mediated with special attention. The ethnographic mode of "silent participation" resulted from a discussion about our respective positionalities vis-à-vis the patients. While it is common for psychiatrists to maintain a professional distance, anthropologists usually try to delve into their interlocutors' lives as deeply as possible to achieve an "ethnographic closeness". It was paramount to discuss clear responsibilities and boundaries at the beginning within the team and with the patients, as reciprocal trust and empathy may blur professional relations. Interventions and crisis response were solely the psychiatrists' and psychologist's responsibility, which the whole team strictly adhered to. Thus, the psychiatrists and the psychologist also set individual boundaries and pointed out potential pitfalls for ethnographic encounters with respective patients. Our research was made more productive through constant dialogue about the advantages and disadvantages of our method, about our multiple interpretations and the transparent handling of affective relationalities.

The heterogeneity of our field demanded a holistic approach in which we considered the biographical backgrounds of the patients, their social embeddedness and their sensorial navigations, medical conditions, psychological resources, and challenges. Our multi-perspectival method afforded us a deeper understanding of the patients' affective processes and their impacts on mental health as well as on psychotherapeutic dynamics and outcomes. In our context, a multi-perspectival approach to observation and analysis, along with a prudent synthesis of different researchers' accounts, meant striving for the maximum benefits of collaboration between the disciplines of anthropology and psychiatry.

Notes

1 The first specialized outpatient clinic for Vietnamese migrants opened in 2010 at the Department of Psychiatry and Psychotherapy, Charité-Universitätsmedizin Berlin, Campus Benjamin Franklin (CBF) and the second specialized outpatient clinic opened in 2012 at the Department of Psychiatry, Psychotherapy and Psychosomatics, Evangelic Hospital Königin Elisabeth Herzberge (KEH) (Ta et al., 2015; Hahn et al., 2016).

2 Based on our research focus, we pursue the question of how *actors* perceive affective efforts of migration. According to our interdisciplinary outline, we will talk of actors as our research participants in two ways: we speak of actors as *patients* in clinical encounters, whereas we term actors as *interlocutors* while accompanying them during ethnographic encounters.

3 Our team consists of diverse academic professions, research interests, ages, socialization, and genders, to facilitate a multiplicity of perspectives and to complement our

theoretical assumptions: Thi Minh Tam Ta, a Vietnamese-born and trained physician, achieved her specialization in psychiatry in Germany as a cognitive behavioral therapist (CBT), specializing, moreover, in the treatment of post-traumatic stress disorders (PTSD). She pursues affect- and emotion-focused individual and group therapy and shares the experience of migration. Eric Hahn is a German psychiatrist with a proficiency in the Vietnamese language who specializes in cultural psychiatry and Global Mental Health. He works bilingually in both hospitals the Charité and KEH, in both in- and outpatient settings. Thi Main Huong Nguyen is a German-born psychologist, trained in mindfulness-based approaches, who focuses on surveying patients' explanatory models. Due to her own parents' different migration biographies – her father came as a refugee to Western Germany and her mother as a contract worker to Eastern Germany – she contributes personal knowledge apart from her professional training. Anita von Poser is a psychological anthropologist with expertise in relatedness, empathy, care, and aging. Within the project, she focuses on the growing number of Vietnamese social care workers in Berlin who serve as intermediaries between clinical spaces and everyday lifeworlds. Jörg-Christian Lanca is an area specialist on Southeast Asia, focusing on gender issues and conducting ethnographic research among former contract workers. Both Anita von Poser and Jörg-Christian Lanca are German-born with one parent having a migratory biography. Edda Heyken is a German anthropologist with research experience in forced migration, memory, remembrance, and the anthropology of psychiatry. She is conducting ethnographic research with actors who arrived as refugees.

4 Before approaching the patients, our team applied for the ethical approval of the ethical committee of the Charité - Universitätsmedizin Berlin. Medical research involving humans has to meet the standards of the Declaration of Helsinki by the World Medical Association (WMA, 2001), which comprises fundamental ethical principles respecting each person and his/her right to self-determination. In the application, we described the theoretical background as well as our assumptions, aims, the criteria for participation, the selection process, and the research procedure. According to the laws of the federal state to protect the anonymity of the participants at all times, data security forms an essential part of the research. As we set foot into a "vulnerable field", the psychiatrists pre-selected the patients on the basis of their psychiatric stability and individual biographies. Criteria to exclude patients from our research were neurodegenerative diseases, acute intoxication, acute suicidality, severe aggressive behavior, and severe psychotic symptoms. Participants in the survey could later be excluded or refrain according to the course of their illness.

5 The therapy is conducted by one psychiatrist while the second psychiatrist and the psychologist function as co-therapists and are also able to engage in participant observation during the session.

6 The differentiation between "refugees" and "contract workers" is not to be regarded as exclusively but as a constructed category: with the separation of Vietnam in 1954, approximately one million people fled from the North into the South. Additionally, also people stemming from the former South were sent to the GDR with temporary work permits (see also Nguyen, DT, 2017).

7 For detailed information, see www.sfb-affective-societies.de/en/teilprojekte/A/A02/index.html. (16 January 2019).

8 Intervision is a standard method within psychiatry and psychology in which clinicians and researchers exchange experiences and discuss critical issues at eye level (see Toman, 1996).

References

Blix Bergman, S 2015, 'Emotional insights in the field', in H Flam & J Kleres (eds.), *Methods of Exploring Emotions*, pp. 125–133, Routledge, New York.

Dreher, A, Hahn, E, Diefenbacher, A, Nguyen, TMH, Böge, K, Burian, H, Dettling, M, Burian, R & Ta, TMT 2017, 'Cultural differences in symptom representation for depression and somatization measured by the PHQ between Vietnamese and German psychiatric outpatients', *Journal of Psychosomatic Research*, no. 102, pp. 71–77. Available from: DOI: 10.1016/j.jpsychores.2017.09.010 [17 July 2018].

Flam, H 2015, 'Introduction: Methods of exploring emotions', in H Flam & J Kleres (eds.), *Methods of Exploring Emotions*, pp. 1–22, Routledge, New York.

Gelso, CJ & Hayes, J 2007, *Countertransference and the Therapist's Inner Experience: Perils and Possibilities*, Erlbaum Publisher, Mahwah.

Hahn, E, Burian, R, Dreher, A, Schomerus, G, Dettling, M, Diefenbacher, A, von Poser, A & Ta, TMT 2016, 'Beurteilung depressiver und somatischer Symptome mittels des PHQ-9 und PHQ-15 bei ambulanten vietnamesischen und deutschen Patientinnen', *Zeitschrift für Psychiatrie, Psychologie und Psychotherapie*, vol. 64, no. 1, pp. 25–36. Available from: DOI 10.1024/1661–4747/a000257 [17 July 2018].

Halpern, J 2001, *From Detached Concern to Empathy: Humanizing Medical Practice*, Oxford University Press.

Hinton, DE, Hinton, L, Tran, M, Nguyen, M, Nguyen, L, Hsia, C & Pollack, MH 2007, 'Orthostatic panic attacks among Vietnamese refugees', *Transcultural Psychiatry*, vol. 44, no. 4, pp. 515–544. Available from: DOI:10.1177/1363461507081640 [22 July 2018].

Hinton, DE & Kirmayer, L 2017, 'The flexibility hypothesis of healing', *Culture, Medicine, and Psychiatry*, no. 41, pp. 3–34. Available from: DOI: 10.1007/s11013-016-9493-8 [17 July 2018].

Hollan, D 1997, 'The relevance of person-centered ethnography to cross-cultural psychiatry', *Transcultural Psychiatry*, vol. 32, no. 2, pp. 219–234. Available from: http://journals.sagepub.com/doi/pdf/10.1177/136346159703400203 [17 July 2018].

Kirmayer, L, Lemelson, R & Cummings, C (eds.), 2015, *Re-Visioning Psychiatry: Cultural Phenomenology, Critical Neuroscience, and Global Mental Health*, Cambridge University Press, Cambridge.

Kleinman, A 1980, *Patients and Healers in the Context of Culture: An Exploration of the Borderland between Anthropology, Medicine, and Psychiatry*, University of California Press, Berkeley, Los Angeles, London.

Kusenbach, M 2003, 'Street phenomenology: The go-along as ethnographic research tool', *Ethnography*, vol. 4, no. 3, pp. 455–485. Available from: http://journals.sagepub.com/doi/abs/10.1177/146613810343007 [17 July 2018].

Littlewood, R 1980, 'Anthropology and psychiatry – an alternative approach', *British Journal of Medical Psychology*, no. 53, pp. 213–225. Available from: https://doi.org/10.1111/j.2044-8341.1980.tb02544.x [17 July 2018].

Littlewood, R 2010, 'Plädoyer für eine kultursensible Psychiatrie', in T Hegemann & R Salman (eds.), *Handbuch Transkulturelle Psychiatrie*, pp. 20–40, Psychiatrie Verlag, Bonn.

Mattes, D & Dinkelaker, S 2019, 'Failure and attunement in the field', in T Stodulka, S Dinkelaker & F Thajib (eds.), *Affective Dimensions of Fieldwork and Ethnography*, Springer, New York.

Mattes, D, Kasmani, O & Dilger, H 2018, ' "All Eyes Closed": Affective dynamics of sensing and Dis-sensing in comparative fieldwork on religious experiences', in A Kahl (ed.), *Analyzing Affective Societies*, Routledge, New York.

Nadig, M 2006, 'Transkulturelle Spannungsfelder in der Migration und ihre Erforschung – Das Konzept des Raums als methodischer Rahmen für dynamische Prozesse', in

E Wohlfahrt & W Zaumseil (eds.), *Transkulturelle Psychiatrie – Interkulturelle Psychotherapie, Interdisziplinäre Theorie und Praxis*, pp. 67–80, Springer, Heidelberg.

Nguyen, DT 2017, 'Zwei Communities. Theorie und Erfahrung', in B Kocatürk-Schuster, A Kolb, L Thanh, G Schultze & S Wölck (eds.), *Unsichtbar. Vietnamesisch-deutsche Wirklichkeiten*, pp. 300–315, edition DOMiD, Berlin.

Nguyen, TMH, Hahn, E, Wingenfeld, K, Graef-Calliess, IT, von Poser, A, Stopsack, M, Burian, H, Dreher, A, Wolf, S, Dettling, M, Burian, R, Diefenbacher, A & Ta, TMT 2017, 'Acculturation and severity of depression among first-generation Vietnamese outpatients in Germany', *International Journal of Social Psychiatry*, vol. 63, no. 8, pp. 708–716. Available from: DOI:10.1177/0020764017735140 [17 July 2018].

von Poser, A 2018, 'Affective lives im Vietnamesischen Berlin. Eine emotionsanthropologische Perspektive auf Zugehörigkeiten, Alter(n) und (Im-)Mobilität', *Geschichte und Gesellschaft*, vol. 44, no. 2, pp. 285–311. Available from: https://doi.org/10.13109/gege.2018.44.2.285 [18 July 2018].

von Poser, A, Hevken, E, Hahn, E & Ta, TMT 2019, 'Emotion repertoires', in J Slaby & C von Scheve (eds.), *Affective Societies. Key Concepts*, Routledge, New York.

von Poser, A, Lanca, JC & Heyken, E 2017, ' "Endlich drüber reden können" – Psychiatrie als affektiver Artikulationsraum und die Formierung transkultureller Emotionsrepertoires im Migrationsprozess', in B Kocatürk-Schuster, A Kolb, L Thanh, G Schultze & S Wölck (eds.), *Unsichtbar. Vietnamesisch-deutsche Wirklichkeiten*, pp. 256–273, edition DOMiD, Berlin.

Redman, P 2009, 'Affect revisited: Transference-countertransference and the unconscious dimensions of affective, felt and emotional experience', *Subjectivity*, vol. 26, no. 1, pp. 51–68. Available from: https://doi.org/10.1057/sub.2008.34 [22 July 2018].

Slaby, J, Rainer, M, & Philipp, W 2017. 'Affective arrangements', Emotion *Review*, pp. 1–10. Available from: https://journals.sagepub.com/doi/pdf/10.1177/1754073917722214 [13 December 2018].

Slaby, J 2016, *Relational Affect*. Working Paper SFB 1171 Affective Societies, 16 February. Available from: http://edocs.fu-berlin.de/docs/receive/FUDOCS_series_000000000562 [17 July 2018].

Slaby, J & Röttger-Rössler, B 2018, 'Introduction. Affect in relation', in B Röttger-Rössler, B & J Slaby (eds.), *Affect in Relation – Families, Places, Technologies. Essays on Affectivity and Subject Formation in the 21st Century*, pp. 1–28, Routledge, New York.

Spencer, M & Davies, J 2010, *Emotions in the Field. The Psychology and Anthropology of Fieldwork Experience*. Stanford University Press, Stanford.

Stodulka, T 2015, 'Spheres of passion: Fieldwork, ethnography and the researcher's emotions', *Curare – Journal for Medical Anthropology*, vol. 38, no. 1 + 2, pp. 103–116.

Stodulka, T, Dinkelaker, S & Thajib, F 2018, 'Fieldwork, ethnography, and the empirical affect montage', in A Kahl (ed.), *Analyzing Affective Societies: Methods and Methodologies*. Routledge, New York.

Svašek, M (ed.), 2012, *Moving Subjects, Moving Objects: Transnationalism, Cultural Production and Emotions*. Berghahn Books, New York, Oxford.

Ta, TMT, Neuhaus, AH, Burian, R, Schomerus, G, von Poser, A, Diefenbacher, A, Röttger-Rössler, B, Dettling, M & Hahn, E 2015, 'Inanspruchnahme ambulanter psychiatrischer Versorgung bei vietnamesischen Migranten der ersten Generation in Deutschland', *Psychiatrische Praxis*, vol. 42, no. 5, pp. 267–273. Available from: DOI:10.1055/s-0034-1370008 [17 July 2018].

Ta, TMT, Spennemann, N, Nguyen, TMH & Hahn, E 2017, 'Psychische Beanspruchung durch Migranten am Beispiel vietnamesischer Migrant_innen', in B Kocatürk-Schuster, A Kolb, L Thanh, G Schultze & S Wölck (eds.), *Unsichtbar. Vietnamesisch-deutsche Wirklichkeiten*, pp. 240–255, edition DOMiD, Berlin.

Toman, W 1996, 'A plea for more intervision', *Contemporary Family Therapy*, vol. 18, no. 3, pp. 385–392. Available from: https://doi.org/10.1007/BF02197049 [17 July 2018].

Wettergren, A 2015, 'How do we know what they feel?' in H Flam & J Kleres (eds.), *Methods of Exploring Emotions*, pp. 115–124, Routledge, New York.

Whelton, WJ 2004, 'Emotional processes in psychotherapy: Evidence across therapeutic modalities', *Clinical Psychology and Psychotherapy*, no. 11, pp. 58–71. Available from: https://doi.org/10.1002/cpp.392 [17 July 2018].

Chapter 15

'All Eyes Closed'

Dis/sensing in comparative fieldwork on affective-religious experiences

*Dominik Mattes, Omar Kasmani
and Hansjörg Dilger*

Today, I took a different approach. I tried to join in, not only to clap my hands and sing, but also to pray and keep my eyes closed as much as possible. It felt good, somehow invigorating. . . . In any case it was a lesson in empathy, an approximation of how it might feel to embrace all this with full commitment. With my eyes closed, it was easier for me to concentrate on myself and God, secluded from the many external visual influences.

(Field notes, Dominik Mattes, prayer meeting, 19 August 2016)

More than 40 people joined the *zikr* today; the *halqa* (circle) was quite big. Again, very powerful, a lot of screaming, bawling and people in fits. . . . While performing *zikr*, I thought about how sound helps override particulars of language; also for the researcher. At one point, everyone is part of a body of sound, words recede and a sonic experience comes to the fore.

(Field notes, Omar Kasmani, *zikr* gathering, 26 February 2017)

Introduction

Religious sites, practices, and materialities appeal to the senses. Together, they also shape the specific ways in which senses become entwined with human experiences and articulations of affect and emotion. The relationship between sensation and materiality is central to Birgit Meyer's (2010, 2012) understanding of religion as a form of mediation. Based on her empirical work on neo-Pentecostal religious practice, she argues how respective groups rely on various types of sensational forms – language, texts, sounds, images, etc. – in order to establish a direct connection between the members of a congregation and the intangible spiritual world (Meyer, 2010; see also Promey, 2014). Ideas of such mediation find an echo in Amira Mittermaier's work on Sufi religious dreams that dialogically tie religious sites' tangible materialities with an "Elsewhere" (Mittermaier, 2012). Thus, a focus on sensational forms opens up ways to explore comparatively how particular religious experiences are generated, and how these come to link bodies and materialities with what lies "beyond the ordinary" (Meyer, 2012, 26).

In this chapter, we discuss how a focus on the researcher's own senses facilitates the comparative study of affect in the context of religious gatherings and practices in the city of Berlin. We draw on our fieldwork in the framework of an ongoing research project on *Embodied Emotions and Affective Belonging in Migratory Contexts: Sufi Orders and Neo-Pentecostal Churches in Berlin* since 2015.[1] The project explores how affective experiences and practices are shaped and embodied in distinct ways in a neo-Pentecostal church that is mostly attended by West African migrants (Dominik Mattes) and a predominantly Turkish-speaking Sufi group, comprising mainly young men born and raised in Germany (Omar Kasmani) (see Dilger, Kasmani, & Mattes, 2018). We proceed from the assumption that affectivity is "an as of yet indeterminate unfolding of forces" (SFB Affective Societies, 2016, 3), which "evade[s] specific forms of reflective representation", whereas emotion is the "culturally shaped conceptualization" of affect (ibid., 5). It is of particular interest to us how members of these two religious communities perceive affective intensities that arise during prayer gatherings in their mutual entanglement with the apprehension and articulation of such experiences through the language of emotion.

However, in the course of our fieldwork, it turned out that our interlocutors found it difficult to describe in precise terms how they felt during particular affective situations that regularly occurred as part of the prayer sessions we observed. Even though we had expected this to some degree, as there are limits to how affect "can be readily verbalized" (Wetherell, 2013, 350), it presented a significant methodological and conceptual challenge. How were we to study affect if our interlocutors were not willing or able to put their experiences to words? Would we have to accept the assumption of Brian Massumi and others that "human affect is formulated as a kind of 'extra-discursive' event" (ibid.), and thus ultimately non-representable through language?

In this chapter, we suggest that the binary opposition between affect as the unspeakable, unstructured experience of feeling, on the one hand, and emotion as its codified form, on the other, is better viewed as a continuum in relation to practices as they unfold in specific empirical configurations. As the case studies from our two field sites show, affect is represented, even triggered by spoken words – in fact, it is always culturally mediated as "talk, body actions, affect, material contexts and social relations assemble *in situ*" (ibid., 351). However, rather than exclusively listening and observing in the field – the core methods of ethnographic fieldwork – we highlight the importance of using the researcher's own bodily perceptions, that is, her/his ways of 'sensing the field' as a crucial means for understanding and representing the affective atmospheres prevailing in religious gatherings (see also Mossière, 2007).

With this approach, we follow Paul Stoller's (1997) call for a sensuous scholarship, which relies on the researcher's body with "its smells, tastes, textures, and sensations" (ibid., XV) in order "to eject the conceit of control in which mind and body, self and other are considered separate" (ibid., XVII). We also rely on Sarah Pink's (2009) work on sensory ethnography, in which she argues that we need to investigate the full potential of "attending to the senses in ethnographic research and representation" (ibid., 7) as a way to open up "new routes to knowledge" (ibid., 8, see also Feld, 1996).

The following two case studies show that the potential of accessing affect through the researcher's body and senses was enhanced by the researchers' decision to close their eyes as part of the believers' practices in both the neo-Pentecostal church and the Sufi circle. Thus, the decision to close one's eyes led to a sharpening of the aural – as well as other more-than-visual modes of sensing and feeling the gatherings' atmospheres – and opened up researchers' access to some of the ways in which members of these groups may also have been affected. This enabled us to come closer to such atmospheres' affective power that includes sensations of intensity, intimacy, energy, and immediacy, but also resonances of bodies, bonding, and belonging. Furthermore, in both sites the decision to close one's eyes enhanced the researchers' sense for how believers *may* apprehend things, events, and beings – the 'hidden realities' of the immaterial world – that they would not otherwise see or sense.

Moments of enhanced empathy[2] (Harvey, 2011, 231) in the context of religious ritual and our attempts to embrace their full affective power do not imply that the researchers have the 'same' affective experiences as other participants of the religious gatherings (see concluding remarks). Nor does the researcher's bodily involvement with all his or her senses entail the complete surrender of the ethnographer's agency (Stoller, 1997, XVII) or his or her capacity to reflect on the events in which one has agreed to immerse oneself.[3] Thus, as we illustrate in the following two sections, such moments of closing one's eyes in our two field sites – and the struggle and reluctance to do so – included sensations of vexation, awkwardness, curiosity, discomfort, doubt, unease, and resistance on the part of the researchers. Moreover, the exposure to sensorial abundance required a considerable amount of trust from the side of the researchers to yield full or even partial control of the situation – if only momentarily. As we argue in the concluding discussion, such trust and the various sensations and feelings the immediate experience of religious affectivity may entail are closely tied to the researchers' positionalities and their ways of relating to spiritual and ideological world views of particular denominations or religious groups.

Sensing Pentecostal choreographies of intensity (Dominik)

> Spirit of the living God! Every works of darkness around me, burn them with your fire! Burn them with your fire! Spirit of the living God! I'm coming back home! . . . I'm a child of God! I'm a servant of the mighty God! Spirit of the living God! . . . Take away every works . . . of darkness! . . . Let your fire fall! Let your fire fall! Let your fire fall!

My eyes closed, I am subjected to the pastor's prayers. I feel shaken by his powerful voice, ear-piercingly amplified by two powerful loudspeakers in the front of the prayer hall. Some 60 fervently praying believers around me stamp their feet on the floor, beat their fists into their hands, swing their arms back and forth, incessantly shake their heads. They all contribute to the noise of exalting the divine, filling the otherwise plain room with their rhythmically enunciated, at times hissed, supplications. Invisible energetic bonds between us set my own body in motion. I am immersed in this soundscape and the mass of moving bodies, myself praying, albeit in less expressive ways. "Spirit of the living God, wake me up! Wake me up! Wake me up!", the pastor exclaims, setting an ever-faster pace for his highly receptive audience.

> The days of sleeping are over! Wake me up! Wake me up! Expose the devil! . . . Expose the fires of darkness! . . . Expose the works of Satan against my life! . . . Spirit of the living God! He's here! He's here! Let him come upon you! Let him come upon you! Let him consume you. Are you tired, are you tired, are you tired? Say you're thirsty! Lord I'm thirsty! Lord I'm thirsty! . . . Let your fire! Let your fire! . . . The Pentecostal fire! . . . Let it fall! Let it fall! Let it fall!

The atmosphere seems to be on edge. Somewhere behind me, a woman avers her unconditional surrender to Jesus singing loudly with a voluminous, almost operatic voice. Across the aisle, a man slumps to the ground. I open my eyes, his head rolls to and fro on his forearm, tears run down his cheeks. As the congregants' arousal reaches its peak, the pastor puts the microphone away and wipes tiny beads of sweat off his forehead. With an enraptured smile on his face, he lets his gaze wander over his ignited congregation for a short while, before he loudly exclaims a protracted "In Jeeeeeeesus' naaaaaaame we praaaaay!"

Within seconds, the body of noise extending to every corner of the room implodes, all bodies stand still. "Your eyes closed," the pastor interjects into the sudden quietude. He now speaks with a very sonorous, soothing tone of voice. "Now look at yourself," he whispers into the microphone.

> You committed yourself to God because I stood here and I told you God was in need of a committed man, a committed woman . . . and you have raised your hand and said I am one of them! God will take care of you! (Congregation: Amen!) God will defend you. (Congregation: Amen!). God will protect you. (Congregation: Amen!). He will be an enemy to your enemy (Congregation, ever more loudly: Amen!). . . . He will not let you down! (Congregation: Amen!)

Sunday services and prayer meetings at this church include numerous such waves of aural-kinaesthetic intensity. In the absence of strong visual features like paintings, sculptures, or illumination, the affective strength and potential of these gatherings predominantly resides in the sonic and bodily movement – both intimately intertwined. Congregants' heightened sensorial engagement is effected not only via the semantics of the pastor's words but also by their acoustic characteristics.

The most obvious of these is the modulation of his voice's pitch and volume. Both carefully phrased *crescendi* and the sudden eruptions of high-pitched exclamations punctuating the tapestry of the congregants' calmly dabbling prayers create suspense in equally effective ways. However, the frequency and density of the pastor's utterances also contribute to a felt increase in intensity. Towards the culmination of the prayer waves, his language picks up velocity and features more and more repetitions and anaphors.

Aside from such phonetic cues, the pastor also guides the praying crowd's bodily, sensorial, and emotional performance by occasionally prompting individual believers to express their commitment with more physical engagement, carry out particular bodily movements, and adopt the desired emotional attitude. Such guidance not only generates affective arousal. After the climax of the prayer waves, it also creates an atmosphere of intimacy and trust. These moments of affective respite often begin with the pastor's request to have "all eyes closed", to enter into a dialogue with God unaffected by any exterior influence and protected from the gaze of others so as to freely open up to the Lord one's innermost concerns.

Unable to ever know precisely how church members perceive these choreographies of intensity, attending to my own feelings, bodily reactions, and perceptions during the services and prayer meetings certainly helps me gain a sense of how powerful and effective, how moving in both senses of the word these are. It was after I had decided to engage more actively and physically in the church's liturgical practice – to stand up, close my eyes, pray, and sing with the congregants – that I noticed being affected much more than when I had remained seated, watching, taking notes. My body unavoidably started swinging in particular patterns during prayers, and I felt great joy in joining in the congregants' polyphonic worship songs and syncopated clapping. Occasionally, I perceived sudden heat and would begin to sweat. At other moments, shivers ran down my spine; and once I felt a lump in my throat with my eyes tearing up. The most moving moments, however, were those in which the pastor specifically addressed me in his prayers, referring to me as "our researcher" or "brother Dominik". The Lord's mission for me on earth, he once emphasized, was far greater than any scientific accomplishment.

> I pray for my brother Dominik. He cannot come to all these processes and go to hell. Lord, before the end of his writing, you will transform him. . . . You will save him. . . . Lord, when we will get to heaven, we will see him there. Help him to be free from shame. Help him to be free from mockery. And through him . . . light will spread into German society. Through him, life will spread into the city of Berlin. Jesus, tonight, as he's going to sleep, let him see you!
>
> (Sunday service, 16 October 2016)

In this moment, when the church members' hands turned towards me, I gained a sense of the enormous affective power that sprang from such collective prayers for individual congregants, a practice I had witnessed several times before.

At the same time, on occasions when the pastor presented the prospect of me belonging to "the most miserable ones on earth",[4] should I not learn my lesson, eventually convert, and become a born-again Christian – always followed by the congregation's loud and unison "Amen!" – I developed distinct feelings of dis-sense in the face of what I perceived as rather disturbing to my sensibilities. I read truth claims implicit in such moments as being tied to a logic of moral supremacy vis-à-vis other religious and moral orientations (see also Marshall, 2016), which in turn evoked a sense of disconnect where I felt subjected to a practice I could only passively endure. This affective reaction at times corresponded with – and was amplified by – my unease regarding particular sensorial qualities of the prayers and sermons. The moderately pitched, repetitive, almost meditative singing of worship songs, and calm self-reflections revolving around themes such as one's personal humility or capacities of forgiveness, for instance, were quite appealing to me. But collective endeavors to deliver oneself and one's surroundings from the dark powers of Satan by way of clamorous prayers and vigorous bodily gestures caused me consistent disconcertion.

My dis-sense in these situations can certainly be ascribed to how I had been socialized into the sphere of the religious and to my own previous religious engagements and experiences. I was raised by a father who was a teacher of Roman Catholic religion, a regular church-goer who wholeheartedly embraced the Catholic doctrine, placed great emphasis on the adherence to religious liturgy, and irrespective of our choice made me and my siblings attend Sunday service well into our early youth. Also influential is the fact that my mother, who was brought up in a Protestant family, had always adopted a critical position vis-a-vis Catholic religious routines and the largely violent history of the Roman Catholic church. Leaning towards agnosticism, she always made great efforts, wittingly or not, to foster our capacities for critical self-reflection, implanting in us the seed of tolerance in regard to others' diverging religious orientations and, in a more general sense, attitudes to life.

The clash between my resulting fundamental conviction of the importance of 'moral relativism' and more or less explicit ideas of moral superiority inherent in religious teachings were also the reasons why I eventually distanced myself from Vaishnavism, a Hindu tradition and practice I had engaged in during my early adulthood. What remained from it, however, was a profound affinity with the soundscape of *kirtan*, a sung form of worship. Perhaps, this is one reason why I was able to appreciate the congregation's melodious singing of worship songs much more than the excited and high-pitched episodes of certain prayers at the church.

In conclusion, my regular participation and multisensorial engagement in and with the congregation's religious practice has enabled me to come into contact with church members' "affective habitus" (Reckwitz, 2012, 255). I believe that this methodological "fusion of the intelligible and the sensible" (Stoller, 1997, XV) and the epistemological reflection thereof allows me to gain a sense of where, how, and to what effect affect unfolds and materializes in the congregation's gatherings. More than a mere focus on spoken representation, it helps me apprehend how church members are moved by and within their religious experience. Moreover, while it does so *in spite of* my own moral and sensuous dissonances, these moments of dis-sensing hold in themselves the potential for more nuanced inquiries in the field. It was precisely my own occasionally felt sensuous-moral divergence, for instance, that impelled me to probe in interviews with individual congregants, whether or not at times they had similar experiences. Had I not drawn on my own manifold perceptions of the field in this regard, I would probably have missed the opportunity to intersubjectively explore dynamics of authority and compliance in the church context.

A taste of the unseen: scenes from a Sufi circle (Omar)

It is my first time in the circle. For almost 20 minutes, in this mosque that doubles as a gathering place of the Sufis in Neukölln, their *hoca*, an elderly teacher, delivers a *sohbet* (talk) in Turkish. I do not understand a thing he says, so I try and fight off wandering thoughts. I spend my time inspecting the circle, arresting the relative lull, observing how men in the group listen with their heads lowered, their bodies almost curled out of deference to their spiritual master. At some point, heads rise and all eyes converge at me when from within this talk in a language I do not follow, the words "anthropologist", "tasawwuf" (Sufism) and "university" stick out. The *hoca* signals for me to draw closer. As I sit right before him, he recites a small prayer. I return to take my spot in the circle, authorized as though to join the group in *zikr*, a sonic and corporeal ritual of remembrance that follows the weekly gathering of *sohbet*.

Now tightly knit, the circle feels denser than it did during *sohbet*. A quieter phase of inward reflection is leading to a rhythmic repetition of the names of Allah. Soon enough, men are on their feet and the circle turns incrementally intense. The *hoca* introduces lyrical verses that float over a heavy tide of collective chants. I find it harder to keep pace. The energy is overwhelming, the thick sound of breathing is unmissable, not least the forceful swivel that pulls me in directions both left and right. I am struggling to hold my ground. In this room, carpeted wall-to-wall in a shade of green, all eyes are now closed. Mine too, but rather intermittently. In watching, I betray the circle; with eyes shut, I feel I am not doing what I'm supposed to do as an ethnographic observer. Neither can I take notes, so I try making mental ones. That does not help much either. Thoughts charge at me from every side: How did I land myself a place in this circle? How do I observe with eyes closed?

Months into the research, I was still curious as to how believers relate to not-seeing during *zikr* or how their experiences could help me make sense of my own challenges in the field. It had become a regular point of conversation with my interlocutors. "He sees you, you don't see Him, we're all together, it's love" – 29-year old Hasan was describing his experience of *zikr* in German as we caught up in a noisy kebab shop. Yet this wasn't the first time a Sufi follower had spoken to me about sensing the unseen. Neither was what I was encountering in conceptual terms exactly new. For several years I had researched with Sufis in Pakistan, allowing me to cultivate a sense of appreciation for their devotional and charismatic lifeworlds (Kasmani, 2016). For instance, I was easily, almost instantly, drawn to the lyrical and sense-aesthetic qualities of *zikr*, often finding myself taking joy as I indulged in its sonic atmospheres. Yet, there were things that kept me cautious and at bay. Contrary to my experience in Pakistan, the discourse I often encountered in *sohbet* gatherings in Berlin through the help of an interlocutor was strict and conservative in its interpretation of religious doctrine, at times contributing to my sense of unease in the circle. Questions of access and distance were now more pressing than ever, not least because when it came to researching ritual I had not allowed myself to participate to this extent before. I had been at best skeptical of such methods. And yet here I was, standing in a circle with some 30 men, our arms locked with one another, reciting names of Allah, our bodies pacing up with the intensities of chanting. Such advanced access however meant that week after week, in a ritual I was now privy to, I was in the company of young men like Hasan who would chant, sing, scream, laugh, howl, or simply fall on the ground reacting to affective intensities that arose and waned during *zikr*.

That men in the circle longed to see during a ritual, which required them to close their eyes, wasn't entirely odd to me. Through my observations of the ritual but equally in our conversations beyond the ritual setting, it was becoming evident that there was more to the circle than met the eye. When followers spoke of the intensities of *zikr*, they often insisted on an extended feeling of togetherness. They described how one was potentially in the company of saints and holy beings, a presence many longed to sense but only a few had witnessed. "It's possible that one, that a few, see things which one normally doesn't see," Hasan had told me. "Angels! . . . people who have lived 500 years ago! Saints, they are there, and they perform *zikr* with us". In fact, in our very first conversation, the *hoca* had evoked the well-known Sufi metaphor of the veil, which when lifted, reveals, only to the initiated, the hidden realities of the world. As I understood, this wasn't simply a matter of seeing but of witnessing with one's senses. If indeed the separation of the here and the hereafter – in his words, two seas, one sweet, the other salty – was upheld by a *Vorhang* (*lit*. curtain), the ultimate goal of the Sufi was to overcome this divide in order to *taste* the fruit of higher truth. Witnessing exceeded seeing.

Even if I didn't share their persuasions, each week, as I joined these men to sing and chant praises of saints and holy men, I worried if I was indeed getting the technique right. I feared my clumsy movements disturbed the continuity of the circle. I strived to keep up the coordination of the chanting with the swaying. And all this while curbing the urge to watch how others moved: Whether men lifted their feet or not, if indeed their eyes were properly closed, or who among them seemed the most talented. If learning had to do with doing, how could the skill of doing be acquired in the absence of watching, I wondered. In my conversations with men of the circle, the question of why we had our eyes shut during *zikr* kept returning. While some thought it was necessary for concentration, others had pointed to the intimacies of *zikr*. In their view, a ritual as emotionally disclosing as *zikr*, even though collectively performed, demanded that it be done while others weren't watching one's every move.

Not watching required learning new skills in the field. Every now and then, when someone would experience an emotional outburst or the circle would turn intense at one of its many points, it became all the more difficult to contain the impulse to see what had just occurred. There was certainly something sneaky about being in the circle and observing men who all had their eyes closed. Such occasional peeking also meant that my impressions of what came to pass in the circle were indeed episodic, a series of briefly caught scenes at best. In moments when I had let myself observe with eyes open, or at times half-open, I had seen people make mistakes, and much like myself, their failures to synchronize were visible too. Also, the extent to which people moved varied tremendously: the jerk of the head, the to-and-fro of torsos, the movement of arms back and forth. I could see how some had their fists tightened, some had their palms open, some moved their heads more rigorously, some very lightly, some moved their heads back and forth, some right and left, and some barely moved. It was only on occasions when I closed my eyes following those whom I was observing in this weekly circle of remembrance that I purposefully allowed the watching ethnographer to recede. Colors, textures, bodies, and gestures that had until then cluttered my field of vision were quickly giving way, letting a sonic singularity emerge in its stead: A singularity not in the sense of a flat plane of sound but experienced as a complexly layered ensemble of all manner of sounds, turning my attention to rhythms, melodies, and resonances, deftly inter-woven, densely scored. What was lost in vision was gained in resonances of the body; the multitude of dissimilar movements and gestures that visually constituted the moving circle now registered itself differently, traveling through the chain of bodies as men locked their arms with one another. Saintly encounters that participants of the circle described as "the shock of one's life" were audibly traceable in the sonic architecture of *zikr* gatherings.

It has to be said that there is a perceptible difference in how I observed with eyes closed, primarily because one's aural access to the world is differently structured, influencing also how affective knowledge is registered, airborne in inflect-prone waves rather than fluid streams of uninterrupted vision (see also Kasmani, 2017). Knowing through affect isn't a claim for knowing affect itself, just as doing as one's interlocutors do isn't an exercise in sharing affective worlds. Because even in moments when I let the watching ethnographer recede, I was involved not as a follower but as an ethnographer, insisting on observing otherwise, longing to witness, arguably like my interlocutors, but to radically different ends.

Witnessing in the field has to be forever caught somewhere between a Geertzian assertion that one has truly *been there* and "a seeing that doubts itself" (Taussig, 2011, 1). Just as the work of ethnography only affirms that "actual, existing circumstances are always imbued with the possibility of being otherwise . . . that the real is always more than what is actually present somewhere" (Pandian & McLean, 2017, 19). The *hoca* had it right. There were seas that separated the visible from the real. There were fruits to be tasted on the other side. It was during these ritual gatherings when I had stopped seeing that I first began to witness how and why *zikr* was more than a collective exercise of a mindful remembrance of Allah. With its sonic and corporeal structures, its propensities for release and contact, and its capacities to generate moods, the ritual presented itself as a routinized possibility of immersing oneself in incrementally charged and sensorially abundant atmospheres. Veils were momentarily lifted, leaving the circle of men – researcher as well as the researched – though visibly in bouts of exhilaration, altered in their affective knowledge of the world and hence also of themselves.

Concluding discussion

In a world so inter-affectively charged, so porously imagined, and where the agency of religious individuals cannot only be a question of their acting in the world but equally of being acted upon (see Mittermaier, 2012), driven as much as driving subjects, the work of the anthropologist must also shift gears. And such adjustments extend beyond the analytical labor that goes into making sense of the field remotely to include the work of participation and 'being' in the field itself. In this regard, the researcher's embodied immersion serves as a crucial instrument for sensing the immediacy and affective power of religious performances as well as for subsequently articulating and representing such sensations.

To the extent that this reflection is about limits of participation and discusses the researcher's body as a valuable resource in affect-rich religious contexts, there are obvious parallels to be drawn with Mikkel Rytter's (2015) account of his fieldwork with Danish-Pakistani Sufis. However, it also diverges from it in significant ways. Unlike Rytter, our participation in religious gatherings is not a form of 'imitating' whose goal is to eventually experience what our interlocutors describe; neither are we inquiring after possibilities of being affected by the phenomena we study (p. 141). In other words, concerns of how to receive, experience, and communicate the non-representational experience of affect do not take center stage here. They are only indirectly addressed through a discussion of otherwise foreclosed forms of access that open up particularly through constraints of sensing and also dis-sensing – in affect-abundant situations.

In all these regards, it is important to emphasize that the involvement of the researchers' bodies with all their senses during fieldwork represents only *one* part of our project's methodological repertoire. The insights that we gather through this method always acquire meaning in relation to, and simultaneously inform, our other sources and methods of fieldwork. These include various types of interviews and non-formal conversations with members and leaders of the two religious groups, as well as the exploration of religious practices and experiences through video- and sound-recordings, and the contextualization of religious practices in regard to the groups' wider socio-urban environments and their trans-national religious networks.

This being said, a more pronounced focus on the senses allows us to tap into our field sites' affective dynamics as various sensational forms impactfully coalesce in particular moments: authoritative language and instructions of the *hoca* and the pastor; the pitch and modulation of their voices; the percussive use of chants and exclamations; the evocative recourse to metaphors and melodies; all contribute to the at times excessive soundscape in the Pentecostal church and the rather spirited atmosphere in the Sufi circle. By yielding control, opening up to the unexpected, and subjecting ourselves with all our senses, we are able to advance our access to the understanding of religious experience in embodied, more than cognitive ways.

With this, we do not wish to suggest that we experience religious practices and atmospheres in the exact same way as members of the groups we study. Nei-ther do we necessarily ascribe the same meaning to our respective experiences. Rather, we consider our varied physical-emotional reactions as significant to the affective dynamics that we as researchers experience in the company of believ-ers. In the case of Dominik, this became manifest in his reactions to Pentecostal prayer waves – his shivers, sudden attacks of sweating, and instances of being moved to tears. For Omar, it was given in the dual registers of feeling included – for instance, the extent to which he, like others around him, took pleasure in the lyrical-melodic structures of the ritual – while also worrying if his physical move-ments interrupted the continuity of the Sufi circle.

Sensing the field, however, also includes instances of dis-sensing. Our sense-perception of the field – that is, the extent to which we are able to see, hear, smell or taste – is largely shaped by the sites' sensorial regime, but also by our prepar-edness to abide by it. A clear example of dis-sense that we can identify in our fieldwork is not being able to visually observe *zikr* gatherings and prayer meet-ings with our eyes closed. Omar's strong curiosity to see what was happening in the circle while others had their eyes closed, his concerns of not adhering to the *hoca*'s instructions, and its accompanying sense of betrayal to the circle as well as to his task as an ethnographer is one instance where particular forms of sensing may draw feelings of conflict in the field. Dis-sensing, however, also occurs in our individual responses to what we encounter and deem personally dissonant in sen-sorial terms. Dominik's unease with congregants' loud and vigorously gestured efforts to deliver themselves from the powers of darkness and Omar's difficulties to morally align with the conservative discourse of *sohbet* gatherings may serve as a case in point.

As our ethnographic accounts show, the dynamics of sensing and dis-sensing in our field sites is closely entwined with our personal life histories. Our own religious socialization, for instance, in the case of Dominik, and previous experi-ences of fieldwork, as was the case with Omar, shape the emotional and cognitive stance we adopt towards the communities we work with. In the social scientific study of religion, this question of positionality has been discussed prominently with regard to the researcher's perspective of agnosticism or atheism (Blanes, 2006; Ewing, 1994) – as well as his or her decision to engage in a kind of "methodological ludism", which allows for the performing of appropriate roles in the field even though one may not share certain commitments and convictions (Harvey, 2011, 224).

However, as our focus on the researcher's own bodies and senses in doing fieldwork demonstrates, such positionalities are also deeply embodied and involve more than a cognitive alignment with or dissociation from a certain religious ideology or practice. A focus on sensing and dis-sensing is not to be understood thereby in a binary opposition to intellectual reflection on ritual practice in the moment it takes place; neither among the researchers nor among our interlocutors (Dilger et al. forthcoming). This means that one does not come before the other, that reflecting, sensing, and feeling occur complementarily – and often simultaneously – and are in a dialectical relationship with each other (ibid.). Having the researcher as a resource while being an object of study thus helps blur the lines between experience of the field and knowledge about it (see Papageorgiou, 2007). The embodied ways of knowing arising out of such methods offer also the possibility to transcend distinctions between cognition and emotion (see Mossière, 2007), eventually covering some measure of distance between researchers and the researched.

Notes

1 The research project is funded by the German Research Foundation (DFG) in the context of the Collaborative Research Centre (CRC) *Affective Societies* at Freie Universität Berlin. Dominik Mattes and Omar Kasmani are the postdoctoral research associates of the project; Hansjörg Dilger is the principal investigator.
2 Following Harvey (2011, 243), we understand empathy here as "the practice of assuming an attitude of interest in other people's lives and concerns", which is "developed by feeling or thinking oneself into others' habitual and motivational lives".
3 For a thorough theoretical discussion of 'immersion' in relation to 'affect', see Mühlhoff and Schütz (2017).
4 As the pastor clarified in a discussion of this text before publication, he explicitly used this drastic language in reference to the bible verse 1st Corinthians 15, 19 where Apostle Paul states: "If in this life only we have hope in Christ, we are of all men most miserable".

References

Blanes, RL 2006, 'The atheist anthropologist: Believers and non-believers in anthropological fieldwork', *Social Anthropology*, vol. 14, no. 2, pp. 223–234.

Dilger, H, Bochow, A, Burchardt, M & Wilhelm-Solomon, M (eds.), forthcoming, *Affective Trajectories: Religion and Emotion in African Cityscapes*, Duke University Press, Durham.

Dilger, H, Kasmani, O & Mattes, D 2018, 'Spatialities of belonging: Affective place-making among diasporic Neo-Pentecostal and Sufi groups in Berlin's cityscape', in

B Röttger-Rössler & J Slaby (eds.), *Affect in Relation: Essays on Affectivity and Subject Formation in the 21st Century*, pp. 93–114, Routledge, Abingdon, New York.

Ewing, K 1994, 'Dreams from a saint: Anthropological atheism and the temptation to believe', *American Anthropologist*, vol. 96, no. 3, pp. 571–583.

Feld, S 1996, 'Waterfalls of song: An acoustemology of place resounding in Bosavi, Papua New Guniea', in S Feld and K Basso (eds.), *Senses of Place*, pp. 91–135, School of American Research Press, Santa Fe.

Harvey, G 2011, 'Field research: Participant observation', in M Stausberg & S Engler (eds.), *The Routledge Handbook of Research Methods in the Study of Religion*, pp. 217–244, Routledge, Abingdon.

Kasmani, O 2016, *Off the Lines: Fakir Orientations of Gender, Body, and Space in Sehwan Sharif, Pakistan*, PhD thesis, Freie Universität, Berlin.

Kasmani, O 2017, 'Audible spectres: The sticky Shia sonics of Sehwan', *History of Emotions – Insights into Research Blog*, blog post, October. Available from: www.history-of-emotions.mpg.de/en/texte/audible-spectres-the-sticky-shia-sonics-of-sehwan [24 July 2018].

Marshall, R 2016, 'Destroying arguments and captivating thoughts: Spiritual warfare prayer as global praxis', *Journal of Religious and Political Practice*, vol. 2, no. 1, pp. 92–113.

Meyer, B 2010, 'Aesthetics of persuasion: Global Christianity and Pentecostalism's sensational forms', *South Atlantic Quarterly*, vol. 109, no. 4, pp. 741–763.

Meyer, B 2012, *Mediation and the Genesis of Presence: Towards a Material Approach to Religion*, Universiteit Utrecht, Faculteit Geesteswetenschappen, Oratie 19 October.

Mittermaier, A 2012, 'Dreams from elsewhere: Muslim subjectivities beyond the trope of self-cultivation', *Journal of the Royal Anthropological Institute*, vol. 18, pp. 247–265.

Mossière, G 2007, 'Sharing in ritual effervescence: Emotions and empathy in fieldwork', *Anthropology Matters*, vol. 9, no. 1. Available from: www.anthropologymatters.com/index.php/anth_matters/article/view/59/113 [22 September 2017].

Mühlhoff, R & Schütz, T 2017, *Verunsichern, Vereinnahmen, Verschmelzen. Eine affekt-theoretische Perspektive auf Immersion*. Working Paper SFB 1171 Affective Societies 17 May. Available from: www.sfb-affective-societies.de/publikationen/workingpapers eries/wps_10/index.html [24 July 2018].

Pandian, A & McLean, S (eds.), 2017, *Crumpled Paper Boat: Experiments in Ethnographic Writing*, Duke University Press, Durham.

Papageorgiou, D 2007, 'Field research on the run: One more (from) for the road', in A McLean & A Leibing (eds.), *The Shadow Side of Fieldwork. Exploring the Blurred Borders Between Ethnography and Life*, pp. 221–238, Wiley-Blackwell, Malden.

Pink, S 2009, *Doing Sensory Ethnography*, Sage Publications, London.

Promey, S (ed.), 2014, *Sensational Religion. Sensory Cultures in Material Practice*, Yale University Press, New Haven.

Reckwitz, A 2012, 'Affective spaces: A praxeological outlook', *Rethinking History*, vol. 16, no. 2, pp. 241–258.

Rytter, M 2015, 'The scent of a rose: Imitating imitators as they learn to love the prophet', in B Knudsen & C Stage (eds.), *Affective Methodologies: Developing Cultural Research Strategies for the Study of Affect*, pp. 140–160, Palgrave Macmillan, London.

SFB Affective Societies 2016, *A Glossary. Register of Central Working Concepts*. Working Paper SFB 1171 Affective Societies, 16 January. Available from: www.sfb-affective-societies.de/publikationen/workingpaperseries/wps_1/index.html [24 July 2018].

Stoller, P 1997, *Sensuous Scholarship*, University of Pennsylvania Press, Philadelphia.
Taussig, M 2011, *I Swear I Saw This: Drawing in Fieldwork Notebooks, Namely My Own*, University of Chicago Press, Chicago.
Wetherell, M 2013, 'Affect and discourse – What's the problem? From affect as excess to affective/discursive practice', *Subjectivity*, vol. 6, no. 4, pp. 349–368.

Chapter 16

Fieldwork, ethnography and the empirical affect montage

Thomas Stodulka, Samia Dinkelaker and Ferdiansyah Thajib

Introduction

It is striking that anthropological discussions about epistemology and ethnographic writing seem to have little impact on similar debates in the wider arena of the social and cultural sciences. This is surprising, given that these longstanding debates in anthropology straddle the concerns of reflexive epistemologies (Davies & Stodulka, 2019; Sluka & Robben, 2012). Moreover, anthropology's partialism and particularism seem to have trickled into critical public discourses about subjectivity, hybridity and culture theory (Liebert, 2016; Reckwitz, 2000, 2008; Slaby, 2016a, 2016b, 2016c). Despite this, anthropology's contribution remains undisclosed, and isolated at best. *If* anthropological practices of researching and writing are acknowledged within interdisciplinary and public debates of methodology and epistemology, it is predominantly restricted to one concept: 'ethnography' (Gable, 2014; Ingold, 2014).

Some anthropologists argue that the term 'ethnography' has been applied to such a variety of settings and scientific practices that "*ethnographic* [emphasis added] appears to be a modish substitute for qualitative, [and] offends every principle of proper, rigorous anthropological inquiry – including long-term and open-ended commitment, generous attentiveness, relational depth, and sensitivity to context" (Ingold, 2014, 384). Anthropologist Tim Ingold provocatively suggests giving up the term 'ethnographic' altogether, because its intellectual erosion no longer does justice "to the fieldwork in which these encounters take place, to the methods by which we prosecute it, or to the knowledge that grows therefrom. Indeed, to characterize encounters, fieldwork, methods and knowledge as ethnographic is positively misleading" (ibid., 385). We share Ingold's concerns, but instead of refuting the term, we intend to formulate a 'call to arms' that challenges anthropologists to better communicate what is at stake when they *do* ethnography, in a language that also speaks to non-anthropologists. Many anthropologists have defined ethnography in negative terms – it is *not* qualitative social science, it is *not* travel writing, it is *not* fiction, it is *not* science, it is *not* art (Ingold, 2014; Sanjek, 1991). Others have highlighted its long-term and open-ended commitment that does not end with fieldwork, its ethical responsibility, participatory-observation mode, holistic attentiveness, or the 'dilemma' of simultaneously seeking affective immersion with and detachment from interlocutors and informants (Candea et al., 2015; Cook, 2016; Ingold, 2014; Fabian, 1983; Jackson, 1989; Okely, 2012; Sluka, 2012; Stoller & Olkes, 2012).

While building on this literature, this chapter also argues that the epistemological potential of fieldworkers' affects and emotions has been insufficiently discussed in empirical terms, and that its links to a systematic methodological heuristic have been overlooked (Davies & Stodulka, 2019; Lubrich, Liebal, & Stodulka, 2017; Stodulka, Selim, & Mattes, 2018; Stodulka, Dinkelaker, & Thajib, 2019). We hypothesize that enhanced emotional literacy and a methodology that takes ethnographers' affects and emotions into account, assists in translating field experiences (observations, participations, conversations) into a language that speaks to those who have not "been there" (Hollan, 2008). The systematic methodological and epistemological focus on the affective dimensions of fieldwork practice fosters a transparent communication of ethnographers' simultaneous immersion and detachment during field research encounters and, as we shall outline, positions anthropology back at the center of transdisciplinary methodological and epistemological debates.

These heuristic aspirations gave incentives to design emotion diaries that assist fieldworkers in the systematic documentation of their affective experiences and hence extend the interpretation of fieldwork encounters and data to its affective dimensions. This chapter proposes *Empirical Affect Montage* as a technique to bring the researchers' affects and emotions in dialogue with more traditional accounts of the phenomena they study (e.g. field notes, interviews, memory protocols, transcripts, photographs, video, etc.). We propose emotion diaries as pragmatic aids to support fieldworkers in training their capacities to reflect and document affective experiences in the field. By offering a tangible device, we respond to earlier calls for fieldworkers to "becom[e] participants and observers not only in field relations but also in [their own] subjectivity" (Spencer, 2010, 20).

Rear view: reflexive ethnography and the 'literary turn'

Anthropologists and sociologists have compellingly highlighted the intersubjective dimension of ethnographic data and narrative (Berger, 2010; Bonz et al., 2017; Burkitt, 2016, 2012; Clifford & Marcus, 1986; Desjarlais & Throop, 2011; Hastrup, 2010; Herbrik, 2013; Hollan, 2008; Jackson, 1989; Rosaldo, 1989; Wikan, 1992). During the so-called *literary turn* of the 1980s, anthropology went through a cathartic 'vale of tears' where fieldworkers' (post-)colonial complicity, ethnographic authority and the *raison d'être* of ethnographic research were radically deconstructed. When compared to sociology, political science or area studies, anthropology has celebrated this as a unique self-reflexive movement. The objectivity paradigm was rejected along with ethnographers' authority over the production of data about society, culture and experience. Most of anthropology has since produced an academic regime of reflexive fieldworkers that cannot but produce "partial truths" (Clifford, 1986a). Until recently, the discipline's epistemology has been dominated by subsequent calls for ethnographic writing that is experimental (Marcus & Fischer, 1986; Behar & Gordon, 1995; Pool, 1991; Poewe, 1996; Amit, 2003), dialogic (Crapanzano, 1980; Michirina & Richards, 1996; Gergen & Gergen, 2002; Tedlock & Mannheim, 1995), multi-vocal and polyphonic (Clifford, 1982, 1986b; Tobin, 1989; Ellis, 1997; Lassiter, 2011). In retrospect, the blurb on the back cover of the edited volume by James Clifford and George Marcus, *Writing Culture – The Poetics and Politics of Ethnography* (1986), has set the trail for anthropology's postmodern, postcolonial and post-structural epoch, wherein "Western writers no longer portray non-Western peoples with unchallenged authority" and "the process of cultural representation is now inescapably contingent, historical, and contestable". The reverberations of this *Writing Culture Debate* may have led to initial splits between followers and opponents, framed as 'intellectual deliberation of colonialism' vs. 'navel-gazing'. Yet, ethnographic fieldwork and writing has significantly changed in the aftermath. 'Doorstep anthropology', 'anthropology at home', 'multi-sited research', 'urban anthropology', and 'science and technology studies', to name just a few, have flourished over the last decades. Obviously not just a consequence of this *literary turn*, the discipline's epistemology has changed fundamentally since the 1980s, due to significant shifts in globalized transnational communication, mobility and labor regimes with all their consequences (Appadurai, 1996). Accordingly, the genre of ethnographic writing has equally changed: the 'ethnographic present' has been refuted as essentializing jargon; the number of ethnographies written by a first-person narrator has significantly increased when compared to monographs written from a *pluralis auctoritatis* perspective; and notes, sometimes chapters, even whole books highlight the researcher's self-reflexivity in evocative ethnographies that have outnumbered formerly authoritative scientific anthropology over the last 30 years (Lehmann, Lubrich, & Stodulka, 2018).

Methodological consequences: positionality reconsidered

Reflexive ethnographers agree that ethnographic knowledge is always situated and positioned (Haraway, 1988). Renato Rosaldo's definition of 'positionality' may be one of the most cited terms of anthropological method chapters, when anthropologists describe their subjectivities vis-à-vis the persons and phenomena they study.

> The ethnographer, as a positioned subject, grasps certain human phenomena better than others. He or she occupies a position or structural location and observes with a particular angle of vision. . . . The notion of position also refers to how life experiences both enable and inhibit particular kinds of insight.
>
> (Rosaldo, 1993 [1989], 15)

This classical definition hints at researchers' synchronic and diachronic double-bind. It also highlights the ethnographer's subject positions. Age, the social marginality of being an 'outsider' to the researched community, the hegemony of being affiliated with postcolonial regimes, gender and other contexts, have a major impact on fieldwork encounters and the ways in which informants and interlocutors reveal their experiences and narratives. The *literary turn* has taught anthropologists that narratives, stories and observations emerging from fieldwork are always 'particular' and 'partial' (Behar & Gordon, 1995; Clifford, 1986a). As such, they must constantly be juxtaposed with data constructed from other fieldwork encounters, by including various interlocutors' perspectives on a particular phenomenon, or drawing on other dimensions of data – an approach sociologists call 'methodological triangulation' (Rothbauer, 2008). 'Positional-ity' has been extended to the discussion of fieldwork ethics (Castillo, 2015; Dilger, Huschke, & Mattes, 2015; Sakti & Reynaud, 2017). Yet little attention has been paid to its affective dimension and how ethnographers deal with their ascribed positionalities in methodological terms. The psychoanalytical concepts of 'transference' and 'countertransference' remain persistent theoretical references in this field of discussion (Crapanzano, 2010; Devereux, 1967; Erdheim, 1988; Nadig, 2004). So too do sociological discourses of research as relational or 'emotional labour' (Burkitt, 2016, 2012; Barbalet, 2004; Irwin, 2007; Knoblauch, 2014; McQueeney & Lavelle, 2017; Pollard, 2009). We, however, choose a pragmatic and practice-oriented path lying at the crossroads of these schools of thought.

Anthropologists James Davies (2010a), Dimitrina Spencer (2010) and Maruška Svašek (2010) have paved our way by addressing the methodological significance of emotions as embodied social communicators between ethnographers and their interlocutors. They have set the path for inquiring into a practice-oriented emotional reflexivity that does not begin at our desks, but starts during ethnographers' encounters in the field and the ways these encounters affect them. Indeed, anthropology's disciplinary rationale calls for researchers to immerse themselves in others' lives and affectively relate to those lifeworlds as empathetic and compassionate fieldworkers. Only in so doing can anthropologists 'blend in' enough to grasp informants' ways of feeling-thinking, narrating and navigating through their local worlds. It therefore seems only logical to pay careful attention to these affective and emotional practices. Nevertheless, attempts to systematically attend to fieldworkers' affects and emotions have remained rare when compared to the abundance of critical discussions about ethnographies as partial, particular and positioned representations of the 'Other'. What *has* remained a powerful narrative within anthropology's emotional regime is that fieldworkers are expected to metamorphose into detached analytical scientists upon return to the academic site, where their emotions and immersions are transfigured as scientific disturbances (Davies, 2010b). Since fieldwork produces positionalities that can be particularly affective, a methodologically informed documentation of and reflection about researchers' affective and emotional positionalities promises to open up complementary and candid pathways to ethnographic data construction.

Epistemological consequences: taking researchers' affects seriously as epistemic emotions

Emotions can be defined as embodied social and relational processes (Burkitt, 2014; Röttger-Rössler & Stodulka, 2014; Stodulka, 2017a, 2017b, 2017c). In our understanding, emotions are complex products that link affects – as bodily, sensory, inarticulate, nonconscious experience – with surrounding local worlds, by way of mutually shared modes of communication, articulation and feeling. Emotions are linked to cultural repertoires that enable persons to express their own and label others' observable or imagined affects and feelings. Such expressions can occur through shared and communicable emotion words, through gestures, symbols or body movement. Emotions can be performed without significant changes in a communicating person's physiological arousal and experience. Emotions motivate action and interaction, and relate to social, cultural, economic and physiological needs and wants. Their display and articulation are affected by and affect others. They are critical in relating people to or disconnecting them from each other. Considering their experiential, psychological and social qualities, their understanding is vital in navigating and making sense of our everyday lives and environments. In short, everything emotions can do should be considered directly relevant to an ethnographic fieldwork practice spanning the encounters with persons, places and objects that shape our method toolkits (e.g. interviews, FGDs, systematic observation, participatory approaches, or field experiments).

We consider the transfiguration of so-called "field emotions" into "epistemic emotions" to be a considerable heuristic first step. Many anthropologists have experienced and documented what we define as "field emotions": the excitement and anxiety of arriving at field sites; the happiness and relief after establishing social relations; the pride of 'belonging' to host communities; the fear of not producing enough data or of doing fieldwork 'the wrong way'; the boredom when repetitively waiting for informants or interlocutors; the distress related to playing many different social roles; the annoyance of being addressed as an 'outsider'; the disappointment when we feel that we never really belonged to our host communities; for some, the guilt related to colonial heritage and/or privileged life compared to many of our research subjects; the insecurity about how to reciprocate hospitality and shared knowledge; or the panic that sneaks in when we feel we are not doing enough, or realize that we have to 'wrap up' and leave soon. Sometimes reflections on field emotions are translated into the introductions or method chapters of ethnographies. This has become inevitable rhetoric where ethnographers demonstrate their ethical propriety while in the field and their literary reflexivity according to the *literary turn*'s legacy when 'writing up'.

We thus argue that "field emotions" are fundamentally epistemic. As such, they are relational, contextual, culturally coded through the researcher's socialization, and particular to our research environment, or the 'field'. As we have mentioned previously, emotions arise from and influence social relationships and encounters with informants, interlocutors, collaborators, research partners and spaces. Treating researcher emotions as epistemic and understanding them as relational data can be scientifically rewarding. Emotions as we understand them here are phenomena that relate us with others, and relate others with us.[1] They are important in ascribing meaning to the phenomena and the affects we experience as researchers. To enhance researchers' emotional reflexivity, it is therefore advisable to train fieldworkers' emotional literacy – or, the capacity to discern and name affective experience in relation to someone or something – by encouraging techniques to document their emotions systematically.

Consequential synthesis: emotion diaries and empirical affect montage

Emotion diaries

Discussions about researchers' affects and emotions have illustrated their methodological and epistemological potential (Davies & Stodulka, 2019). They have pointed to a lack of anthropological training that "develop[s] one's senses, perceptions, the imagination, and self-awareness" (Spencer, 2010, 24). And they have identified training in psychotherapy as a fruitful measure for enhancing ethnographers' qualities (ibid., 23). As a concrete and tangible contribution to these discussions from within anthropology, we designed templates for semi-structured emotion diaries based on focused group discussions with colleagues of the collaborative research project *The Researchers' Affects*.[2] We have used and evaluated these templates during our respective fieldwork in Indonesia and East Timor, before we invited over 20 other ethnographers (mainly anthropologists) to regularly use them according to their own preferences during fieldwork.

The proposal to use emotion diaries rests on the premise that the researcher's emotional literacy and reflexivity can be trained through regular documentation of affective experience (whether unsettling, overwhelming, difficult, pleasurable, or simply ordinary). The act of documenting it helps it become a habitual mode of affectively aware perception and attention to the researched phenomena. More precisely, we discern at least three purposes of the emotion diary. The first purpose is psychological. Emotion diaries assist ethnographers to 'let off steam' in a productive and structured way. This is crucial, since most novice ethnographers face emotionally challenging situations in the field, even in the most ideal settings where psychological trainings, counseling meetings and attuned academic supervision are made available before and after the journey to the field. There is a noticeable lack of psychological support in contemporary academic landscapes (Heaton Shreshta, 2010; Spencer, 2011), and our collaborating ethnographers have underscored the imperative for such support. The second purpose of emotion diaries is epistemic. The diaries help to document 'uncanny' and 'enigmatic' experiences in ways that serve the interpretation of field relations and data analyses during and after fieldwork. Attending to and documenting affective experience during fieldwork fosters understandings of field relations, while preserving them for later-stage analyses. Lastly, a third purpose of emotion diaries is strategic. Through an enhanced understanding of particularly emotion-laden moments in the field, emotion diaries can strategically foster affectively attuned ways of navigating field encounters. These three purposes interrelate and converge in the aim to nurture emotionally reflective fieldwork practice.

Emotion diaries must necessarily come in different and contextualized forms, since there is not one format that fits all ethnographic projects or researchers. Our collaborators have used structured, semi-structured, open or clean sheet written, spoken or visual documentation, with or without quantitative self-evaluation checks. The template that was most widely used is structured around seven open questions (see Figure 16.1) as related to the aforementioned three dimensions. We encouraged our collaborators to adjust the diary according to their preferences over the course of their fieldwork, delete, adapt, or add their own questions.

The first two questions (1 and 2) take a psychological approach: *What do I have to write down here and now?* and *Which feelings describe me best today? Can you describe why?* are designed to help reflect retrospectively on a day's fieldwork in a structured manner. Taking into account Andrew Beatty's (2005) observation that affects are hard to articulate into words, the template incorporates techniques such as drawing or sketching. Incited by the invitation *This is me in the field. . . . Try to describe or sketch yourself,* question 5, sketching offers an additional technique to depict and reflect on affective experiences (see Causey, 2016). Since we emphasize both fieldwork and emotion as relational experiences and practices, questions 2, 3 and 4 were key when designing the emotion diary: *What feeling describes me best today (can you describe why)?, Is that feeling related to a particular situation or person (when did that happen? Can you describe it briefly)?, Who or what has surprised or impressed me today?* In reflecting subjective feelings and translating them into narratives, we targeted detailed descriptions on the affective dimensions of interacting with persons, objects, narratives, or spatial environments that had presumably triggered them. The last two questions (6 and 7), *What am I longing for?* and *What I will do tomorrow is . . .* pertain to the diary's strategic dimension in sometimes messy fieldwork trajectories.

Emotion diaries assist fieldworkers in chronicling their emotions. They help navigate field encounters in an affectively aware manner. And they facilitate a methodologically grounded attention to the otherwise 'uncanny' affective dimension of fieldwork encounters. What remains is the question, 'How can fieldworkers make use of their emotion diaries after fieldwork?'

Empirical affect montage

Our approach to montage differs from traditional understandings. Montage has traditionally been regarded suspiciously as "a disruptive principle that potentially

Emotion Diary

Date: Time:

Where are you now?

Who else is here:

---

1. What do I have to write down here and now?

2. What feeling describes me best today?
Can you describe why?

---

3. Is that feeling related to a particular situation or person?
When did that happen? Can you describe it briefly?

4. Who or what has surprised or impressed me today?

---

5. This is me in the field...
Try to describe or sketch yourself.

6. What am I longing for?

---

7. What I will do tomorrow is...

Further comments:

Figure 16.1 Emotion diary.

could pollute the direct correspondence between scholarly representations and the social world, thereby obstructing our possibilities for understanding human life across the boundaries of culture" (Willerslev & Suhr, 2013, 1). We hold the opposite to be more adequate. The montage of different data dimensions 'thickens' ethnographic accounts and increases their transparency. We contend that it is through the technique of montage that fieldworkers can make accounts of their affective experience epistemologically productive, without falling into the trap of self-indulgence. We underline that the use of self-reflexive field material in writing up ethnographies pertains "only to the point that the author shows its relevance to the production of knowledge" (Leibing & McLean, 2007, 13).

The juxtaposition of montage components has been described as an "opening up of a gap or fissure, through which the invisible emerges" (Willerslev & Suhr, 2013, 1). For our own purposes, we borrow this assertion and accentuate that by juxtaposing affective field accounts with classic data, ethnographers can make the relationality of fieldwork more discernable. From an abstract perspective, this resonates with George Marcus' proposition to juxtapose different localities of fieldwork as a method to "examine the circulation of cultural meanings, objects and identities in diffuse time-space" (1995, 96). Marcus' project of "multi-sited ethnography" grasps relationalities between local scales, and global discourses and structures, between phenomena that occur across times and spaces, or between the study of lifeworlds and spaces of academic knowledge production. We, on the other hand, endeavor to capture and communicate field relationalities through a systematic focus on ethnographers' affects and emotions.

We propose *Empirical Affect Montage* as an extension of more traditional epistemologies in our attempt to systematically juxtapose fieldworkers' affective experience with accounts of the lifeworlds of those with and about whom they study. In reference to our own ethnographies, juxtaposing our affective experiences and emotional reactions to the emotional labor of interlocutors and informants has proven productive in the formulation of anthropological theory that attends to affects and emotions and social interaction practices in the context of asymmetrical power relations and positionalities (Stodulka, 2015a). In a research project on young men's challenges and affective practices when coming of age on the streets in Yogyakarta, Indonesia, Thomas made sense of street-related[3] young men's ways of coping with scarce economic, material and kinship resources through a close reading of his emotion diaries and subsequent juxtaposition with the analyzed narratives of his interlocutors and informants.

Paying attention to his affective experiences related to encounters with his interlocutors has enabled Thomas to foster valuable empirical and theoretical insights that led him to formulate a theory of 'emotional economy' (Stodulka, 2014, 2015b, 2017c). In this, he explains the resilience and skills of his interlocutors and informants to transform scarce resources, marginality and stigma into affective bonds and vital socioeconomic cooperation with various actors of their widespread social networks. By relating to, affectively bonding with and emotionally attuning to particular persons who could provide them with medication, admission papers to hospitals, healthier food, job opportunities and money, the young men managed to transform social ties into material goods, money and increased well-being. While coming of age on the streets, they continuously refined their social skills of empathetically assessing and framing encounters with various interaction partners. The social, cognitive and affective knowledge inherent in these skills of perspective-taking distinguished these young men from their peers who were not living on the streets. Their ability to adequately relate to and interact within highly diverse social fields was amplified by the men's constant exposure to others within the public space, where the refinement of social encounters was an important strategy of survival.

Through *Empirical Affect Montage*, Thomas also understood the motivations of activists, artists, researchers, or students to remain involved with the young men, despite their ongoing complaints about them. Similar to himself, the street-related young men's interaction partners did not empathize without reason. They were not only 'exploited', as some of them had repeatedly claimed during interviews and conversations. NGO activists, journalists, travelers, anthropologists, street-related women or shop owners pursued their own motivations, tasks and targets in their social encounters with the young men. They equally benefited from and created their own emotional economies. Whereas the young men initiated and translated affective bonds into social and economic capital on the spot, the actors on the other side of the interactive spectrum often profited in the long run. In Thomas' case, these artifacts transformed social capital generated from his fieldwork into cultural capital in a strictly Bourdieusian sense, materialized in the form of educational qualifications (Bourdieu, 1986, 47), and subsequently, into economic capital by means of his employment.[4]

In a similar vein, fieldworkers' experience of embodied learning during and after fieldwork could be brought into dialogue with protagonists' and interlocutors' modes of relating to others in a variety of research contexts (Stodulka, Dinkelaker, & Thajib, 2019). Therefore, we suggest that montage can be used as an epistemological technique to combine various data formats during analysis, as a writing strategy that allows the author to selectively "put [herself] into the data" (Ghodsee, 2016, 23), or as a way to highlight particular aspects of field relationality.

Indeed, there are manifold ways of incorporating researchers' affects and emotions through Empirical Affect Montage. As clearly suggested by the term, our proposed framework rests on the premise of opening up ways for fieldworkers to communicate what was 'at stake' in their multiple encounters with the local worlds of their protagonists to readers who have not 'been there'. Within an edited volume titled *Affective Dimensions of Fieldwork and Ethnography* (Stodulka, Dinkelaker, & Thajib, 2019) that grew out of our research project, the 20 collaborating authors have engaged in empirical affect montages in a variety of ways. Common to all chapters is that they analyze and describe crucial research results through systematically practiced emotional reflexivity. Some authors analyzed individual passages of their emotion diaries in a hermeneutic-interpretative manner vis-à-vis their research questions. Others subjected them to a qualitative content analysis. Still others replaced their conventional field diaries with emotion diaries that they adapted to their own needs and preferences in hybrid terms. Depending on methodological convictions, theoretical training and genre conventions, the Empirical Affect Montage took place in a variety of ways. It could take place directly during participant observation, merging emotion and the field diary, or as *ad-hoc* analyses in the field involving comparative readings of emotion diaries and conventional data. It might develop at the desk following the fieldwork, by analyzing the emotion diaries and comparing them with conventional data. It sometimes took the form of a dialogue between two researchers, through exchanging and then mutually interpreting their emotion diaries. Or it might be a mixture of all mentioned possibilities. The Empirical Affect Montage is an extension of more traditional methodologies and epistemologies, rather than a prescriptive compulsion that follows concise rules.

Conclusion

We have argued that a systematic and practice-oriented focus on researchers' emotional literacy and reflexivity can sustain the methodological transparency of ethnography. Recent debates have demonstrated the importance of communicating the heuristics 'behind' ethnographic practices, in order to counter their intellectual exploitation (Ingold, 2014) and the suspicion towards them (Kuipers, 2013; Stoller, 2015). This chapter proposed a candid heuristic that explores how an Empirical Affect Montage might transpire as anthropological practice – rather than a phenomenological *thought experiment* – when conducting fieldwork and making sense of ethnographers' multifarious encounters and experiences. More precisely, we have argued that ethnographic research that intends to analyze others' experiences stands in need of a more robust relational methodology that pays attention to the affective dimensions of research encounters and how fieldworkers make use and sense of them.

We consider ethnographers' affects and emotions as epistemologically beneficial aids in the study of human experience. If we agree that ethnographic data is positioned, hence relational, then ethnographers' affects and emotions cannot be left unattended. They call for systematic documentation, interpretation and representation. This means incorporating self-reflexive hermeneutic circles of interpretations and memories when 'writing up', as some emotions take time to be fully understood and articulated in written form. However, we also argue for a systematic 'writing down' of affective experience at the time of the fieldwork encounters, since affective positionalities are best attended to during the fieldwork itself.

The focus on relational experience triggers ethical concerns in order not to project the ethnographers' subjectivities on others, or put our interlocutors and informants at risk due to the intimate, personal and political dimension of shared narratives. By being attentive to their affective responses to environments, places, situations and people, and learning to describe these more thoroughly, ethnographers can train their analytical gaze and skills of documenting, describing and translating human experience and narrative into comprehensible and lively anthropological analyses.

We would like to conclude on a brief psychological note that had emerged from our fieldwork experiences and from the collaboration with other fieldworkers. Besides epistemological and strategic benefits, we consider the documentation of affects and emotions to be psychologically rewarding.[5] How often do anthropologists struggle to communicate their experiences during fieldwork with family, friends, peers, colleagues or academic supervisors? And how often would documented affective experience be of help when trying to explain what 'ethnography' is, and seeking psychological or other support in the wake of overburdening field experiences?

Notes

1 See Stodulka, 2017a, 2017b, 2017c for an extended theoretical discussion on affect, emotion, feeling and emotive.
2 see www.loe.fu-berlin.de/en/affekte-der-forscher/unterprojekte1/ethnologie/index.html.
3 We use the term 'street-related' very broadly in relation to persons, who have left their families or primary caretakers either through exclusions, self-conscious decisions, or combinations of both during childhood, adolescence or later stage in life; who use the streets in ways that are considered socially and culturally inadequate when compared to their local peers; who integrate themselves in fluid communities whose members do not only share similar past experiences, but also future-oriented targets and motivations to make a living; who identify themselves with and who share a temporary feeling of belonging to these communities (Stodulka, 2017c, 21).
4 Some of the passages on 'emotional economy' have been published in Stodulka, 2015b; for a detailed analysis, please see Stodulka, 2017c.
5 We have also discussed the potential drawbacks of using emotion diaries and over-focusing on the affects of researcher-researched encounters, such as 'lack of time' to add another format of fieldnote writing to already existing genres, and an 'over-emotionalizing' of researchers at the expense of more pragmatic fieldwork trajectories. This will be addressed in relation to feedback sessions with fellow anthropologists in Stodulka, Dinkelaker, & Thajib, 2019.

References

Amit, V (ed.), 2003, *Constructing the Field: Ethnographic Fieldwork in the Contemporary World*, Routledge, New York.

Appadurai, A 1996, *Modernity at Large: Cultural Dimensions of Globalization*, University of Minnesota Press, Minneapolis.

Barbalet, J 2004, 'Consciousness, emotions, and science', in JH Turner (ed.), *Theory and Research on Human Emotions* (*advances in group processes, vol. 21*), pp. 245–272, Elsevier, Amsterdam.

Beatty, A 2005, 'Feeling your way in Java: An essay on society and emotion', *Ethnos*, vol. 70, no. 1, pp. 53–78.

Behar, R & Gordon, DA (eds.), 1995, *Women Writing Culture*, University of California Press, Berkeley.

Berger, P 2010, 'Assessing the relevance and effects of "key emotional episodes" for the fieldwork process', in J Davies & D Spencer (eds.), *Anthropological Fieldwork: A Relational Process*, pp. 119–143, Cambridge Scholars Publishing, Newcastle.

Bonz, J, Eisch-Angus, K, Hamm, M & Sulzle, A (eds.), 2017, *Ethnografie und Deutung: Gruppensupervision als Methode reflexiven Forschens*, Springer VS, Wiesbaden.

Bourdieu, P 1986, 'The forms of capital', in J Richardson (ed.), *Handbook of Theory and Research for the Sociology of Education*, pp. 241–258, Greenwood, New York.

Burkitt, I 2012, 'Emotional reflexivity: Feeling, emotion and imagination in reflexive dialogues', *Sociology*, vol. 46, no. 3, pp. 458–472.

Burkitt, I 2014, *Emotions and Social Relations*, Sage Publications, London.

Burkitt, I 2016, 'Relational agency: Relational sociology, agency and interaction', *European Journal of Social Theory*, vol. 19, no. 3, pp. 322–339.

Candea, M, Cook, J, Trundle, C & Yarrow, T 2015, 'Introduction. Reconsidering detachment', in M Candea, J Cook, C Trundle & T Yarrow (eds.), *Detachments: Essays on the Limits of Relational Thinking*, pp. 1–31, Manchester University Press, Manchester.

Castillo, RC 2015, 'The emotional, political, and analytical labor of engaged anthropology amidst violent political conflict', *Medical Anthropology*, vol. 34, no. 1, pp. 70–83.

Causey, A 2016, *Drawn to See: Drawing as an Ethnographic Method*, University of Toronto Press, Toronto.

Clifford, J 1982, *Person and Myth: Maurice Leenhardt in the Melanesian World*, University of California Press, Berkeley.

Clifford, J 1986a, 'Introduction: Partial truths', in J Clifford & GE Marcus (eds.), *Writing Culture: The Poetics and Politics of Ethnography*, pp. 1–26, University of California Press, Berkeley.

Clifford, J 1986b, 'On ethnographic allegory', in J Clifford & GE Marcus (eds.), *Writing Culture: The Poetics and Politics of Ethnography*, pp. 98–121, University of California Press, Berkeley.

Clifford, J & Marcus, GE (eds.), 1986, *Writing Culture: The Poetics and Politics of Ethnography*, University of California Press, Berkeley.

Cook, J 2016, *Ethnography: Translation*. Available from: https://culanth.org/fieldsights/874-ethnography-translation [17 July 2018].

Crapanzano, V 1980, *Tuhami: Portrait of a Moroccan*, University of Chicago Press, Chicago.

Crapanzano, V 2010, '"At the heart of the discipline": Critical reflections on fieldwork', in J Davies & D Spencer (eds.), *Emotions in the Field: The Anthropology and Psychology of Fieldwork Experience*, pp. 55–78, Stanford University Press, Stanford.

Davies, J 2010a, 'Disorientation, dissonance, and altered perception', in J Davies & D Spencer (eds.), *Emotions in the Field: The Anthropology and Psychology of Fieldwork Experience*, pp. 79–97, Stanford University Press, Stanford.

Davies, J 2010b, 'Introduction: Emotions in the field', in J Davies & D Spencer (eds.), *Emotions in the Field: The Anthropology and Psychology of Fieldwork Experience*, pp. 1–31, Stanford University Press, Stanford.

Davies, J & Stodulka, T 2019, 'Emotions in the field', in *The SAGE Encyclopedia of Social Research Methods*, Sage Publications, Thousand Oaks.

Desjarlais, R & Throop, CJ 2011, 'Phenomenological approaches in anthropology', *Annual Reviews of Anthropology*, vol. 40, pp. 87–102.

Devereux, G 1967, *From Anxiety to Method in the Behavioral Sciences*, Mouton, The Hague.

Dilger, H, Huschke, S & Mattes, D 2015, 'Ethics, epistemology and engagement: Encountering values in medical anthropology', *Medical Anthropology*, vol. 34, no. 1, pp. 1–10.

Ellis, C 1997, 'Evocative autoethnography: Writing emotionally about our lives', in WG Tierney & YS Lincoln (eds.), *Representation and the Text: Re-framing the Narrative Voice*, pp. 116–140, State University of New York Press, Albany.

Erdheim, M 1988, *Psychoanalyse und Unbewußtheit in der Kultur: Aufsätze 1980–1987*, Suhrkamp, Frankfurt am Main.

Fabian, J 1983, *Time and the Other: How Anthropology Makes Its Object*, Columbia University Press, New York.

Gable, E 2014, 'The anthropology of guilt and rapport: Moral mutuality in ethnographic fieldwork', *HAU Journal of Ethnographic Theory*, vol. 4, no. 1, pp. 237–258.

Gergen, KJ & Gergen, M 2002, 'Ethnography as relationship', in AP Bochner & C Ellis (eds.), *Ethnographically Speaking. Autoethnography, Literature, and Aesthetics*, pp. 11–33, Alta Mira Press, Walnut Creek.

Ghodsee, K 2016, *From Notes to Narrative. Writing Ethnographies That Everyone Can Read*, University of Chicago Press, Chicago.

Haraway, D 1988, 'Situated knowledges: The science question in feminism and the privilege of partial perspective', *Feminist Studies*, vol. 14, no. 3, pp. 575–599.

Hastrup, K 2010, 'Emotional topographies: The sense of place in the far north', in J Davies & D Spencer (eds.), *Emotions in the Field: The Anthropology and Psychology of Fieldwork Experience*, pp. 191–211, Stanford University Press, Stanford.

Heaton Shreshta, C 2010, 'Emotional apprenticeships: Reflection on the role of academic practice in the construction of "the field" ', in D Spencer & J Davies (eds.), *Anthropological Fieldwork: A Relational Process*, pp. 48–74, Cambridge Scholars Publishing, Newcastle.

Herbrik, R 2013, 'Das Imaginäre in der (Wissens-)Soziologie und seine kommunikative Konstruktion in der empirischen Praxis', in R Keller, H Knoblauch & J Reichertz (eds.), *Kommunikativer Konstruktivismus: Theoretische und empirische Arbeiten zu einem neuen wissenssoziologischen Ansatz*, pp. 295–315, VS Verlag für Sozialwissenschaften, Wiesbaden.

Hollan, D 2008, 'Being there: On the imaginative aspects of understanding others and being understood', *Ethos*, vol. 36, no. 4, pp. 475–489.

Ingold, T 2014, 'That's enough about ethnography!' *HAU Journal of Ethnographic Theory*, vol. 4, no. 1, pp. 383–395.

Irwin, R 2007, 'Culture shock: Negotiating feelings in the field', *Anthropology Matters*, vol. 9, no. 1. Available from: www.anthropologymatters.com/index.php/anth_matters/article/view/64/123 [17 July 2018].

Jackson, M 1989, *Paths Toward a Clearing: Radical Empiricism and Ethnographic Inquiry*, Indiana University Press, Bloomington.

Knoblauch, H 2014, 'Reflexive Methodologie. Sozialwissenschaftliche Hermeneutik und kommunikatives Handeln', in R Hitzler (ed.), *Hermeneutik als Lebenspraxis*, pp. 117–129, Beltz, Weinheim & Basel.

Kuipers, J 2013, 'Evidence and authority in ethnographic and linguistic perspective', *Annual Review of Anthropology*, vol. 42, pp. 399–413.

Lassiter, LE 2011, ' "Reading over the shoulders of natives" to "reading alongside natives", literally: Toward a collaborative and reciprocal ethnography', *Journal of Anthropological Research*, vol. 57, no. 2, pp. 137–149.

Lehmann, J, Lubrich, O & Stodulka, T 2018, 'Formatierung von Emotionen: Paratexte in der Ethnographie', *Interdisziplinäre Anthropologie*, no. 6, November.

Leibing, A & McLean, A 2007, 'Learn to value your shadow! An introduction to the margins of fieldwork', in A McLean & A Leibing (eds.), *The Shadow Side of Fieldwork. Exploring the Blurred Borders Between Ethnography and Life*, pp. 1–28, Wiley-Blackwell, Malden.

Liebert, W 2016, 'Kulturbedeutung, Differenz, Katharsis: Kulturwissenschaftliches Forschen und Schreiben als zyklischer Prozess', in F Vogel, J Luth & S Ptashnyk (eds.), *Linguistische Zugänge zu Konflikten in europäischen Sprachräumen: Korpus – Pragmatik – kontrovers*, pp. 21–41, Universitätsverlag, Heidelberg.

Lubrich, O, Liebal, K & Stodulka, T 2017, 'Affekte im Feld – Ein blinder Fleck der Forschung?' *Interdisziplinäre Anthropologie*, vol. 5, pp. 179–197.

Lubrich, O & Stodulka, T 2018, *Emotionen in der Wissenschaft – Methoden für die Feldforschung. Pocketbook*, Transcript Verlag, Bielefeld.

Marcus, GE 1995, 'Ethnography in/of the world system: The emergence of multi-sited ethnography', *Annual Review of Anthropology*, vol. 24, no. 1, pp. 95–117.

Marcus, GE & Fischer, MMJ 1986, *Anthropology as Cultural Critique. An Experimental Moment in the Human Sciences*, University of Chicago Press, Chicago.

McQueeney, K & Lavelle, KM 2017, 'Emotional labor in critical ethnographic work: In the field and behind the desk'. *Journal of Contemporary Ethnography*, vol. 46, no. 1, pp. 81–107.

Michirina, BP & Richards, CA 1996, *Person to Person. Fieldwork, Dialogue, and the Hermeneutic Method*, State University of New York Press, Albany.

Nadig, M 2004, 'Transculturality in process: Theoretical and methodological aspects drawn from cultural studies and psychoanalysis', in HJ Sandkühler & HB Lim (eds.), *Transculturality, Epistemology, Ethics and Politics*, pp. 9–21, Lang, Frankfurt am Main.

Okely, J 2012, *Anthropological Practice: Fieldwork and the Ethnographic Method*, Berg, London.

Poewe, K 1996, 'Writing culture and writing fieldwork: The proliferation of experimental and experiential ethnographies', *Ethnos*, vol. 61, no. 3, pp. 177–206.

Pollard, A 2009, 'Field of screams: Difficulty and ethnographic fieldwork', *Anthropology Matters*, vol. 11, no. 2. Available from: www.anthropologymatters.com/index.php/anth_matters/article/view/10/10 [17 July 2018].

Pool, R 1991, 'Postmodern ethnography?' *Critique of Anthropology*, vol. 11, no. 4, pp. 309–331.

Reckwitz, A 2008, *Unscharfe Grenzen. Perspektiven der Kultursoziologie*, Transcript Verlag, Bielefeld.

Reckwitz, A 2000, *Die Transformation der Kulturtheorien. Zur Entwicklung eines Theorieprogramms*, Velbrück Wissenschaft, Weilerswist.

Rosaldo, R 1993 [1989], *Culture and Truth: The Remaking of Social Analysis*, Beacon Press, Boston.

Rothbauer, P 2008, 'Triangulation', in L Given (ed.), *The SAGE Encyclopedia of Qualitative Research Methods*, pp. 892–894, Sage Publications, London.

Röttger-Rössler, B & Stodulka, T 2014, 'Introduction: The emotional make-up of stigma and marginality', in T Stodulka & B Röttger-Rössler (eds.), *Feelings at the Margins: Dealing with Violence, Stigma and Isolation in Indonesia*, pp. 11–29, Campus Verlag, Frankfurt am Main, New York.

Sakti, V & Reynaud, AM 2017, 'Understanding reconciliation through reflexive practice: Ethnographic examples from Canada and Timor Leste', in G Millar (ed.), *Ethnographic Peace Research: Approaches and Tensions*, 159–180. Palgrave Macmillan, Cham.

Sanjek, R 1991, 'The ethnographic present', *Man*, vol. 26, no. 4, pp. 609–628.

Slaby, J 2016a, 'Mind invasion. Situated affectivity and the corporate life hack', *Frontiers in Psychology*, vol. 7, pp. 266–279. Available from: www.frontiersin.org/articles/10.3389/fpsyg.2016.00266/full [17 July 2018].

Slaby, J 2016b, *Relational Affect*, SFB Affective Societies Working Paper 2, Berlin. Available from: https://refubium.fu-berlin.de/bitstream/handle/fub188/17927/SFB1171_WP_02-16.pdf?sequence=1&isAllowed=y [17 July 2018].

Slaby, J 2016c, 'Die Kraft des Zorns – Sara Ahmeds aktivistische Post-Phänomenologie', in I Marcinski & H Landweer (eds.), *Dem Erleben auf der Spur. Feminismus und Phänomenologie*, pp. 279–303, Transcript Verlag, Bielefeld.

Sluka, JA 2012, 'Fieldwork relations and rapport. Introduction', in A Robben & JA Sluka (eds.), *Ethnographic Fieldwork: An Anthropological Reader*, pp. 137–142, Wiley-Blackwell, Chichester.

Sluka, JA & Robben, A 2012, 'Fieldwork in cultural anthropology: An introduction', in A Robben & JA Sluka (eds.), *Ethnographic Fieldwork: An Anthropological Reader*, pp. 1–45, Wiley-Blackwell, Chichester.

Spencer, D 2010, 'Emotional labour and relational observation in anthropological fieldwork', in D Spencer & J Davies (eds.), *Anthropological Fieldwork: A Relational Process*, pp. 1–47, Cambridge Scholars Publishing, Newcastle.

Spencer, D 2011, 'Emotions and the transformative potential of fieldwork: Some implications for teaching and learning anthropology', *Teaching Anthropology*, vol. 1, no. 2, pp. 68–97.

Stodulka, T 2014, '"Playing it right": Empathy and emotional economies on the streets of Java', in T Stodulka & B Röttger-Rössler (eds.), *Feelings at the Margins: Dealing with Violence, Stigma and Isolation in Indonesia*, pp. 103–127, Campus-Verlag: Frankfurt am Main, New York.

Stodulka, T 2015a, 'Spheres of passion: Fieldwork, ethnography and the researcher's emotions', *Curare: Journal of Medical Anthropology*, vol. 38, no. 1+2, pp. 103–116.

Stodulka, T 2015b, 'Emotion work, ethnography and survival strategies on the streets of Yogyakarta', *Medical Anthropology*, vol. 34, no. 1, pp. 84–97.

Stodulka, T 2017a, 'Towards an integrative anthropology of emotion – a case study from Yogyakarta', in A Storch (ed.), *Consensus and Dissent: Negotiating Emotion in the Public Space*, pp. 9–34, John Benjamins, Amsterdam.

Stodulka, T 2017b, 'Storms of slander – relational dimensions of envy in Java, Indonesia', in R Smith, M Duffy & U Merlone (eds.), *Envy at Work and in Organizations*, pp. 297–320, Oxford University Press, Oxford.

Stodulka, T 2017c, *Coming of Age on the Streets of Java. Coping with Marginality, Stigma and Illness*, Transcript Verlag, Bielefeld.

Stodulka, T, Dinkelaker, S & Thajib, F (eds.), 2019, *Affective Dimensions of Fieldwork and Ethnography*, Springer, New York.

Stodulka, T, Selim, N & Mattes, D 2018, 'Affective scholarship: Doing anthropology with epistemic affects', *Ethos*, vol. 46, no. 4, pp. 519–536.

Stoller, P 2015, 'Alice Goffman and the future of ethnography', *Huffpost Blog*, blog post, 15 June. Available from: www.huffingtonpost.com/paul-stoller/alice-goffman-and-the-future-of-ethnography-_b_7585614.html [17 July 2018].

Stoller, P & Olkes, C 2012, 'The taste of ethnographic things', in A Robben & JA Sluka (eds.), *Ethnographic Fieldwork: An Anthropological Reader*, pp. 465–479, Wiley-Blackwell, Chichester.

Svašek, M 2010, '"The Field": Intersubjectivity, empathy and the workings of internalised presence', in D Spencer & J Davies (eds.), *Anthropological Fieldwork: A Relational Process*, pp. 75–99. Cambridge Scholars Publishing, Newcastle.

Tedlock, D & Mannheim, B (eds.), 1995, *The Dialogic Emergence of Culture*, University of Illinois Press, Urbana.

Tobin, JJ 1989, 'Visual anthropology and multivocal ethnography: A dialogical approach to Japanese preschool class size', *Dialectical Anthropology*, vol. 13, pp. 73–187.

Wikan, U 1992, 'Beyond the words: The power of resonance', *American Ethnologist*, vol. 19, no. 3, pp. 460–482.

Willerslev, R & Suhr, C 2013, 'Montage as an amplifier of invisibility', in C Suhr & R Willerslev (eds,), *Transcultural Montage*, pp. 1–15, Berghahn Books, New York.

Chapter 17

Investigating emotions by using computer-assisted qualitative data analysis software
A methodological approach

Elgen Sauerborn

1. Introduction

Qualitative research into emotions is usually not associated with computer-assisted qualitative data analysis software (CAQDAS). Since researching emotions includes the investigation of personal experiences, meanings, interpretations and views, any kind of feelings turn out to be a very sensitive research topic. To understand emotions sociologically, it is often inescapable to consider in-depth interpretations and the emotional connection between the researchers and the participants (Fitzpatrick & Olson, 2015; Arditti et al., 2010).

It seems fair to say that most sociologists of emotions would agree with the assertion that social interpretations, culture, socialization and social environment have a huge impact on the emergence, appearance and experience of human emotions (Stets & Turner, 2014; Hochschild, 2003; Illouz, 2007; Thoits, 1989). Hence, if emotion researchers use qualitative methods, they often draw on constructivist or phenomenological ideas of emotions. These notions imply that subjective and individual interpretations and the ways humans make sense of their world and of their sensate bodily feelings turn out to be significant in qualitative emotion research. Considering emotions as a social construct that is inextricable from meaning, sociological analysis must include definitions and interpretations of emotional experiences (Weigert, 1991). But investigating emotions requires more than merely asking participants about their feelings and assuming their answers to reflect exactly the way emotions appear. Researchers, in fact, often aim to reconstruct meaning or structures and their interplay with emotions. Therefore, qualitative emotion research is often based on interpretative or hermeneutic approaches and methodologies.

However, at first glance, these methodologies seem to be inconsistent with CAQDAS, as software is more likely to be used in the context of qualitative methods that focus on rather quantitative aspects and approaches (van Manen, 2014). Interpretative qualitative researchers are, with good reason, reluctant to adopt the various quantitative data analysis tools CAQDAS provides, such as features to measure word frequencies or coding relations. They argue that the complex and unstructured nature of qualitative data analysis is simply incompatible with technology or computers in general (Roberts & Wilson, 2002). Similar justifiable criticism points to an alleged possibility of standardization of qualitative research processes, which the use of technology and software might suggest (Knoblauch, 2014). These criticisms often refer to the incapacity of software to actually interpret the data.

Investigating emotions, moreover, requires a consideration of the researcher's own emotions as well as her emotional biography (Clarke, Broussine, & Watts, 2015). Just like in any other field of research, emotional processes and dynamics are inevitably involved in qualitative social sciences. The impact of emotions on findings and results may be unpreventable, but transparency through reflexivity is a well-esteemed approach to deal with this condition (Munkejord, 2009). But reflexivity as a highly subjective and emotional process seems again to be inconsistent with the logic of computer software.

However, this does not suggest that CAQDAS should be avoided in emotion research. On the contrary, in this chapter, I want to show how emotion research, including all the methodological controversies mentioned here, can benefit from the use of software.

Ironically, the initial concerns that CAQDAS might not be able to 'think', or to undertake the researcher's task of interpreting, highlights the importance of using a tool like CAQDAS in the first place. In particular, it demonstrates how the standardization of qualitative work is a consequence of poor methodological rigor, rather than an unavoidable consequence of using computers. Fears about the automation of qualitative research are often connected with a lack of exposure to robust and accessible research about CAQDAS as a qualitative tool, thus leaving researchers with the faulty impression that CAQDAS threatens to take the analytical work out of the researchers' hand. However, this is a misnomer. Qualitative researchers should not expect CAQDAS to carry out their interpretations and their data analysis. Qualitative data analysis (QDA)-software remains a tool that frames and in many ways aids and simplifies qualitative analysis, but it could never substitute scholars' interpretational work.

Given that, I will show that these criticisms are mainly based on methodological discrepancies. Therefore, it would be misleading to blame tools aiming to modify and simplify qualitative data analysis in general. In this respect, I will argue, CAQDAS' capabilities of possible applications for qualitative analysis are often underestimated and should not be limited to single methodologies or paradigms. Or as Weitzman (2000) puts it: "It is important to emphasize that software is not now, if it ever was, something that is relevant only to 'positivist' or 'quasi-positivist' approaches to qualitative research" (p. 804).

However, this raises the question as to how these implementations concern qualitative emotion research itself. In the following sections, I show how QDA-software can be useful for visualizing the researcher's interpretations and analysis as well as the discursive and interpretational structure in the data that is subject to emotions per se. Thus, software can help identify emotions in the data that are often not obvious at first glance. This chapter seeks to illustrate ways to use these software packages in order to take advantage of the benefits QDA-software offers. By drawing on Konopásek's (2007) ideas of "making thinking visible" through CAQDAS and of considering computer-assisted analysis as "material practices", the chapter shall examine how emotions can be traced from the data. It shall further be demonstrated how the materialization of interpretations can facilitate reflexivity as part of qualitative emotion research.

To do so, I first very briefly introduce QDA-software in general and the basic tools it offers. I will concentrate on the coding procedure as a basic function of CAQDAS. Although a large number of CAQDAS tools are predominantly used for deductive research processes, I want to highlight those functions that are advantageous for inductive and interpretative methods. I shall illustrate how software facilitates the use of a variety of data sources and how emotion research can benefit from it. While ideas about the modification of data through these material practices apply to all kind of unstructured qualitative data, the focus in this chapter lies on textual data. Second, I will demonstrate how qualitative researchers broaden their own data with their interpretations, and outline why it is easier to grasp emotions if the researcher's interpretations and linkages are visualized. Finally, I want to address the significance of the researcher's emotional biography, and how software can increase transparency through reflexivity. In that regard, I examine how feelings *towards* the data can be treated in qualitative interpretations with CAQDAS.

2. Computer-assisted qualitative data analysis software

Various kinds of QDA-software can be utilized for qualitative data analysis. The most widespread ones such as NVivo, MAXQDA, NUD*IST, The Ethnograph, QDA Miner, HyperRESEARCH, or Atlas.ti support basic features that are advantageous for qualitative or mixed-methods research. These applications are also used for managing and organizing data, mainly if research requires the use of a big range of data such as written words, videos, pictures, tables, or social media data. There is a growing interest in using mixed-methods approaches to integrate quantitative and qualitative methods. Thus, more qualitative data analysis programs include the possibility to evaluate surveys as well (Kuckartz, 2014; Creswell, 2011).

Most programs are built on a similar architecture. Subsequently, the interface consists of different windows displaying general data sources, the specific data that is currently edited or analyzed by the researcher(s), the attached codings and a list of all created codes. Most software packages allow the researcher to decide which windows and information are displayed on the monitor, so the same data might look disparate to different researchers.

One of the main functions of QDA-software is certainly the code-and-retrieve process of qualitative data. To code data means to label segments with abstract categories, concepts or anything else that might be of use for the analysis. For instance, this might include assigning codes only referring to structural aspects of data, such as different speakers, forms of speech or simply descriptions of what can be observed in visual data. While coding, qualitative researchers tag a particular segment of a document, table, image or media clip with at least one code. These codes can then be organized into a hierarchical structure while several subcodes are assigned to one main code. During and after coding, CAQDAS allows the researcher to retrieve the data. In this context, retrieval means collecting identically tagged passages and classifying it within one window. It provides a better over-view of data that is assigned to identical codes, topics, concepts or descriptions.

A majority of the tools for advanced analysis depend on codes and codings. Many tools that facilitate quantifications and even statistical analysis of qualita-tive data are reliant upon the previous assignment of codes to data segments. Cod-ing is predominantly, but not necessarily, a manual procedure. Indeed, functions to automatize the coding process exist, but this is mainly based on the presence of specific words, phrases or sentences that are only useful for textual data. These cannot replace qualitative interpretations, but a general requirement for most of the advanced and more sophisticated functions is the preceding subjective or inter-subjective data interpretation of one or more researchers. In this respect, Saldaña (2016) understands coding as heuristic and as a technique that cannot follow algo-rithms. He asserts that coding is "not just labeling, it is linking". This approach includes the idea of coding as "the initial step toward an even more rigorous and evocative analysis and interpretation" (p. 9). While I recognize the concern that CAQDAS promotes falling into the "coding trap"[1] (Gilbert, 2002), I will follow Saldaña's understanding and consider codes and codings as both a foundation and consequence of subjective and intersubjective, in-depth data interpretation.

Other useful CAQDAS tools include functions to comment on any kind of data segment and codes but also to draft free memos. Writing memos is certainly a cru-cial part of qualitative research (Strauss & Corbin, 1990). As this procedure alone is a way to visualize thoughts, it should not be underestimated and equated with note-taking. There are indeed various ways of writing memos (Hutchison, John-ston, & Breckon, 2010). This is why CAQDAS can clarify the researcher's role in the analysis process through options to systematize different kind of memos, such as questions, reflections, abductive inferences, literature-related remarks, concep-tual thoughts, interpretations and so forth.

Memos can be linked to different data sources or can be categorized and organ-ized in different tables or maps. The same applies for codes and codings, com-ments and so on. Simply put, CAQDAS provides the linking and connecting of any kind of data with outcomes of the researcher's analysis, and visualizes, clas-sifies, organizes and – if needed – even quantifies it.

2.1 Using a variety of data

One main advantage of CAQDAS over the traditional "pen, paper, and scissor approach" (Séror, 2005) is certainly the possibility to work with a great range of data sources. Computers facilitate simple but essential steps of analysis, such as writing memos, searching text or themes, and classifying concepts. Keeping track of different sources and quantities of data, moreover, seems to be nearly impossible without using technical devices. Various tools of CAQDAS offer aid in monitoring and systematizing data. Visual tools are one example of functions that help researchers to display data in condensed or arranged systems like matrixes, maps, tables, diagrams or networks. The ease of connecting different data sources invites researchers to use more data for their research, which they otherwise might avoid (Goble et al., 2012). This is not necessarily an advantage, as it could lead to an imbalance between data collection and data analysis, in my view, but it broadens opportunities of qualitative research to include more data in the analysis. This choice must be weighed with due methodological diligence.

2.2 CAQDAS and the materialization of interpretation

The use of CAQDAS for qualitative research affects not only the sort and amount of data that scholars use but also the way they perceive and look at the data. Hence, software applications change "our being-in-the-world as qualitative researchers" (Goble et al., 2012, paragraph 5). In this regard, I will draw on Konopásek's (2007) idea of qualitative analysis as a set of material practices. Following this understanding, CAQDAS cannot be considered as a meaningless tool that simply aids researchers to organize and analyze their data but rather as "complex virtual environments for embodied and practice-based knowledge making" (ibid., 276). Software and analytical practices such as coding, writing memos and linking data include the material modification and extension of the original data. Different codings, links and written comments, which are created by the researcher(s), become part of the data itself. Thus, the data is modified and altered with every single step of analysis and interpretation. The researcher "inscribes him- or herself into the studied material" (ibid.). The interpretation's materialization, which manifests in visible analysis practices on the screen, makes the interplay of 'original' data[2] and scientific interpretations more graspable. Drawing on Latour's (1995) ethnographic account, Konopásek highlights the importance of research practices that translate reality into words: "we can follow numerous small practical operations by means of which reality is more and more loaded with meaning and progressively de-materialized so that it becomes increasingly 'textual'" (Konopásek, 2007, 280). This chain of translations of reality into texts, videos or pictures may mean that some material gets lost or sidelined along the way, but it also creates new material. Each step of data collection and data analysis comprises the change of the data itself. Transmitting the collected data into software means creating a new kind of materiality that can actually be seen on the screen. For example, a complex interview situation including all the countless characteristics of the specific field, the voices, the physical appearances of the participants or the atmosphere of this setting is progressively reduced until it can be viewed on a monitor. But what can be seen here is a new construction that did not exist when the interview was conducted. Hence, new material is produced.

In this view, it is worth scrutinizing certain assumptions about the disembodiment of computerized methods (Sohn, 2017). In fact, working with software yields outcomes scholars can actually see on the screen(s). These are understood as physical results, which are hardly incorporeal. Now the question might arise as to why the materialization and visualization of interpretations in qualitative research processes should be relevant at all. I argue that reflecting on the researcher's role as a part and co-constructor of the data, as Charmaz (2006) has it, is an indispensable component of the research process that is particularly vital for understanding emotions. CAQDAS facilitates researchers to literally see their interpretations and change the initially 'nude' data. When addressing emotions and emotion research, the fundamental assumption of CAQDAS as part of knowledge making leads to the question of how these kinds of feelings can be identified by practices in qualitative research. To answer this question, a theoretical modification of Konopasék's approach is needed since emotions cannot be reduced to a kind of "thinking" or to merely cognitive phenomena, as I shall elaborate as follows. Therefore, I argue that CAQDAS is not only useful to visualize a researcher's interpretations, or what Schütz (1962) calls "second-order constructions", but also for visualizing first-order constructions as well. Second-order constructions refer to a researcher's attempt to reconstruct "first-order" meanings in order to understand common sense, types and patterns. Those first-order constructions include subjective interpretations and the meaning actors attribute to something. Thus, while reconstructing meaning in terms of first-order constructions, the researcher's interpretations must be understood as "constructs of the constructs made by the actors on the social scene" (ibid., 59). While Konopasék mainly refers to those second-order constructions, I argue that CAQDAS also aids to visualize and materialize first-order constructions, such as culturally established definitions of feelings, or the biographical and social contexts that shape emotions.

The following sections shall suggest that researching emotions qualitatively cannot be separated from reconstructing meaning, that the researchers' own emotions are significant for their interpretations, and that CAQDAS can be used on both fronts.

3. Identifying emotions in the data

Emotions can be studied within a variety of disciplines, such as psychology, neuroscience, sociology, political sciences and cultural studies, to name a few. Hence, research on emotions can focus on numerous aspects and dimensions. That is why, unsurprisingly, different scholars have different understandings of what it means to investigate emotions. Thus, theoretical and epistemological positioning becomes inevitable. The following considerations are based on sociological approaches to the social and cultural construction of emotions.

Considering emotions as a social construct means acknowledging the relevance of individual interpretations, understood here as the "cognitive labeling" (Shott, 1979) of physiological arousals. That means that the way people make sense of bodily sensations, as well as of the situation from which this feeling emerges, is crucial to the lived experience of emotions. The sociology of emotions seeks to understand how emotions are systematized as well as the modes and varieties of feelings as lived experiences (Sturdy, 2003). Sociologists of emotion regard emotions as "individual, intentional, episodic, and categorical" phenomena (von Scheve, 2018, 45).

Following Weigert (1991), I understand emotions as "socially constructed definitions of feelings that link body and situation in a system of meaning" (p. 15). My definition includes the culturally established categorization and labeling of a certain subjective feeling. 'Feeling' is used here to refer to the bodily felt experience of, for instance, an emotion. Thus, emotions are integral to meaning, while meaning, in turn, is progressively constructed and "interactively realized" (ibid.). Consequently, methods and methodologies dealing with this approach to emotions must reconstruct meaning in order to disentangle and identify emotions. The aim is to reveal social characteristics of emotions and ways in which "emotions can be 'known'" (Sturdy, 2003, 86). Yet in a social constructionist sense, emotions cannot be separated into isolated components, such as bodily sensations and interpretations of the situation. In light of that, how can qualitative research investigate emotions as an entity?

To answer this question, it is necessary to understand that even scholars who share the idea of a social construction of emotions draw on different approaches. While some highlight historical variations of emotions (Reddy, 1997; Rosenwein, 2010; Frevert, 2010), others address normative (Hochschild, 2003), symbolic-interactionist (Shott, 1979) or discursive (Harré & Gillet, 1994) aspects of feelings. They all share the idea that emotions are based on sociality, but they stress different characteristics. Frevert (2010), for instance, points out that first-order interpretations of feelings are historically variable, thus calling for an understanding of emotion as an acquired phenomenon. This, in turn, means qualitative researchers need to understand the contexts and situations in which emotions emerge in order to investigate those feelings themselves. Similarly, Harré and Gillet (1994) consider physical arousals as an emotion's underpinning, but state that their meaning is defined by discursive interactions. This means that a shared language and knowledge are indispensable for building a comprehensive interpretation of emotions. Consequently, researchers must take note that we usually cannot investigate emotions per se, but rather their indications and manifestations. In order to understand emotions as a second-order construct, we need to gain a narrative explanation of this feeling and integrate it within its discursive and social structure (see Weber-Guskar, 2009). This is essential for interpretative researchers who try to avoid attaining a merely descriptive characterization of emotions but rather seek to actually understand them in an interpretative manner.

Outside interpretations of physiological arousals, intentionality signifies a pivotal characteristic of emotions (Solomon, 2007). If emotions are always directed towards an object, an event or a person, then they cannot be regarded as isolated inner experiences since they only emerge due to an intentional relationship. This understanding of emotions allows scholars to focus on the intended object, or rather the participant's interpretations of it. Gill's (2015) suitable methodological proposition in this context is to begin studying the event without presupposing the role of specific emotions. In this case the researcher should not ask for definite emotions in her research question, but for particular events that are most likely accompanied by the emergence of emotions. While this surely offers one approach to researching emotions qualitatively, I want to focus on the reconstruction of meaning, as well as on norms and structures that underlie emotions. Obviously, qualitative analysis alone cannot be used to research bodily sensations and physiological states such as altered heart rates or flushing. But it certainly can be a valid instrument to reconstruct the interpretations and meanings of the emotions and actions that are caused by them. To understand those individual feelings, it is important to recognize the historical, cultural and biographical contexts, as well as the norms and discourses, in which feelings are embedded.

3.1 Visualizing emotions in the data

As I have argued, comparing the use of CAQDAS with material practices does not necessarily make it possible to visualize emotions in the data. However, using software can be a way to illustrate structures of meaning and linkages to broader social contexts in a number of ways.

First, it can make it easier to disentangle different types of interpretations and meaning, such as first- and second-order constructions. This is particularly important in light of the researcher's role in co-constructing the data. Examining single steps of analysis is also beneficial to the endeavor of actually *doing* something with the data. For instance, using CAQDAS – in comparison to the traditional pen-and-paper approach – enables scholars to take a step backwards without destroying all the previous analytic work. Sometimes qualitative research simply requires hiding analysis steps that have been done already. This is the case when researchers sense they are on the wrong track and want to redo parts of their analysis. In such an instance, software can allow one to conceal selected parts, such as certain codings, linkages or memos, with a single click, while also leaving open the possibility of undoing this step later if necessary.

Second, new meaning can be gathered through the process of modifying or "manipulating" the data (Konopásek, 2007). According to Konopásek, it is "only thanks to these manipulations" that "we can see (and show) differences and similarities, emerging patterns, new contexts" (p. 281). In the context of emotion research, this means that material practices in qualitative analyses can disentangle first-order constructions of emotions as well as norms, values and discourses that might impact the emergence of feelings. Seeing the structures of individual interpretations is also useful for identifying the structures that underlie emotions. As I have argued, emotions can hardly be analyzed without taking into account the social, cultural, historical and often biographical contexts of their emergence.

So, if researchers sincerely seek to analyze feelings in qualitative data, it seems imperative to consider those environments. To demonstrate the importance of visualizing contexts and meaning-making in order to reconstruct emotions, it will be helpful to consider the following example. Figure 17.1 shows a segment from an interview that was imported into the QDA-software MAXQDA. The interview is not yet analyzed. All that can be seen is the 'original' data (which, as outlined earlier, is not original at all, but this term shall make this example more comprehensible).[3]

After doing analytical work, which Konopásek defines as material practices, several effects can be noted. The data gained meaning in terms of the researcher's second-order constructions. Moreover, the data *looks* different, since the steps of interpretation and analysis are visualized. Numerous codes and links to other documents have been added. Some parts are highlighted in different colors, and several memos and comments have been written that can be reached with one click (Figure 17.2).

But how can this material modification be used to investigate emotions? The text in this example includes a narrative from a woman called Teresa, who recalls an incident when a fire in her neighbor's apartment led her to move from her apartment to her parent's home. She says she has a "weird feeling" about moving back and feels "miserable" since the fire occurred five years ago. Teresa talks a lot about her feelings and emotions without explicitly naming them. So, small practices that

Figure 17.1 Not yet analyzed data in MAXQDA

Figure 17.2 Analyzed data in MAXQDA

include the researcher's interpretations in the form of codings, memos or linkages contribute to a more comprehensive understanding of Teresa's emotions. Here, anxiety is interpreted as a pivotal emotional experience for Teresa. It becomes manifest because of her own interpretations of the situation, as well as of her family ties and the way she makes sense of it as part of her biography. Actually seeing the different dimensions and interpretations of emotional experiences makes it easier for researchers to disentangle and make sense of emotions' various components. Significantly, Konopásek (2007) calls the work with the software Atlas.ti a "travel in time and space" (p. 284). This characterization highlights how CAQDAS can further facilitate analyses of different but connected data sources and contexts. In this regard it is important to note that any kind of data can be useful for contextualizing emotions. A variety of information about participants as well as about broader contexts is accessible on the same screen. These could be field notes, research diaries, newspaper articles, pictures or videos. Regarding someone's own analysis as part of the data also entails including researcher's own memos from the research process as data in its own right that can be used in further analysis. Again, the linkages between different data segments can actually be seen, and this, in turn, simplifies the understanding of patterns. Different colors can illustrate different contexts, while the linkages among several data sources can visually render the complexity of the emergence of emotions. This might be a part of an interview, linked to biographical aspects of the participant, linked to field notes including the tone, voice or the audio recording of the interview situation, linked to theoretical texts about the context of the research topic, and even linked to variables like sociodemographic data. All of these connections are crucial for understanding emotions, but can barely be grasped without actually materializing the analysis on the screen.

Indeed, the ease of coding and quantifying qualitative data involves the danger of routinizing and oversimplifying processes of analysis. The decision alone to use QDA-software changes research practices and outputs (Woods, Macklin, & Lewis, 2016). This, in turn, changes the way researchers see, use and often interpret their data. In many respects, the use of technology certainly makes researchers a "tool of [their] tools" (Sohn, 2017, paragraph 7), but it is hard to believe that this would not be the case with non-technological tools. Likewise, the use of pen, paper and scissors influences researchers in their analysis. In fact, I would argue that this influence can be even more harmful for qualitative research, since it is even harder to comprehend or to reverse single steps of analysis. Most qualitative researchers might know the discomfort of acknowledging that they have been on the wrong track and did a lot of work for nothing. It might be even harder to accept this insight when the work cannot be reversed with a single mouse click but only with long, tedious efforts.

The decision to use software also affects the way emotion researchers design their research. The great range of technical possibilities QDA-software provides might tempt emotion researchers to quantify data by equating emotion words with emotions. Undoubtedly, occasional research questions require such methods, but this seems to apply to a restricted range of emotion research. This is a problem that can only be solved by the researcher's methodological reflexivity and a profound examination of the research question and topic. This, in turn, is also influenced by the use of software: studies show that the decision to use CAQDAS impacts researchers reflexivity in qualitative analysis. Thus, authors examine how the use of software can enhance reflexivity because they have to make fundamental decisions by choosing the right software and functions for their research and certain analysis steps (Woods, Macklin, & Lewis, 2016). In this regard, one can claim, again, that CAQDAS cannot necessarily be blamed for the 'wrong' choice of method in emotion research.

4. Researcher's emotions and their impact on interpretations

Discussing emotion research and the impact emotions have on nearly any aspect of sociality requires considering the relevance of the researcher's own emotions. Feelings wield influence over nearly every step of the research process (Clarke, Broussine, & Watts, 2015; Whiteman, Müller, & Johnson, 2009). Yet this does not mean it is easy to figure out the appropriate way to look at and interpret data for individual emotions.

I want to outline two ways the researcher's emotions can influence the interpretation process and the role CAQDAS can play in this process. First, I will examine how the researcher's emotional socialization and felt experiences guide the kind of meaning they ascribe to their participants. Second, I shall outline how the researcher's feelings *towards* the data are crucial for understanding the resulting scientific interpretations.

4.1 Considering the emotional biography of the researcher in emotion research

I have suggested that investigating emotions with qualitative data requires understanding the meanings and first-order interpretations that are essential for emotion's emergence. But understanding emotions also requires reflecting on the researcher's own emotional biography. This distinguishes emotions as a research topic from examining other phenomena. Given that qualitative researchers are only capable of exploring meaning, and not emotions as an entity, it is crucial to determine whether the researcher herself ever felt the emotion she believes to discover in the data. Having experienced the feeling of certain emotions as a qualitative emotion researcher can be both useful and misleading. Personal experiences with a similar emotion certainly foster the understanding of participants' emotions, even though it is impossible to experience exactly the same feeling (Weber-Guskar, 2009). When two individuals feel envy, for instance, they might experience it in completely different ways and – perhaps more importantly – link utterly distinct narratives and meanings to their experiences. If the participant's individual experiences with envy do not match the researcher's experience, she may overlook this emotion in the data. This makes it even more important to unfold different kinds of interpretations and include the knowledge of comprehensive narratives in the analysis.

How can CAQDAS help researchers reflect on their own emotional biography and disentangle the hermeneutic interpretations and meanings that underlie emotions? One possibility is based on the idea of writing memos as a means of facilitating the qualitative research process as well as recording the researcher's reflections (Strauss & Corbin, 1990). Simplifying the arrangement of memos, and seeing those arrangements on the screen, can help structure qualitative research practices. This can also motivate researchers to create more memos and to write down their reflections about their interpretations with more precision and regularity. This might appear obvious, but researchers are often tempted to skip this analysis step since it is time-consuming, and because the purpose and utility of writing memos might not be immediately apparent to them. Nevertheless, memos should not be underestimated as an instrument for reflecting on and interpreting data. If researchers can use CAQDAS to quickly create and organize different kinds of memos, this might well lead them to use memos more often. On the other hand, without CAQDAS, one is faced with the daunting prospect of organizing a big amount of different, and perhaps even hand-written, memos on paper, or in common writing software, and with the physical difficulty of linking these memos with certain data segments. Some software allows the use of a variety of memo types, which can often be labeled individually. Researchers could use certain colors or labels to highlight different kinds of memos: some could contain reflections on the research process, others ideas about one's own emotions or the analysis, which can also help to grasp reflective practices. The process of writing memos is not only a pivotal part of creating in-depth interpretations, but is also crucial for the subjective modification and manipulation of the data through the researcher's analysis. While drafting memos or comments, "the researcher inscribes him- or herself into the studied material so that it becomes more and more under control" (Konopásek, 2007, 289). The analyzed data becomes increasingly enmeshed with the researcher's own ideas, views and feelings. She not only reconstructs the meaning that underlies the emergence of emotions, but also inscribes her own feelings into the data. In so doing, her emotional biography as well as her feelings towards the data expand the 'original' data. As outlined earlier, this is an inevitable part of every qualitative research process, but the use of CAQDAS makes it easier to reflect on these developments and to disentangle different kinds of data from the interpretations.

Exchanging with other researchers also fosters improved reflexivity about emotional biographies. This is because interpreting data from different perspectives makes it easier to and more likely for researchers to disentangle interpretations that are affected by individual experiences. In this regard, Rademaker, Grace, and Curda (2012) examine vividly how by "playing around" with the software through CAQDAS can facilitate discussions from multiple perspectives as well as alter interpretations. The ease of working on the same qualitative data set with multiple researchers enhances the possibility of reconsidering single interpretations. While trying to find emotions in qualitative data, it is useful to see how others might have interpreted specific data segments in order to prevent misconceptions resulting from the assumption that a participant's emotional experiences are equivalent to one's own.

4.2 Revealing researcher's emotions towards the data

The role of researchers' emotions in fieldwork has attracted scholars' attention (Davies & Spencer, 2010; Arditti et al., 2010; Munkejord, 2009; Kleinman & Copp, 1993). Yet the feelings toward the conducted data themselves remain understudied. Although idealistic beliefs about objective research may contradict this view, it cannot be denied that feelings accompany any researcher's analysis process, and qualitative researchers are no exception. These feelings are not equivalent to the feelings one has about research in general, but are specific to those about the data. Feelings towards the data impact interpretations and outcomes of qualitative research, and change when CAQDAS is utilized. For instance, researchers might have a feeling that some concepts are significant because they occur in a relevant context. Or they could feel that topics or concepts are somehow linked, but without being able to articulate how and why this connection should exist. Different CAQDAS tools for material research practices could help reveal patterns in the data which would otherwise remain concealed. Various tools that visualize structures in the data could help researchers see what they might merely have felt before. If researchers work in a team, which is indeed helpful for fostering multiple interpretations, CAQDAS could aid by identifying intercoder agreements. Even qualitative researchers who strictly reject positivist approaches might be aided by the simplest amount of certain codes, arising as a result of in-depth interpretations. Such codes could help them see and grasp structures, patterns or linkages that would have otherwise stayed hidden and invisible to them.

Although this chapter is based on Konopásek's idea of the visualization of thinking with CAQDAS, I disagree with him on one point. Konopásek states that the decision to add new links, codes, comments or memos to the data should be based on a cognitive appraisal of the analysis' worthiness:

> But what could be a feasible criterion for decisions about whether to link two quotations or codes or not? Some would suggest various kinds of rational criteria, but I recommend a pragmatic (and almost mechanical) one: is there anything worth of putting down about this particular text passage or connection? If yes, then let us create the link with confidence and make the respective comment. But if we are unable to write a comment on the considered link at the time, and only have an uncertain 'feeling' or 'sensation', then we should hesitate.
>
> (Konopásek, 2007, 290)

I would argue the opposite. If the researcher has a "feeling" or a "sensation" towards any data segment, she should deem this a reason to modify the data with a link, comment or code. If it eventually turns out that it did not lead to any new patterns or ideas, it can easily be deleted or concealed, but often a feeling alone is the only indicator for some hidden patterns in the data, a sensation that cannot be named in the first place but has the potential to be revealed through material practices. In this regard, I argue that CAQDAS enables researchers to visualize their feelings towards the data, which are often the source of relevant and significant ideas, patterns and interpretations.

5. Conclusion

This chapter has argued that CAQDAS is not merely a tool for positivistic research, but also a highly useful application for qualitative research design. As such, its applications should be considered as more than simple tools to classify, quantify or organize specific data segments. Understanding CAQDAS use as a set of material practices offers qualitative emotion researchers with many possibilities to grasp emotions in their data.

In this regard, emotions must be distinguished from other cognitive phenomena. Because emotions rely on physical arousal, they are quite difficult for qualitative research to truly 'measure', but emotions are never comprised of bodily sensations alone, as they rely on some cognitive interpretation of the situation. Thus, in order to interpret their data, qualitative researchers of emotion need to concentrate on the reconstruction of meaning. However, these individual first-order constructions often need to be integrated into social, cultural and historical contexts in order to elucidate the emergence and experience of feelings. Using a variety of data to structure and link different characteristics, hints and interpretations can be advantageous on that front. As interpretations and single analysis steps can be visualized through software, the meanings, norms discourses and cultural contexts that underlie emotions can come into the researcher's view and build the ground for in-depth qualitative analysis.

Nevertheless, utilizing CAQDAS carries the risk of considering qualitative data analysis as an impartial or objective process. While technology is not capable of undertaking (inter)subjective interpretations in this field, the researcher's role as a feeling and passionate co-constructor of the data requires a high level of reflexivity at every step of the research process. This is certainly nothing that can be automated, but the use of CAQDAS can help researchers construct their own emotional biography and holds the potential to reveal the feelings scholars have towards their data.

Working with CAQDAS makes it possible to visualize the structures that are connected to the sociality of emotions. Thus, treating the work with CAQDAS as a material modification of the more-or-less 'original data' contributes to a better understanding of emotions in the data. This approach can also offer researchers a powerful tool for reflecting on their own feelings, on their impact on qualitative research results.

Notes

1 As Gilbert (2002) notes, the "coding trap" is a manifestation of too much closeness to the data. One result, for instance, could be that coding becomes too technical or mechanical.
2 The term "original data" might be confusing since every kind of data record implies the loss of other data. A transcript of an interview or a video recording, for instance, is far away from being "original" considering that so many aspects of the field cannot completely be reflected in a transcript or a recording (see Konopasék, 2007).
3 Special thanks to Christina Silver and Ann Lewins for allowing the use of their example data set, which they created for the book: *Using Software in Qualitative Research*, 2nd edition, 2014, Los Angeles/London//New Delhi/Singapore/Washington DC: SAGE Publications Ltd.

References

Arditti, JA, Joest, KS, Lamber-Shute, J & Walker, L 2010, 'The role of emotions in fieldwork: A self-study of family research in corrections setting', *The Qualitative Report*, vol. 15, no. 6, pp. 1387–1414.

Charmaz, K 2006, *Constructing Grounded Theory. A Practical Guide Through Qualitative Analysis*, Sage Publications, London, Thousand Oaks, New Delhi.

Clarke, C, Broussine, M & Watts, L (eds.), 2015, *Researching with Feeling. The Emotional Aspects of Social and Organizational Research*, Routledge, London, New York.

Creswell, JW 2011, 'Controversies in mixed methods research', in NK Denzin & YS Lincoln (eds.), *The SAGE Handbook of Qualitative Research*, 4th edn, pp. 269–284, Sage Publications, Thousand Oaks.

Davies, J & Spencer, D (eds.), 2010, *Emotions in the Field. The Psychology and Anthropology of Fieldwork Experience*, Stanford University Press, Stanford.

Fitzpatrick, P & Olson, RE 2015, 'A rough road map to reflexivity in qualitative research into emotions', *Emotion Review*, vol. 7, no. 1, pp. 49–54.

Frevert, U 2010, 'Gefühlvolle Männlichkeiten. Eine historische Skizze', in M Borutta & N Verheyen (eds.), *Die Präsenz der Gefühle. Männlichkeit und Emotion in der Moderne*, pp. 305–330, Transcript Verlag, Bielefeld.

Gilbert, LS 2002, 'Going the distance: "Closeness" in qualitative data analysis software', *International Journal of Social Research Methodology*, vol. 5, no. 3, pp. 215–228.

Gill, MJ 2015, 'A phenomenology of feeling: Examining the experience of emotion in organizations', in CEJ Härtel, WJ Zerbe & NM Ashkanasy (eds.), *New Ways of Studying Emotions in Organizations*, pp. 29–50, Emerald Group Publishing, Bingley.

Goble, E, Austin, W, Larsen, D, Kreitzer, L & Brintnell, S 2012, 'Habits of mind and the split-mind effect: When computer-assisted qualitative data analysis software is used in phenomenological research', *Forum: Qualitative Research*, vol. 13, no. 2, art. 2.

Harré, R & Gillet, G 1994, *The Discursive Mind*, Sage Publications, Thousand Oaks.

Hochschild, AR 2003, *The Managed Heart. Commercializiation of Human Feeling*, University of California Press, Berkeley, Los Angeles.

Hutchison, AJ, Johnston, LH & Breckon, JD 2010, 'Using QSR-NVivo to facilitate the development of a grounded theory project: An account of a worked example', *International Journal of Social Research Methodology*, vol. 13, no. 4, pp. 283–302.

Illouz, E 2007, *Cold Intimacies: The Making of Emotional Capitalism*, Polity Press, London.

Kleinman, S & Copp, MA 1993, *Emotions and Fieldwork*, Sage Publications, Newbury Park, London, New Delhi.

Knoblauch, H 2014, 'Qualitative methods at the crossroads: Recent developments in interpretive social research', *Forum: Qualitative Research*, vol. 14, no. 3, art. 12.

Konopásek, Z 2007, 'Making thinking visible with atlas.ti: Computer assisted qualitative analysis as textual practices', *Historical Social Research*, vol. 19, Grounded Theory Reader, pp. 276–298.

Kuckartz, U 2014, *Mixed Methods. Methodologie, Forschungsdesigns und Analyseverfahren*, Springer VS, Wiesbaden.

Latour, B 1995, 'The "pédofil" of Boa Vista: A photo-philosophical montage', *Common Knowledge*, vol. 4, no. 1, pp. 144–187.

Munkejord, K 2009, 'Methodological emotional reflexivity: The role of researcher emotions in grounded theory research', *Qualitative Research in Organizations and Management: An International Journal*, vol. 4, no. 2, pp. 151–169.

Rademaker, LL, Grace, EJ & Curda, SK 2012, 'Using computer-assisted qualitative data analysis software (CAQDAS) to re-examine traditionally analyzed data: Expanding our understanding of the data and of ourselves as scholars', *The Qualitative Report*, vol. 17, art. 43, pp. 1–11.

Reddy, WM 1997, 'Against constructionism: The historical ethnography of emotions', *Current Anthropology*, vol. 38, no. 3, pp. 327–351.

Roberts, KA & Wilson, RW 2002, 'ICT and the research process: Issues around the compatibility of technology with qualitative data analysis', *Forum: Qualitative Social Research*, vol. 3, no. 2, art. 23.

Rosenwein, BH 2010, 'Thinking historically about medieval emotions', *History Compass*, vol. 8, no. 8, pp. 828–842.

Saldaña, J 2016, *The Coding Manual for Qualitative Researchers*, 3rd edn, Sage Publications, London.

Schütz, A 1962, *Collected Papers, Vol. 1, The Problem of Social Reality*, Martinus Nijhoff, Den Haag.

Séror, J 2005, 'Computers and qualitative data analysis: Paper, pens, and highlighters vs. screen, mouse, and keyboard', *TESOL Quarterly*, vol. 39, no. 2, pp. 321–328.

Shott, S 1979, 'Emotion and social life: A symbolic interactionist analysis', *The American Journal of Sociology*, vol. 84, no. 6, pp. 1317–1334.

Sohn, BK 2017, 'Phenomenology and qualitative data analysis software (QDAS): A careful reconciliation', *Forum Qualitative Social Research*, vol. 18, no. 1, art. 14.

Solomon, RC 2007, *True to Our Feelings. What Our Emotions Are Really Telling Us*, Oxford University Press, New York.

Stets, JE & Turner, JH (eds.), 2014, *Handbook of the Sociology of Emotions*, vol. II, Springer, Dordrecht.

Strauss, AL & Corbin, J 1990, *Basics of Qualitative Research: Grounded Theory Procedures and Techniques*, Sage Publications, Newbury Park.

Sturdy, A 2003, 'Knowing the unknowable? A discussion of methodological and theoretical issues in emotion research and organizational studies', *Organization*, vol. 10, no. 1.

Thoits, PA 1989, 'The sociology of emotions', *Annual Review of Sociology*, vol. 15, pp. 317–342.

van Manen, M 2014, *Phenomenology of Practice: Meaning-Giving Methods in Phenomenological Research and Writing*, Left Coast Press, Walnut Creek, CA.

von Scheve, C 2018, 'A social relational account of affect', *European Journal of Social Theory European*, vol. 21, no. 1, pp. 39–59.

Weber-Guskar, E 2009, *Die Klarheit der Gefühle. Was es heißt, Emotionen zu verstehen*, De Gruyter Verlag, Berlin, New York.

Weigert, AJ 1991, *Mixed Emotions: Certain Steps Toward Understanding Ambivalence*, State University of New York Press, New York.

Weitzman, EA 2000, 'Software and qualitative research', in NK Denzin & YS Lincoln (eds.), *The SAGE Handbook of Qualitative Research*, 2nd edn, pp. 803–820, Sage Publications, Thousand Oaks.

Whiteman, G, Müller, T & Johnson, JM 2009, 'Strong emotions at work', *Qualitative Research in Organizations and Management: An International Journal*, vol. 4 no. 1, pp. 46–61.

Woods, M, Macklin, R & Lewis, GK 2016, 'Researcher reflexivity: Exploring the impacts of CAQDAS use', *International Journal of Social Research Methodology*, vol. 19, no. 4, pp. 385–403.